D0403368

SUTHERLAND AND BONYNGE

Also by Quaintance Eaton

Opera Caravan

The Miracle of the Met: An Informal History of the Metropolitan Opera

A Pictorial Guide to Opera

The Boston Opera Company

Opera Production I and II

The World of Music (editor)

Sutherland
and
Bonynge

An
Intimate Biography

Quaintance Eaton

DODD, MEAD & COMPANY   *New York*

Copyright © 1987 by Quaintance Eaton
All rights reserved
No part of this book may be reproduced in any form
without permission in writing from the publisher.
Published by Dodd, Mead & Company, Inc.,
71 Fifth Avenue, New York, N.Y. 10003
Manufactured in the United States of America
Designed by Mark Bergeron
Production supervision by Mike Cantalupo
First Edition

1   2   3   4   5   6   7   8   9   10

Library of Congress Cataloging-in-Publication Data

Eaton, Quaintance.
    Sutherland and Bonynge.

    Includes index.
    1. Sutherland, Joan, 1926–   .   2. Bonynge, Richard.
3. Singers—Biography.   4. Conductors—Biography.
I. Title.
ML394.E28   1987   782.1′092′2 B)   87-13725
ISBN 0-396-08945-3

Contents

viii / CONTENTS

PART TWO

Acknowledgements

THE NAMES OF MOST OF THE PEOPLE TO WHOM I AM indebted appear in the text. However, I wish to give special thanks to the Australians who were so charming and helpful—the New York office of the Information Service, the comparable groups in San Francisco, Sydney, Melbourne, Canberra, and Adelaide, and the Australian Opera press crew and the Opera House staff, especially Ava Hubble and David Brown. And not to forget the courtesy of Qantas. Those two stages of the pilgrimage were fruitful and happy indeed.

Other management and press experts were invaluable—in every city I visited on the trail of the prima donna, initially the backstage heroes of the Metropolitan Opera. I owe heartfelt thanks to Barbara Fischer-Williams and John Owen Ward, both of whom read the manuscript and did not spare their criticism. And lastly, thanks to *Opera News* for permission to reprint an adaptation of "Operation Hoffmann" from their issue of February 2, 1974, which started the whole thing.

Quaintance Eaton

Overture

THIS BOOK IS DIVIDED INTO TWO PARTS, THE FIRST DEAL-
ing with Sutherland's and Bonynge's career until the time of the
Hoffmann experience. The second part is largely derived from personal
encounters, chronicling my adventures with the couple in many operatic
centers; also, the consideration of high points among the soprano's roles.

The *Hoffmann* chapters reveal what is the true life of the dedicated
performer, a day-by-day, grueling, hour-by-hour of hard work, lightened
only by the good spirits of the performers themselves. Here the diary
form seems most appropriate.

Knowing how I relish observing and reporting the inside story of
the buildup of a production, Gerry Fitzgerald of *Opera News* had been
trying for quite a while to give me a backstage assignment. I had done
it years before for *Musical America* when the unique Ljuba Welitsch
made her debut as Salomé with Fritz Reiner in the Met's orchestra pit.
That was, of course, in the old house on Thirty-ninth Street and Broadway.
I had consumed pages of rehearsal details and wise sayings from Herbert
Graf, the vintage stage director. Then the New York City Opera's first
production of Prokofiev's *Love for Three Oranges* underwent the same
dissective process, with hilarious moments gleaned from director Val
Rosing's imaginative and almost unintelligible Russian-English vocabu-
lary. I had done the same for NBC's television production of Benjamin
Britten's *Billy Budd*, writing half a dozen articles about the mysterious
goings-on in the control room, but I had never done such a story for
Opera News.

Several ideas were aborted because they came too late. A new
production at the Met starts building months (even seasons) ahead, and
actual on-the-spot rehearsals begin anywhere from three to six weeks
before opening curtain. Missing the challenge of August Everding's and
Gunther Schneider-Siemssen's *Tristan und Isolde* in 1971–72 was a dis-

appointment. It turned out to be the most stunning and evocative of any up to that time in the new house, rivaled only by Strauss's *Die Frau ohne Schatten*.

The next thought was Donizetti's *Daughter of the Regiment*, which was the first to prove Joan Sutherland capable of comedy, with sprightly, if somewhat balloonlike, partnering by Luciano Pavarotti. That inspiration also dawned too late, so I missed the opportunity to watch in rehearsal the statuesque lady cavort gracefully through regimental rataplans and comic music lessons.

Then Sir Rudolf Bing was gone, and Goeran Gentele seemed destined to brighten many dark corners. Being something of a Swedophile, I conceived the idea of covering this Scandinavian's first *Carmen* in depth—a new general director stage-directing his own first night in a new production of the world's most popular opera! A natural!

Opera News bought the idea, and I interviewed the charming Herr Gentele before taking off for the summer of 1972. The shock and dismay of his tragic death in an automobile accident on July 18 carried with it the realization that the story could not be done—at least, not by *Opera News*, where it was contended that there was too much uncertainty about the production at that time. So I shelved my chagrin, only to feel it all the more when Harvey Phillips, an excellent writer, made the exploration I had wanted to and put the *Carmen* rehearsal experience in the hard covers of a book.

It was Offenbach's *Les Contes d'Hoffmann* that won the toss in the long-delayed project for *Opera News*; *Hoffmann* was to have its opening on November 29, 1973, preceded by a month's rehearsals. I wrote Richard Bonynge, Sutherland's husband, who was to conduct a "new" version, and received a reply from his secretary, Paul Garner, granting me permission to attend rehearsals. I showed up at the designated spot on October 29, when Bonynge was taking his first orchestra rehearsal.

All that month, I practically lived in the opera house, taking off three Sundays, Thanksgiving Day, and one Saturday, when to everyone's relief expected rehearsals were canceled. I missed only some technical run-throughs, which I would have understood only dimly anyway, and a few of the "room" rehearsals, at which individuals, both principals and "covers," dig deeply into their roles and would have no doubt felt discomfort at the presence of any stranger.

When Gerry had proposed *Hoffmann*, he added: "I know you'll like it because you love Joan so." Now, at that time, "love" was not exactly my word for Miss Sutherland. I respected her as one of the greats, was in awe of her fantastic technique, which I had first experienced through her album, "The Art of the Prima Donna." Other recordings came along, and then the broadcast of her Met debut role as Lucia, on December 9, 1961, which quite overwhelmed me as I listened from the artists' colony, Yaddo, near Saratoga Springs.

I had, in fact, already encountered her "live," so to speak, at the Carnegie Hall repeat on March 1 of her February 1961 Town Hall concert success, *Beatrice di Tenda*, which she performed with the now-defunct

American Opera Society. I joined in the rapturous, wild applause for her thrilling performance of Bellini's music, and admired her red hair, piled high in queenly style, and her graceful black gown with its flowing panels faced in vivid emerald green.

My first face-to-face meeting with the prima donna must have been at the beer-and-hot-dog party for the entire Met company in the winter of 1963, when the social rooms of the old house were wide open and the ballet swung until dawn. She was standing in the doorway to the crowded Sherry's bar. The late Francis Robinson, the courteous press chief, introduced us. Like any fan, I asked for her autograph, but this was really special, for I carried around my *Opera Caravan*, the book about the Met's tours, and snared every possible autograph all over the pages. (It should be a collector's dream by now.) Cheerfully the tall redhead scrawled her name on the inside front cover above Dorothy Kirsten and opposite Anna Moffo, Henry Butler, stage director, and Charlie Riecker, at that time assistant administrator.

I interviewed Richard Bonynge for *Opera News* just after his Met debut (December 12, 1966) conducting *Lucia*. His wife, of course, was in the title role. They lived at that time in a narrow complex on West Ninth Street, crammed (as are all their habitations, I was to learn) with the booty from Bonynge's obsessive antique collecting. Madame appeared only briefly on her way to the hairdresser (a nagging preoccupation with the opera singer, whose head is more often bewigged than not), wrapped in luxurious mink, but with the titian crown uncovered. She said only a few words and vanished.

That day Richard was nervous at first. A spry little photographer, perching monkeylike here and there to get angle shots, did not make things any easier. But I think I established a friendly rapport. At least he remembered the interview (titled "Man of Instinct") when the later assignment turned up.

On another occasion, an intermission during the Juilliard Opera Theater's presentation of Stravinsky's *Rake's Progress* in 1969, I encountered Madame, momentarily alone, quiet and stately in a long flowered silk gown. I rather foolishly asked her what she thought of the opera.

Her eyes slid sideways under lowered lids, her mouth, too, dropped to one side as she muttered conspiratorially: "What a bloody bore!"

It was obvious that Sutherland is no lover of contemporary music. I learned later that one of her most distressing experiences had been a tussle with Michael Tippett's *Midsummer Marriage* at Covent Garden.

A closer view of the couple was afforded when I was lucky enough to be an honored guest along with the Bonynges and Marilyn Horne (after their blazing *Norma*) and George London at the Waldorf-Astoria luncheon given by the New York Singing Teachers Association. I sat next to Richard and joined in his wonder about just what Harold Schonberg could possibly have meant by his repeated *Times* criticism of the conductor's "accented upbeats." (Schonberg since admitted some virtues in Bonynge's conducting.)

These brief scattered encounters constituted my entire experience with the Bonynges before the *Hoffmann* assignment, although, of course, I had heard her *Lucia*, her *Sonnambula*, and the marvelous *Norma*.

Meanwhile I had become involved with the New York City Opera (as a founder of its Guild and editor of its newsletter), and, consequently, familiar with its *prima donna assoluta*, Beverly Sills. Beverly came to personify the warm, impassioned singing actress, while Joan still bore the sobriquet "Ice Maiden." It is a shame, but these polarizations do exist in the world of prima donna advocates and detractors—you are not supposed to like one when you are loyal to another.

Joan's voice still possessed too much of that "mourning-dove" quality noted by critics in England as well as in the United States. I rather thoughtlessly joined the ranks of those who noted these shadows in what was assuredly the most shining international career of any woman singer. In 1970 I was one of 342 pilgrims who jetted to witness Sills's debut in Covent Garden as Lucia—a challenge (although the idea remained unspoken) to Sutherland on her home grounds and in the very role that had made her famous in 1959. I listened, and probably put in a word or two, to the debates over the relative merits of the two stars, and remember rather resenting the coolness of some scribes and some of the listeners (outside of the rather obvious 342) to the "interloper."

Joan, I believe, does not know about this shady past of the follower who has faithfully traipsed over three continents and into more than a half-dozen opera houses to observe her life and good times.

The idea for attempting a book about the Bonynges assumed shape during the *Hoffmann* rehearsal period, especially when I learned they were taking the opera to Australia. I had encountered a slim volume by Edward Greenfield, critic of the *Manchester Guardian*, and thought it unsatisfactory, in spite of considerable detail about the recording processes in which the Bonynges participated. At the time, I did not know of an earlier biography by Russell Braddon, which, however, took the couple only up to 1961.

A good many second thoughts have occurred to me since undertaking this account. Writing a book about a "celebrity," one must cope not only with the dual personality of the subject—artist versus human being—but with one's own schizophrenia. Friend or observer? . . . (spy, if you will). It is a dilemma between whose two horns one vacillates. The choice is not as easy as Truman Capote made it . . . write and let "friendships" fall where they may.

I remember that a strict credo of "hands off" was practiced, or at least proclaimed, by the late Oscar Thompson, music critic of the New York *Sun* and also, at the time I knew him, editor of *Musical America*, where I was his associate. I found out why he had to assert a rigidity about associating with performers. Once in Europe he had shared a taxi with among others Maria Jeritza, and that gorgeous blonde had sat on Oscar's lap. He told the story with lips visibly smacking. We all thought it quite funny, until photographs of the lovely Maria began appearing in every possible (and some not so possible) connection month after month in *Musical America*. It was the same with a charming but unknown American soprano whom Oscar had met in Europe. She was just beginning a career, and talented as she proved to be, did not quite belong in the upper strata on the illustrated pages of our magazine. Despite his professed credo, Oscar could be had.

While realizing the dangers, I have sometimes walked the tightrope. I had made "friends" with a few operatic celebrities—Lawrence Tibbett and his wife Jane, John and Carla Brownlee, Jussi and Anna-Lisa Björling, and most of all with that wonderful gentleman and artist, Set Svanholm and his wife Nini. I had had to write about them occasionally, but it never seemed to affect our friendship.

I was willing to take the risk. Perhaps it is valuable to know as much about one's subjects as possible and to try to sort out the purely artistic from the sometimes impure human qualities. I know this is not *comme il faut* with most critics, but I have long since detached myself from any consistent participation in that grind.

One time I did get my comeuppance and had a rude truth brought home. Early in her American career, a singer who later became the rage and attracted a visible cult was quite friendly. I championed her beginning career in America, went to all of her concerts, heard her at the opera, and watched her attain the highest rank as an "artist." Going to parties at her home was fun; I met some rather rare musicians and show-biz folk there. She and I exchanged Christmas gifts, too. Then I left *Musical America*. Busy with books rather than news accounts and reviews, I didn't see her for quite a while. Meeting her backstage at the opera one day, I remarked on the long absence one from another. She looked up and said: "But you don't write anymore."

I trust that my account of the many worlds of Joan Sutherland and Richard Bonynge will display the best of both worlds—the cool observer's and the warm friend's.

One of the first things I learned about the couple was that their life is lived ninety percent of the time in the underground of a dozen or more opera houses. Their emergence into the blaze of light onstage, of which the Met *Hoffmann* experience is typical, is the icing on the cake.

It is safe to say that there has never been an unfavorable reaction from any audience before which Joan has sung. Not so with the critics. Here the opinions diverge as widely as do the personalities and habits of the individuals—the training, experience, and personal prejudices of each listener who is privileged to comment in the public press.

Therefore, it seems unnecessary, even redundant, to delve into audiences' approval on most occasions; we can take it for granted that the peerless star will be rapturously received. It is more diverting, although in the last analysis not necessarily more accurate, to sample the sayings of the ladies and gentlemen of the press. The myriad facets to one's career may be thus revealed, and, as the opinions are set off against each other, some semblance of a true picture of an artist's performance may be perceived, even if dimly.

SUTHERLAND AND BONYNGE

PART
ONE

CHAPTER

1

Songs My Mother
Taught Me

❋ IT WAS CHRISTMASTIME, 1974. JOAN SUTHERLAND
stretched out on the chaise longue in the dressing room of
her Switzerland home and told me about her early life in Australia.
Her bare toes curled up dangerously near the tape recorder as if
to send it spinning off onto the floor at any moment. But it stayed
safely there.

. . .

The house on Queen Street, No. 115, in the Sydney suburb of
Woollahra, still stands, though "propped up by chicken wire," Joan
joked. There is a white fence surrounding it, but otherwise the
house that holds most of Joan's youthful memories seems much
the same—shabbier, to be sure, than it was even when Sutherland's
mother moved into it after her husband's death on November 7,
1932, Joan's sixth birthday.

William McDonald Sutherland, master tailor, had suffered
from a chain of misfortunes common to a modest craftsman in a
depression: lawyers and doctors and dentists and others did not
get paid, so, in turn, neglected their tailor's bills. Without telling
his wife, he had twice mortgaged the house in Point Piper, one of
Sydney's most attractive suburbs. (Sydney is a patchwork of these
suburbs, the central city itself is quite small.) The Sutherlands'
house stood at the top of a bluff, 111 steps leading down to a private
beach on Sydney Harbour, where three of the children—Joan,
Barbara (four years Joan's senior), and stepbrother Jim (eight years
older)—swam daily. Climbing those stairs put the final strain on
William's heart that November morning.

The family cracked open after the father's death, splitting into natural halves: the children by his former marriage (his first wife, Clara, had died in 1919) went their own way, and Muriel Alston Sutherland, Joan, and Barbara moved into the Alston family house on Queen Street. Heather, the oldest stepsister and Joan's favorite, quickly made her way as an architect and married her boss. Nancye had already become involved with a young man whom she married in 1933. Ailsa, the only one alive at this writing, was working as a dental nurse in a hospital. Even young Jim had flown the nest, attending an accountancy school. Later, a former friend of his father's took him into his firm as an office boy. He became a secretary, worked hard at night school, and rose to head the business—a typical Alger story.

Joan missed Heather and Jim, but had plenty of company in the new old home. The residence was one of several built by her maternal grandfather and his father. Already occupying the house on Queen Street were Muriel's brother Tom and her sister Ethel, both older than she. Ethel had long ago suffered the indignity of being nicknamed "Blossom" by Tom, and, worse, of having it shortened to "Bloss." These two, good-natured Aunt and eccentric Uncle, formed a steady backdrop for Joan's young life. Tom, as the saying goes, had no visible means of support.

Joan's grandfather, displaying a lack of foresight atypical of the canny Scot, had died intestate, leaving his property to be managed by Tom. "Manage" is hardly the accurate word: Tom just let things happen. Very soon, wartime restrictions forbade property owners from raising rent; the tenants became richer than the landlords. It was also against the law to sublet, yet the extra revenue was essential to the Alstons, who had no business head among them. When Joan began to make a salary, she begged them to hold on, to let her pay the taxes and keep the property. Nevertheless, the family sold the house—"just to get rid of their problems."

Goaded by the stress of war, (Jim was listed as "missing" in Malaya) Tom went to work with a strong will and never returned to idleness. He amused himself by gardening and teaching his niece old English music-hall ditties, a unique and savory brand of musical culture that verged perilously on vulgarity. Joan loved them, and to this day might just break out into "My old woman's an awful boozer" when specially inspired. To balance this influence, Muriel's Cousin John paid periodic visits, bringing along his American wife and their collection of phonograph records, which gave the youngster her first taste of grand opera. There were all the oldies: Caruso, McCormack, Tetrazzini, and even Australia's own

Nellie Mitchell, who, as Nellie Melba, went by a version of the name of her hometown, Melbourne. Then there were some of the middle period as well: Tibbett, Rethberg, Elisabeth Schumann. More to the fancy of the growing Joan was the birdlike voice of Amelita Galli-Curci. Joan herself was beginning to mimic the birds.

With the memory of her kind but elderly and strict Presbyterian father fading, Joan's lodestars were her mother and her sister Barbara. The two girls were not given any special treatment or regarded as prodigies; Joan grew up singing and Barbara showed a natural grace. Joan believes Barbara could have managed very well on the stage either as actress or dancer—if things had been different. Barbara's talent was obscured by a veil of embarrassment. Barbara suffered from epilepsy, and, because of the ignorance about that disease at the time, the secrecy that shrouded it, and the shame that attended it, the moody girl withdrew further into herself, and at last from life itself. In her deep love and admiration for her sister, Joan still feels the wound of Barbara's tragedy. (It was a shock to have my taxi driver one day in Sydney point out, and ask if the visitor would like to go closer to the very spot, Watson's Bay, at the head of Sydney Harbor, notorious for this very grimness, from which Barbara had leaped or fallen to death. I refused, shuddering.)

Still, it was Joan's mother, the tall, imposing, rather formidable Muriel Alston Sutherland, who mattered most.

"She thought along Victorian lines," Joan recalled, "and believed that girls should find well-to-do husbands who would take care of them, settle down, and all that. Of course, they should give up careers, if any. I don't think she was keen on either Barbara or me really being performers. She believed it was a very dicey sort of career, and wanted for us something much more down to earth, less flighty.

"It wasn't a religious discipline she inflicted on us. She went to church, having been in a family that adhered strictly, but she herself was not particularly devout. Oh, sure, we made weekly pilgrimages to church, though she never forced it, and she resented anything said against religion. She couldn't abide bad language. But that was more a matter of taste."

There was plenty of personal discipline, however. This hour to get up . . . that hour to go to bed . . . lights out . . . all were monitored and yet not so strictly as Muriel's own habits as a child. Joan believes that her mother resented having been kept in such firm control and rebelled—just as each generation rebels against its particular restrictions. "She was really rather willful herself and did pretty much what she wanted to," said Joan.

School years passed in more or less humdrum fashion. At St. Catherine's Church of England School for Girls, located at Waverley, Joan was a bright pupil in everything but French. To this day she confesses she has no ear for it and that she must toil over its light accents, the occasional purr, and the vowel sounds through which the Australian twang and diphthongs often break. If she had only had a teacher observant enough to take trouble with her . . . but Australia seemed too far from France—and opera in French —to matter.

She had come into the world at eleven and a half pounds and expanded steadily, until, at sixteen, she weighed one stone (fourteen pounds) for each year of her life. No doubt her heft proved a handicap, instilling some insecurity in the otherwise happy and carefree girl and conditioning her approach to everything from early sports to stage deportment. It was not until after the success she herself could hardly believe that she was able to come to terms with and ostensibly conquer this diffidence. She demurs at reports by her first teachers that her mother and aunt treated her as a clumsy person, saying: "Don't let Joan handle that, she'll drop it!" Nor, says Joan, did her mother encourage her to "feel small." Rather, Muriel would urge her to stand up straight, saying: "You're a tall girl, make the most of it!" Certainly, somewhere along the line she became reconciled to her imposing height—even evinces a certain pride in it. "It's a great advantage—you can see over everybody," she declared, only half in jest.

Joan cannot remember when she did not sing. "Mother noticed right off. Of course, I had her as a model." Muriel's voice was a great, warm mezzo-soprano, lush in tone, pure in quality, effortlessly produced. "She had studied with a pupil of Mathilde Marchesi and could have had a fine career, but, true to her principles, remained at home. She was very much against young voices being trained beyond their capacity, so she didn't set out to 'train' me. In fact, she actually said she didn't at all, but I don't go along with that, because she did, without realizing it. I sang all the things she sang, and she would correct me and tell me how to do it better, both vocally and physically."

Joan never stopped "singing around the house." What did she sing? "Everything I heard. Old songs, arias I learned from records—a mishmash. I used to imitate Galli-Curci, but never thought of being a coloratura. I had my heart set on Wagner."

What else could a tall sixteen-stone young lady with a rib cage that held what must have been the most voluminous female lungs in the world have aimed for? A young lady with what one doctor later called "the most perfect vocal cords he'd ever seen"? One deterrent still lingered: a progressive infection of the sinuses and ears that showed up as early as her fifth year and was allowed to remain for fear that any operation would damage the vocal cords. This neglect was later to prove nearly fatal to her career at the very moment her success seemed assured.

Her love for singing notwithstanding, there was a living to be made. Singing remained a thing to occupy one's leisure hours, if any, and to dream about. At this point, Joan's dreams transported her no farther than Sydney Town Hall, although an occasional mad fantasy put her before a cheering audience in some glamorous opera house, or on a silver screen, svelte and melodious. It was to be work and nothing much else for quite a while. She gave up school as an academic discipline and turned to practicalities—shorthand, typing, and tailoring (in her father's image) so that she could make her own clothes instead of buying them off the rack. She learned enough to land a job in 1944 as typist for the Council for Scientific and Industrial Research at Sydney University, which dealt with radiophysics. At the end of the year, she switched to a country supplies firm, becoming adept at rabbit traps and combine harvesters.

Tailoring turned her out in serviceable but awkward and unbecoming skirts and coats—unimaginative in cut, drab in color, clumsy in material. Style? No thought of it. Once referring to the first time he saw her, Richard Bonynge said she "looked as big as a house." Joan reacted defensively but conceded: "It was ghastly material, herringbone, now that I think of it, very masculine . . . did absolutely nothing for me." At least it was her own, and thrifty, too.

Into this rather monotonous life (dominated in daylight by farm machinery and the rush to get home on crowded trains, and in evenings by study and perhaps some music) came a ray of promise—an advertisement in the *Sydney Morning Herald*. Two singing teachers, Aida and John Dickens, were looking for prize pupils. In fact, they would grant a two-year scholarship to the winner of a competition. Joan was the forty-first to enter and she won. How unlikely it had seemed! The great, awkward girl had stood before Aida at the piano. John was by his wife's side, she looking kind, he, fierce and dominating. Joan's homemade dress sat nowhere comfortably on her Junoesque figure. Her hair—not the glorious red we know today but the shade uncharitably referred to as "mousy"—was rather messily attended to; a nervous smile exposed imperfect teeth; her feet fidgeted; and her hands (well, what to do with them was always a problem) twisted and separated and came convulsively together again with a life all their own. But there were her fair and unblemished skin, with no overlay of makeup, her glorious eyes under extravagant lashes, and then the voice itself sang for her and settled everything.

Out it poured . . . creamy, pure, secure on the breath as her mother's had been, and, of course, in the mezzo range . . . deep, warm, pulsating. No matter that it was an aria from Saint-Saëns's *Samson and Delilah*, in customary English disguise as "Softly Awakes My Heart." It awoke amazement and eagerness in the hearts of Aida and John. There could be no doubt about the choice of their scholarship pupil.

The Dickenses' credentials were sound. He was the grandson of Otto Vogt, thorough musician and organist, who had even tried to teach that king of instruments to a young tomboy named Helen Porter Mitchell (later Nellie Melba). Aida was a professional pianist and singer. They had married in 1940 and moved from Melbourne to Sydney in 1944.

The first step toward higher realms for their new protégée was an upward one indeed. They determined that her voice, patterned all her life after her mother's, must be lifted into the stratum where it belonged—a high soprano. They detected dramatic possibilities, Verdian heights, even Wagnerian kingdoms.

Joan demurred. Until proven desirable to her, she habitually resisted change, often to a point where tears would shatter what little composure she possessed. It was not altogether stubbornness; more likely, insecurity. After all, what previous successes did she have to build on? She was venturing timidly on unknown terrain that could easily prove to be quicksand.

Moreover, there was Muriel in the background. What would she say? Muriel left no doubt in anyone's mind about her opinion. Joan's voice was a contralto, like hers, or at least a mezzo. She objected strenuously. She had been against the idea of strangers' taking over Joanie in the first place. "I don't know who they are," she remonstrated. "And if they ruin your voice, you can't get it back."

Her daughter, too excited to give up, countered with a question: "Who, then?" . . . Muriel could not put her finger on any name. (This friend—no good; that one—I didn't like the way they sang.) The outcome was: "Oh, well, maybe it's better to trust someone you *don't* know; you can always leave them without embarrassment."

So at age eighteen Joan began a four-year stint with the Dickenses: Aida, firm, clear, setting down principles that worked; John, a tyrant whose rantings and pronouncements terrified the girl. "He just tied me in knots," she realized many years later. "I dreaded lessons when he was there; only enjoyed them when he wasn't. But they did lift my voice. I worked with them till they went back to Melbourne."

How did they regard their prize pupil? In 1974, I met with them in their Melbourne studio, one room icy, the other uncomfortably warm. Aida sat and spoke quietly, interrupted and overpowered in every utterance by her forceful spouse, who stood by the piano conducting the scene.

Their first impression of Joan? Her size, and the combination of eagerness and reluctance she showed. She worked very hard, they agreed, although there was an "enormous amount of being pushed into it, as though she really didn't want to do it all. Gauche, naive . . . still she did everything she possibly could . . . yet, if left to herself, she'd slow up."

Aida ventured a remark about a lot of "sit-you-eye-shuns" Joan had had to accept, leaving this mysteriously in the air. Possibly she meant the mother's disapproval, but it is more likely that she was referring to their eventual resentment of Richard Bonynge's influence. This broke through their surface caution every so often. John interrupted, as usual: "But she was more than straightforward . . . probably the most enormous sense of character I've ever experienced in a woman . . . my wife is the same," he hastened to add, still not softening the male chauvinism. "Joan was able to override anything . . . had to sort of brainwash herself, putting up with what every prima donna has to. Look at Callas and her publicity. If *she'd* stuck with Meneghini, she'd be singing today. Onassis unsettled her . . . led her into paths no singer should be led into."

"Joan never had any vocal troubles here," Aida resumed. "When we were in London one time, she'd had an illness, and everybody in Covent Garden was telling her what to do. Her middle voice was gone, and, without a middle voice, there's nothing at all. So she started to work on it." Referring to this same period, Bonynge claims that he was instrumental in repairing this vital stretch of the vocal road. There is no doubt that, as he was Joan's husband and coach by that time, the Dickenses' advice may well have been only coincidental with his.

It was obvious that John, at least, had looked for more dramatic and heavy roles for this girl with the big voice, and that he thoroughly disagreed with her accession to the "coloratura stuff," blaming Bonynge as a matter of course. He admired the *Turandot* (only recorded, never sung on stage) over the *Lucia*, the (Handel) *Rodelinda* over everything, and when *Puritani* was mentioned, he muttered: "Should think she'd get away from all that rubbish!"

Weren't they proud of her?

"We don't take it that way. Not like fans. We look on her as family. But not many get close to her."

Surely she was very warm and outgoing?

"That's just surface stuff," asserted John. "I don't know anybody who's really close to her. She doesn't admit people . . ."

When he walked me out to the street, John added a few more cautions about Bonynge, in terms that left no doubt why their object returns their uncomplimentary opinions.

Just what was the Dickens method?

I put this question to Joan one day when were talking in the Bonynges' Switzerland home.

She laughed. "It turned out to be what one professor called 'the iniquitous form of forward production.'" She laughed again, and asked rhetorically: "But how else to sing? Yes, I feel the voice coming very much from the 'masque,'" she said, pointing, then posing her fingers on her high cheeks over the sinuses. "If I feel it in my throat, I know I'm singing badly. No matter what anyone says, I do exactly the way I did at first—throw my head back and sing. It may strain the muscles, I don't know, but it's a habit by now. Perhaps [I'm] singing to the gallery and not wanting to look the stalls in the face. I've neither cultivated it nor tried to stop it. Occasionally, I use the chest voice. But the trouble comes when you take that too high and you're very much in the middle of the voice and hear the gears grinding even when you're singing a middle G."

What about the "break" between registers?

"Mother always told me to iron it out as much as possible. The voice is one line from top to bottom and back again. And you work on it to make it even. And keep on working."

Joan used to sit for hours watching her mother, noting how she breathed. Of course, she herself has the rib cage and lungs that offer the perfect machinery for the vital business of singing.

"It's a matter of diaphragm support," she asserted. "Not so much 'breathing' as how you release the breath, sustain it . . . it's proper support. Nothing else. The sound sits on top of the breath and you don't have to do another damned thing—it's the whole basis of singing."

Such simplicity must be quite inspiring to struggling young ones and infuriating to those further along who have found the pathway rugged and toilsome with "methods." Not everyone is blessed with such superior basic equipment or early guidance.

Richard and Joan have come to speak of "The Voice," as if it were an entity apart from the human being who possesses it. As indeed it is. They are accustomed to living with it, but treat it with respect and consideration, if not the awe that observers are apt to show for its puissance and beauty

"One hundred percent natural!" Richard is likely to exclaim, mentioning those perfect vocal cords. "Of course she's developed technique, so that she doesn't come offstage, even after *Norma*, vocally exhausted—physically, maybe, but not vocally."

"One thing she did have to learn," he added, "the difference between a trill on a whole tone and one on a half-tone." That she did by slow motion, taking one note at a time.

As Joan pointed out, she cannot remember when she did not sing, and when she didn't trill—the perfect trill that has astonished the cognoscenti. Mother did that, too. Daughter imitated. (One tenor partner of many operas begged her to teach him and later boasted that she had. Joan confessed that she still did not find his trills absolutely perfect.)

One climactic question to our interview that day: Does she feel the process of singing entirely physically or is it a mental thing, too? Does she do it consciously, intellectually?

"It's a mental thing," she said. "But you have to convince the physical mechanism. It really comes down to 'mind over matter' in more ways than one."

Back in her girlhood days, the voice was still based on the model of her mother's. The Dickenses' opinion that it had to be raised finally overcame Mrs. Sutherland's objections, though never stilled them completely. Muriel thought they were taking the girl too fast, but Joan was more philosophical.

"Either I go up or I don't," she figured. And this expansion of the voice might be a good thing. Otherwise, there was nothing so very contrary to her mother's ideas: she rationalized that the teachers merely explained things differently. Joan went on—combining her teachers' strictures with her mother's methods and exercises, and it seemed to come out pretty well.

After the Dickenses moved back to Melbourne, Joan coached with Adrian Holland, who had played accompaniments for Isobel Baillie and several other English singers. Meanwhile, she had begun to think about trying her newly acquired skills in the public arena.

2

On with the Quest

NOW BEGAN THE PART OF JOAN'S LIFE THAT WAS TO build up experience and knowledge—long days and weeks and months of doing what came along, learning, stumbling, and painfully getting up again, taking the insignificant along with the important and trying to sort it out.

No one is really discovered overnight—or at least no one who has learned a lesson. Those meteors who flash across the sky and are soon gone have not spent the years of toil, inching toward the zenith; and, unless they retire for a while from their own dazzlement to put a foundation under their success, they become quick flashes indeed.

How many child prodigies have gone through swift success to become true artists? A few distinctive instrumentalists; almost no singers. Remember Marion Talley? Or Felice Lyne (who, before World War I, was hailed as a second Patti?) The voice is a late bloomer, anyway, and should not be forced. Very intensive preparation for a singer is difficult, because it is usually begun late. Lucky are those who have already started on piano or violin before their teens and the "discovery" of a voice. Lucky are those who have before them an example and inspiration such as Joan's mother, or who have the indestructible will and talent of a Bubbles Silverman, who also had a forceful mother to help her turn into Beverly Sills.

Undeterred by her new job with another country wholesaler whose genial senior director, "Pop" Clyde, even abetted a growing number of absences from her secretarial desk, Joan went to work at the profession that was to absorb her entire life. The first entry in her scrapbooks is a letter from one O. King, president and founder of Singers of Australia, a "national society for the encouragement of singers and advancement of the art of singing." It read:

> Dear Joan,
> It is very important that I should hear you sing. Could you come to my place for a few minutes on Monday evening, the 30th inst., with Wagnerian song . . .

The result was a concert on March 22, 1947, at Sydney Town Hall. Joan had gained at least one objective (besides a fee of £10, 10s). Here she was, at last, singing in that bright, almost steely voice that the Dickenses had drilled into her such items as Senta's Ballad from *The Flying Dutchman*, the *Lohengrin* Bridal Scene with Ronald Dowd (destined to become one of the Australian Opera's cherished tenors), and with other colleagues the Quintet from *The Mastersingers*.

Henry Krips, brother of the Josef known in Europe and America, conducted. "Henry was a matinee idol," Joan later remembered, "with a fetching Austrian accent. I adored him and was brokenhearted when he got appointed conductor of the Adelaide Symphony."

Next day, a photo in one paper heralded a "New Voice," and a review in the Sydney *Sun* called that voice "powerful and warmly resonant, responding to pressure without stridency." One demurrer pointed the way to the future: "But her head tones, of much beauty, can be made more secure." Another critic agreed: the weight of the metal in the head range needed to gain. A genuine carper maintained that "a Wagnerian soprano must be able to relish the high B and C—to blow the roof off the Town Hall. Sutherland had replaced a high B with a G. How would the young lady, if ever placed in the terrible position of singing *Lohengrin* right through, cope with the finale of the first act?" Still another commented that nobody seemed to have realized the potential in the top voice.

"Least of all me," remarked Joan.

Prior to this, she had already won second place in two of the dozens of competitions that showed Australia's concern for building up an autonomous musical life: the Opera Aria Contest and the Dramatic Soprano Championship. (Australian sports terminology and psychology carried over into budding cultural consciousness.) She placed fourth in the most important, the Mobil Oil Quest. Everyone entered these feats of endurance. There was even an

Eisteddfod, named after the famous Welsh contest. Joan won in Sydney one time. Not only did triumph mean cash prizes and some acclaim, but, as Joan recalled, these competitions provided a way to perform under harassing conditions that stood one in good stead for facing the professional world later.

In and around these high points flowed dozens of appearances, chiefly in the "music club" network that spanned most of New South Wales. Sprinkled throughout the scrapbooks are names like Wagga Wagga, where Joan enthralled them with Santuzza's "Romance" (everything had to be put in sensible English); "Softly Sighs the Breath of Eve" (which turns out to be "Leise, leise," from *Der Freischütz*—or rather, *The Freeshooter*); Sibelius's *The Tryst*, and Liszt's *Lorelei*.

She offered the same fare in Narrandera, Leeton, and Cootamundra.

Talking with her one day, I reminded her of those names and that repertoire. Joan exclaimed in a sort of disbelief: "Oh, God!" It can be unnerving to look over one's shoulder at the long-ago.

"For auditions, we had no choice," she explained. "Oley Speaks's *Morning* was a set piece. Imagine having to hear seventy to eighty singers do that!" Also, there was Ernest Charles's "When I Have Sung My Songs," and Dido's lament, "When I Am Laid in Earth" by Purcell, and Bach's "Wert Thou but Near," and Handel's "O, Sleep, Why Dost Thou Leave Me?"

"I was always singing songs that began with 'O'—'O, That It Were So,' by Frank Bridge, and, most of all, that real old sentimental, 'Oh, Could I but Express in Song!' " and she sang the following line: "Oh, could I but tell you in sorrow!" "Malashkin composed that one," she added and then warbled a few bars of Harriet Ware's "This Day Is Mine."

The music clubs' programs progressed little beyond this rash of ballads, hardly a repertoire to build on, Joan reflected. "I learned much better stuff from my mother—arias and oratorio pieces."

One aria pursued her—or she it—until she must have felt like its protagonist, La Gioconda. "Suicidio!" was constantly called for. It has a brave, startling beginning and a dramatic finish, and she invariably made a hit with it. Gradually, she added this and that for the edification of the music club ladies. At the Lunchtime Music Club it was Sibelius's *Tryst*, Delius's *Homeward Way*, and Hageman's *Do Not Go, My Love*. (So many hackneyed American songs found their way down under—La Forge, Charles, Ware, Malotte, Worth, Speaks—and quite a few English ones, too.)

Things looked up a bit with the Singers of Australia performance of *Acis and Galatea* at the Eastwood branch, but fell down several notches when Joan vied for attention with the xylophone soloist and the Grand Organ and Military Band. Also, it was judged hardly a competition when she bravely offered "Elizabeth's Greeting" (as "Dich teure Halle" was translated) at a concerto competition, at which the violinist won with Mendelssohn. Joan may not even remember that Eugene Goossens conducted. The debonair Belgian-Englishman had headed the Sydney Conservatory for several years and was to play a role in her operatic aspirations. At least, this concerto occasion prompted what must have been her second "publicity" photograph, the first having accompanied the account of her Wagnerian stint with the Singers of Australia. This one showed her hair shorter and not so curly.

She reverted to the mixture of arias and songs for the suburbs Manly and Ryde, adding "Porgi Amor" (*Figaro*), "Il est doux, il est bon" (*Hérodiade*), and three Richard Strauss songs, but giving Killara only Strauss and tidbits.

Winning the first heat of the Mobil Oil Quest, Queen of Contests, brightened her sky a little. She had sung Aida's "Ritorna vincitor" (quite naturally known as "May Laurel Crown Thy Brow"—same number of syllables), eliciting from the *Radio Times* the prediction: "Here is a successor to Marjorie Lawrence." Experts hailed the sensational new soprano, who went on to the Grand Finals past eighteen heats and 1,829 other contestants. Meanwhile, she revisited Leeton and Narrandera and Wagga Wagga and Cootamundra, reaping compliments on her "almost miraculous development."

Then came the finals, on September 15, in Melbourne's Town Hall. The prize was to be £1,000 and a tour. Where did Joan place? Fourth, with £50. Ronal Jackson, bass-baritone, had come in first; Trudy Daunt, soprano, was second; William Smith, bass-baritone, third. Perhaps a bit of regionalism cropped up here. Both men hailed from New South Wales, as did Joan, and Victoria needed to be represented in there somewhere. Daunt lived in Melbourne.

At any rate, Joan profited from the publicity and the many recitals that resulted. In one of these, she sang Tosti's "Goodbye," a good old tearjerker that had been a favorite with Melba and other luminaries. For Joan, although she may not have meant it to, the "good-bye" signaled the abandonment of her regular job to concentrate at last on "career." Pop Clyde wished her well.

At first, she was left in the shade by condescending reviews, which found that she "pressed on her vocalism," "took on a certain hardness in *fortes*," "possessed little sign of the richness expected of a really great voice." Ronal Jackson was the ideal for opera, the papers asserted.

Just about then, Aida and John Dickens decided that their star pupil had to branch out into the wider world of language mastery, and, to Joan's horror, acting.

A Miss Judy Rathbone Lawless (no getting away from the oddity of English names) had come out from the mother country and had started an "elocution school." It was called the Rathbone Academy of Dramatic Art. Rather artlessly, the initials suggested the Royal Academy of Dramatic Art in London, always known as RADA. To this emporium Joan was committed, balking all the way. She was made to prrro-nounce and differentiate between vowel sounds; to try to move, sit down, stand up, and even fall, with a certain amount of grace she didn't possess; and, in short, to endure twice-weekly torture for the sake of her "art."

Joan had set her heart on winning the Sun Aria contest, in which she had competed and lost twice. John, Aida, and Miss Lawless bombarded her with advice; only reluctantly did she accept the crowning bit—to wear long white gloves with her black velvet dress.

Whether or not her affected sophistication added importance to her "glorious voice, temperament, and intelligence" (as one reviewer put it), she won first prize, singing the *Aida* and *Tannhäuser* arias, adding Bantock and Charles songs.

"She'll be equally famous in *Lied* and opera" was one verdict (but where the basis for the judgment on *Lied*?) The reward was a whopping £300, her first important money, which was promptly banked.

Another event that autumn proved fateful. On November 28, 1949, Joan shared a Lithgow Celebrity Concert with a young pianist who had just won the City of Sydney Open Grand Championship (sports terminology again). He was a pale, thin youth, with a handsome, rather sulky face, enormous eyes, and short black hair, nervous until he got to work at the keyboard. There he gave a satisfactory account of Beethoven, Chopin, Weber, and Albeniz. Joan obliged with her familiar arias and songs.

And what was her first impression of young Richard Bonynge, who was to become her life companion?

"Rather self-opinionated" was all she would say when I asked.

The two would appear several times together before Richard

sailed for England, most notably at his farewell concert. Many of the young aspirants in Sydney were often thrown together in the crop of competitions they tried out for, and, also more informally, at the request of a lady named Gladys Hart, an accompanist for one of the music clubs. She busied herself by arranging little club entertainments and coaxed all the reluctant singers, pianists, and violinists into performing. They loathed it, Joan remembered . . . the ladies gobbling up sandwiches and rattling teacups, not a bit interested in the music going on over in one corner . . . poor competition. "But it was terribly good for you," she said, "because you got conditioned for the outside world by performing in front of indifferent people. And the five-guinea fee helped."

The youngsters pitied poor old Gladys and almost invariably said "yes" to her pleas. "Besides, she was a damned good cook, and at Christmas, or when some of the students had done something particularly spectacular, we'd all end up at her house for a splendid feed."

Perhaps even as enticing as the food was the chance for young people of a like persuasion to talk shop. Hardly a one of them could count on being understood at home; nor did most of their friends share their preoccupation with music, which set them apart.

"Gladys would get us together, and even when we met at each other's houses, we still had that sense of belonging," Joan recalled.

Between her Sun Aria triumph and the decisive moment of the Mobil Oil Quest lay almost a year of the grind to which she had become accustomed—music clubs all over the place with a few juicy additions to the repertoire: some Wolf, Rachmaninoff, and Gretchaninoff songs, and the soprano part in *Elijah* and *Samson* (though in the latter, a pettish critic thought she might as well be singing "Hey-nonny-nonny.")

Steadily becoming salient in this small pond, Joan was chosen more than once to partner Richard Bonynge in various benefit concerts. One at the Conservatorium, under the patronage of Sir Eugene Goossens, benefited a hospital for women and children. The young people plied their arts, sharing the stage with a violinist, Ronald Woodcock. This event resulted in the special distinction of a newspaper photograph that showed Richard sitting with his eyes closed and Joan leaning over his shoulder—not entirely flattering to either.

The end of the year brought Richard's farewell to Australia for fifteen years. At twenty, he had won a scholarship to the Royal

College of Music in London, and was to be fêted. These demonstrations seemed to speak of the Australian people's pride in homegrown talent, along with an undercurrent of rue that they might never see this talent on native soil again. All too many had departed, never to return.

The Mobil Oil Quest was the highest pinnacle to be attained by a young Australian singer. The Vacuum Oil Company had already shown its concern for opera in a series of network broadcasts, translated into performances "in the flesh." The second annual Quest drove its hundreds of young singers through the summer of 1950 to the Grand Finals in September. Joan survived all the way, past 874 other strugglers, sharing the final laurels with four men, all from Victoria except the baritone David Allen. Edwin Liddle was the only tenor. William Smith had been a previous finalist, and the fourth was Robert Allman, the only name that appears in Joan's later lexicon. He sang at Covent Garden and became a valued member of the Australian Opera.

Hector Crawford, longtime mentor of the contestants' dovecote, had conducted the Australian Symphony Orchestra all through the eighteen heats, the semifinals, and now the Grand Finals, which he also judged. Joan remembers him with gratitude, and had occasion later to know several of the judges better, especially Mrs. Frank Tait (later to become Lady Tait) and Dr. Percy Jones. Lady Tait is the widow of the impresario who was to bring Joan and Richard back in 1965 with their own company for a triumphant tour. Percy Jones, a jovial priest who is at home in the opera houses of the world, more recently served the Melbourne Conservatory. I spoke with him and he remembered Joan on that portentous night.

"First-class people are always simple. Even though I can't abide Wagner, I had to admit that Joan had the voice for it—a wealth of warmth and power. And that build!" She sang "Dich teure Halle" and "Voi lo sapete" (still in English), and the Ernest Charles song for the test.

As in other competitions, the verdict was announced excruciatingly with the low winners first. Liddle, Allman, and Smith were all called and the drawn breaths in Melbourne's Town Hall became audible. When the call for Allen at £300 came out, only one conclusion was possible: Sutherland was first with the £1,000 victory!

Flushed and girlish, she showed such obvious delight and goodwill toward her fellow competitors that their bitterness in defeat was softened. They congratulated her with sincerity.

The aftermath brought about the usual rash of press photographs, one showing Joan blowing kisses at her fellow contestants, another placing her on a piano bench singing to the janitor (that one a bit farfetched).

"No, she hadn't even thought of marriage." "Yes, she had a good-luck charm, a four-leaf clover in her glove." "Not temperamental, but emotional; never loses her temper" . . . and on and on. Some discouragement also nestled in the heart of newspaper encomiums: "the contest was at best amateur . . . they should use fully professional standards . . . after all, music is not an entertainment but an art . . ." thus revealing the self-conscious inferiority feelings of a provincial nation that had to insist on something superior without realizing exactly where it stood. After all, what are contests for, one might argue, except to expose talent that can and will become professional? And, if one talent of Joan's caliber emerges in a hundred tries, it can be said to be worth it.

The heroine of all this to-do went happily about her business, which at the time consisted of a sponsored tour to all the states with her two cowinners. Brisbane proved rather stuffy; Newcastle gave the break to its hometown Smith; Kalgoorlie, way out in western Australia, found Joan, in her gold-beaded green crepe ensemble with white gloves, singing gloriously. There were duets with Smith that ended with an arch bit called "Ah still suits me."

Adelaide thought the soprano had gained in poise and sensibility, "occasionally falling off in quality and flexibility," but prophesying that, when she fully liberated her range of emotions, a true Wagnerian would emerge. Clouds of "Glorious!" trailed her path.

Even now, although she had made the great decision to go to London, she was not spared the round of club concerts, jamborees for the Scots or the Irish, and skirmishes with xylophone and banjo virtuosi. Through the early spring they persisted. None of this activity gave her much time to fatten her repertoire, except that in her farewell concert she added arias by Peri and Arne, and, to establish another Wagnerian beachhead, the "Liebestod" from *Tristan and Isolde*. For this one special occasion, both Aida Dickens and her other coach, Adrian Holland, accompanied her.

The most startling development so far had been the request from the great man, Sir Eugene Goossens, that she sing the title role in his new opera, *Judith*, in the Conservatorium which he headed. She could not imagine why he had chosen her, except perhaps that he had noted all those benefit concerts and marked that she had shown up on time and seemed to know what she was doing. Certainly, she appeared to be an unlikely seductress-murderess. Goossens's librettist, Arnold Bennett, had provided for a decapitation scene in plain view, not even sparing the audience the goriness, as Oscar Wilde had done in *Salomé*. After the flourish with the knife, Judith was supposed to wave aloft a papier-mâché replica of Holfernes's head. Joan stifled her doubts and at least tried with her strong arm to do the deed. But Holfernes, played by a singer even more corpulent than his lover, rolled off the bed for all to see, his head still on his body. Nothing could save the situation. Joan had to take her curtain calls with a fiery face, only less suffused than the real head of her victim.

The papers called the production "hesitant and unimaginative." But Goossens had judged the musical abilities of his protégée correctly: Joan "declaimed freshly and well . . . sang broadly and boldly with dignity and style." Still, of course, she was "histrionically defeated, in a part that would have taken Sybil Thorndike to make plausible."

For her farewell concert on April 20 in Sydney Town Hall, three hundred tickets went for £3 apiece. Both the Sun and Vacuum Oil companies sponsored, giving her £350, more than enough to make up for the tax bite on her winner's purse. By now her bank account also harbored the bonus thousand promised by her Cousin John if she won the competition. It was a splendid nest egg for her London sojourn.

Now only a few concerts remained before her scheduled departure. In Brisbane, for the Murwillumbah Music Club, the exhilaration of it all went to Joan's head, and, for an encore, she tossed off "One Fine Day" from *Madama Butterfly* without ever having studied it. "A fit of madness," she explained. Her spirits could hardly be contained.

Muriel was not to be left behind, nor was Joan to be allowed to cross the terribly wide oceans and enter the strange, daunting bigness of London alone. Joan said later that she took her mother along to give Muriel something in return for all that she had done. It is true that Muriel would have been very lonely at home without her one fledgling.

On July 14, 1951, Joan and Muriel were "farewelled" by their friends on the old P. and O. liner *Maioja* with the assurance that in London they would at least have the standby assistance of Vacuum Oil, which looked after its chicks long after they hatched.

Off into the future she sailed, with high hopes and £2,000-plus in the bank.

CHAPTER

3

Young Maestro Takes Over

LONDON DID NOT SEEM SO FORMIDABLE AFTER ALL. Met at the dock by Vacuum Oil bigwigs, with limousine and flowers laid on, Joan and her mother were made to feel very important, even when deposited at their minimum-rate hotel. But the cocoon of security and prestige woven by their auspicious welcome soon dropped off, and they were left to face day-by-day living—cheerfully and hopefully, to be sure. Prepared to face it with them was a young compatriot. Richard Bonynge sought out the Sutherlands the very day after their arrival and soon became attached to the ménage, following them to successive dwellings and making himself very much at home.

Joan welcomed her young colleague warmly; Muriel, a trifle less so, perhaps with premonition. The boy was in the throes of frustration and indecision. His scholarship to the Royal College of Music had soured. They would not let him study Mozart with Kathleen Long, and worse, would not hear of his trying to be a conductor. He hared off to private lessons with one Herbert Fryer.

Nothing happened fast enough for him. Bonynge is an impatient man; he was an impatient youth.

There was always more to do than he could get done in one day—or a lifetime. A whole world of music, dance, theater, pictures, things to collect and cherish, a million things. So he started early.

Not a blazing prodigy, such as Mozart or Menuhin or a few others who have startled the world practically at babyhood, Richard nevertheless possessed the extraordinary gift that sets individuals apart. "I didn't choose music; it chose me" is his explanation. His father, Carl, had played the piano a bit, but there was nothing in the Bonynges' placid life to prepare them for a little three-year-old picking out nursery tunes on the upright keyboard. Instinctively, Richard went for the most pleasing sounds—the intervals of thirds and sixths.

The old piano, a German Romisch, so enormously heavy that it took four men to move it, was not used much after Richard went away. When I visited his parents, a quiet, gentle couple, I could see that it served as a simple shrine to what their only child meant to them. Photos of the boy, the man, his celebrated wife, and the grandson Adam sat atop it, as well as a drawing of Adam "made by someone in Melbourne when they were all here in 1965," explained Carl Bonynge.

The older couple's suburban house in Epping was like them: neat, modestly trimmed, solid. Carl was the spokesman; Betty sat silent for the most part, putting in a word or two now and then, hesitantly answering a direct question. One could see where Richard got his shyness.

Puffing on his pipe, Richard's father renewed his memories of the boy's talents. "I knew he had music in him," he said, "but we didn't push. He chose his own path. When he was four, a great-aunt gave us a gramophone. Richard would stand on the arm of a big chair and watch it in utter fascination. He just couldn't figure out where the music was coming from. It wasn't 'pop' music, you know, but folk tunes and such. No opera yet.

"Then there was a teacher who played the violin. Rick said, 'I can play that.' She told him to try, and he did. But the violin wasn't really for him. And he couldn't get enough out of the piano by himself. So he asked for a teacher—at four, mind you. We took him to Miss Crocker, a good sound teacher. But Rick said, 'I need a man.' Miss Crocker understood and recommended Lindley Evans, who had been Melba's last accompanist. That's when the boy started to develop. He got a good sense of values from Evans."

Always restless, at twelve Richard discovered a new world. He filled in for an opera-class accompanist and lost his heart to the singing voice. Within two years, he had acquired a sizable string of pupils whom he coached in opera. The die was cast.

Ballet, too, fascinated him, and this passion led to his deep and sensitive understanding of dancers and his numerous recordings of their music, so sympathetic that famous ballerinas swear by him.

But that lay beyond. Early, in Sydney, the boy was prey to

annual bronchitis and even asthma. Deeply disturbed by this and finding that standard treatment did no good, his parents decided to move away from their suburb by the sea to the home inland. Richard was sixteen. Hay fever has occasionally plagued him since, but the more severe infections have not recurred.

Betty and Carl each told a story about Richard's babyhood. "He just loved to drop eggs and see and hear them smash," related his mother. "Yes, eggs. He'd cry: 'Whoosh! What a lovely noise!' " To save the family budget—and the cleaning up—Mother would have to hide the eggs up high.

Carl added his bit: "One day I was planting beets, digging little holes in a row. Rick was with me, and awfully quiet. I looked back, and the child was pulling up every beet as I planted it. I'm afraid I yelled: 'You little bastard!' He didn't have the slightest idea what that meant, but he drew himself up right haughtily and yelled back at me: 'I am *not* a little bastard.' "

In his midteens, this gifted youngster turned nervously about, undecided on a future course. He completed an aptitude test, and it came out "music, music, music!" Away went thoughts of a diplomatic career: "I am probably the least diplomatic man in the world," he confessed later. And banished were visions of gliding gracefully down a mountain and teaching others to ski. His legs simply do not coordinate as well as his muscular conducting arms. (Now, if he zips down a mountain, it's on a sled, and there's less of that sort of thing with every passing year.)

Lindley Evans's home is on the way to the Bonynges, in a pretty suburb. When I visited there in 1974, from the house came piano music of the utmost loveliness and sensitivity. Evans rose from the keyboard, a tall, very thin, white-haired man of great, though rather reticent, charm. We sat on the porch, which overlooked the water; trees dappled with sunshine.

"Richard was one of the most versatile lads I've known," began Richard's former teacher, "and he's a gentleman—comes from gentle folk. He's a thoughtful man and a fine musician. That arrogance he displayed was a cover for lack of experience and real shyness. He really had to go through the hoops: When he began to enter the contest, he almost won a concerto test. Funny, but the girl who took first place is just modestly teaching somewhere now— and look at Richard!"

Mrs. Evans brought out an old scrapbook that contained mementos of Richard. Evans read an early letter from London, reprinted in a small newspaper, that described a vacation visit by

Joan and Richard to Switzerland, particularly the promontory of Chillon and the castle where the hero of Byron's *Prisoner of Chillon* was incarcerated. (The Bonynges' own home would one day be close by.) They had missed the little boat that would take them back to the steamer, and had frantically hired a taxi to the quay. But the boat had pulled out. Somehow they found a launch and drew alongside the vessel, whereupon a rope ladder was lowered for them. Imagine Joan scrambling up that! Luckier passengers lined the rails and cheered them on their tricky climb, taking photos like mad.

Another reprinted letter commented: "There are a lot of pianists over here not worth their salt." But Richard added high praise for Gina Bachauer. The young maestro was already beginning to assert his independent taste.

Then Evans chuckled and read out a review of Joan's very first opera venture, that Goossens melodrama glorifying Judith's foul deed. It went something like this: "I suppose it was necessary for Judith to learn the slightly uncomfortable art of decapitation, which is not usually among a singer's capabilities. She accomplished it satisfactorily. The corpse lay on the bed headless until the final curtain, which came back up too soon. She, running off stage, stopped for the applause. Now he, being headless, should he respond to Joan's invitation to share the approval? Apparently yes, for the big man rolled off the bed and came up with his head intact. Quite a trick."

"Of course, we consider Richard really responsible for Joan's enormous success," Evans concluded. "We couldn't believe in what he was doing until some friends invited us to hear a new batch of records she'd made. We were stunned! It was the first time we had heard that high-flying Joan. She had, after all, been a contralto and then a dramatic soprano. It was Richard who spotted her potential."

. . .

Their first summer day together in London, Richard, with characteristic thoroughness, trotted Joan off to a couple of museums, determined that she should broaden her artistic perceptions. She remembered it to me with wry humor.

"He took me to every museum. You name it, we went—as many as we could each day: the Tate, National Gallery, Royal Albert, places around Chelsea . . . but not the British Museum. I can't quite think why. Just the two of us. He walked my legs off. There were other outings, too. The politicians connected with the

Mobil Quest organization took me out, but I don't think I was quite ready for that—posh restaurants and all."

Richard, already disillusioned with the Royal College of Music, thought Joan was foolish to aim for it. "He was absolutely right about himself," Joan said. "He got fascinating results from Herbert Fryer, a marvelous old boy not actually in the College. Bertie and Rick got along very well. They were silly at the College to make him take theory and harmony all over again. He never would have won his scholarship if he hadn't mastered them already. He was furious; said people in the conducting class couldn't do any better than he. I said just the wrong thing: 'You've got to let them be the judge.' That infuriated him a little more."

Joan is as stubborn in her own way. John and Ada Dickens had made an appointment for her with Clive Carey at the RCM, and she kept it. Carey, who had studied with the illustrious Jean de Reszke, was greatly impressed by the quality of her voice and her seemingly endless breath. He realized that her faults were deficiencies that could be supplied—confidence, poise, security in her high voice, which she had always neglected in favor of her mezzo range. She was admitted right away to the Opera School. Almost immediately, to her horror, she discovered that her great body, which she felt to be incurably clumsy, was to be put to the rigors of ballet training.

"Ballet! Me! The ballet mistress made us do unimaginable things. Another Australian girl, rather tall, and great big David Ward, the bass, and I—all being butterflies and fairies. What a fool I felt!"

Both the uncertainties and the virtues were reflected in the progress reports issued by Carey (after a time in which Richard got in his nagging): "Joan is capable of the brilliant coloratura demanded by Bellini and Donizetti. If she fully realized the importance of relaxation, she could no doubt find her way to the very top. There is nothing she couldn't do . . . There is stiffness of body to contend with, but she has already gone far toward release . . . she must continually give her mind to improvement, on her own. . . . Good stage sense; gained in expressing emotion . . ."

Drama director Miss Wodeman thought Joan had made "remarkable progress. She has a feeling for the stage and a fine presence, and is beginning to realize how to use her assets—humor, warmth, and a capacity for emotion—and bring them into her work. She needs fluidity and ease in movement and gesture, and to get rid of the tendency to stiffen when she is nervous. Very cooperative."

Richard must have smiled like the Cheshire cat at Carey's reference to Bellini and Donizetti. He was already urging her toward these highland pastures. She had fallen into the habit of, with Carey's approval, taking him along to her singing lessons. "That's right, bring your boy." It amounted to a conspiracy.

"Yes, it's true that Ricky tricked me," admitted the prima donna, confirming the oft-told story. "He thought I had the voice to sing certain things—not exactly what I had in mind, of course. I've not got absolute pitch [the ability to pluck a tone out of the air or to identify one without peeking], so he sent me to the other side of the room, away from the piano, and told me I was singing in the key of C when it was really E-flat. I just didn't know the difference. But when I hit a high F, he managed to convince me. It hadn't been so hard. I thought I couldn't do better than a B, and now I could be certain of at least a C-sharp."

I asked her if she felt the difference in her head.

"Not really. But if I had known . . . one's always a little bit inhibited, afraid of going beyond what one thought possible. And you can make some awful sounds when they aren't supported. Oh, yes, I did that, too. But you don't need bad sounds to convince yourself there are good ones."

.   .   .

By now, the young man had practically abandoned his own career and constituted himself a one-man steering committee for Joan's. The fact was that Richard had always had a passion for the human voice. His own boyhood soprano had turned into what he described as a croaking old crow. It was the one real cause for dissension between him and Joan: "We really used to row about my singing. I wasn't mediocre; I was ghastly," he told a Canadian interviewer. "Joan would holler: 'Shut up and stop making that noise.' " He had found a friend in Terence McEwen, who later became the artistic director for Decca-London Records and subsequently shepherded the flock of discs made by Joan and Richard. Both young men confessed to being "record nuts," and spent many hours listening to great voices, comparing, criticizing, adoring. McEwen thought Richard a frustrated prima donna anyway. It was inevitable that he turn his growing expertise to his tall soprano friend.

Richard had always been fascinated by the early nineteenth-century operas, particularly those of the period known as *bel canto*. The term in Italian means simply "beautiful singing," but its implications range far beyond the definition to include perfect execution of florid music, as well as a long, flowing, and unbroken lyrical line. Richard came to it from an early infatuation with the piano music of Chopin, which is redolent with these characteristics.

"I think he latched on to the idea that I was the reincarnation of Giuditta Pasta or Maria Malibran, one of those legendary singers of his favorite period," laughed Joan when we spoke of it, "and he really wanted to express himself through that music—better than anything remotely connected with the piano—and to re-create the theatrical scene of the 1830s. He had to have a singer to do it. And there I was."

So they started to work seriously on the higher range. Bellini's *I Puritani*, which became one of Joan's cherished favorites, was early on the new agenda. For the BBC, Joan sang what she described as music dug out of the library and cooked up by various conductors—collections of songs and so on, which all went to prove that Richard was not as crazy as she had thought.

Alternately coaxing and bullying, never allowing her time out for trivialities or self-pity, he became the real master of the situation. The comparison with Svengali and Trilby was too great a temptation for the press, which later found the couple headline fodder. It has always distressed Joan a little, understandably; she is a strong-willed lady in her own right, and only yields when she is convinced the "irresistible force" is right. Trilby, after all, had no real voice until Svengali hypnotized her.

"Svengali? I don't think so," Joan commented during one of our visits together. "Richard had his own ideas of what I should do, and wouldn't take no for an answer. I could say 'No, I won't!' all I liked. But next day, I'd be doing it." She laughed again. "If he'd been another kind of personality and I'd had a different temperament . . . but what good are all those 'ifs'? He simply had the ability to get the best out of me, and I'm not the only one. Look at all the singers he's 'discovered' and helped!"

• • •

Almost immediately after their arrival in London, Joan and her mother moved from their modest hotel to a charming place arranged by a friend. They stayed only a fortnight, however. Muriel, ever cautious, thought it too expensive. Instead, they got a flat at the head of Kensington High Street, at Notting Hill Gate—"the wrong part of London. It was the very top attic, with three nasty flights of stairs. We shared it with a girl who worked in the Foreign Office. But we were mostly alone, away from the rest of the house. [We] had a piano and an extra little room up there, instead of just one big bed-sitter, so Mother had a separate room. The kitchen, which was in the middle of the row of rooms, we shared with the girl. It was good that we were right up there; we heard no noise but our own."

Joan was very happy to have her mother with her. Back home she had never been able to persuade Muriel to take much for board, and felt that she owed her a great deal. Muriel really enjoyed herself in London, apart from worrying about pence and pounds and Richard. "She went to Australia House, little functions once a month," recalled Joan. "And she'd visit friends at the Victorian League and in Kew Gardens and get on the Green Line Bus and take little jaunts.

"But I really felt badly about those three flights she had to climb."

All this time, Muriel's daughter was toiling at the Royal College and taking barrages of advice and criticism from young Bonynge. He, more often than not, would accompany his "protégée" home after bouts with museums or concerts or cheap seats in the "gods" at Covent Garden. There he would conduct his lectures, "and incidentally," said Joan wryly, "get a free meal."

All of this did not sit particularly well with Muriel. Here was this upstart trying to convert her daughter's voice from the deeper realms where it belonged to altitudes undreamed of. And, he was "pushy."

Meanwhile, Joan plodded on, and one day no less than astounded Professor Carey by singing the vocal fireworks of the aria "Qui la voce sua soave" from *I Puritani*. He had been working to lighten her middle voice and to coax her to sacrifice a bit of her phenomenal breath control now and then for the sake of expressiveness, but all to the end of fashioning a dramatic soprano. Her perfectly articulated arpeggios and trills, her dazzling ornamentation of the line of the Bellini aria, and the pure high E-flat at the end bowled him over.

Yes, the swan was beginning to emerge from those drab duckling feathers. Slowly, but inevitably, Richard Bonynge was getting his way.

CHAPTER

4

Covent Garden at Last

JOAN FELT SHE WAS NOW READY FOR THE CHAL-lenge of the Royal Opera House. It took her three tries, each one as discouraging as the one before. She got her first audition on the strength of a letter from Eugene Goossens, who praised her "dramatic soprano voice." The members of Covent Garden's administration, who had heard her in Wigmore Hall, the principal recital hall, were left bewildered with her choice of music as dramatic as Wagner and as high-flying as Bellini. Who in the world these days could encompass those extremes, except that rare bird Maria Callas? And *she* was one of a kind, probably never to be duplicated. Covent Garden's repertoire could not open up for those old-fashioned pieces. *Norma* was as far as they would go, even for the inimitable Callas.

The report slammed the door on Joan: "A ring in the voice, but very little experience or gifts of nature," the kind of gifts, in other words, that would allow her to make a presentable appearance on stage. After all, Covent Garden had only four "resident" so-pranos, taxing their versatility to the limit. Joan simply did not fit their requirements.

Six months of hard work with both Carey and Richard went by before Joan applied for a second audition. It was granted. This time, again in the small hall, she ranged from Wagner to Mozart, finishing with the fiendishly difficult "Non mi dir" from *Don Giovanni*, with all the embellishments Richard was sure Mozart had intended. It left the auditors breathless—if not the singer—but still puzzled. They asked her to sing again, this time for the administrator, David Webster, and filed a private report that showed their confusion. It criticized her Wagner, but added: "You should take her."

A third chance came. Here she was singing on the very stage she had dreamed about since childhood, even if it was only with a work light and to a darkened auditorium. She was asked to begin with "Non mi dir." Then she relapsed into the heavy dramatic arias her mother had drilled into her.

Again the reaction was ambiguous. "Stylish. Very good diction [note this for future reference]. Top quite good. Sympathetic. Middle very good. But is she a proposition for the theater?"

Convinced that it was all over, she chugged on through her routine at the Royal College, enlivened by an occasional performance. In May 1952, one of these was a hearty affair called *All at Sea*. The libretto and lyrics were written by the well-known British actor-author Sebastian Shaw and his then wife. (He was later to marry Joan Ingpen, an artists' agent who was to become a potent influence in Sutherland's life.) The music was by Shaw's father, Geoffrey. David Ward, later prominent at Covent Garden, portrayed an old sea captain. Joan sang the small part of Mrs. Empson, which Joan Ingpen insisted was in the mezzo range. Alexander Gibson, who was to become noted as the music director of the Scottish Opera, conducted the piano accompaniment. Nothing much more than hilarity is roused when the occasion is mentioned in the company of either of the two Joans.

Joan finished her school year singing Giorgetta in Puccini's *Il Tabarro* in a student performance. One of Covent Garden's future conductors, Edward Downes, heard that performance. Talking about Joan some twenty years later, he recalled to me that it seemed as though she sat on that barge in the River Seine and did not move the entire night. But the voice was fabulous, and he believed then, and still believes, that Joan should have been the greatest Verdi singer who ever lived, although Puccini was decidedly "not her world."

In the meantime, Covent Garden had finally come to a decision in regard to Joan. That third audition proved to have been the clincher. A telephone call eventually summoned an amazed Joan to the Garden for the somewhat less than seraphic salary of £10 per week, £15 on tour. Ecstatic, she would almost have sung for nothing; but, of course, Muriel would not have heard of that.

Here she was, straight from "down under" and terribly green, wildly enthusiastic, but trying not to show it; timid; gawky; unused to the breezy camaraderie of backstage opera; and unable on her first day to find the "loo" in the dungeon labyrinth of the old, ramshackle opera house—but altogether blissful. She had been asked to learn the roles of the First Lady in Mozart's *Magic Flute*, the nurse Clothilde in Bellini's *Norma*, and the Priestess in Verdi's *Aida*—all small roles, but with potential. Her fellow artists proved unexpectedly kind. In spite of her size, Joan inspired others to help, to protect, to push her along on her chosen path.

She got through those first three roles with no disaster. The purity of her voice as the *Aida* Priestess, the beauty of it as it floated in from backstage, had been noted in several important quarters. What's more, she had come under the influence of the great Callas, for La Divina had been engaged to sing *Norma*.

Edward Downes had been engaged as an Italian prompter. Odd as it seems, there had never been one at Covent Garden, but Callas insisted upon it. He arrived on the scene the very same day as Joan. "We had heard about this extraordinary tigress, Callas," he recalled, "and Joan and I became absolutely besotted with this phenomenon. I still have the present Joan gave me then—Callas singing *Puritani*."

On November 8, 1952, beside her idol—the enormously heavy but utterly regal Maria Callas—Joan shivered with nerves and anticipation. The revered woman was no termagant; on the contrary, she had proved to be a genuinely good colleague, down-to-earth and easy to work with. She had even agreed that Joan might emulate her someday. Joan's question to her was an indication that Richard's constant nagging was beginning to take effect.

By now, it was apparent that Joan stood in need of help. Her gaucheries, her incessant mugging when she made mistakes (never to be completely eliminated), her uncertainty about her own bodily presence in stage situations, all spoiled the stage picture.

Norman Feasey, Covent Garden chief coach, was drilling her in such unlikely roles (at least for the present) as the Marschallin in Strauss's *Der Rosenkavalier* and the other German repertoire that was his specialty. Downes, who also had her on his list, actually despaired. The final straw was Joan's sluggish learning ability, a characteristic that has lasted throughout her career and for which she has had to compensate.

Downes told Webster that they should dismiss her—she would never make an opera singer. "What I meant in my naive, youthful way," reflected Downes, "was that she was not going to make the sort of opera singer I dreamed about—an Isolde and an Elektra with a little Aida thrown in." This was treated very seriously by Webster and Steuart Wilson, his deputy director. "They very certainly took note of what I said, but also took note of my callow age and my reasons." Fortunately, they felt they knew better. Joan remained, singing in dozens of performances that Downes conducted, first as Frasquita, then Micaela in *Carmen* ("which she sang beautifully," said the now repentant Downes), Olympia in *Les Contes d'Hoffmann*, Gilda in *Rigoletto*, and Desdemona in *Otello*.

On the provincial tour, the local reports had it that she sang the Countess in Edinburgh's *Le Nozze di Figaro* "without any undue mishap" (what is a "due" mishap?). At the home opera, she once learned the taxing role of Amelia in Verdi's *Un ballo in maschera* in six hours to replace an ailing soprano. For this unwonted effort, in December 1952, she won these words: "Not sensational, but acquitted herself creditably." This noble effort convinced Downes that she was a real trouper. He became her faithful friend and adviser. At about this time, he was forced to coach her in the seemingly impossible role (and with almost no time to do it!) of Brangaene in *Tristan und Isolde*. This was impossible, at least from Richard's point of view, because it is a heavy mezzo part and Wagnerian at that. This happens to be Downes's favorite opera, however, and the distinguished conductor Sir John Barbirolli had specially asked for Joan. He admired the mezzo quality in her voice, having evidently heard her in an occasional concert. Downes took on the chore cheerfully. Slow learner or not, she mastered the part over the weekend, "swotting by the hour." The part actually consists of only two "warnings" in the second-act love scene, sung offstage. Joan remained in her plain black suit and did not even take a curtain call.

Everyone but Richard seemed to like it. Here, ironically, for a part she would never sing again, were some of her first real press notices. The *Daily Express* spoke of the "round and confident voice that rose above the strength of the full symphony orchestra . . . heartwarming." The *Guardian* called it "memorable, enriched by just sufficient a vibrato to give it sensuous beauty."

In May, Joan was among the group of singers for a concert to welcome the new Queen. In July and August, she joined a small band (including the Australians Monica Sinclair, Ron Jackson, and John Lanigan, and the Americans Frances Yeend and Jess Walters) who played at the Royal Theater in Bulawayo, Rhodesia, to celebrate the centenary of Cecil Rhodes. Joan sang the *Figaro* Countess, and, for the first time, the role of Lady Penelope in Benjamin Britten's *Gloriana*, which had been written expressly for the coronation of Queen Elizabeth II. It had been given its premiere at Covent Garden on June 8, with Jennifer Vyvyan singing the part Joan later took over. She welcomed the sort of review she got: "A handsome figure, as well as singing some exceptionally difficult music."

Not that she cared for this "difficult" music very much. Never, in fact, would she feel really at home in new idioms. She said as much to Lord Harewood, who, at age thirty, had joined the company as Controller of Opera Planning in the spring of 1953.

"I was terribly shocked by this blasé young singer," recalled Lord Harewood when I met with him later, "I remember thinking: 'Well, she's not very much!' But then, just a fortnight later, I met her in a corridor. Typical of her, she was able to go back on what she'd said, and acknowledged that the part was marvelous and she was enjoying it.

"This was always the good thing about her: she knew that she was valuable, but with absolutely no side—isn't that an American expression, too?"

An early instance of this trait occurred at a party after a benefit concert at Royal Albert Hall. Lord Harewood was standing by Joan as the guests were thinning out. A young person approached the singer for an autograph. As Harewood told it:

" 'Oh, Miss Sutherland,' the girl said, 'you were so wonderful. I do so admire you, and my mother was such a fan of yours!' This was too much for Joan, who collapsed with a *whoosh* of laughter in a heap on the floor!" The girl got her autograph, and one for her mother as well.

· · ·

Joan Ingpen actively entered Joan Sutherland's life in 1953. A musician by training and an artist's agent by choice, she headed the enterprising firm of Ingpen and Williams, managers of opera singers. (The "Williams" of the partnership, by the way, was neither man nor woman, but Ingpen's dog. She thought the firm name sounded prettier than with her name alone.)

For the new *Ring* cycle at Covent Garden Ingpen had booked the German producer Rudolf Hartmann and came by the Garden one day to take him to lunch. Waiting in the auditorium, she listened to the eight Valkyries vocalizing on the rocky heights.

"Who is that girl singing Helmwige?" she inquired backstage. It was then that she encountered Joan for the first time.

"I remember I took her on," Ingpen recalled, "and tried to talk about her all over the place. It was an era when nobody believed British singers could be any good. It took a little while."

The first breakthrough was an SOS from Cologne, where a soprano had canceled out of a Handel opera. "How about this marvelous girl you keep talking about?" it asked. Joan went over and made a big success. Although noted little at home, it was very soothing to her amour propre. She came back to Covent Garden remarking that it was very nice to go somewhere where she was treated as an important visitor.

The next emergency found her less ready. Ingpen had tried, without any luck, to land a BBC date for her new protégée. Then, on a week's notice, a soprano reneged on an assignment for the Beethoven *Missa Solemnis*. Ingpen assured the radio authorities that her new soprano could handle the job—and then proceeded to convert Joan to the idea.

"But I've got my mother sick with flu and Richard is away," Joan protested. Both were important, Joan's devotion to her mother a notable factor, and Richard's guidance in learning anything new indispensable. "I've never even seen it. How could I learn it?" Joan agonized.

Ingpen soothed her, and then took the score, underlining all the soprano parts in red. She promised: "I'll sit with your mother."

Joan made her trembling way to the BBC studio and sang "marvelously," Ingpen later recalled.

There was to be no more trouble with the BBC after that.

. . .

If Joan had found Britten's music uncongenial at first, worse was in store. Lord Harewood had persuaded Michael Tippett to write a formidable part for her in his *Midsummer Marriage*, which was coming up shortly. Joan never did fathom this peculiar role. Tippett told her not to bother, just to sing as beautifully as she could. However, she worried constantly about climbing a stairway that ostensibly led to a higher world, but in reality ended in midair. The result: Lord Harewood thought Joan magnificent; so did some of the critics.

Sprinkled among these regular stints were occasional odd jobs that added experience, and, in a few cases, caught important eyes and ears. She shared a Celebrity Carol Concert in Orpington Civic Hall with Alfred Deller, counter tenor, and Heddle Nash, tenor, soaring above them in Bach and Mozart. Her *Madama Butterfly*, over the BBC General Overseas Service, fluttered few sensibilities; and she did nothing for herself by Lisa's aria from Tchaikovsky's *Queen of Spades* at a Prom Concert; but her Mozart *Exultate Jubilate* galvanized a Concerto Orchestra concert as *Alleluia*, the third element of that wonderful piece, had previously done. She even filled in as Aida for her countrywoman, Joan Hammond, on one occasion.

Meanwhile, she was assigned to Agathe in Weber's *Der Frei-*

schütz, scheduled for May 1954. It was a role that called for more than singing; a little acting would be a good thing, too, and, by universal opinion, Joan did not know how to walk across a stage. The higher-ups decided to pay for a course in acting for their promising ugly duckling. Christopher West, Covent Garden's resident producer (director, to Americans), had too many chores on his list and passed this one to a friend.

Webster phoned Norman Ayrton, former actor-teacher, and now coaching drama: "We have a young girl here, an Australian, and we think she has a voice of potential world promise. But she's got a lot to learn—just doesn't know a thing about acting. If you ask her to be a tree, you won't get much result. Do take her on."

Ayrton agreed and set a date. He recalled it vividly to me. It was February 12, 1954. He was late getting to his studio, which was upstairs in Upper Baker Street. There she stood, this girl, looking out the grimy window at dustbins. She wore a tacky black coat trimmed with braid, and a velvet hat that looked "like an inverted saucer . . . not terribly becoming," Ayrton put it politely. Her hair was a mousy color, pulled rather tightly away from her long face.

"She looked at me, I at her," he continued. She was obviously unwilling to go on, but finally agreed to two or three sessions a week. Then Ayrton sat and listened to her sing (she chose "Leise, leise," from *Freischütz*); he swallowed hard and said: "Ah, now we know where we are."

Thus began a pull-and-haul operation that left both of them exhausted; Joan usually rebellious, but gaining slowly. Her coach would ask her to do things that embarrassed her, and she was scared of the whole thing. She couldn't move without fear, was acutely conscious of her size, and apparently had no physical imagination. Embarrassment triggered a defense mechanism, until battles ensued, one strong will against another. Richard had discovered that the best way was to make her genuinely angry, agreeing with W. H. Auden, who wrote on the subject of anger in a delightful little book, *The Seven Deadly Sins*:* "Anybody, like a schoolmaster, a stage director, or an orchestral conductor, whose business it is to teach others to do something, knows that, on occasion, the quickest—perhaps the only—way to get those under him to do their best is to make them angry."

* *The Seven Deadly Sins*, William Morrow, Sunday Times Publications Ltd., 1962.

The inevitable result was a flood of tears and repentance. Then Norman—and Richard—knew she was ready to start again. It was often difficult to get her mind to focus on the exercises she didn't want to do. She would find any excuse to circumvent Ayrton. Underlying her contrariness was, of course, the uncertainty, the extraordinary lack of self-confidence.

Joan was frightened at the beginning of anything untried. Hours were spent over her climb of the eerie staircase in *Midsummer Marriage*, and she had to get through the *Freischütz*. They tried it out in Manchester in March, and there were compliments for Joan. Then, in London, at least one critic approved her "ravishing voice, a voice to watch, firm, well focussed, with rare purity and warm artistry." So far, so good.

Freischütz is a *singspiel*, which means that spoken dialogue alternates with singing (just as in the French opéra comique and a later descendant, the American "musical"). It was this dialogue that Joan never really mastered without a strong Australian streak. The performance was in English (Edward Dent's translation), so the words should have been at least as understandable as any operatic text, given the musical demands and singers with good diction. After long hours of training, Ayrton gave up.

"Keep your Aussie twang," he advised. The rest of the cast was polyglot, so that Joan did not obtrude unduly.

Gradually, Ayrton (who belied his mild, blond appearance with a firmness that occasionally amounted to whiplash) saw this Galatea take shape. She learned not to semaphore her arms meaninglessly, but to make a gesture with her hands express something; to walk smoothly or precipitately as the action called for; even to glide effortlessly over the ground in a swoop reminiscent of a bird's flight. This move became unforgettable in the *Lucia di Lammermoor* Mad Scene and in the doll scene in *Tales of Hoffmann* (thanks also to the later good offices of Franco Zeffirelli and Tito Capobianco).

Best of all, to Joan's way of thinking, she learned to fall gracefully and without injury. It is startling to watch this statuesque beauty suddenly go limp and collapse quite slowly to the floor in one fluid motion. She also learned how to kneel, and equally important, how to get up. One director with whom she has since worked a great deal invariably has his characters kneel. Joan can do it, no matter how encumbering the skirts, how turbulent the action.

Soon, the critics began to wake up to the presence of a new voice and personality. Andrew Porter, one of the first to appreciate her, wrote of Joan's Antonia in *Tales of Hoffmann*: "Tall, with pre-Raphaelite looks, as sweetly attractive as her voice. She acted convincingly, sang with artistry, and beautiful tone." Points scored for size and acting.

She took over the courtesan Giulietta for another singer in Scotland and Manchester, but it was the doll Olympia that first woke up the public to the higher reaches of her coloratura. (She was not to sing all three of Hoffmann's loves in one performance until much later.) In the role of Giulietta the producer Günther Rennert required her to throw herself on a pile of cushions while laughing seductively. There were hysterical moments in her music room with Ayrton coaching, Joan giggling, balking, then finally letting go and flinging herself down. It was worth it. She made the greatest impression on Scotland as an actress. Another point racked up.

All was not so serene in *Carmen*; Joan had graduated from Frasquita to Micaela, José's country sweetheart. Rafael Kubelik, the Czech conductor, had decided to do the Bizet opera in its original version, with the dialogue that had been prescribed by the composer for its premiere at the Opéra-Comique in Paris. For a subsequent performance in Vienna, after Bizet's death, his friend Ernest Guiraud had composed the singing conversation or recitatives, and this version had persisted thereafter everywhere except in France. (Recently, it has become fashionable to revert to the dialogue, to the distress of many singers. The operatic voice does not readily change gears into speech. It was the talk and not the "popular" songs that troubled Ezio Pinza in *South Pacific*.) Joan hated dialogue, shrinking from the exposure of her broad accent. Suddenly, she was confronted by the *Carmen* maestro with the request: "Where's your dialogue?" just as she was about to embark on the third-act aria, the one that invariably brings down the house for Micaela—Joan's only real chance to shine in this role. She had already conquered one obstacle; they had not wanted her to do Micaela, because she towered over the Gypsy heroine, Carmen (in this case, Regina Resnik, the American mezzo, buxom in her own right, but lacking the inches to match her "rival"). Joan had made good in the part, however, still rather stiff, but singing her aria magnificently. But to speak? She was totally at a loss, waiting for the orchestra to play the passages that preceded her aria. Sparks began to fly. Kubelik insisted; Joan resisted. Finally, she fled in distress to Webster's office. "She walked out on Maestro!" everybody whispered in shock.

The mouse had roared, a very big mouse, to be sure, but heretofore so meek. It was the first time (it was to happen yet once more) that the soprano balked at the man in the pit. And what was to be done about it?

Webster, with that tact that is inborn in an opera impresario, settled the fuss by having Joan omit the preliminary to her aria and utter neither dialogue nor recitative. Kubelik was pacified, as famous conductors must be, and the Micaela's misgivings and temper were soothed. Joan has become noted for the evenness of her disposition, but, once in a while, if pushed too far, "I stamp my foot," she says, only half in jest. She would encounter the other maestro who called forth this unaccustomed rebellion only after she had become a star on her own.

This had been Regina Resnik's first acquaintance with Joan. To one schooled in opera hierarchies, as she was, this flouting of a conductor, especially by a "minor" singer, was unheard of, even if one were a Geraldine Farrar, as in the classic story. (Farrar got her comeuppance when she defied Arturo Toscanini and proclaimed herself *the* star. The great conductor's withering reply: "Signorina, the only stars are in heaven.") Yet, after hearing Joan sing the aria, relieved of the burden of dialogue, Resnik capitulated and the two have been friends and respected colleagues ever since. As for Kubelik, all was forgiven; he was to preside over Joan's *Meistersinger* and *Dialogue of the Carmelites* in perfect harmony in the near future.

She was beginning to emerge out of the medium-to-good class, and it would be her two mentors, David Webster and Lord Harewood, who would give her the final push upward into stardom.

"But you must remember," Lord Harewood cautioned, "that the world is full of people who helped 'make Joan what she is!' And some of them, if they tell the story often enough, begin to think she could not have done it without them. I don't belong to that school. I think she always had it. The moment anything happened to kindle the spark, she had it. Many people made things possible for her. Perhaps she is a lazy responder and needs something to respond to, but she's always had it."

CHAPTER
5

Marriage and Other Milestones

WHILE JOAN'S CAREER PROCEEDED IN WHAT MIGHT be called fits and starts, and Richard devoted less and less time and love to the piano and more and more to buoying and bullying Joan, their respective home lives left something to be desired. She grew weary of the confines of her flat, with its inadequate kitchen, and he of the time and energy consumed getting across London from his flat to hers.

One day, Joan came up with the idea of renting a house. She didn't have to consult her mother; that formidable lady had gone off to Australia to care for her elder sister, Bloss, and would not return for several months. With her own inborn caution, Joan approached David Webster at Covent Garden for advice. Could she afford such a move? Webster thought she could. After all, she would be in line for bigger things, and soon, he hinted. So she used part of Cousin John's gift of £1000 to take a seven-year lease on a house at 20 Aubrey Walk, still in Notting Hill Gate.

An eccentric old lady by the name of Miss Horne had owned the house, Joan was told. The mistress of a friend of Keats, she had been also a devotee of music, and, though there was not a bed in the house, a piano had formerly adorned every room. Joan, Richard, piano, and chaperone—a Mrs. Fox—moved in. "We were all very young," sighed Joan. "I owed Richard so much, but he would not take any pay. So at least he could save carfare, share the rent, and have his meals in nice surroundings."

The marriage seems to have been broached in a rather offhand manner, but Joan bridled at the suggestion that she did not have a bona fide proposal.

"You bet I did!" she retorted, when I ventured to ask. "Richard came stalking in one day—I was ironing one of his shirts—and blurted out: 'This is silly. You know your mother isn't going to like me living here like this. Why don't we get married?' "

Joan said she gasped at the abrupt quality of the proposal, but with her usual control of her feelings, managed to sound just as casual in her acceptance. They decided the following Saturday would do. No use in waiting. Clive Carey, who gave the bride away, and David Webster, who sent a bouquet of red carnations, were the only ones in on the secret. Even the newspapers did not find out until later. The happy couple telephoned two friends the next morning with the bulletin: "We're married." Norman Ayrton was one of those favored. "It came out of the blue," he told me.

The other friend to be telephoned was Elizabeth (Betty) Allen, remembered from Australian competition days. After winning the Mobil Quest in 1953, she had come to London to seek her fortune. She was to remain on the scene until 1958, witnessing Joan's trials and triumphs and experiencing a few of her own. In that time she married and divorced (although Richard thought Mme. Wocejewicz, her married name, to be a marvelous one for the stage). Joan and Richard were to throw both a kitchen "shower" and a wedding breakfast for her. A photograph of the latter shows Joan wearing a most unbecoming hat—flat as a board and perched uncompromisingly on her tightly bound hair, leaving the long face to seem even longer. Richard later told her to burn that hat, arbiter as he had become of every detail of his wife's appearance.

What did Joan wear at her own unusually "quiet" wedding? Not white and orange blossoms, you may be sure. "A red corduroy deal and a great big hat." (The same one? She does not remember.) And how were her clothes in those days?

"Monstrous!"

Immediately after their unceremonious ceremony, they cabled Richard's parents. They were delighted, although Richard's young aunt, Jane Roughley (known as "Weenie"), later to become very involved in their careers, cabled back that she would have preferred a contralto. Muriel Sutherland's reply to her cable showed that she had swallowed only a little of her disapproval: "You naughty children. Watch yourselves. Love."

The new couple invited a few friends over for dinner. The next night they attended a big party at Adele Leigh's, a charming soprano who sang at Covent Garden. Joan recalled to me: "Muriel Kerr, Webster's secretary, called for silence, and introduced 'Mr. and Mrs. Richard Bonynge.' Everybody fainted."

Muriel was not reconciled all that quickly. "Her idea had been for me to marry somebody who would support me—that had been her own problem," Joan said. "One of her big worries about Richard and me was that we were both stupid musicians. I don't think she need have worried so much. At least I had managed to solidify my position. And Rick was on his way. But of course in our day little girls were brought up to be housewives. It is ingrained."

Housewifery—the other side of Joan's nature—tried to reassert itself in the new surroundings whenever a minute could be snatched from the grind of study, rehearsal, and performance. And it was a grind. Muriel did not quite understand the necessity for a professional singer to spare her energy and spend it at the right times. After a strenuous rehearsal or coaching session, Joan would find that Muriel expected household chores of her. "All this when she was just emerging into success and needed every ounce of her strength," commented Ayrton. Cheerfully Joan accepted these duties, but at the expense of fatigue. "And in the new house," Betty Allen recalled, "there was kitchen furniture to paint, a tiny garden to dig and plant—always some little task for poor Joan."

Richard at the time was playing a few concerts and broadcasts, but his talents were gradually being turned entirely Joan's way. She, ever the peacemaker, diplomatically fostered his self-esteem while fending off her mother's disdain. Muriel did not bring her opinion of Richard entirely out in the open, but she would grumble to Betty Allen, who had moved in to take care of her during a spell of illness. Her habit of referring to him as "Mr. Sutherland" rankled. He was not a gentleman. He did not get dressed in the morning, but showed up for breakfast in his dressing gown. Gentlemen got up at a proper hour, bathed, and got dressed before they showed themselves. And almost worst of all, he wore suede shoes!

Between coaching sessions with his wife, with Betty Allen, and with a few other young aspirants, this nongentleman succeeded in making the house beautiful with old prints, posters, porcelain figurines—the beginnings of a fabulous collection. He and Betty would roam through the junk shops, Richard invariably lighting on some obscure treasure that turned out to be "real." It was lots of fun, Betty thought. One picked up the collecting bug just from Richard's sheer enjoyment.

Joan's work became even more strenuous, more concentrated. In an effort to minimize her height, she had formed the habit of slouching and bending her knees. Ayrton told her grimly that she looked like a camel. Unfortunately, much of this valuable training in the studio fell by the wayside when she confronted those puny tenors, those shorter mezzos and baritones on stage.

This slouch made her seem even older than her thirty-one years, a decided detriment, as most of her parts were young or youngish women. Ayrton drilled her day after day for suppleness, straight and upright carriage, lighter movement.

"I had always *sat* up straight," maintained Joan. "Mother made me."

But her self-consciousness ran so very deep. It would all have to be taken care of somehow.

The voice also encountered problems. A *Times* critic had spotted it. "At present she is inclined to spoil the vocal line in the middle and low registers by throwing the tone back into the mouth." He did add that at the top there were flexibility, power, brilliance, and beauty of tone, "but she still has much to learn about style. Gluck, Mozart, Bellini, and Liszt [this referred to a concert in Wigmore Hall] were all much of a muchness, and likely to remain so until she attends to her words—there is no thought of interpretation."

Well, Richard would fix all that. He was as persistent as a drillhammer on every point of music, of tone, of phrase, and of nuance. His shouting and verbal abuse would reduce her to tears, but she always came up for more. Thus were the refinements of *bel canto* literally and unrefinedly pounded into the budding coloratura.

At about this time, her nagging husband also turned his attention to Joan's appearance. The hair . . . something must be done about it. It made her look excessively plain, minimizing her strong and handsome bone structure, her fair and perfect skin, that pair of glorious hazel eyes.

"Dye it!" commanded the stern mentor. She went off to a beauty parlor and came back as a blonde. It was some improvement, but not entirely satisfactory. No more money could be spared, however, so as a blonde she appeared (somewhat to the shock of her companions, it must be said), and short and curly to boot, until a year or so later. Again she put herself trustfully into the hands of a beautician. Red, red, *blazing* red this time. Fearfully, she confronted Richard. To her astonishment, he rather liked it. And glorious red it remained, although the superabundant length to which she had let it grow has since been cropped.

Still in her blond incarnation, the months went by with the calendar showing the usual provincial tours and a little Wagner, which, of course, Richard frowned upon. They were small parts to be sure: Woglinde, the first Rhinemaiden in *Das Rheingold* and *Götterdämmerung*, Helmwige, one of the shouting Valkyries in *Die Walküre*, and, more importantly, the Forest Bird in *Siegfried*. She was later to record this in illustrious company, herself almost too illustrious to be cast in such a minor role.

Now her pregnancy became noticeable to an alarming degree. Fortunately, there were plenty of Micaelas in flowing peasant skirts. One February evening, after a supper of baked beans, she said: "Let's go to a flick." She and Richard saw a horror film, a strange prenatal influence by any prescription. Joan began to feel pains. She thought it was indigestion, but Mother knew better. Off to the maternity ward in Queen Charlotte's Hospital Muriel and Richard packed her. A boy, whom they named Adam Carl, was born February 13, 1956. Several of her friends called on her in hospital, and found her beaming with joy.

"It was difficult at first to think of Joan as a mother," recalled Norman Ayrton. Joan took it very seriously, even though it became necessary to engage someone to look after the baby. With the kind of fortune that seems to pursue them, Joan and Richard found a Swiss girl, Ruthli Brendle, who remained with them through the years, surrogate during the parents' long absences.

"It didn't do to take Adam around with us," said Joan. "He started playing up to all the old ladies and fans and photographers and was really becoming a little monster in a very short time. He went to a day school until he was twelve, then to a boarding school."

The lack of an orthodox home has been accepted by all three, parents and son, as the inevitable hazard of this kind of career.

Joan Ingpen recalled afterward a typical incident in Adam's first days.

"I had sent my car to a friend who was going to the hospital to have a baby. When Joan heard that the baby was born, she said, 'Oh, may I come in to see her?' It was a great occasion. All the nurses remembered her and she had a big ovation. She hadn't had Adam in a private room but in a public ward. I was astonished to hear that. 'Of course!' she insisted. 'I was only earning £10 a week!'"

Meanwhile, Joan's teeth—ragged, uneven, discolored—remained the one flaw in her facial beauty. She had tried not to smile openly, a nervous habit that made her even more self-conscious than normally, but she could not conceal the offenders when singing. Her first appearance at the revered summer festival of Glyndebourne had suffered from this cosmetic fault. Lord Harewood, who kept a constant and fond eye on Joan's progress, had heard her sing the demanding aria "Martern aller Arten," from Mozart's *Die Entführung aus dem Serail*, at a concert and a subsequent broadcast. Overcome by her brilliance, he had recommended her for the part of the Countess in Glyndebourne's *Le Nozze di Figaro* in this Mozart bicentenary year of 1956. Glyndebourne, the spacious estate of John Christie, could be a prestigious step for Joan. The beautiful house and grounds, some miles from London in the countryside of Sussex, had been turned by their master into a showcase for his wife, Audrey Mildmay, a soprano of some ability. He surrounded her with the best singers in the world in an ambience that was at once bucolic and sophisticated. Stage equipment was excellent, the stage and theater itself charming. Eager pilgrims from the city would take the short train ride dressed in evening best; many carried picnic baskets to share on the lush green lawns, others dined in the rambling brick edifice. Glyndebourne had become an international cachet, esteemed by buffs and bigwigs alike.

Behind the scenes, all was not the best possible world for the newcomer. Joan felt her size more keenly here; the stage was so small. The producer, Carl Ebert, had little time for her individually, and she found the coaches stern and unhelpful. Chief of these, a crusty little Hungarian, Jani Strasser, really wielded a big stick and intimidated her still further. He was to coach every role she undertook from then on in this halcyon byway, and to become a staunch friend and supporter.

(After his death in 1978, a former protégé, Martin Isepp, wrote in *Opera News*: "His similes were mostly visual and frequently unprintable . . . To resent his autocratic approach was to misunderstand his humility when perfection was within his grasp. He loved his position as enfant terrible!")

Although Mrs. Bonynge felt hopelessly lost, none of her trepidation showed on stage at Glyndebourne. The audience and critics found her Countess "dazzling," "enchanting," the "Dove sono" "one of the loveliest things of the evening." That individual "mourning dove" tone, so laden with melancholy, was first noticed here —highly appropriate for the Countess's sadness (it was to persist for a long time). Vittorio Gui was the conductor, and he would later lead for her Donna Anna in *Don Giovanni*.

Joan also took on the extra bit of the First Lady in *Magic Flute*. Richard remembers the odd trio made by those Ladies— Joan so tall, Monica Sinclair fairly tall, and, in the middle, a tiny Dutch girl, Cora Canne-Neijer, "a valley between two mountains." What a bevy of accents in that production, all singing German:

Joan and the Monostatos (Kevin Miller) were Australian; Sinclair; the Papagena (Maureen Springer) and the Speaker (Thomas Hemsley), English; the Papageno (Geraint Evans), Welsh; the Queen of the Night (Mattiwilda Dobbs), American; the Pamina (Pilar Lorengar), Spanish; the Sarastro (Drago Bernardic), Yugoslavian; the First Priest (John Carolan), Irish. Somewhere in the middle of it all was a Scotsman in a couple of small roles. It was, indeed, one of those vaunted Glyndebourne international casts.

Joan was not asked back. Joan Ingpen, who now handled her, broke the news that it was the fault of her unsightly teeth. Characteristically, Joan did something about it. She consulted a famous surgeon, Henry Pitt-Roche, and decided to place herself in his hands, even though it would cost at least £700 and would involve a torturous process she could not have fully anticipated. That agonizing period may be quickly passed over here; but it encompassed capping every tooth and extracting an impacted root that had penetrated an antrum. Her lower jaw, already so prominent, had to be built up so that it would not contract and give her the profile of a witch. It is enough to say that, beginning with a seven-hour ordeal and continuing with twice-weekly bouts of two to three hours each, the painful business consumed an entire year.

Now Joan could go out smiling confidently into her world. Not so happy a change was fated for another part of her well-shaped head. Its interior was a mess. How anyone could sing as she did with the horrors that existed in sinus cavities and teeth was a miracle to both of the doctors who wrestled with them. Ivor Griffiths was Covent Garden's particular medico to whom every opera singer rushed at the slightest hint of trouble in trachea, throat, or nose. For months Joan had been his charge, regularly and with incredible stoicism sitting through the torture of having those sinuses scraped. The London damp had aggravated a condition she had suffered since childhood. Eventually she was to undergo the most dangerous operation possible for a singer—the complete clearing out of those infected cavities, which carried the fear that "the most perfect vocal cords in the world" might be irrevocably injured.

For the moment, Sutherland was a happy mother and wife, and a fixed star, if not yet blazing, at her favorite opera house.

Her own domicile had grown to seem inadequate. The Bonynges decided to own a house instead of renting one. They abandoned their lease on Aubrey Walk, changing three stories for six, and took a mortgage for a home at 36 Cornwall Gardens in Kensington (the overall price was £20,000). They moved *en famille* when Joan was ready to leave the hospital. The entourage included (in addition to Muriel) a German maid, a Swiss nanny (Ruthli) and Richard's aunt, Anne Roughley.

Richard had no trouble in decorating the mid-Victorian freehold, with its fifteen rooms, five bathrooms, and an L-shaped drawing room big enough for two pianos. At the same time, they hired a press representative, Walter Price.

Joan was soon singing a broadcast (Lord Harewood remembers it as the part of Vitellia in Mozart's *La Clemenza di Tito*) and then, in Covent Garden, she graduated from the First Lady to Pamina in *Magic Flute* in November 1956, winning from Andrew Porter the credit for bringing "a world of sweetness and serene light into a basically wrong production." He cited Kubelik, West, and Piper (designer) as "agents of darkness." In spite of the dismal production, he claimed that Sutherland sang exquisitely, artistically, with "uncommon refinement of technique and expression," and with an especially lovely B-flat.

Five distinct peaks were part of 1957. First came a *Meistersinger* (January 28), scrupulously prepared by Kubelik, but in the English translation so often required at the Royal Opera. It was almost enough to convince Joan for good that Wagner had best be left alone. Richard, of course, was secretly gleeful when she was dubbed "not quite equal to the part."

Quite a different story was the Handel Society's *Alcina* on March 19 at St. Pancras Town Hall, revived after almost two years. Joan nearly refused to take it on in the press of learning Gilda for the month of May. But this was Richard's dish, and he insisted. Not only did *Opera* magazine reward her with the most flattering words ("she surprised even her warmest admirers with an ease and assurance not yet seen at Covent Garden, but she looked both regal and attractive, moved with ease and dignity"), but they emblazoned their cover with a color photo of her.

Monica Sinclair, her colleague, and the Boyd Neel Orchestra under Charles Farncombe also were the recipients of warm words, but Joan swept the boards. Peter Heyworth, who had already begun to notice her, wrote in the *Observer*: "A most remarkable performance . . . lovely silvery quality of tone, melodic line not only deeply impressive but immaculately clear . . . handled tricky vocal ornamentation with such ease and grace, for once not like something gratuitous stuck on, but an essential part of the melodic flow." He also commented that she moved with an ease in St. Pancras

Hall that had not yet been visible at Covent Garden. This critique was important not only for those perceptions, but for the notice given to the ornaments with which Joan henceforth embellished florid music. The art was a passion of Richard's, whose study and employment of it were to command increasing attention and respect.

Joan's first scheduled venture into a leading Verdi role (the *Aida* Priestess had been minor, and the *Aida* and *Masked Ball* fortuitous) came off beautifully. This was her Gilda in *Rigoletto*. The customary adjectives were now being applied to this new vocal phenomenon, and one paper shouted: "Room at the Top for Joan!" Only Porter discovered a certain self-consciousness in the "Caro nome," the aria by which most sopranos win or lose this opera. Joan was still finding the natural movements of a very young girl not quite conquerable, and Gilda is very young, and very gullible.

Madame Herz, on the other hand, is a virago, a flaming prima donna. She contends with a rival for a job in a provincial opera company, with the harassed impresario trying to make peace. The opera: *Der Schauspieldirektor* (*The Impresario*). The composer: Mozart. It was a little past his centenary, but he was always welcome at Glyndebourne. And so was Joan by now, with her pretty new teeth. She got them into this part with a will. For the first time, her high Fs catapulted into an astonished world. She impressed everyone, and felt vindicated. The Vancouver Opera director heard her, and promptly bid for her services.

Then, Edward Downes conducted Joan in a Verdi opera (where he had thought all along she belonged). Desdemona in *Otello* calls for no florid singing, but the drama is explicit, the tension is terrible, and the tone must remain pure and floating. Joan was rehearsing rather dispiritedly for the December 21 premiere, standing like a rock and mumbling her words. Probably the huge, virile Otello cowed her. This was Ramon Vinay, a handsome, well-built Chilean quite tall (praise heaven!), with black curly hair, snapping eyes, and a smile that could be sweet or cruel. He was very good for Otello. Gentle enough in person, he could be a tiger on the stage.

Norman Ayrton summoned Joan to a coaching session. "It was so dreary," he told her. "Look at him now, that rather tough, sexy tenor. For God's sake, there's a huge black man you're madly in love with. He's not just a tenor, but the love of your life. Show it!"

The exhortation did not really work. At dress rehearsal, the exasperated tenor seized his Desdemona and flung her from him in a fit of passion, smashing her into a pillar. Joan bounced back, eyes blazing, temper thoroughly aroused. The result: she sang and acted aroused and blazing.

"See?" teased Norman. "Now you've done it once, you can do it again." And reflected yet again on the value of anger.

Still, the lesson had not apparently sunk in far enough for at least two critics. Felix Aprahamian of the *Sunday Times* qualified his praise: "If she masters the stage as well as the vocal part, she may become a Desdemona of international repute." And the *Daily Telegraph and Morning Post* found her "chilly and rather colorless," though she steadily grew in confidence and dramatic vitality.

No "ifs" for Noël Goodwin, who crowed in the *Daily Express*: "She carried her fast-growing reputation up another notch." The *Daily Mail* noted that her voice "seemed to strengthen for Verdi."

So 1957 had come up as a vintage year. It brought a personal satisfaction as well. Margreta Elkins turned up in London. She had met Joan back in Australia in the Mobil tours that had followed the contests. She had disregarded Joan's advice not to marry. "I dragged my husband, Ike Elkins, an export-import man, to London. He liked it well enough during my ten years at Covent Garden," she explained. Upon meeting her, she hardly recognized the then blonde Joan, who, by this time, had lost a few pounds and, under Richard's goading, had found a flattering dressmaker. Margreta went through the same mill that Joan had been through, her first assignment identical to Joan's, the Priestess in *Aida*—not normally a mezzo role. "It's a matter of having the feeling for it," said Elkins. In her decade, she was to sing Octavian (*Rosenkavalier*), Amneris (*Aida*), Ulrica (*Masked Ball*)—"though I shouldn't have, it was too low"—and Marina (*Boris Godunov*). Between the two tall Australian women developed a friendship that remains probably Joan's closest. They were to be associated professionally many times, particularly in their homeland, where Margreta returned for good.

Another visitation, not quite so satisfactory, was from Ada and John Dickens, who found their fledgling chick surprisingly grown up. Very proud they were of Joan, too, though they disclaimed it, saying rather gruffly, as they later repeated to me, that they considered Joan "family" and that they were not "fans." John was disturbed at Richard's success in raising Joan's voice. But their rather dispiriting opinions made little impact at this time. Joan was now set firmly on the upward path, and nothing would pull her down from the dizzying heights.

CHAPTER
6

Six Thousand Miles for a Debut

A DEFINITE TURN IN THE PRIMA DONNA'S PATH CAME in 1958. Joan was to travel out of England—and six thousand miles at that—engaged for the first time by a non-British opera company and to be treated as a Very Important Person instead of Good Old Joan. Furthermore, plans established earlier were beginning to ripen toward reaching just such stardom status at home.

The year began propitiously with a new production of Poulenc's *Dialogues of the Carmelites*, which had had its premiere in Milan just a year previously. The affecting story concerns a Carmelite convent whose nuns are forced to disband during the French Revolution and to go one by one to the guillotine. Joan sang the part of the Prioress Marie, the "most lyrical, and sung with the utmost purity of tone and sensitivity," said *Music and Musicians*, which also placed her in color on its cover. Six of the cast were from "down under." Elsie Morrison was chief among them, along with Sylvia Fisher, that leading lady whom Downes thought Joan would one day replace. Martin Cooper, often a critical dissenter, thought the opera monotonous, but a letter from Sister Mary of Christ affirmed that the costumes were exactly right and that Joan had the ideal face for her role.

A March *Rigoletto* in Oxford drew from Andrew Porter the remark that Joan was maturing, her exquisite voice showing more heart, more warmth. Her tenor on this occasion was a Maltese with the imposing name of Oreste Kirkop.

Deeply impressed by her astonishing performance in *Der Schauspieldirektor* at Glyndebourne, Irving Guttman, the Vancouver impresario, had invited her to sing Donna Anna in Mozart's

Don Giovanni for a July festival. The two outstanding arias, especially "Non mi dir," had become old favorites to Joan, who used them in concerts and auditions. But she had not tackled the entire opera, which calls for enormous presence, reserve, and stamina, as well as flaming temperament. A problem arose later in the spring. It looked as if Joan would have very little of the needed stamina. Her persistent sinus trouble flared up, causing abscesses in both ears, which poisoned her whole system, causing her legs to swell to elephantine proportions. Despite the pain and awkwardness, she completed a recording session, singing two arias from *Alcina*. (Her first record had been of a Bach cantata earlier in the year, and she would also put a song recital on disc, with Richard accompanying).

A hospital doctor made the horrific demand that she rip out her new teeth. This was too much to bear. Affronted, she went back to her dentist and to Ivor Griffiths at Covent Garden. They agreed that the teeth should stay, but that sooner or later—and Griffiths vainly prescribed sooner—something drastic would have to be done with the interior of her head. Her fortitude now bolstered by the sweet promise of glory, Joan managed to stick it out for almost another year, undergoing periodic cleaning of the sinuses and agonizing through a plane trip and the Vancouver experience with legs so painful she could not stay in any one position overlong.

Vancouver's first International Festival marked a high point for the beautiful city surrounded by sparkling waters and aglow with pride. For Joan, it was an elevation to that fame which very soon would surround her. She had to enjoy and endure it without Richard, who could not afford the trip, but she was fortified by the extra work she had done to perfect her middle voice, which had weakened under the pressure of illness. Furthermore, she had her new teeth and titian hair to comfort her.

Almost more significant than the esteem of her colleagues and the public was the opportunity to work steadily with a producer who would concentrate on every detail of her performance. Günther Rennert bestowed on her the attention he or others had never been able to give her in Covent Garden's mad schedule or in Glyndebourne's brief span, where Carl Ebert was too rushed. She learned a valuable lesson. From now on she would balk at scanty direction or lack of attention to motivation and action. Seldom again would she have to submit to it.

In a local interview that found her "more smiley and friendly than many interviewees," she acknowledged her temperament.

"You take so much, and then you've got to let fly. It's only natural in the sweat and hope and fury of high-pressure rehearsals," she admitted, no doubt remembering Kubelik's *Carmen.*

Joan found her fellow singers congenial and delighted in working with an artist of the stature of George London. Leopold Simoneau (Ottavio) and Jan Rubes (Leporello) she was to meet again. London wrote on Joan's program: "The ideal Donna Anna and a charming human being."

The versatile Rubes, who has since become Canada's best-known figure in opera and educational projects, later remembered Joan as feeling lost without Richard, and depressed over her costly dentistry. "She thought she would have to go to Nicholas Goldschmidt, our impresario, and ask for a raise.

"We were both staying in a little eight-story hotel, then the highest building on English Bay—now it's surrounded by skyscrapers—and we used to sit on a lonely beach and commiserate with one another. I have pictures of Joan and me, walking hand in hand for companionship to the Capitol Theater, where we played. In her short street clothes, with no makeup, she looked like a big little girl. Then Ita Maximova took over. It was probably the first time a woman had had a good look at Joan's possibilities. When she first appeared in Anna's black lace costume, with her hair high and a tiara in it, she looked absolutely regal, magnificent. She moved in a sovereign way." And, of course, she sang with a new confidence.

Very little acid dripped into the honey ladled out by the press; in fact, Joan's very first American criticism, from Irving Kolodin in *The Saturday Review*, hinted at what was to come. He thought the production rigidly Teutonic, the cast only capable. But about Joan he wrote: "Least expected and almost unexceptionable was the Donna Anna . . . used her voice with remarkable poise and musicality." Did it matter that Arthur Jacobs of the London *Evening Standard*, in a broadcast over CBC that was printed in a local paper, spoke of a small lapse of memory? Furthermore, he thought the conductor, Nicholas Rescigno, insensitive. "He stopped for applause," he wrote, outraged, and also ignorant. It is customary in this opera, with its distinctly separated "numbers." Otherwise, he patted the Vancouver effort rather patronizingly on the shoulder: "It would be an honor in a European city, and you're new to the game at that." He still thought the singing in Italian a mistake— a kind of inverted snobbery.

Joan's new feeling of freedom and exaltation could well have been dashed by an audition at the Metropolitan that took place on her way home to England. George London had phoned John Gutman, Rudolf Bing's associate manager, about her. Richard Leach, a clever young man in management (later to become director of the Metropolitan Opera Guild), made some of the arrangements. It was in the doldrums of summer and Joan was exhausted by a flight that immediately followed her last performance in Vancouver. She was summoned for ten o'clock in the morning. She sang the "Non mi dir" and, willfully, against Richard's cabled advice, Gilda's "Caro nome" in English. Bing was among the missing—but Walter Surovy, Risë Stevens's husband, was there. He told his wife that nothing would ever come of this aspirant, as Risë confessed to me many years afterward.

Also present in that darkened auditorium were the conductor, Erich Leinsdorf, and John Gutman. "Decent, but will not do" was the verdict. Gutman did not even report the audition to Bing. He remarked to me later that, at that time, nothing could have been worse for her "if we had taken her." It would, indeed, have brought her prematurely to light, and undoubtedly would have proved disastrous.

Leinsdorf was even a trifle contemptuous. He recalled a recent cartoon in *The New Yorker* that showed two fat, bored gentlemen chomping at huge cigars as they left a theater where the play had got raves from its out-of-town tryout. Leinsdorf quoted the caption, which read: "Sides must split easily in New Haven."

Joan went home and dismissed the incident. Even the Covent Garden routine could not quite squelch her new spark. She was soon called to Dublin, where Joan Ingpen occasionally booked singers, finding it a convenient place for tryouts.

"It was called the Dublin Grand Opera Society," said the manager. "For three spring weeks a year it would assemble an *ad hoc* company of Italians, Rumanians—whoever—and the government would sponsor it. In the fall they used more or less British singers. Nobody had one penny to scrape against another, and they were always cutting fees, cutting fees.

"There was a *Don Giovanni* performance, so I got Geraint Evans and Joan to go. Geraint was dying to do Giovanni—he had become quite a famous Leporello, but always yearned to be the 'master.' I thought, 'Oh well, it will give him pleasure.' I believe it was the only time he sang the Don."

Joan did very well as Donna Anna, and, flushed with success, attended a party where the Lord Mayor of Dublin was present.

Sebastian Shaw, who had recently married Joan Ingpen, said to the heroine: "I'm no musician, but everybody tells me how difficult that role is, especially the second aria, and here you were so marvelous in it."

Joan replied airily: "Oh, that's just a cup of tea for me!"

"We couldn't help shouting with laughter," concluded Ingpen. A fateful moment occurred later that month. Joan was among a distinguished list chosen to perform at Covent Garden's Centenary Concert. Maria Callas, the avowed star of the event, heard her former Clotilde rehearsing an aria from Balfe's *Bohemian Girl* with the tenor John Lanigan. La Divina, sitting in the back of a box without her glasses, did not recognize Joan, but she immediately spotted her quality and stayed to listen.

The event itself, however, fizzled as far as Joan was concerned. The Queen had to leave at an appointed time, so Joan's aria was cut and cut again. She could not be said to have been at her best.

Nor did a *Rheingold* Woglinde brighten her horizon.

It was a short time later, however, that she dazzled everyone with the Israelite woman's aria, "Let the Bright Seraphim" from Handel's *Samson*, at the Leeds Centenary Music Festival. This time the Queen and the Duke of Edinburgh really heard her. The excitement rose as loftily when she repeated the work at Covent Garden on November 15. Andrew Porter thought the Handelian trumpet should emulate her phrasing. Noël Goodwin, still her champion, wrote prophetically soon after:

"I predict that, if Maria Callas, now thirty-four, goes on performing at the present rate, she will have left no professional singing voice by the time she is forty. Joan Sutherland, now preparing for *Lucia di Lammermoor*, will, within five years, be acclaimed as famous an international star as Maria Callas is now, but she will no longer be a member of the Covent Garden Company."

Crystal ball indeed. And a revelation of Joan's next step.

As early as 1955, Lord Harewood and David Webster began to realize that in their midst dwelled an emerging swan, and that no proper pool existed to reflect her stately beauty. They did not think of it quite that way, of course. What to do with Sutherland? was more likely how they thought of it. Richard, in his privileged position as husband and coach, badgered both administrators whenever he could. Even Joan, never one to complain or overassert herself, had hinted at something beyond the miscellany they seemed to be throwing at her—an unhomogeneous mixture that had no focus.

Looking at the possibilities for a coloratura role, they washed out *Traviata* without hesitation. Joan certainly was not ready for *that* combination of drama, pathos, fire, and fireworks. *Lucia* was mentioned, but Harewood recalled in horror the previous disastrous venture into the misadventures of Donizetti's heroine thirty years before—a single fiasco that had cast a cloud of superstition over the opera, resulting in there being only one performance. Few memories went back to the earlier reign of Nellie Melba. Donizetti's fancywork now simply enjoyed no favor.

Still, the example of Callas's brilliance in this repertoire stood before them. Even if the Covent Garden board scoffed at the idea that Sutherland would be another Callas, Webster and Harewood felt more sanguine. Yet, a new production would set them back at least £20,000. At the suggestion of the board, the management somewhat feebly offered Joan a *Louise*. Sets from a previous production of Charpentier's opera slumbered in the warehouse.

A more unlikely choice can hardly be imagined. Joan's figure and French would be cruelly exposed in this French sample of *verismo*, or real life. Nevertheless, she and Richard agreed to take a look at the scenery. Standing amid the rags and tatters of poor old Paris, Joan for once stamped her foot. She would not appear in that scenery, even if it meant her dismissal from the Garden. She had her way, and *Lucia* was now definitely waiting in the wings.

She continued to wait (though Richard at once began to prepare his wife for Donizetti's rigors) because the whole idea had to be postponed. It happened that an Italian troupe came to town with *Lucia* in its repertoire, and Lord Harewood, unable to persuade the visitors to drop Donizetti, quietly shelved his own plan for a year and a half.

The breathing space proved the best possible luck for Joan's future. The original idea had been to let the audience in on Lucy's woes by means of a specially commissioned English translation by Christopher Hassall. Painstakingly, Richard drilled Joan in the meaning of the Italian words—word by word, phrase by phrase. Laboriously, they fine tooth-combed the music, seeking perfection in every lyric moment, every silvery glissando, every trill.

The delay caused a shift in management's thinking as well. They determined to go "all out," to do the opera in Italian and to secure the most illustrious conductor and producer to do it. The answers were not far to seek: Tullio Serafin would have to preside, and the young genius Franco Zeffirelli must design and produce.

Such magnitude cowed the complaisant Joan, but Richard exulted. Now we will see something, he thought, and buoyed his wife's spirits with his confidence and assurance.

As early as 1948, Zeffirelli had already cut his operatic teeth at La Scala, enhancing his reputation as an individualist, a veritable iconoclast. He came to Covent Garden especially to see Joan before he signed the contract. Their first meeting was not exactly propitious; the big clumsy girl was suffering from a cold and was swaddled against the damps of the old opera house in layers of wool; the young, fierce, ebullient Italian's every gesture and word came from a territory outside the Australian's experience. Both were appalled by one another. Joan had practically no other option, but Zeffirelli could have bowed out. The opportunity to practice a little of his Pygmalian talent and carve something glorious out of this unprepossessing woman must have appealed to his daring nature. He patted her on the shoulder with effusiveness, which also required some getting used to on the part of this undemonstrative Australian.

The encounter with Serafin went off more reassuringly. Joan and Richard flew to Venice for two weeks, but needed only a few days, as it turned out. The venerable maestro, kind but demanding, was enchanted by the Sutherland voice, respected the preparation Richard had been responsible for, and admired Joan's determination to work as hard as he himself did. He found a few flaws in her otherwise excellent Italian diction, lapses that could not be cured because of her new tooth structure. Otherwise, he gave her a passing grade in short order.

Deeply impressed by Zeffirelli's inventiveness, Bonynge later wrote an article for a local magazine, outlining his attributes:

> In rehearsal he is consumed with boundless energy and is tremendously excitable, communicating his excitement to the artists . . . Always completely natural and friendly, in this way he manages to inspire confidence and affection in all those who work with him. His attention to detail is nothing less than phenomenal and there is no small task he will not perform himself in order to get a perfect result.
>
> Before *Lucia di Lammermoor* he went personally to the Scotch House in Knightsbridge to select the Hunting Fraser tartan for the Bucklaws and the red Innes tartan for the Ashtons . . . A costume fitting with Zeffirelli can be an exhausting affair . . . His sense of color is always exciting and truly dramatic. He loves shaded whites and "false" blacks, ambers and champagnes. Who does not remember that striking mo-

ment in the wedding scene in *Lucia* when the Bucklaws entered dressed in steel blue contrasting so wonderfully with the tans and maroons of the Ashtons?

Now the real intensive work could begin at Covent Garden itself, with February 17, 1959, set as the goal. Sets were executed from Zeffirelli's bold designs and assembled for final effect. His costumes for Joan, combinations of becoming colors and brilliant tartans, were cunningly corseted and fitted. For the first time in her career, her costumes were actually conceived with her own body in mind. They featured flaring skirts that hid her heavy hips. Zeffirelli's decision to show the crazed Lucia, after the murder of her new husband, in a bloodstained white robe nearly caused a break with Serafin, who professed outrage at the veristic horror. The designer's decision prevailed, and it was one of the most tradition-breaking bits of theatricality.

The subject of madness induced by the frustrations and suppressions of the Northern countries had long held a fascination for the warmhearted Italians, who seldom go mad, rather acting out their emotions, spewing out like a volcano and thus relieving tensions. Joan, of Scottish Presbyterian stock, accustomed to holding emotion strictly in check, had always found it difficult to let go in the outspoken, passionate way that Italian opera demanded. Now she was really up against it—emote or fail.

Fortunately, Zeffirelli was there to help her. First of all, the volatile genius possessed one quality that would prove a godsend to his recalcitrant pupil. Feeling his own genius strong within him, he stood tall in the saddle, completely disregarding his own physical height—somewhat less than the soprano's. By his own conviction he made her seem small, a delicious sensation she had never experienced before. After her customary balking at anything new she was called on to do, she reacted with an entirely new freedom of movement, and, backed by Norman's patient drilling in posture and the art of falling gracefully, appeared a different creature on the stage. This was particularly evident in the Mad Scene, where Zeffirelli had her moving erratically among the horrified guests, looping and darting like a crazed bird, searching for her true bridegroom, listening with a startled turn of the head to the summoning flute, echoing and imitating it, always in fluid motion. It was a revelation to the audience, to all of her colleagues, and, it must be said, to Joan herself.

That Mad Scene was to be the pattern for all others to follow, except in a few hidebound great opera houses, where tradition is more important than excitement. Few coloraturas thereafter dared to stand stock-still, facing the audience and the flute, and merely utter birdlike tones. That scene had to be acted. Callas had led the way; Joan followed ardently, and the train of "acting singers" was established.

Christmas 1958 passed, with a few snatched moments of celebration in the Bonynge household, to which Muriel's sister Bloss had been added. January was soon upon them. Exhilarated by the swirl of activity with her at its center, Joan almost forgot about the surgeon's knife, held over her head like Damocles' sword.

February 1959 arrived. Now the seventeenth would tell the story.

7

The Mad Scene Heard 'Round the World

✸✸ OPERATIC GRAPEVINES ARE WONDROUS NETWORKS ✸✸ of communication, faster, it seems, than electronic circuits, or even the speed of light. Before *Lucia* rehearsals had gone very far, the word was out. Something extraordinary was about to happen. Of course, the old walls of the opera house in Covent Garden could not contain such news, which leaked out as if by osmosis, until the very air of the nearby market seemed charged with electricity.

Every factor that chance, or fate, could have contrived fell into place. The postponement, the decision to do the work in Italian and to draw in the most brilliant Italians, Joan's own sharpened senses and expanding skills—all were working in her favor. Now an additional element provided a grace note. Maria Callas came to town to make recordings. The gossip reached her instantly, and she remembered the voice she had approved at the Queen's concert. The diva arrived at the dress rehearsal, more an object of attention than the unknown quantity who was nervously getting ready backstage. Along with the beautiful German soprano Elisabeth Schwarzkopf and her husband Walter Legge (at that time head of Columbia Records), Callas witnessed the miracle on stage and unbegrudgingly acknowledged it. "The tigress sheathed her claws and purred," as one scribe colorfully put it. Graciously, she swept backstage, surprising and flustering the fledgling in her tatty dressing gown. The Great One consented to be photographed with Joan and two famous poses are recorded for posterity: one showed the cool Callas and a grinning Joan, with Richard smiling contentedly in the background. The other caught Joan wagging her finger at an unsmiling Callas. Joan had just said: "That photo showed your good side—now let me show mine." Joan, too excited to realize that she had possibly presumed too much, still blushes at the remembrance.

Covent Garden went slightly mad on its own that night of February 17. Such an avalanche of printed praise had probably not descended on any singer since the days of Nellie Melba. Fifteen or so music critics can cover quite a few columns when they have something exciting to write about. The Bonynge scrapbooks for 1959 attest to this, with page after page headed "New Prima Donna," "A New Melba," "Covent Garden at Her Feet," "The Toast of London."

From those who had previously sensed Sutherland's potential greatness came a certain amount of "I told you so," most notable among these Harold Rosenthal of *Opera*, who preened himself on his prior engagement of Joan for one of his lecture recitals. It was even more gratifying to read those who had previously belittled—or ignored—her.

Philip Hope-Wallace was one of the latter. "She had seemed previously tall and used to look gauche—now she is beautiful, like an old print of, say, Persiani," he admitted without rue in *Time and Tide*. In the Manchester *Guardian*, he added that Joan had surprised even her most ardent admirers. He, as did others, credited much of her success to Zeffirelli's absolute mastery. For one thing, it was the most satisfactory solution of the Scottish costume problem. "A joy from beginning to end—makes most of the Covent Garden productions look like try-outs."

Another early doubter also ate his words in the *Sunday Times*. "A triumph for Joan Sutherland, soprano, and also for a previously unknown creature, Joan Sutherland, the tragic actress." It was also a triumph for Tullio Serafin and the forces he so admirably controlled. Zeffirelli's conception of unity was deeply satisfying, the sombre, realistic mood never losing in a splendid series of stage pictures. "His bold concept of the Mad Scene could not have been achieved without a Lucia of first rank," added Desmond Shawe-Taylor, and continued, covering the ground with admirable thoroughness:

> Some singers, like Mary Garden or Rosa Ponselle, burst on the world as stars; others serve a long period of apprenticeship. Even then, there is nearly always a moment at which the butterfly emerges from its chrysalis, and that brilliant and delightful phenomenon we just witnessed.

Joan Sutherland had previously given grounds for high hope, but never quite shaken off a certain angularity of vocal and dramatic deportment. Now all is changed. The voice, always pure, has gained richness and color and remarkable fullness in the upper register. The vocalisation is brilliant but never merely decorative. Both style and accent are convincingly Italian. The singer is appropriately and touchingly beautiful, while her acting underlined at every point the pathos of this ill-used but by no means insipid heroine of the North. In the cold grey light of the steps of the spiral staircase, we know Ravenswood Castle will shortly have a second and more terrifying ghost.

Sutherland's performance was all of a piece, the writer went on, the music exquisite, the drama veracious and intense. He did have a reservation or two. Perhaps his foreknowledge of the imminent sinus operation exerted an influence. "Her highly accomplished singing was not quite flawless. The arpeggios were marvelously rapid and distinct, the scales a little less so. She trilled at full volume on B-flat, but tended to reduce the tone when lower. At 'Alfin son tua, alfin sei mio,' some miscalculation occurred. I am not sure if the voice sounded tired or the attempted effect of broken pathos failed. In very soft *sostenuto* singing she sometimes allows the tone to sag—but these are small flecks on a lovely performance."

What of her early admirer, Andrew Porter? Then, as later, he was to make his trademark by beginning with a survey of the work and its background. Soon he got down to particulars.

The young Australian soprano becomes one of the world's leading prima donnas. The surprise of the evening was her new dramatic power. Since the war, no one but Callas has received such ovations. New beauty shone in her face. Her gestures, bearing, were unfailingly expressive. The singing was exquisite; notable were the sustained notes followed by an octave drop. The decorations [ornaments of the vocal line devised after arduous study by Bonynge] were tastefully and justly conceived and beautifully executed. The arpeggios delicate and lovely, trills confident. Beyond all this, there was meaning in everything she did. A singer who can make florid decorative bursts in thirds with a flute heartrending in effect has understood the secret of Donizetti's music.

After the February 26 performance, Porter embellished his own bright medallion of honor: "No soprano in our country has recorded the great scenes of *Lucia* with so rare and precious a combination of marvelously accomplished singing and dramatic interpretation. Tears and fire commingled in her tones."

Porter had always been a champion of *ottocento* opera. Others were not, agreeing with George Bernard Shaw that these works were not for "cultured" listeners, but for the self-ravishment of "a dynasty of execrable imposters, in tights and tunics, interpolating their loathsome B-flats into the beautiful melodies they cannot sing."

At least, Shaw had acknowledged that the melodies were "beautiful." Many Londoners would not go even this far. Even among those who owned a disposition to accept Bellini, Donizetti remained unacceptable.

Now all this had changed. It was not only the discovery of a brilliant gem in Covent Garden's jewel box, but a boost for the house itself and a vindication for the admirers of *bel canto* opera.

The Queen magazine brought out an amusing anecdote (which had long been forgotten) to surround acclaim for the ripe gifts of the conductor: "Not since the memorable night in 1925, when Toti Dal Monte took the law into her own hands and conducted the orchestra across the footlights with her fan," had such responsibility for conducting rested upon a singer. The veteran Tullio Serafin conceived the opera, "not merely as a vehicle for acrobatics, but as a tenderly moving drama, pulsing with life and human feeling." (Incidentally, Dal Monte's not unprecedented, but certainly unusual, usurpation of authority accounted no doubt for the cancellation of any subsequent performances of *Lucia* that had been planned. Still, it is hard to understand why her capriciousness should have reacted so unfavorably upon the opera itself.)

Joan was not alone in her triumph. Three fellow Australians shared in it. Only twenty-four hours before the curtain, Kenneth Neate was brought in to replace the Brazilian Joao Gibin as Edgardo, no doubt adding to the prima donna's nervousness. He came off very well. Joan's chum, Margreta Elkins, sang the Alisa, Lucia's confidante, and Raymond Nilsson had the smaller part of Normanno. Often dominating the stage, Geraint Evans, the bluff Welsh baritone, showed his usual dramatic punch and authority as Enrico. (Later, a more suave tenor, Alfredo Kraus, took over as Edgardo, and an even more blustery John Shaw replaced Evans.)

One might think that all this hoopla and adulation would upset any budding prima donna. According to the *Sketch* reviewer: "Sutherland's previous joyful exuberance now became triumphant radiance. One of the most compelling things is her delight in everything. She is supremely happy, abundantly fulfilled."

The public could not have known how this happiness, this radiance, was manifested on the "morning after."

Norman Ayrton went to call. His mother was rather seriously ill in the hospital, but he wanted to stop off to congratulate his protégée. Joan, after all, was in the habit of referring to him as "our oldest friend."

"There she was," Norman related, "rubber gloves on hands, scrubbing the bathtub and singing away at the top of her lungs. Singing what? *Lucia*, of course, all over again. Ricky had always claimed he could tell when Joan was well and happy by the birdlike trills around the house. Happy she was. There were mountains of flowers all over. Joan instantly grabbed the biggest bouquet I'd ever seen, thrust it into my arms, and insisted I take it to Mother. I could hardly wrestle it into the cab. Well, Mother almost had a relapse when she saw it, from sheer amazement. Everybody in the hospital, learning about it, tiptoed in for little visits. Joan's unbelievable thoughtfulness never deserted her, even in such a moment."

Now it was all about to begin. A headline, "Everyone Wants Joan," sums it up. The offers poured in—Glyndebourne, Vienna, La Scala, America . . .

Before any of this international gold dust could shower down on Joan's white shoulders, however, the dreaded operation had to be undertaken. The risk had now tripled; those vocal cords to which some damage might be done had suddenly become so much more precious. Ivor Griffiths, in spite of his own misgivings, urged on by Joan herself, who thought she might as well get it over with, went ahead into the perilous undertaking. The month of March 1959 marked the turning point. After the gruesome two-and-a half-hour operation itself, when the infected sinuses were completely cleared, the outcome still lay in doubt for a week or so. Joan tried her voice, and it came out a croak. Frightened out of her wits, she begged Griffiths to help. Reassured that the cords had not been damaged and that her head was free for the first time in her life, he counseled her to keep on trying. At last, the voice came clear; all the fears and agonies of uncertainty were put behind Joan and Richard. Joan would never again be entirely clear of the poison that had so firmly entrenched itself in her system, but, as Griffiths promised and Richard affirmed, she could sing as long as she wanted to.

More splendid than ever, was the popular verdict after a *Rodelinda* at Sadler's Wells and a *Samson* at Covent Garden, thus confirming several critics' opinion that Handel was Joan's strongest province.

Then in the fall, the overseas trials began, out of which she came triumphant—a Donna Anna in Vienna's Staatsoper, with a cast that included such good names as Anton Dermota, Hilde Gueden, Eberhard Wächter, and Walter Berry, with Heinrich Hollreiser as conductor. Joan reaped all the headlines. An *Otello* in December took her back to an earlier role; she was called "ein englischer Engel als Desdemona."

But now another hurdle reared up on her home grounds. She had agreed joyfully to sing *La Traviata* at Covent Garden, but was not really prepared for it. This opera has undoubtedly been Joan's severest challenge through the years. And no wonder. The Verdi setting, which the librettist Piave based on *La Dame aux Camélias* by Alexandre Dumas, *fils*, requires every ounce of a prima donna's resources. The heroine Violetta has to sing dazzlingly, tenderly, defiantly, and brokenheartedly, exploring the giddy heights of coloratura, the lengths of lyricism, and the depths of tragedy. It follows that she should be an actress, although Verdi himself thought little of the role as an exercise in intelligence, saying that even a mediocrity could shine in that part, while being very bad in others. Still, we have come to expect very near the impossible from our Violettas.

Joan tried on the courtesan's joys and miseries before she was ready for them. Zeffirelli, who would never, in spite of her repeated pleas, produce *Traviata* for her, told her she was tempting fate. Covent Garden, obviously relaxed from the high-strung concentration on *Lucia*, trotted out a production in tatters—what one critic called the wreck of the Tyrone Guthrie–Sophie Fedorovitch staging for Schwarzkopf twelve years before. The producer, so inept that no credit appeared in the program, remained anonymous in all accounts, and better that way. Joan so despaired of finding any direction that she secretly consulted Norman Ayrton every night after rehearsal frustrations at Covent Garden. Not only did the producer let her down, but the pit was occupied by a gentleman who was to spark Joan's one serious walkout in her career in a Venice imbroglio—Nello Santi. He never seemed to agree with the star on tempi. The strain told, and she went on the London stage shaking with confusion and ridden with a cold that settled in her throat.

January 8, 1960, became a night to forget. Until that Friday evening, wrote Desmond Shawe-Taylor in the *Sunday Times*, one had supposed *Traviata* to be one of a small group of indestructibles. "One was surprised to learn that it can be long-winded and dull." He attributed this to the conductor and the anonymous nonproducer, recognizing that Sutherland had been left pretty much on her own. To make matters absolutely their worst, Joan had to compete with a strangely insistent prompter, whom she had actually asked for. She did not trust her memory, even though cues were pasted on the scenery all over the stage. The man in the box did his duty so heartily that at one vociferous moment a cry came from the Grand Tier: "Silence the prompter!"

Instead, the star was silenced. She went to bed immediately after the show with an attack of laryngitis. As soon as she could totter around, Joan called Ayrton in to work on Violetta's emotions and motivations.

Not many critics witnessed the transformation on January 30, but Andrew Porter in the *Financial Times* took back all he had said previously. Gone was the monotony of tear-laden timbre, the wilting gentleness, that too-persistent pathos. In Act II, she was loving with Alfredo, dignified with Germont in phrase and gesture, realizing the creation of Verdi's imagination. The dramatic intensity of her acting in the next scene was remarkable, and in the last, there was not only the pathos of resignation, but also moments of fierce defiance, of the will to live. She regained all the necessary color and technique for the music, with delicate portamentos, subtle and supple phrasing, and a long sustained trill at the end of "Ah fors è lui." In short, she revealed consistent dramatic progress.

This conversion of near failure into triumph was not generally observed by the press, but Lord Harewood remembers the early *Traviata* only as a success. He was close to the scene, yet had some perspective on it. It was perhaps the cornerstone of his belief in her ability as an actress.

The impression that her Violetta was lukewarm, with the pathos missing, stayed with the press even for her return to the role in 1962. Yet Philip Hope-Wallace in *Opera* and Arthur Jacobs in the *Financial Times* leaped to the affirmative side, the former seeming to hear a new voice, ravishing, doleful, that might have been a viola. Jacobs believed that Sutherland had made the vocal part her own, but that she had not quite reached the point of realistic acting.

This time, Ayrton received a credit for "production rehearsal," and it was Ayrton's imprint that remained with Joan in an early American performance of the opera. But, by 1963, when she sang her first Violetta in Philadelphia, Bonynge had been conducting for her here and there, and the improvement was apparent. Gerald Fitzgerald wrote in *Opera News* that it was no secret that Sutherland sang better for her husband than for anyone else. Bonynge's seamless line breathed in time with his wife's every phrase, and there was no hint of indulgence, except for an ornate cadenza and trill in "Ah, fors' è lui." The interview with Germont was warmly felt, and the death scene eloquent. For once, Joan's diction was complimented. She would never receive full marks in this department, but now and then someone claimed to understand at least every other word.

There have, of course, been later Violettas in the Sutherland calendar, but this was how a solid foundation for what would undoubtedly become one of her cherished roles was built.

8

La Stupenda is Crowned

ON THE SCREEN, THE MASSIVE LOCOMOTIVE ROARS into the night. Falling softly and fading one by one, names and scenes of cities flash by—Paris, Rome, Vienna, Prague . . . It's a hackneyed movie device for showing the lapse of time and the parade of place, the climb upward and onward of career, with no bother for details.

So it would have been with this newest rising star in the season of 1959–60. Joan Sutherland's flashing parade, with jet planes replacing ground transportation, would read: Vienna, London, Venice, Palermo, Genoa, Paris. It had begun: that endless round of international flight, the pauses in great and lesser capitals, the glories of the stage, the toil to make ready, the frustration of travel, the adulation, the crowd outpourings, the reams of paper consumed in expressing it, the weariness—and always on, on, to the next trial and triumph.

Joan could hardly believe it at first. Like the little old lady in the nursery rhyme, she would look at what was happening all around her and wonder: "Laws-a-mercy, can this be I?"

The amount of money people were prepared to pay her took her breath away. Richard was less fearful, more assured. He had known it would happen. His confidence had never wavered, and his pride, almost arrogance, followed as naturally as sunrise. The money he could deal with; he had always known how to spend it.

A somewhat dazed Joan stepped onto the merry-go-round that was to whirl her through time and space for as long as she could remain aboard. After the Vienna *Don Giovanni* (pulling a success right out from the Mozart stronghold) and *Otello*, and a return

Lucia at Covent Garden (better than ever), came Venice.

Franco Zeffirelli, still enamoured of his protégée, daringly introduced George Frideric Handel to this most Italian of cities, with a dazzling production of *Alcina*. Joan was timorous: "They've never liked Handel; will they like me?" Franco reassured her with his usual bravado: "We'll make them like it!"

Joan had sung the splendid Queen in 1957 in one of her greatest, most secure hours on the stage. It had been a Handel Opera Society revival of the opera after more than two hundred years, in the less than luxurious surroundings of St. Pancras Hall, and it had kindled a fire of enthusiasm there for the ease and assurance of this regal, attractive large person. Joan had loved it. The role fitted her in size, sentiment, and dignity; she felt perfectly at home on a stage, perhaps for the first time.

Joan almost did not make it to Venice for *Alcina*. The first indications of an arthritic back sent her into a realm of pain that forbade movement. It was only calmed by a strange doctor recommended by Joan Ingpen—an unorthodox fellow who seems to have anticipated acupuncture in the West.

Joan Ingpen recalled the incident to me.

"I got on to this old man in Kent. He came up with a nurse from his nursing home and I picked them up at Charing Cross Station. He had some sort of magnet and passed it up and down Joan's spine, looking at a little black box the while. Finally he found a spot that seemed the right one and inserted a kind of scalpel. After doing this twice, he told Joan to bend over and touch her toes."

After an initial attempt that failed, Joan tried again and found she could. The doctor warned her not to faint or fall—it would hurt. She sang at Covent Garden that night anyway, and made a deep curtsy at a curtain call.

"Richard and I sat together and held our breaths," said Mrs. Ingpen. "Joan did go to that old man several times, but he put her off by insisting that she exercise and not lie in bed all morning after a performance. She didn't like that."

Joan resorted to masseuses after that, finding a favorite one in every country where she spent any time. No more little black boxes for her.

"But the black box was only a diagnostic tool," insisted Mrs. Ingpen. "That old doctor had an ingenious theory about such ailments as Joan's. Most of these things are like the situation when the hair gets on the wrong side of an accustomed parting—it's painful. The muscles are the same. Anyway, I believe that anything that cures you is all right."

At last, in February 1960, Joan ventured into the Aegean climate, seemingly so alien to Handel's soaring music, her only bulwark Zeffirelli's sumptuous production, outrageous courage, and constant supervision. Rehearsals raged from ten A.M. till after midnight for days on end. When the date arrived, some costumes were still held together with safety pins.

The upshot was an explosion of joy in La Fenice such as only the Italians can summon up. "Venice was purring," one Englishman commented. Then it happened. Noël Goodwin of the London *Daily Express* overheard one worshiper call Joan "La Stupenda." He wrote home about it, and Joan Sutherland was crowned La Stupenda!

Renata Tebaldi had been dubbed "Blue-eyed Angel," and Maria Callas owned the rights to La Divina, but La Stupenda went one better. Joan was now moving into the throne space formerly occupied by these two ineffabilities.

It was hard for her to realize, but, as the work mounted and the kudos and the bank account accumulated, she began to believe that she could not go on quite as independently as before. She needed at least a semblance of a retinue. Richard, of course, was always there, but obviously needed attention himself. The Bonynges have always passionately guarded their privacy and have welcomed into it as few as possible. Ruthli stayed on first as Adam's nurse, later as housekeeper in Switzerland. There was at this early time a secretary in London for Joan's correspondence.

Now Richard's young aunt, Ann Roughley, came into the picture. She could not be faulted for congeniality or expertise. A former nurse, she took on a great deal, always excepting the actual managerial tasks of booking and haggling. These fell to Joan Ingpen, and in the United States, the firm of Henry and Ann Colbert, introduced by Ingpen. The latter had taken Ann Colbert in 1959 to hear Joan in *Rodelinda*. The voice bowled Colbert over. So the nucleus of the Bonynge troupe was formed, and remained intact for a good many years.

*   *   *

In the meantime, there was Venice, after which they set off for the Teatro Massimo in Palermo, to do a *Lucia* with Zeffirelli-Serafin backing and a whole new cast to work into.

Fortunately, the Sicilians were charmed, overwhelmed, by the revelation in *bel canto*. Callas's name was murmured here and there in a comparison favorable to the newcomer. Then Genoa's public was conquered, and it was on to Paris for Joan's twentieth *Lucia* and Paris's three hundred and first!

Here was a whole new ambience. Paris has its own moods and, fickle as she is, can turn surly on cue. Veritably, it was April in Paris. One English critic, however, found the whole setting bursting at the seams with noisy English school parties and exhausted-looking German honeymooners; furthermore, the interior of Charles Garnier's ornate palace of an opera house seemed chilly and even hostile.

Joan was happily installed in the most famous dressing room in the building, that of the legendary Fanny Heldy. It had remained practically Heldy's personal property (her name was on a brass plate) and she had the right to determine which prima donna might occupy it. Callas had been favored; Tebaldi had not. Graciously, Heldy, who was now sixty-eight, opened its door for Sutherland. She had chosen to decorate it herself, in festoons of rose satin and a tentlike ceiling. She even came to one of Joan's performances. Famous for her Tosca, Manon, Thaïs, and Louise in the first decades of the century, Fanny had been forgotten outside her own country. Joan thought the room a bit fussy, but to assume the mantle of a prima donna also entailed dwelling within the fripperies of a revered predecessor. She dared not minimize the honor.

To reign with any authority in such a bastion of tradition is not the easiest task for a stranger. The Paris public was notably captious. Joan must have wondered what lay ahead when the harp tinkled her entrance as Lucia into the haunted park of the Ravenswoods. The house was instantly silenced, only to break out in a storm after her first cabaletta, "Quando rapita in estasi." She was in! No doubt about it, even though it had been the English visitors, not the French, who had shown such bad taste as to applaud in the middle of a *scena*.

Zeffirelli had devised some additional, more telling, movements for the Mad Scene. The crazed Lucia ran in and out of the horrified crowd as if hearing strange voices, and her facial expressions were quite terrifying to those fortunate enough to see them. All the while, she sang effortlessly, radiantly. The inevitable applause (from the English) in the middle of the scene, always so disruptive, yet serving to give the singer a moment to catch her breath, was so quickly cut short by French shushing that the usual respite did not arrive. Joan had to go on to the exhausting climax without a breather, not exactly happy at this manifestation of audience circumspection.

Several other innovations marked this production, including a few changes in Joan's costuming—the omission of tartan scarves and a different headdress for the wedding (a simple circlet of flowers and a veil). But the strangest bit was Lucia's ghostly apparition that seemed, just as Edgardo was about to stab himself at the family tomb, to welcome him into her arms. Paris, used to apotheoses after a century of *Faust*'s Marguerite, did not mind. Someone noted that Joan got more applause than had Tebaldi in the previous year for *Aida*.

Lucia itself had not always fared so well in the Gallic capital, where several hoity-toity critics had not concealed their contempt for Donizetti's masterpiece. The illustrious Marc Pincherle wrote in *Les Nouvelles* that, if anybody had told him he would not only listen to *Lucia* without a single moment of weariness, but that he would do so with the kind of emotion one feels when confronted with the greatest of lyric works, he would have been dumbfounded. Sutherland's magic had succeeded in creating for him a genuine drama from pieces of sheer virtuosity.

The sets and costumes had been those used in Palermo, but every other element was strange to the central figure. The conductor was a Frenchman, Pierre Dervaux; the Edgardo, Alain Vanzo ("almost first-class," remarked one observer condescendingly); the Enrico, "one of the finest baritones," Robert Massard; the Raimondo, Joseph Rouleau, whom Joan would meet often thereafter. The chorus had not bothered to learn Italian, so chirped away in native French.

Joan came out of it dubbed as "one of the greatest singers of the epoch." One ecstatic fellow thought that, since Maria Barrientos, he had never heard a trill like this—not amplified vibrato, but alternation of two distinct notes. In short, there was not one dissenting vote.

A mark of this newcomer's eminence was Parisians' rush to name things after her, particularly the restaurant owners, who never missed a trick. Witness Pêche Melba, Chicken Tetrazzini, and any number of Caruso-honoring viands. Upon Joan was bestowed a L'Aile de Bresse Sutherland—homely chicken wings braised in "the loveliest sauce ever," said the honored one, as she sampled the dish with Decca Records executives at Laserre Restaurant.

The popular press was also beginning to pick up its pens. What higher accolade could one wish for than Elsa Maxwell's gush in the New York *Journal American*? *Variety*, the show-biz bible, got in its typical licks. "Joan Sutherland's Mad Lucy a Click as Paris Borrows Sicily's Scenery," ran the head over the story that proceeded to review the sets, rather than the performance, considering *Lucia* a "pretty silly opera."

Paris had fallen for Joan. Now only two traditional strongholds remained: La Scala in Milan and the Metropolitan in New York. All that would come to pass in 1961. Meanwhile, there was a *Traviata* to prove itself at Covent Garden, and after that two new roles to master and take around the circuit, which now included her own Covent Garden, Glyndebourne, revisits to Palermo and Genoa, and a first call on Barcelona. Both new roles were in operas by Vincenzo Bellini, Richard's idol. He had fallen in love with *I Puritani* at the age of thirteen. Now Glyndebourne wanted to mount it for Joan, and Covent Garden proposed to do *La Sonnambula*, opening with a gala performance for the Queen. *Bel canto* was assuredly in, now that Joan, succeeding Callas, was around to sing it.

Puritani came first. Bellini's final opera, rated only second to his *Norma* by those who could bear the genre at all, is the kind of music that creeps up on one, luring the sensibilities into the simplicity of its melodies, which then expand into long, flowing, supple, sinuous lines so fervently elongated that one's own breath catches in wonder. Coupled with this pure linear flow is the higher realm of birdsong—florid, unending, glittering, and sparkling in the sun. Just made for Joan, this music. Also made for her is the role of the trusting, slightly unstable Elvira; she is mad only for a short time when her lover abandons her. When he returns, she is driven sane, so to speak. Her temporary derangement serves only to bring on some effulgent flights of song. Joan has always loved the part.

Puritani's hero, Arturo, is called on for spectacular doings also, not only high Cs by the cupful, but two enormous inescapable Ds. In fact, there is one impossible high F, but few essay it. The Ds are tricky enough, usually coming out like raw gashes in the earth—not at all pretty sounds—and to sing them in unison with a voice like Joan's, one has to hit the pitch squarely and maintain enough volume as well. It is no cinch, this role. Tenors have suddenly fallen ill just before performances of *Puritani*, perhaps more often than before any other opera.

Scoffers call the plot silly, absurd. That is nothing new in opera. Still, one must exercise an unusually large suspension of disbelief for the tale of a gentle girl, a feckless hero, the vengeful, rejected suitor, and the general sweetness and light of the denouement.

Just as Donizetti had gone out of style, so had Bellini, except for an occasional *Norma*. *Puritani* had not been seen in over seventy years, when, as one observer wrote in May 1960: "Nightingales descend on Glyndebourne." Joan's performance elicited a whole column in *The New Yorker* from Mollie Panter Downes, who usually held forth on affairs of state or other peculiarities of life in London. Joan's melting purity of line and dazzling trills stopped the show. Flitting in gauzy, disheveled draperies across the stage, she looked, with her long auburn hair and long, pale Pre-Raphaelite face, like a Millais Ophelia. She was in perfect voice and with a new relaxed style of acting. The producer, Gianfranco Enriquez, may have had something to do with this, but it is certain that Joan was finding new self-assurance.

Further comment on her vocal progress noted the control, the sense of style, the latent power. This, thought Spike Hughes, was no timid tinkle, no Ponslike, larklike sound, but solidly cast, and with absolutely effortless breathing. There were always alternatives in her solos: if she gets bored holding a note, she can come off of it; if she likes, she can hold it. If the idea of hitting a high note does not appeal, she can take a lower one; if she is feeling in tremendous form, she can up everything an octave and ensure that a good time is had by all. Perhaps this was treating Bellini—and the artist's integrity—a trifle cavalierly, but Hughes did admit that in ensembles one had to sing what the composer had written, unless one kept quiet and pretended.

Despite the praise for Joan, people were still not taking Bellini seriously. But, it was noted, quite remarkable was the pathos that he—and Donizetti—could express, a pathetic otherworldliness of its own, which Joan's voice suited to the seams.

Before the next Bellini, *Don Giovanni* at Glyndebourne provided Joan with another chance to show her Donna Anna, again with Rennert directing, as in Vancouver, and with John Pritchard conducting. A name that was later to flare across the opera horizon was Mirella Freni, the Zerlina. That model of English diction, tenor Richard Lewis, sang Ottavio's arias prettily, and in the background loomed the John Bull figure of John Christie, the founder-patron of the beautiful opera resort, and the squat, indefatigable "backroom boy," Jani Strasser. Strasser has appeared at intervals throughout Joan's career, coaching with a will of iron, never letting up his severe regimen.

Joan had already sung before the Queen Mother and the Princess Royal, at a recital in St. James's Palace, when Royalty

again decided to use the panoply of opera to entertain the King
and Queen of Nepal. A specially constructed royal box in the center
of the Grand Tier held these personages, who sat with Queen
Elizabeth and Prince Philip.

Sonnambula, chosen for the occasion, had also been out of
fashion, having not been heard in London since 1910. Serafin was
brought back to preside beneficently in the pit. The command
performance on October 19 went off brilliantly, but at the first
public showing two days later, which brought the critics, Joan found
herself in trouble. One of the nasty colds that never ceased to
plague her had hit at this inopportune time. Yet she gave a masterly
lesson on how to nurse a suffering voice through three acts of high
notes, high strain, and a walk across a high bridge in her (theatrical)
sleep. She conquered the first two heights, at the outset by sheer
caution and technique, then with gradual warm-up and application
of all her skill. But she simply did not dare "walk the plank," as
the innocent Amina is supposed to do. Joan played it safe and
merely felt her way along the edge of the roof from the balcony
devised by the designer Filipo Sanjust. The voice regained its
strength and sheen toward the last. In spite of her eventual vocal
triumph, the histrionic side remained in doubt, as it would throughout the years to come. The belief persisted that no one with such
manifold vocal talents could act as well. It was expressed rather
caustically at this time in *John O'London's Weekly*:

> Does she stand quite still and sing? She does not. Some fool has
> come along and told her she could act, and, since her roles incline
> towards simple village maidens going nuts in ample nightdresses, she
> has taken to hanging that large head sideways and carrying on like
> Miss Muffet after the episode of the spider. The result is very painful
> and a wicked waste. A singer has been given a voice to do this acting
> lark for her, and often with a great singer, a great artist, and great
> music, it is better so.

Variations of this opinion would persist, regardless of the opposite claim that Joan's acting improved, that it had become subtle,
very expressive. There has over the years been a faint rumor that
Bonynge is inclined to believe that the voice is enough. Whatever
the truth, Joan continues to try. And in many opinions, La Stupenda has become a truly well-rounded performer, expert in all
aspects of the characters she portrays.

9

"Big D" and Other Compass Points

✳ IT WAS PROBABLY THE EAGER AMBITION OF ONE impresario and the laissez-faire policy of another that brought Sutherland to Dallas for her United States debut rather than to New York. Lawrence Kelley had proven his mettle over and over in the Texas city after splitting with Carol Fox of the Lyric Opera of Chicago; snatching an international star was nothing new to him. (He had caught Callas thrice previously, and it was from his stronghold that La Divina's press war with Rudolf Bing had been waged in 1958.) In New York, Bing was notoriously indifferent to providing "firsts" for the Met, especially singers. San Francisco and Chicago had beat him to it many times.

Joan would conquer Dallas, as well as San Francisco and Chicago, before reaching the third of her highest goals, the house on Thirty-ninth Street and Broadway. She even stormed the walls of La Scala before broaching the Met.

"Big D" was just the place for Big Joan. Everything Dallas did was outsize, from the ceremonial reception that greeted the Bonynges at the plane with a presentation of Honorary Citizenship and a welcoming dinner (which the couple had to refuse because of jet fatigue), to the presentation of a personal wardrobe designed by various distinguished Texans. This included a *peau de soie* ball gown of blue-green, a white boucle dinner dress, a black cocktail dress, a rehearsal costume with a divided skirt for freedom of motion, and several casual costumes of jersey and nylon, all of which were described in delicious detail by the local newsgatherers.

With typical enthusiasm, Dallas stamped and roared for Joan's

Alcina in Zeffirelli's Venice production. Inevitable comparisons with Callas were whispered; a few journalists tried to fan a feud between the two ladies, but Joan was not having any of that. Harold Schonberg of *The New York Times* traveled to Dallas and weighed the situation thus: Sutherland was the more accurate singer, with better vocal technique, the pitch in her higher voice more secure; but she will never possess Callas's temperament and stage magnetism, he declared. Her acting remained rather rudimentary—she was unable to make the dramatic impact Callas achieves. Very well. Joan was used to it by now and determined never to give up in those departments.

Behind stage, Zeffirelli had worked his magic without stop. Blanche Thebom, the beautiful mezzo-soprano who sang the part of Ruggiero, remembered long afterward that Franco had spent endless moments getting just the right light on the right angle of Joan's comely face and elaborately costumed body. Thebom had never seen anything like it at the Met. The result, of course, was a stunning picture, regardless of Schonberg's comments.

Monica Sinclair made her American debut on this occasion, and others in the cast were Joan Marie Moynagh, Luigi Alva, and Nicola Zaccaria.

Zeffirelli went away before Joan's Donna Anna, but Rennert's firm directorial framework remained to give her a feeling of security. Zeffirelli had given her a high collar and sumptuous gown, so that even Elisabeth Schwarzkopf as Elvira could not eclipse her glamor. Dallas was doubly enchanted.

At about this time, two developments occurred that were to make profound changes in the Bonynges' life, both professionally and personally. After *Lucia*, London Records, temporarily awaking to the presence of the jewel in their midst, put some Donizetti and Verdi arias into circulation, but with the intransigent Nello Santi as conductor. During the rest of 1959, Joan recorded Handel's *Acis and Galatea* with Sir Adrian Boult; Beethoven's Ninth Symphony (of all things) under Ernest Ansermet; and a complete *Don Giovanni* under Carlo Maria Giulini, with Wächter, Schwarzkopf, and Cappucilli among the singers. These were on the Angel label.

London Records came to life again in the summer of 1960, and allowed Richard to make a daring leap into the void. This was the two-part set of "The Art of the Prima Donna," in which Joan committed to posterity an appropriate aria for each of fifteen divas of the past, presumably in her style. Although he did not conduct it (not yet ready for *that* leap into space), Richard masterminded the perilous undertaking. The two albums were beautifully produced, with photographs and descriptions of the various prima donnas, from Pasta to Patti and on, and with Joan's perfect singing to illustrate them. The sensation was worldwide, paving the way for the singer's presence in any opera house or concert hall. Like so many artists before, her ensuing career was built on those flimsy discs as ambassadors. The recording would be steady and assured in the years to come, following inevitably on the performances of each new role, and sometimes repeating one in a new version.

That was the professional aspect. The personal one was to move headquarters out of London. Ten winters in that damp and fog contributing to Joan's series of malevolent colds, ear abscesses, and arthritic back were enough. Furthermore, with their newly enriched income and glittering prospects, the nightmare of English taxes and death duties was frightening. At this rate, Adam would not get much after they had gone. The ideal answer was, of course, Switzerland, where taxes were negligible, and where the Bonynges' particular brand of privacy could be firmly established. They rented a fourteen-room villa, Rocca Bella, over Lake Maggiore. It had a sun balcony, two lodges in a park, and eighteenth-century bits of furniture. Originally, it had been built for a prince and was once the home of the Swiss president; more recently, it had been the home of an engineer of the Simplon tunnel.

Their first summer in the splendid new villa proved anything but peaceful, with friends and an assortment of colleagues stumbling over each other in a wild picniclike atmosphere. Soon thereafter, Joan and Richard learned to invite only those with whom they could cope, employing charm and thoughtfulness, and giving a measured amount of their time and attention.

Another landmark in 1961 was a first call at Barcelona. After some more *Lucias* and *Sonnambulas* at Covent Garden (it seemed she was always dashing home to reaffirm her supreme achievement within those old walls), she set out for Spain on December 26, 1960. In the Gran Teatro del Liceo she sang *Puritani* three times, gaining not only another roof under which she would always be welcome, but also a mascot that still remains with her. Uneasiness beset her during her first performance; her breath came short, and she felt unaccountably low-spirited. Her Spanish dresser consoled her with the gift of a small figure of the Madonna of Montserrat and placed some flowers before it. Mysteriously comforted, Joan went on for the second act and found herself in prime form. The next day, she paid tribute to the real Madonna with a bouquet, and the dresser presented her with the replica, which has since almost invariably had its place on her dressing table along with a single red rose. Singers are not always superstitious, but sometimes there are certain little things . . . like the sixpence Serafin had handed her for her high E-flat in *Lucia*. One rather scoffs at it, but, all the same . . .

Barcelona was properly wild about the new sensation, calling for an extra special gala, in which Joan would duplicate Melba's old feat (singing the Mad Scene from *Lucia* after a full performance of *La Bohème*) by encoring the famous aria from *Sonnambula*, "Ah, non giunge." Such practices are no longer permitted in the colder Anglo-Saxon climates, but the hot-blooded Spaniards adored it, and gave her a gold medal and a whole garden of flowers.

Serafin himself was on hand for her beginning of the year 1961, and Zeffirelli, too, for the *Puritani* in Palermo. This town, already ecstatic over its recognition of the new star so early in her career, called her "La voce dell'anno."

The year 1961 should have been secure but it was then and there that her first excruciating ear abscess left her in pain and totally deaf. She sang under this terrible handicap, following the conductor's beat and trying to hear the pitch from her tenor and baritone. In the middle of the second act, with the piercing E-flat of Elvira's mad scene, the abscess broke from the vibration. Blood streamed down her cheek. The relief of it was exquisite. She turned her head away from the audience, never missing a note, and finished the opera in triumph. The company knew, although the audience did not suspect, and Richard recalled the terrifying incident to me long afterward. Stoically, Joan realized that her path would probably be menaced by these illnesses whenever a cold germ came along. The decision to move permanently out of London was solidified.

The road now led to New York. She anticipated the Metropolitan by making her New York debut in an American Opera Society Town Hall presentation of Bellini's *Beatrice di Tenda*, another neglected masterpiece created for just such a singer.

The American Opera Society, fostered and ruled by a rather enigmatic person, Allen Sven Oxenburg, gave New York a series of concert presentations of little-known operas; a boon to aficionados, although too often one luminous star was surrounded by lesser lights. Whether these were the wisest auspices for Joan's New York debut is debatable. The absence of staging left her in a steady spotlight, but lacking costumes and a character to act out with something more than a voice. Joan has never been entirely at home on the concert stage. It is often a *faute de mieux* situation with her, to be met with a grain of resignation (but the pay is very good indeed).

Here she was in the company of several singers not quite in her league, although it may come as a surprise that, sharing the tag "New York Debut" was a rosy-cheeked mezzo, rather short and stocky, named Marilyn Horne. Richard Cassilly was (and is) a serviceable tenor, but Enzo Sordello, only a loud bass. Both men bellowed, which is no treatment for *bel canto*. Joan shone forth as the bright particular star in this evening of often beautiful Bellini, occasionally dull in an absurd story (as all such plots seem to be). It is all very tragic, and the heroine goes to her death after singing an elaborate aria and cabaletta.

None of this need have clouded the occasion, but sad news had come from overseas. Muriel Sutherland, whom Joan had left in good health and spirits, at age seventy-four had awakened on the Monday morning tired and listless. Before the doctor could answer the summons by Muriel's sister, Muriel had closed her eyes and was gone. Auntie Bloss cabled Ann Colbert, who quickly notified Terry McEwen, who, as London Records' representative and good friend to the Bonynges', immediately sought out Richard. They decided they must tell Joan, and broke the news as gently as possible. Now, of course, it was a question of whether the show should go on or not. Joan remained firm in her intention to sing; her mother would have approved. She performed that Thursday night. Few in the audience knew, but Schonberg of the *Times* did, and professed to believe that "obviously she could not have been in any emotional state to give her all to Bellini." Others suspected no cloud. But Schonberg, drawing on his Dallas experience, now vouchsafed an opinion that he held firmly thereafter. She may well be the unique singer of her genre in the world today, he thought; a singer who can handle coloratura with complete ease, and yet whose voice was big enough to take on roles like Donna Anna and Norma. It is a beautifully colored voice, he continued, one that ascends effortlessly to the E in alt, and most likely, beyond. Where most sopranos have trouble with B-flats and Cs, Miss Sutherland is at her most secure above the staff. And withal, he added, "she preserves warmth, color, and style. In concerted numbers her voice soars over the ensemble without ever becoming hard or jagged. She is a supreme technician."

Although this occasion found her attacking some notes not

entirely on pitch, he knew from experience that she usually proved flawless in that department, and in musicianship:

> She phrases like an artist, and she never tries to take center stage in ensembles. She has numerous ways of changing the color of her voice in accordance with the stylistic or dramatic needs of the moment. Like all great singers, she plays to strength. It didn't matter that she altered Bellini's score somewhat, adding tasteful embellishments here and there [Of course, this was Richard's domain, the use of ornamentation as tradition permitted—even dictated.]

Despite all this, Joan still had a way to go before she would come back to the house a few blocks south of Town Hall. A long concert tour intervened, during which she met again in Canada Sir Eugene Goossens, her earliest Australian mentor. He professed astonishment at the course she had taken, remaining somewhat dubious about the relinquishment of great dramatic roles. She also returned to New York, to repeat the *Beatrice* in Carnegie Hall with the same cast and conductor (Nicholas Rescigno). The larger audience rose to her superb singing and striking appearance in black satin trimmed in emerald green.

Then she was seaborne again, to Genoa for a Zeffirelli *Puritani* and a *Lucia* in Venice, where Zeffirelli had found a tenor tall enough for her. This was Renato Cioni, whom the Bonynges gave the "family treatment" that was to mark them henceforth. They saw to it that Cioni got engagements here and there wherever they were appearing.

At last they came to La Scala. *Beatrice di Tenda* had been slated for her debut in the revered old house. The celebrated conductor, Vittorio Gui, under whom Joan had sung happily in the Glyndebourne *Puritani*, had exercised his rights over Bellini's score and cut it somewhat fearfully, to Bonynge's taste. The worst mayhem had been done to the cabaletta that ends the opera and presages Beatrice's death. No glory in this death; only mute humiliation. The Bonynges rebelled; Gui stood fast. La Scala management arbitrated: they would do *Lucia*. Still, all was not serene. The horrid splashes of blood on the bride's nightdress after she had murdered her bridegroom offended the Milanese powers-that-be. Joan was told to have her costume cleansed and to appear spotless after the gory deed.

Another trial—she hated her wig, and, after ineffective fussing by the wig-dresser, decided to wear her own hair, something hardly any female singer ever dares to do. The crowning blow was the inability of the follow-spot electrician to catch Lucia's feverish movements through the crowd during the Mad Scene—the chilling effect Zeffirelli had created so dramatically. All the Bonynges' fussing (and the Milanese discredited Richard anyway as a "stage husband") did no good. Lucia had to stand still in a blaze of light and go mad without movement.

The dress rehearsal held problems of its own. From this, the critics wrote; and certain celebrated singers were admitted, revealing jealousy or generosity. The generous ones numbered Antonietta Stella, Renata Scotto, Giulietta Simionato, and Leyla Gencer, veterans all. Callas was absent. But on opening night she sent a telegram warmly wishing triumph.

What of the critics? Joan need not have worried. They capitulated to a man. "The perfect, the ultimate Lucia," they voted. "The voice of Paganini!" Such headlines had rarely been seen in the daily press. Of course, the English writers crowed over one of their own. Not even a murmur from the warring prima donna factions disturbed the sounds of jubilance. There was, after all, only one with whom to compare the newcomer, and her faction ungrudgingly bestowed Callas's own designation, La Divina, on the tall Australian. (As if La Stupenda needed it!) They tore up the house, they shouted, they thundered. Others in the cast shone in reflected glory—Gianni Raimondi, the Edgardo, and the brilliant young baritone Ettore Bastianini—even the venerable Gui yielded place to the prima donna. La Scala has its own way of celebrating triumphs, and they pulled out all the stops. It was Joan's wildest tribute yet, and one she banked in memory against the trials still to come.

They did do *Beatrice* after all, five performances in May. The cabaletta was restored, although some of Gui's cuts remained. The Milanese, now besotted by the new star, attributed to her all the virtues—and then some—of the long-gone Giuditta Pasta, who had introduced the opera in Venice in 1833. Now, La Stupenda was ready for anything.

CHAPTER

10

Intermission: Joan
Takes a Walk

✻ LA STUPENDA WAS READY FOR ANYTHING — ANY-
thing, that is, except a certain conductor. It was unfortunate
that Joan's old bête noire, Nello Santi, had been assigned to her
Sonnambula in Venice in May 1961. Previously unamenable to her
necessities, particularly of tempos, the little Italian now showed
himself arrogant and insulting. Joan was not at her happiest anyway
as she came from Beatrice's woes in Milan. Her own troubles had
multiplied with a fall she had taken in the hotel's slick bathtub;
she had hit her head on one of the faucets and now sported a
flaming shiner. The shock also affected her sinuses. At least, she
thought, she would have a week's respite before Venice. Then
came a request for a special gala of *Sonnambula* in two days' time:
Oh, Madame was not to worry; the production was set, and she
could fit into it beautifully. Ominous words.

The Bonynges found on arrival that one walk-through rehearsal was about all the "fitting" she would get; and the conductor
ruined that by drumming away at the piano, following some inner
voices of his own, and not *Sonnambula*'s. When it became time
for him to raise his baton, it was the same old slowdown he had
tried in London. When Joan politely requested a little brisker beat,
Santi smiled and smiled and agreed, then persisted in his tempo,
which was practically impossible for the fast cabaletta at the end
of the sleepwalking scene, if Joan was to retain her phrasing, her
breath, and the long line demanded by the *bel canto* opera. The
situation worsened as Santi ignored requests from the chorus master. The chorus walked out in a fury.

Joan, determined to make the best of it, politely asked, once again, that the maestro liven it up a bit. Santi continued to smile and went on his placid way, pausing only to remark (in Italian) that this prima donna was in it only for the money.

This was too much. Joan stormed out for a lunch break, during which Richard persuaded her to try once more, and not to let the onus fall on her. At the evening rehearsal, however, when Santi beat out the same old refrain, Joan had had it. She left the stage and hurried to her dressing room. As she was changing into street clothes, the opera general director called, but unlike the tactful David Webster, who had settled a somewhat similar situation with Kubelik on the only other occasion that Joan had rebelled, there was no real apology.

The Bonynges were off for London the next morning. The papers had a field day. Inevitably, there were headlines such as "La Stupenda Does a Callas." That great lady was as notorious for leaving a stage as occupying one.

For all her bravado, Joan's stubborn conscience prompted her to worry that she had done the wrong thing. Venice was threatening to sue, and only withdrew when Joan, with Zeffirelli as a messenger, sent them a doctor's certificate that proved her sinuses had been deeply affected by her tub fall and that she must rest until her next Covent Garden appearance in June. (Then she would have to rush to Rome to record *Lucia* and *Rigoletto*, back to London to record *Messiah*, and, somewhere in there, manage a vacation in her new Swiss home.)

Joan was not reassured by the comments of several of her friends and an interested critic or two. On the one hand, they took it as a joke, which distressed her; on the other, there was polite doubt. One just does not "do a Callas," if one is Sutherland, they seemed to say. Her sense of guilt nagged at her until one night when she went to Covent Garden to hear her friend Margreta Elkins sing Marina in *Boris Godunov*. As she returned to her box after the interval, the whole house rose to greet her, applauded wildly, and, to her blushing confusion, convinced her thoroughly that they were with her. Backstage, it cannot be said that the hero, Boris Christoff, entirely approved of holding the curtain because of this unheard-of demonstration for someone who was not even singing. But, out front, Joan sat back in her seat, moved to tears.

Further soothing any wounded sensibilities was the award of the CBE to Joan in the Queen's Honors list of 1961.

Capping it all, the Fenice management let it be known publicly that Signora Sutherland was welcome in its hallowed halls any time she chose to come. The incident was over, and it was not too long afterward that any quarrel that Joan was to have with a conductor could be settled at home. For it would be her husband, Richard Bonynge, who presided in the pit.

CHAPTER

11

The Met—A New Pinnacle

✳ THE HALF-DOZEN STANDEES SHIVERED IN THE chilly November air, as the Saturday-night performance of *La Perichole* ended at the Metropolitan Opera House on Broadway and Thirty-ninth Street. One of them had been there since the beginning of the opera. The line swelled perceptibly as the hours dragged on. It grew warmer toward morning, and the blankets were thrown back, as tired bodies roused from their camp stools or heavy squatting positions on the cold pavement and stretched out in the pale dawn.

By two P.M., when the doors opened (an exceptionally early time because of the exceptional circumstances; usually, standing-room places were sold only at seven P.M. on the evening of the performance) the line extended all the way back around the corner to the executive office entrance on Thirty-ninth Street at Seventh Avenue. A couple passed the time by scrawling "La Stupenda" in heavy pencil over the posters that heralded the heroine of the evening. Dozens were disappointed. Only 240 of the weary, but eager, pilgrims got places. They scampered off to rest, to eat, to gloat, then to return for the reward of their patient vigil—the Metropolitan Opera debut of the new star, Joan Sutherland.

The old house itself had an air of expectancy about it. The usual purposeful backstage chaos was hidden from the elegantly dressed crowd that filtered through the Broadway and side doors, the noise of their chatter excitedly bouncing off the ochre walls of the corridors and mounting to the dimly seen burnished golden glow of the immensely tall ceiling. Ushers were on the *qui vive*, beaming as they escorted favorite patrons to highly priced seats.

It was, after all, a benefit for the Opera Guild, and the top ticket was raised to an awe-inspiring $25.

Francis Robinson, the ambassadorial press chief, greeted countless friends and colleagues from his little memorabilia-crammed office to the left (as one entered) of the Broadway entrance off the orchestra corridor. This was the very spot from which he had first caught a glimpse of Sutherland. Dressed in becoming black taffeta, she had walked radiantly up the center aisle one night when she had visited the house just before her debut.

Celebrities jammed the house, noted actors and singers among them. Inevitably present were the Australian Ambassador and his wife, Sir Howard and Lady Beale. In their Golden Horseshoe boxes shone Prince Alfonso of Spain, Mrs. Vincent Astor, Mrs. Clarence Mackay (the former singer, Anna Case), and Alfred P. Sloan, Jr.

Behind the scenes, Rudolf Bing seemed calm enough. After all, he was inured to prima donnas and their debuts—although this was admittedly something special.

Bing had never heard Sutherland before she raised her voice in his own house. He had hired her on her reputation, which he admitted was considerable, and he had listened to the recording that swept over the music-loving public like a torrent of melody —"The Art of the Prima Donna," in which Sutherland gave to all the famous sopranos of the past a new voice.

One wonders at his imperturbability. This had been one of those productions thrown on stage with only one day of piano rehearsal and one day with orchestra. Furthermore, Désiré Defrère was listed as director—the old pro who, by this time, was content to watch the singers do pretty much what they wanted. He would give the girls an approving pat here and there and go his merry way. Joan, by her own confession and through testimony of others close to her, has always needed a strong director-producer. She did not get it this time. Fortunately, Zeffirelli's training was still fresh in her mind.

Thus, not quite three years after the Mad Scene shook the world, another vitally important audience capitulated to Joan Sutherland. In that short time, Joan had become the most sought-after singer in the world.

The Metropolitan debut on November 26, 1961, had been long anticipated and eagerly awaited. Between the Lucia of 1959 at Covent Garden and the Lucia at New York's Thirty-ninth Street there had been the debuts in Dallas, San Francisco, and Chicago, and the two appearances in New York as *Beatrice di Tenda*, as well as a concert or two and nationwide exposure on television.

Still, the eruption of feverish joy came as somewhat of a surprise. Even the most staid operagoer could hardly believe that it was really one's own self standing there (standing ovations had been practically unheard-of within current memory)—shouting and beating hands together, even stamping on the thinly carpeted floors of the house. The stamping became so violent that one spectator, perched high in the Family Circle, felt the structure tremble and feared the fate of the Walls of Jericho.

The overwhelming noise of the ovation actually frightened the prima donna as well. She could hardly believe it. She had been visibly disconcerted when applause broke out even before she had opened her mouth to sing, but this was more than she expected.

Still, it was all true and not a wild dream. The operatic world was at Joan Sutherland's feet, as *Opera News* remarked in relative coolness a fortnight later. The daily press had flung its words around more recklessly. Even the rather staid Paul Henry Lang of the *Herald Tribune* caught fire, marking the roars of approval from the audience. "And when some of these untrained vocal cords gave out, there was stamping and all manner of other noisy demonstrations." The enthusiasm was justified, he added, for "Miss Sutherland is a phenomenal singer possessing a phenomenal voice."

Harold C. Schonberg, who had sampled the lady's wares in Dallas, reinforced his earlier opinion. "Along around 10:30 last night at the Metropolitan there was a tiny pause and then the audience went wild. Joan Sutherland had just finished the Mad Scene, topping it with a perfectly placed high E flat. This was not a tentative, mouse-like E flat. It was full, strong, and directly on pitch. It took almost five minutes before order was restored. Then Miss Sutherland went into 'Spargi d'amore pianto,' finishing the scene, and again the house erupted."

The pandemonium (Miles Kastendieck in the *Journal American* called it a "tornado") lasted twelve minutes, during which the heroine took ten fully demanded curtain calls. After the sixth, the few standing patrons were joined by the entire body of listeners. The whole scene was absolutely unprecedented in recent history. "Whatever the house temperature before that, it suddenly jumped up dramatically," marveled Louis Biancolli in the *World-Telegraph and Sun*. "Those haunting curlicues of grief of the crazed Lucy, topped by one dazzling high note, worked like magic."

All agreed that, until the advent of the famous Mad Scene, the new soprano had appeared somewhat tentative, not at the height of brilliance expected from her. Nervousness, no doubt, accounted for her testing of the new and strange waters. She confessed to it. After the initial plunge in the Covent Garden arena, not even La Scala or the other exacting Italian towns, which had fallen like dominoes before her, certainly not San Francisco or Chicago, both of which had preceded New York, had chalked up such a prestigious debut.

When she came to the Mad Scene, in which Zeffirelli had so lovingly coached her, everything clicked. By the third act, she was flawless. "Her cadenza with the flute was as exciting a piece of singing as the lyric stage can show today," acknowledged Schonberg. He added:

> Her well articulated trills, the precision of her scales, the security of her upper range, and, in addition, the good size of her voice were a throwback to a style of singing that is supposed to be extinct. The quality of her voice is one of extreme beauty. Some have called it cool, and it is true that it is produced with very little vibrato. This listener does not find it cool at all. It is silvery, delicately colored, and capable of extraordinary nuance. In addition, the voice has body. In coloratura it does not thin out, but is produced in a full-throated manner. That, too, is something she has in common with singers of a preceding generation, singers who could sing Lucia one night, Donna Anna a few nights later, perhaps Leonora or Elsa after that.

The critic went on to commend the singer's taste, her elegant phrasing, and her effort, "with all her heart, to use her voice to bring out the music meaning. In short," he concluded, "at last we have a great coloratura soprano."

Lang chose to filigree his dominant impression of a voice

> irresistibly pure and insinuating in the upper regions, fully vital in the middle, perhaps a little weak in the lowest reaches, but what captivates most is the effortless gliding . . . She can sing runs like a flute, but the sound is never flutey; she can sing staccatos that cascade like raindrops; her trills are not the usual uneasy vacillation between two neighboring tones, but an utterly musical warbling that a pianist could not execute more securely; and she can make a melody arch as if it were supported by marble columns.

Inevitably, someone said that she came, sang, and conquered. It was Irving Kolodin in *Saturday Review*, who usually commanded more original phrases. However, one of his comments was illuminating and pertinent. He noted her mid-nineteenth-century slant of body to compose her tall figure in an angular attitude of suffering. He added the apt phrase: "Mistress of that ancient, ever-new art."

Apart from Kolodin's comment on her body language and the reference to the use of her voice to color meaning, on this delirious occasion very little mention was made of the prima donna's acting. But the little that was said was not entirely complimentary. This, together with references to diction, constituted a cross Joan would have to bear throughout her career. On this night of nights, it did not matter, and there were other interesting positive reactions to reflect upon. Harriett Johnson in the *Post* thought that Sutherland's "big, gaunt frame was peculiarly suited to the macabre aspects of the role, while her haunted look and demeanor created an atmosphere that was hypnotic the moment she stepped on stage. She made us believe in the idiocy of her encounter with a real ghost. We didn't need a psychiatrist to diagnose that here was a distraught female made-to-order for eventual madness."

"What she possesses in feeling for the word, note, and motivation is precious," commented Louis Biancolli, adding that by popular acclaim, "she is the new reigning queen of song."

From all over—from Germany, Italy, Canada—the scribes flocked to hail what one of them called "a new goddess of song."

Quite naturally, the impressive debut overshadowed the remainder of the participants in the shining night, although Richard Tucker came in for his own kudos. In fact, "he sang his head off," as Robert Landry elegantly put it in *Variety*. Lorenzo Testi, soon to be forgotten, was the Enrico, and the dependables, Thelma Votipka and Nicola Moscona, sang Alisa and Raimondo respectively. It was hardly a night for another debut. Silvio Varviso, a young Swiss whom Sutherland had encountered and liked in San Francisco, kept things under control in the pit. "The orchestra seemed to like him and the audience certainly did," remarked Schonberg.

Rudolf Bing in his box had to be gratified. It goes without saying that Richard Bonynge, who had shepherded this phenomenon for so long, shared the gratification. Soon Richard would be able to participate in the process that brought glory to his wife, coaxing and bullying the best out of her from the commanding position in the orchestra pit. But that was not to happen at the Met for a few years. Now, in the box with Geraldine Souvaine, producer of the intermission features of the Met broadcasts, he grabbed his hostess's hand and squeezed so tightly that it was all she could do to keep from joining the anguished sounds that came from the stage. The Bonynges' son, Adam, aged five, did not feel the full impact of his mother's success. He had come to the States with them, staying with friends in Westchester County, and had attended the dress rehearsal. It was with the greatest satisfaction that he muttered to the soprano Elisabeth Rethberg, who sat beside him, while the mad Lucia was offstage committing her bloody murder: "Now she's cutting him up!"

Joan commented in amusement: "He divides all opera characters into good guys and bad guys and of course he likes the bad ones best."

The crush in the tatty dressing room after the performance was almost lethal. The bulk of Elsa Maxwell filled a good chunk of cubic space. This newspaper columnist-cum-hostess-cum-hero worshiper had forsaken Maria Callas some time before and now fixed on this new sensation. She would give a party, she declared, and was as good as her word, entertaining at the Summit Hotel early the next month. She also managed to get her photograph taken with Joan and New York's Mayor, Robert Wagner.

Outside the Fortieth Street stage door a mob scene was growing. After the last visitor had left the prima donna to assume her own persona, the crowd nearly undid her composure. Richard feared they would never reach their hired Rolls-Royce, so fierce and pressing were the fans. Joan's clothing was even slightly torn, but, at last, they were safely away.

Geraldine Souvaine, who immediately enfolded the couple in warm friendship, gave a great party for them after the show in her apartment in Central Park West. The Bonynges did not get home to their temporary residence in a Central Park South hotel until quite late.

Fifteen hours after the triumphant debut, Joan and Richard, with unusual aplomb, received the press in their hotel suite, which was heavy with the scent of red and white roses. Chatting amiably, the hostess took overcoats and hung them in the closet, also moving chairs around into a circle, until someone told her to sit down and "make like a prima donna." She tried, but it was not easy. She confided that she hoped to take Adam to the new children's zoo in Central Park and to get milk shakes for both of them. She appeared so fresh, so glad to be alive. Here is a perceptive description of her by a reporter from the *Post*:

Joan Sutherland has deserted Wagner, but she has the proportions appropriate for a Valkyrie. She is tall (five foot 8 1/2 [sometimes she was credited with another inch] with a lofty beehive hairdo adding another three or four inches), solid (her weight is down to 170 from a formidable 224), clear browed, dazzlingly fresh complexioned, lavishly dimpled. She is 35, but when she smiles, she acquires a girlish prettiness, even a radiance, that softens the assertiveness of a thin mouth and a strong jaw.

Then, as often before and many times after, she and Richard faced the imputation of his Svengali influence on a passive Trilby. By now, they were used to it and unruffled in their answers. Joan confessed to feeling like Trilby once in a while, but not for long, explaining that Richard had the certain knack of drawing out of her things she did not know were there. Richard put it down to the fact that they had worked together constantly for eleven years and that Joan never worked alone.

Joan had confessed to an earlier inquisitor that she was unhappy at the thought of the old Met disappearing. Plans were indeed ripening for just that demolition.

"Just think! They might have torn the place down before I got there!" she exclaimed. Reminded that the Old Lady of Thirty-ninth Street had some serious flaws and was probably held together with faith and adhesive tape, she brought up the Teatro Fenice in Venice and, above all, her cherished Covent Garden. Both had, and still have, beautiful auditoriums and backstage slums. She moved in perfect happiness through the cramped and almost derelict dressing room and rehearsal facilities in the New York shrine.

Five performances of *Lucia* with their newest goddess were all that voracious Met patrons were allowed. Richard Tucker, whose singing matched Joan's in opulent splendor, was her Edgardo in three of them; Jan Peerce, in splendid voice, took the other two. Lorenzo Testi gave way to Frank Guarerra twice as Enrico; Nicola Moscona had two Raimondos to Bonaldo Giaiotti's three. The broadcast of December 9 spread Joan's fame throughout the hemisphere. Terry McEwen discussed the art of the prima donna in one intermission. When Joan left for the Christmas holidays, Anna Moffo, Roberta Peters, and Gianna D'Angelo each had a Lucia or two.

During all this mad scramble, a Washington concert loomed. The Bonynges arrived at the Union Railroad Station in a shower of roses and steam. The roses were by the order of Patrick Hayes, the indefatigable Washington impresario; the steam, courtesy of the Pennsylvania Railroad. The heroine astonished everyone in the waiting room by discovering a computer that would analyze handwriting. Vastly intrigued, Joan made straight for the machine, stunning the operators by her outgoing, breezy manner. They refused her fee, and she refused to reveal what the analysis had been. At last, it was possible to lead her to the gold-crested limousine of the Australian ambassador, which dropped her at the embassy, the Bonynges' residence during their short stay. The concert was indubitably a smashing success.

Also crammed into the early *Lucia* weeks was an American Opera Society *Sonnambula* in Carnegie Hall, on December 5. Joan "did her considerable bit to reassure a distinguished audience that the age of great coloratura singing was not a lost art," according to one pundit. She was in glorious voice, and once again her sterling musicianship impressed everyone. The surrounding cast did not shine quite as brightly, although Ezio Flagello displayed some bass coloratura of his own, and Betty Allen (not to be confused with Joan's early Australian chum) showed a big rich voice, with real contralto timbre. The conductor was Nicholas Rescigno, "who managed to keep abreast of his forces most of the time."

. . .

It is perhaps understandable that the debuts in San Francisco and Chicago had not registered so high on the applause meter or in the public consciousness. Joan was eight days late into San Francisco, having suffered a miserable bout with abscessed ears in Edinburgh, and Anna Moffo had to take over the opening-night Lucia on September 15. Joan sang only two performances, on September 23 and October 25. Renato Cioni, whom Joan had met when Zeffirelli insisted on a tall tenor for his production of *I Puritani* in Venice, was the Edgardo. The Bonynges liked him, and he partnered Joan in other houses. San Francisco also took to him, Arthur Bloomfield stating that he called a nice truce between refinement and vocal splendor. (The California climate must have suited him, for he fared less well in the December *Sonnambula* in New York.)

This had probably been the first time for Joan's Lucias that the "Wolf Crag" episode was restored. The scene shows the confrontation of Edgardo by Enrico, who challenges the hero to a duel after the turbulent scene in which the Sextet occurs. In later Bonynge performances the scene was included, as well as another between Lucia and Raimondo, the old tutor mentor, which rounds out the plot considerably.

San Francisco's conductor for Joan was Francesco Molinari-Pradelli, an experienced Italian who had been at Covent Garden. He would stay with San Francisco a few years and go also to the

Met and other houses. He was no stranger to the Bonynges; in fact, he had presided over the tremendous task of recording the sixteen representations of bygone singers' art in "The Art of the Prima Donna," as well as the 1961 *Rigoletto*. Richard, in a more reflective mood, professed to respect the conductor's knowledge of repertoire, but at one moment in the San Francisco *Lucia*, the young husband of the prima donna, still inclined to occasional unbridled behavior, lost any sense of caution. Displeased by something the veteran conductor had done (possibly the maestro's disregard of Joan's carefully coached ornamentations), Bonynge leaned over the side of his box and cried: "Porco!" (Pig). It was one of those small incidents that enliven opera houses.

Unfortunately, this conductor had been slated to conduct for Joan's Metropolitan debut. Hastily, in the light of the Bonynges' displeasure with him, he was replaced by Silvio Varviso, who was currently conducting *Le Nozze di Figaro*, *A Midsummer Night's Dream*, and *Rigoletto* in San Francisco, and who, as we have seen, proved to be an acceptable substitute.

These were increasingly hectic days for the Bonynge entourage, which included Anne Roughley, whose earlier skill at nursing had to be called on several times during the frantic schedule of the fall and winter of 1961. Bookings were not the most considerate, calling for dashes back and forth across the continent, and midway stops in Chicago as well as numerous other points where concerts by the newfound prima donna had been hastily booked. Los Angeles and San Diego also demanded the San Francisco *Lucia*.

At least one interval was richly rewarding. After her San Francisco debut, Joan received a letter from her early idol, Amelita Galli-Curci, and an ensuing exchange of letters brought about a visit to San Diego, where the petite prima donna had retired after her active career, prevented from singing by an aggravated goiter condition. Their hostess received them like a pink cloud, dressed from shoulders to toes in that dainty color. Her hair was white by now, but her smile was wide and welcoming as a girl's. Joan will never forget those hours and the wise advice the elder woman offered: "Never worry about critics!" (The San Francisco press had been something less than complimentary about Joan's inclusion of some Tosti ballads in a concert given on her birthday.) "Jus' put on blinders like a 'orse and go straight ahead!"

Going straight ahead in this instance meant more zigzagging from place to place. Between San Francisco opera performances, the Chicago debut was planned. The *Lucia* on October 14 brought one of the most caustic reviews Joan ever received. It came from that grande dame of the Chicago *Tribune*, Claudia Cassidy, universally feared for her propensity to make or break an artist. She had been responsible for the hasty departure of several Symphony conductors, and did not much like many of the reigning singers. Joan got a full dose of venom:

> Miss Sutherland is a tall woman with a great pile of russet hair and a voice, undeniably a voice. But how much of a voice and to what degree a voice for lyric drama I have as yet been unable to discover. In concert her singing was cold and remote, but she had a miraculous trill. In *Lucia* her singing was cold, remote, and dull, until she reached the Mad Scene, and while once more she had the trill, the range, and the fioritura, she created not a ripple of excitement . . . Excitement in music, especially in opera, and even more so in a role such as Lucia, is the projection of character in song.

There was more to this effect, but Richard Tucker provided "the evening's stellar song," and Zeffirelli's settings, imported from Palermo, seemed mostly to be observed under a fog. "Still, that great hall remains the most effective single setting, with its high range of pale windows casting a spectral light."

Musical America and *Opera News* carried the discouraging message to wider audiences: "no fire until the Mad Scene." The remainder of the cast also suffered some hard knocks. Even Tucker received brickbats for his acting, while Mario Zanasi as Enrico and William Wildermann as Raimondo gathered little comfort. Nor did Antonio Votto, the conductor. General Manager Carol Fox, nothing daunted, kept to her own opinions and signed Joan for another season as soon as the travel books permitted. Adler and Fox had so often beaten Rudolf Bing to the post in hiring new and valued singers that it was almost a cliché by now.

Bing was already notorious for his professed distaste for singers—humans with a throat disease, he had contemptuously called them, very publicly. It was questionable sometimes whether he even liked music. His efforts to banish the star system had already flopped rather miserably by the time Joan came onto the Met scene, and he had been known to champion his prize exhibits by challenging his other obsession, the press. "You have to judge singers," he observed, "by noticing not whether they are beloved by the press, but whether they draw a full house."

That Callas and Sutherland, to name just two, had been heard at Chicago's opera before the Met bothered Bing not a bit. Said he: "It's a good thing to let them try out somewhere else first. I have no feeling for this type of competition. I am not a race track."

The upshot of the hectic year of 1961 was three new career anchors for the soprano, of which the Metropolitan would be the most consistent. Soon, too, Richard would be welcomed in the orchestra pit of all three, as well as all over the world.

CHAPTER
12

Three Queens

❄ LUCIA HAD BEEN THE KEY THAT OPENED MANY OF the great opera portals of the world for Sutherland; she had followed up with *Alcina*, *Puritani*, *Sonnambula*, and *Beatrice*, and had conquered *Traviata* almost to her satisfaction. Now, although several of these works would fit comfortably into her opera trunk in years to come, it was time to learn a few new pieces to put on stages that were demanding her presence. The first of these came on January 4, 1962, a Queen of the Night in Covent Garden's *Magic Flute*.

Just ten years after her debut there as the First Lady, and having given them in the interim a perfect Pamina, the prima donna embarked on the most difficult of the three feminine roles in the *Flute*, the Star-Flaming Queen, who sets out to revenge the abduction of her daughter. There are two superb arias for the fierce lady, one of which skitters around high Fs and is the desire and bane of all coloraturas. The first hint of Joan's trouble came when Richard, arbitrarily, it seemed, lowered the pitch a half tone for the first aria and a whole tone for the second. Everyone was scandalized.

Richard defended himself hotly: the pieces were too bloody high and, anyway, Mozart had not intended all those screaming notes. They bore no relation to the rest of the score and were mere show-off stunts. No one took him seriously. Joan was faulted, and in a bland blond wig, she seemed not the strongest Queen ever to dominate the dark skies. Fiery was not her forte. "Although she's been known to hit a high F-sharp when in a rage," added Richard.

What was worse, she was once more inflicted with a slow

conductor. This time it was the venerable Otto Klemperer who wended his way cautiously through Mozart's melodies, nearly driving Joan up the wall. It was the third new production of *Magic Flute* since the war, and not an illustrious credit to the house. The German language was a barrier, for one thing, and the concession to Klemperer was hardly worth it. The result turned out to be an old man's opera, the critics thought, without sparkle, although not without charm.

As for Joan's differences with the conductor, her ideas seemed better. One lone newspaper adored Klemperer, scored Joan, but this sheet, the *Scotsman*, seldom had an encouraging word to say about the new darling of the opera world. There were some excellent singers in the cast: Richard Lewis as Tamino; Joan Carlyle as Pamina; Geraint Evans, a bubbling Papageno. Joan never sang the role again.

Several events that deserved to be colored with a red letter —or a black one—intervened before Joan's next Queen. Although not registered worldwide, the twenty-fifth of January marked a turning point. Richard took up the baton for the first time, at a concert of the Santa Cecilia Orchestra in Rome, with Joan as soloist.

"The first conductor had fallen ill, and the second was run over or something, so they threw me on," Richard confessed. "I'd had no lessons or anything. I would never have attempted it in cold blood."

Sandro Sequi witnessed the affair, which turned out to create proportions of a scandal. The Philharmonic society was very snobbish, very old, and very stylish. They were not very rich—could not pay much, but their prestige, they thought, should go a long way with the fledgling prima donna. Indeed, she had a tremendous success, with arias by Handel, Bellini, and Thomas, but her husband fared badly. When he led the Overture to Offenbach's *La Belle Hélène*, the fashionable audience appeared scandalized that such a piece of fluff should be put before them. *Il Messagero* called Bonynge a café conductor, with the gestures of a ballet dancer. The incident rankled, and Rome was not exactly the favorite city of the Bonynges thereafter, although some time later, Joan did sing at the Academy of St. Cecilia with Richard at the piano.

On July 11, Richard presided over the Los Angeles Philharmonic in Hollywood Bowl. Hedda Hopper attributed to him a mixture of St. Vitus' Dance and the Twist, but thought his good looks ought to get him some Tony Curtis parts. This was a slow road to glory.

As early as March, he had led the recording of *Alcina*; then in September, the *Sonnambula* album appeared. From then on, with very few exceptions, husband conducted wife in recordings. His formal debut in opera remained for Vancouver in early 1963.

.   .   .

Joan had returned to Barcelona in January 1962 for a *Lucia* that bore historical import for a young tenor who sang the part of the ill-fated husband Arturo. His name appeared as Jaime Aragall. As Giacomo he would later appear in the Bonynges' casts. Another obscure Arturo, in Dallas the previous year, had been listed as Placido Domingo, himself destined to light up the hoardings in his own time and fashion and to become one of Joan's favorite tenors. Her Barcelona Edgardo, Lucia's true love, was sung by an old friend, André Turp, later (among other roles) to be Joan's Alfredo in Covent Garden's revitalized *Traviata* in May.

Joan sang a *Sonnambula* at La Scala in February (when Alfredo Kraus's name appeared in the cast); her second new assignment was a May return to Milan for another Queen. This time it was Marguerite of Valois in Meyerbeer's *Les Huguenots*. It proved to be no more lasting an investment than Mozart's leading lady. *Huguenots* is seldom put on the stage to this day; Milan had not produced it in sixty-five years; the Met, for almost a half-century. The reason: the great sprawling score requires seven singers of highest quality—two sopranos, one mezzo, one tenor, one baritone, and two basses. Where to find a bundle like that?

La Scala thought it had just such a constellation, topped by Joan and Giulietta Simionato (deserting the mezzo range for the first time) as the hapless heroine Valentine. Then there were Franco Corelli, in his early and shining promise, as Raoul; Fiorenza Cossotto, comely mezzo, as the page Urbain, who has a complicated piece to do; a baritone named Vladimir Ganzarolli; and the two deep voices, Nicolai Ghiaurov and Giorgio Tozzi. The conductor, Gianandrea Gavazzeni, possessed some distinction, and the sets and costumes were the artful work of Nicola Benois. It looked as though it would make a grand splash.

At dress rehearsal two great Scala prima donnas paid their respects, one in each intermission. Renata Tebaldi came first, remarking: "I'll never forget your singing." Callas (who had been rumored for Joan's part, though nothing had come of it) followed, with smiles and kisses. This kind of tribute at these particular times is apt to be a bit unnerving, even if stimulating. Richard had declared that intermissions should be left sacrosanct; nobody, but nobody, should go near a dressing room for these intended purposes. Nevertheless, prima donnas seem to be exempt from this rule. At any rate, Joan had plenty of attention showered on her, with a seventeen-minute ovation for her and Simionata, whom Richard thought terrific (much better in the higher range than in the later *Semiramide* mezzo part, as he remembered). The occasion was, what one weekly called, "an impossible example of the most glorious kind of Italian vocalism."

What Joan remembers chiefly about that *Huguenots* was having to make her entrance on horseback. Already in pain from her recalcitrant back, she had to be lifted into the saddle practically by derrick, because of her inflexible steel-reinforced corset. There she sat, it seemed for hours, while the horse went through several cycles of natural business and never got properly cleaned up. Her tightly bound torso, the heavy velvet costume of the Queen, and the inescapable odor of the horse nearly undid our heroine.

"It was harder than two *Traviatas* plus two *Lucias*," she commented afterward. The horse's name was George, she added.

Meanwhile, Australia was upset. Here their prima donna was riding around on horseback, even though she had canceled a whole season for them.

Joan's third Queen was to come after an enforced intermission. The *Huguenots* at the end of May was to be followed by a long-awaited trip home. Plans had been laid for a triumphant concert tour of Australia, where the couple had not been since their departure a decade or so previously.

As early as a few weeks after her Met debut in November, signs of trouble appeared. Exhaustion lay underneath it all—the forgetting of words, the occasional race to get ahead of the orchestra, or the slowing down when the orchestra beat her to the end of a phrase. Even cancellation of a couple of dates and a week's rest at home in London did not refresh her, and she carried through the ensuing months with periods of unremitting anguish, relieved only by a dull sort of determination to go on. Injections for the new pains did not help much. In March, the steel corset in which she was forced to sing—and fall—in *Traviata* had been as much burden as panacea. At home once again, her doctor diagnosed arthritis of the discs in her spine. Absolute rest was indicated, even ordered.

Swallowing this bitter pill, Joan gave up the idea of the Australian tour and even wondered if she would sing again on the opera stage. The newspapers, of course, made a great splash of it. In all their headlines, the prima donna was finished.

The summer rest did the trick. By fall she was ready to take on the schedule that had piled up, and by December, her third Queen for the year was in the making. This was the Babylonian Semiramis, whose passions had been set to some extraordinary music by Rossini. La Scala mounted it for Joan, giving her Simionato as the mezzo Arsace (the young warrior with whom the Queen falls in love, only to discover that he is her son by the King Nino, whom she has murdered). Full of blood and battle, the opera provided an enthralling experience for Andrew Porter, who had come from London.

Displaying the scholarship that persisted in his later stint with *The New Yorker*, Porter laid out a neat and knowledgeable essay comparing Rossini and Verdi. He then went on to rhapsodize about Joan—nobody else was worth mentioning. This role, at once most florid and most austere, with an abundance of ornamentation because it had been dedicated to Isabella Colbran (Rossini's inspiration and eventually his wife), provided an Olympian heroine who combines elements of Klytemnestra, Jocasta, Phaedra, and Lady Macbeth—a gaggle of harridans and harpies, to be sure.

Thus *Semiramide* constituted Joan's most decisive step forward since *Lucia*. It was not just brilliance alone, for she dominated the stage against all the distractions that the director, Margherita Wallmann, could devise.

This was a new, glamorous, commanding Joan Sutherland, stronger and fuller in middle voice. The "moony" quality, so disturbing in many previous moments, was gone; so was the rhythmic inertia that had flawed some performances. (Porter singled out the *Rigoletto* recording for this fault; it had been one of the harassing experiences of the summer of 1961 for Joan.) Now she sang freely, astoundingly unselfconscious; had developed new powers; had conquered relative weaknesses and technique (unlike Callas), and could anticipate a long series of artistic triumphs.

Relief at her "comeback" permeated the atmosphere. The five-hour stretch of Rossini's music bothered no one, although Porter believed that the restoration of the half-hour cuts would have made the opera seem shorter. He admired the Benois scenery, based mainly on Sanquirico's for La Scala in 1806, partly on Bagnara's for Venice.

Wallmann was a mistress of distracting detail. At one point, the stage was so cluttered with chorus, ballet, and supers that Joan could not penetrate the mass to make her entrance. She took it humorously, if plaintively. Insisting on getting through the crowd, she was heard to mutter: "After all, I *am* the Queen!"

Of course, there were the usual detractors, not at all happy with the spectacle or the protagonists. Peter Heyworth in the London *Observer* went so far as to dub the opera a white elephant.

In that, he was not too far wrong: *Semiramide* is tricky to mount, but, although the Met shrugged it off, it has had several revivals that provided opportunity for Joan. In fact, Chicago's Carol Fox gleefully seized on it as a showpiece for the incomparable team of Sutherland and Marilyn Horne to open the 1971 season. Of Joan's three Queens of 1962, it was only the Babylonian who endured.

CHAPTER

13

Discovery and Consolidation

✻ THE NEXT TWO YEARS, 1963 AND 1964, AND THE early part of 1965, set the pattern for the Bonynges' future life. For them, and for the managers behind them and the dozens of opera houses and concert bureaus that begged for their very special services, it was a time of fluster, of excitement, of new discoveries. Along with the decisions made and the engagements filled came a sense of consolidation—of digging in and putting down roots in a dozen or more cities to which they would return almost every year. While Europe kept them on a strong tether, with strands of affection, loyalty, and, especially in London, the secure sensation of professional "home," the New World began to demand and get larger and larger chunks of their precious time.

New York quite naturally headed the list, but both Richard and Joan preferred to try out any new work "on the road," so to speak (just as a play is frequently tried out in New Haven or Boston or even Philadelphia before braving Broadway). This not only is a perfectly legitimate process, but enabled several cities to boast of Sutherland premieres. Only occasionally did the complaint arise that a place full of civic pride was being used as a guinea pig.

Vancouver was especially favored in 1963. Marked in red on the British Columbia city's calendar was March 7, when Richard Bonynge commanded the orchestra pit for the first time. The occasion was made more glamorous because his wife was singing her first Marguerite in *Faust*. Five performances confirmed the conductor as a baton man unusually sensitive to singers' possibilities and problems—as could have been expected. New York and London had yet to see it that way, but Bonynge went on to perfect his skills. For a conductor, the only way to learn is by doing. And the first few years were trying for this gifted and ambitious husband of a rising superstar. Vancouver gave him a lift; one observer remarked that, with him in charge, everybody feels opera is fun and nobody minds working twice as hard.

Equally portentous was Joan's first *Norma*, also in Vancouver, on October 17, 1963. Irving Guttman, the producer, had suggested it, and the Bonynges came to the decision that Joan was ready to try this most fiendishly difficult of soprano roles. It was only a first step and received qualified praise. *Musical America* mentioned Sutherland's impeccable control, vocal acrobatics, sweeping lines, and almost perfect intonation, finding only a lack of vibrancy in her veiled tones. This was a quality, more in keeping with eighteenth-century opera, which dampened ardor, despite some wonderful high Cs. Joan, with her height, beautiful features, bearing, and presence, looked regal in a white gown. Her partners in this pioneering effort were the refulgent Marilyn Horne, dubbed the upcoming rage; the tenor John Alexander; and the bass Richard Cross.

These were the soprano's only new roles for North America, but she also penetrated deeper into the Handel treasure house with a *Giulio Cesare* at Sadler's Wells on June 20, 1963. It was not altogether a triumph, and brought about what Andrew Porter called attempts at kittenish behavior that were not exactly happy, but her vocalism remained in no doubt.

Margreta Elkins played Caesar to her Cleopatra. This practice of using a mezzo-soprano to replace the old-time castrato has been advocated by Handel scholars. (Completely at variance was the New York City Opera's employment of the bass Norman Treigle a few years later, when he shared a personal triumph with Beverly Sills, but it made hash of the relative staff-lines.) This is, however, a matter for the pedants. Bonynge has always hewed to the scholarly side, although not he but Charles Farncombe was at the helm for the London performance. Handelians had been previously stimulated by Joan's *Rodelinda* revival in late May and early June, a role she had first graced in 1959.

She glowed with happiness during this time. Perhaps this was relief; for the first time since her enforced vacation in 1962 she felt free of pain, released at last from the horrid confines of a steel corset.

In between these new ventures came *La Sonnambula*, the "opera of the year." The Met gave Joan a new production on February 21, 1963, with Silvio Varviso conducting and Henry Butler directing. Joan's tenor was the indestructible Nicolai Gedda, and Giorgio Tozzi sang Rodolfo. Later, fellow principals were Dino Formichini, tenor, and the basses Jerome Hines and Ezio Flagello. Zachary Solov's choreography, which one writer damned as synthetic rather than authentic, thickly clotted the peasants over the stage (recalling to Joan Margherita Wallmann's crowd scene in *Semiramide*) so much so that Amina could hardly grope her way through the celebrants. In rehearsal, Joan was heard to exclaim in well-carrying tones a few words of uncharacteristic irritation about "that bloody ballet." Henry Butler thought it advisable that the star pacify the dancers, and so she did. Peace was restored.

This was Charles Riecker's first contact with Joan. The Met's artistic administrator had been in the technical department in 1961 at the time of her debut. He had heard the *Lucia*, of course. In 1963 he was helping to coordinate costume fittings, among other duties, and had a chance to observe the prima donna at closer range. He found her to be a wonderful colleague—her reputation backstage, in spite of the little incident quoted above, had already grown; her innate good nature and cheerful working habits impressed everyone.

"When she walked across that bridge—a really high one in Rolf Gerard's setting—we were genuinely frightened. We stood there gasping," he remembered. "But she made it safely—a sleepwalker like Amina fears nothing."

It was almost entirely Joan's show. Here was singing in the grand style, the stuff of which legends are made, the *Times* critic remarked—not only glorious in its E-flats and trills, but also in the musicianship, the turn of phrase, the smooth, effortless line. Schonberg had devoted a Sunday article after the earlier American Opera Society *Puritani* to the restored tradition of ornamenting the vocal line, which Bonynge had certified. It was a good deal closer to the spirit of the music than the work of those present-day singers who are so bound to the printed note that a Houdini could not release them. Dozens of historical examples came to mind. Sutherland was to be complimented on her tasteful use of it.

The 1963 performances brought similar appreciations by alert version-watchers. Irving Kolodin contributed a telling comment on the difference between coloratura singing of other days and Joan's bewitching facility. He wrote in the *Saturday Review*: "When *Sonnambula* was last given here, it was in the lightly embroidered version stitched by Lily Pons in her best *petit point*. By comparison, this is a Gobelin tapestry."

Winthrop Sargeant thought the level of emotional expression too consistently high, but then, since most coloraturas convey no emotion whatever, we should be grateful for a surplus. A few diehards, still insisting that such perfection was mechanical, without heart, all steel springs, refused to be convinced. Most noticeable were *Musical America*, which kept a needle ready for Sutherland, and Alan Rich in the *Herald-Tribune*, notably crochety about this kind of music. He dismissed it with a yawn.

The Bonynges' son, Adam, added a pertinent postscript to all this: "Mummy shouldn't be tired afterward—she was asleep most of the time."

Sonnambula in San Francisco was quite a different proposition. Richard, who had done very well in Vancouver, now faced the challenge of a metropolis, but with his command of the *bel canto* style in his favor. Lotfi Mansouri made his presence known to the Bonynges, who were to encounter him often as director in the future. The settings were fancifully done by Elemer Nagy, one of the first to use rear-screen projections. Renato Cioni and Richard Cross had the leading male roles. When the opera, with its village mill and high bridge, moved to Los Angeles, it was retitled "Bellini's Dream Walking" by Albert Goldberg in the *Times*. The admiring critic called Joan a phenomenon, not only of voice and singing, but an artist with complete conviction and dedication. Bonynge also got a pat on the back for his understanding that shaped the stylistic excellence of the singers, but the writer thought the chorus and orchestra were occasionally at odds.

There was a considerable push toward making *La Traviata* the opera of 1963 and 1964. We have seen that Violetta is Joan's most challenging role in terms of coordinating singing with the portrayal of the abandoned courtesan. This time it was again a tryout situation. The Verdi opera really had more exposure than the Bellini during these months, but not the invariable success. The first United States staging was on November 12, 1963, in Philadelphia, where the Bonynges soon conceived an affectionate relationship with Eleanor Morrison, impresario of the Philadelphia Lyric; they were to go back several times, regardless of other pressures. The first night for *Traviata* in the Academy of Music was followed by a Hartford, Connecticut, showing, for the two cities shared productions. Philadelphia, for lack of a solidly based, full-time company of its own, most often imported several or all elements of a season. This *Traviata* drew Irving Guttman from Vancouver as director, and sets by Robert O'Hearn from Washington. John Alexander and Thelma Votipka (the renowned "Tippy") were the Metropolitan's contributions, as Alfredo and Annina respectively. The distinguished French baritone, Gabriel Bacquier, sang Germont *père*. Max de Schauensee, noted in his own right, was the chief critic in the City of Brotherly Love, a gentleman of the old school, devoted to opera and to singers. For many years he wrote for the *Bulletin* with authority and perception. It is interesting that he thought Joan even managed to suggest fragility as Violetta.

The Met production of this work, first seen on December 14, 1963, was the fancy Oliver Smith–Rolf Gerard–Tyrone Guthrie affair of 1957. There were two massive staircases (Acts I and III), a telephone booth of a summerhouse (Act II), and a sumptuous hotel bedroom far beyond Violetta's straitened circumstances. It was a benefit for the Opera Guild. From the beginning, the management capitalized on Joan's drawing power to the hilt, so that most of her first appearances hiked prices and drew dressy audiences. These factors did not prevent the critics from raising their big guns and firing away.

In the pro camp were Winthrop Sargeant of *The New Yorker*, John Gruen of the *Herald-Tribune*, and Louis Biancolli of the *World-Telegram*. Firmly holding down the negative were Irving Kolodin in *Saturday Review*, and Conrad L. Osborne, the longest-winded writer of all. He said it pithily, however, in the London *Financial Times*: "I look for the emotion honestly felt and not simply understood in an intellectual way. Sutherland misses the boat." He professed to be downright bored by so much good singing producing so little effect. The Sutherland-versus-Violetta fight was well joined, and would last for years.

The "coldness" so often attributed to this new diva possibly arose from such impeccable vocalism. People were used to hearing more effort and less result. Sargeant excoriated this view. When Sutherland's Violetta was brought into direct competition with the great ones, she won hands down. She was not only believable, but extremely touching. It was the most beautiful singing and best acting of our generation. The letter from Germont read in the last act bore the stamp of a consummate actress.

As if pouring on a little additional balm, Schonberg's *Sunday Times* article vowed that this was, indeed, a great Violetta. As for the acting, nobody fussed at Flagstad, who stood quietly and sang. (Of course, this is a trifle beside the point, since Violetta puts out a totally different set of requirements than the Wagnerian characters we were accustomed to see from the statuesque Norwegian.)

Schonberg pointed out something that had relevance—Sutherland's records of the Verdi opera that had preceded her "live" appearance had been of inferior quality and had led him to expect the worst. This was a London set issued in 1962, with John Pritchard conducting and Carlo Bergonzi and Robert Merrill as the Germonts.

Joan did not receive the most illustrious support for her first Met Violetta: Sandor Konya and Mario Sereni. Furthermore, George Schick proved not to be the most sympathetic conductor, either for Verdi or for Joan. Other tenors took over later: Flaviano Labo, Nicolai Gedda, and Richard Tucker. The latter two were decided improvements.

Alternative *Sonnambulas* and *Traviatas* filled the remainder of the Met 1963–64 season, with one addition: a gala on December 14, 1963. Joan was the single star, partnered by Konya in the *Traviata* Act I, Tucker in a scene from *Lucia*, and Gedda in the third act of *Sonnambula*, a neat little package.

Extending its season by two weeks in the spring of 1964, the Metropolitan honored the World's Fair on the centenary of New York's seizure from the Dutch by the English. The sixteen performances were all nonsubscription, so that visitors from all over the world could take advantage of the technical wonders and high jinks at the Fair grounds as well as the highly cultural events on Thirty-ninth Street and Broadway.

Joan's part in this jamboree consisted of two performances of *Sonnambula*. She was also a member of a stellar quartet at a supper arranged by Rudolf Bing. The four fixed stars sat at separate tables, surrounded by hovering satellites. One commentator remarked that Bing's social gamble paid off until Sutherland decided to leave. She suddenly swerved and made a beeline for the table where Renata Tebaldi reigned. All champagne glasses were suspended while Sutherland bent over Tebaldi and a great warm smile illuminated her face. She embraced Tebaldi and was kissed in return. The two great sopranos whispered in each other's ears and giggled like schoolgirls at a prom. An observer noted that Sutherland then swept out, followed by Tebaldi. Anna Moffo left without fanfare; Leontyne Price outstayed everyone; so did Dame Alicia Markova, who doesn't sing, added the observer, but has a fine pair of legs.

Meanwhile, the 1964 season had also encompassed a Covent Garden *Puritani* in March and a *Lucia* in May, as well as a Milan *Lucia* (again with the somewhat less than beloved Wallmann as director).

. . .

By all accounts, Joan had already conquered Boston (at a recital in Symphony Hall in February 1963) when she first encountered the Renaissance Woman of Boston, Sarah Caldwell. Touted as a genius, the portly lady always had a surprise up her voluminous sleeve. The methods she employed were unorthodox as she sprang ever new delights on a wondering public. She seemed to think up new ideas while standing in a reverie, leaving everyone else to stand and wait.

Joan was used to crisper, more forward-moving tactics, but she delivered several vibrant performances for Sarah. *Puritani* led off, on February 12, 1964. (It was not Joan's first *Puritani* in the United States; the first had been the American Opera Society's concerts on April 16, 18, and 24, 1963.) Richard conducted, and those who became "regulars" with the Bonynges were Richard Cross and Spiro Malas. Charles Craig sang Arturo, and the Enrichetta was Dorothy Cole, whom the Bonynges earmarked for what was to be their 1965 Australian tour. It was a triumph for Bonynge—"a marvelous show," the critics thought.

On November 14, *Traviata* was done in San Francisco with Bonynge at the helm. The tenor was unfamiliar to the Bonynges at that time: the Hungarian Robert Ilosfalvy; the baritone, Eberhardt Wächter, had played Don Giovanni opposite Joan's Donna Anna in Vienna, long, long ago in 1959. (Wächter, with his Viennese charm, ended up making other Germonts seem stiff.) Joan, as usual, produced serpentine queues of hopefuls waiting for standing-room privileges. The respected Alfred Frankenstein wrote in the *Chronicle* that Sutherland's Violetta had grandeur and loveliness with equal expressiveness.

The highest honor that the Met could accord a singer was Joan's portion in 1964–65; she opened the season on October 12. It was a return to the familiar *Lucia*, with Silvio Varviso again conducting; but, wonder of wonders, a new production! At last, the Met had thought to mount a fresh show around its most valuable new acquisition. Replacing the rags and tatters that had sheltered Lammermoor's heroine for many years, the new dark, menacing sets were by Attilio Colonella. Margherita Wallmann seemed to haunt Joan. This time she provided action that seldom moved, but sluggishly struck poses and held them, as Alan Rich remarked sarcastically in the *Herald Tribune*. She made the sextet a burlesque.

Konya and Merrill provided Joan's supports. There were eight performances, ending on Christmas Eve, and the customary gala was thrown in on November 29. This time Joan shared the spotlight with two other prima donnas, Renata Tebaldi as Mimi and Elisabeth Schwarzkopf as the Marschallin. Thomas Schippers conducted the act of *Der Rosenkavalier*; George Schick the other two segments.

The year 1965 opened on January 5 with a Carnegie Hall showing of *Alcina*, which, divorced from its sumptuous Zeffirelli mounting, still bombarded a breathless audience with vocal salvos from its heroine. Sutherland and Monica Sinclair were reunited, along with Margreta Elkins, who made her United States debut as Ruggiero. Thanks to Richard Bonynge, *Opera News* remarked, the repetitions in the Handel score were enlivened with vocal embellishments.

. . .

Boston's *Semiramide*, on Feburary 5 and 7, 1965, was not for Joan an American first, as the Los Angeles Philharmonic had put on the Rossini opera in concert on January 29 and 31, 1964. The Boston show brought Marilyn Horne as Arsace to an admiring public. Michael Steinberg, the reigning critic of the *Globe*, went quite dizzy over her singing, stating that there had been none such for 120 years (how could he know? he was a relatively young man). In that cast were André Montal (whose real name was Jenkins), also tapped by the Bonynges for Australia, and Joseph Rouleau, who had sung with the soprano many times.

Another incident that was to prove fateful for the Bonynges, a tenor, and the opera world at large, occurred in February 1965. Joan and Richard were booked for a *Lucia* in Miami. A few weeks before the scheduled performance on the fifteenth, the tenor, Renato Cioni, begged off in order to sing *Tosca* with Callas in Paris. The Bonynges did not begrudge their erstwhile protégé this chance, but where to find a replacement? Arturo di Filippi, the obliging and conscientious general manager, exhausted all his resources; then Bonynge remembered the tenor he had auditioned in London and had already signed for the Australian tour. They got on the line to him, and out came Luciano Pavarotti for his United States debut.

The occasion was entirely happy for all concerned, and for Pavarotti a firm beginning. *Opera News* remarked that no one went home before Edgardo's death scene, a fate that too often overtook tenors in the shadow of a refulgent Lucia.

The exuberant tenor had caught the attention of Joan Ingpen, who had been casting for that *ad hoc* Italian season in Dublin, where she had put Joan as Donna Anna five years earlier. Despite his utter rawness as an actor, the velvety voice as the Duke in *Rigoletto* captured the Irish fancy, and it was then only a step to auditioning at Covent Garden, and later for Bonynge. So was launched the most flamboyant tenor career in recent history. Pavarotti has expressed his gratitude on many occasions, not the least in a book of his own. His adventures with Joan and Richard were to be as many as his (and their) conflicting schedules allowed.

· · ·

There was still much to do before the scheduled takeoff to Australia. Richard consolidated his right to the baton with a *Lucia* in Denmark in late February, but fared less well with a *Sonnambula* in London. There still existed a prejudice against the whole *bel canto* affair, and an extra bit of animosity for this brash new conductor. In fact, a small gang was seen to exist that cherished an implacable grudge against Richard. They got it into their heads that he had too much to say in Sutherland's career. They thought *they* owned the star. They held forth at this *Sonnambula* and would not subside for quite a long time. They cheered Joan as unreasonably as they booed her husband.

Even Joan's stout champion, Andrew Porter, turned against the *Sonnambula*. It was grotesquely cast, he thought. No feeling for Bellini's beautiful line. "Non giungi" was tossed off at top speed. Nothing wrong with Joan's vocal equipment; in fact, she was magnificent. But why appear in such an outmoded production? Why not insist on Serafin and Zeffirelli? As for Pavarotti, he remained totally disengaged.

These cold showers did not appreciably affect the heroine, who moved on to Philadelphia for her first United States *Faust* on March 9. It was an Irving Guttman production. De Schauensee thought the French admirable, which could have placated a good many wounded feelings. Richard Verreau sang Faust, and Margreta Elkins showed up again in a Bonynge cast, as Marthe.

Now it was almost time to realize the long-planned valorous return to their native land.

A one-time role, the Countess in *Le Nozze di Figaro*, Covent Garden, 1953.

Photo: Houston Rogers, courtesy Robert Tuggle.

Sutherland's last Wagnerian role: Eva in *Die Meistersinger,* 1957.

An early venture into the Handel operas that were to become a hallmark: The Israelite Woman in *Samson*, Covent Garden, 1958.

Photo: Houston Rogers, courtesy Robert Tuggle.

As Mme. Lidoine in the British premiere of Poulenc's *Dialogues des Carmelites*.

Photo: Houston Rogers, courtesy Robert Tuggle.

Above: Joan's only Queen of the Night, in Covent Garden's *Magic Flute* of 1962. When chastised for transposing the big aria away from the high F's, Bonynge retorted: "It's just too damned high anyway."

Right: Bellini's *Beatrice di Tenda* at La Scala, 1961.

Marguerite de Valois rides triumphantly onto the scene of La Scala's
Les Huguenots in spite of a smelly
horse (1962).

Photo: E. Piccagliani.

A Zeffirelli version of the Handelian lady Alcina in Venice.

Houston Rogers, courtesy Robert Tuggle.

Cleopatra in Handel's *Giulio Cesare,*
Hamburg.

Photo: Du Vinage.

The breath-holding walk across the narrow bridge by sleepwalker Sutherland in the
Metropolitan's 1962-63 revival of Bellini's *La Sonnambula*. Giorgio Tozzi as
Rodolfo is at extreme left.

Photo: Louis Melançon.

With Regina Resnik as the fussy Marquise in the Met's *Daughter of the Regiment*.
London thought its production a bit vulgar, but New York adored it.

Euridice in Haydn's *Orfeo ed Euridice* at the Vienna Festival, 1967.

Photo: Gretl Geiger.

Lakmé in Seattle, 1967.

Lucia, early and late. *From the left:* That history-making first at Covent Garden, 1959; *Below:* and Australia's elaborate production in the Sydney Opera House Concert Hall.

Photos: Houston Rogers; Branco Gaica.

Violetta, desired and difficult, at Covent Garden, 1960…

Photos: Houston Rogers; Stuart Robinson.

...and in 1975, with Alfredo Kraus.

Two Donna Annas: *Left,* at Covent Garden

Photo by Franco Zeffirelli

Right: The last at the Metropolitan, 1978.

Photos: Zeffirelli's courtesy Opera News; *Metropolitian's by J. Heffernan, courtesy* Opera News.

Rodelina, the Handel Opera Society's London production of 1959.

Norma — the incomparable partnership. Sutherland as the Druid Priestess, Marilyn Horne as Adalgisa, the Metropolitan's *Norma*, 1970.

Photo: Frank Dunand, courtesy Opera News.

The stunning production of Bellini's *I Puritani* at the Metropolitan in 1976, with Luciano Pavarotti as Arturo.

Photo: Frank Dunand, courtesy Opera News.

The enchantress *Esclarmonde* in the San Francisco premiere of Massenet's "Wagnerian" opera, 1974.

Antonia and Hoffmann (Placido Domingo) sing of their undying love in the third act of Offenbach's *Les Contes d'Hoffmann* at the Metropolitan, 1973-74.

Photo: Louis Melançon, courtesy Opera News.

Curtain call for Semiramide and Arsace (Horne) after the performance by the Lyric Opera of Chicago (1971).

With Beverly Sills at last, in San Diego's *Die Fledermaus.* They did not exchange roles as Tito Capobianco planned, however. Sills as Adele and Sutherland as Rosalinda take a happy curtain call (1980).

CHAPTER

14

You Can Go Home Again

✤ THE SUMMER OF 1965 BROUGHT THE FULFILLMENT
of an ambition that had been aborted by Joan's illness three
years previously. The Bonynges were at last going back to Australia.
This time their project came under the most favorable auspices.
Sir Frank Tait, that great gentleman among talent bookers (the
English term) and the American concert managers, would handle
the entire tour—the Sutherland-Williamson International Grand
Opera Company. The Williamson part of it referred to the revered
"Firm" of J. C. Williamson, whose management had brought prac-
tically every musical production and theatrical star to Australia for
the past half-century.

Sir Frank, now eighty, was about to embark on another of his
colossal gambles. The complicated negotiations had gone on since
1963, when the Taits saw Richard and Joan in London during the
Covent Garden production of *Puritani*. The Firm had managed a
few opera tours, notably one for Dame Nellie Melba. She had
returned to her native shores in 1911, at which time John Mc-
Cormack, who was always at dagger points with the prima donna
offstage, stampeded the Australian public with the sheer beauty of
his voice, much to Melba's disgruntlement. Then, in 1924, the
London impresario Henry Russell organized another Melba company that included Toti Dal Monte and the international celebrity,
Prince Obolensky. The aging prima donna sang some Mimis and
Marguerites, but was quite put out that the younger Dal Monte
received the rave headlines and audience cheers. Russell immediately got into hot water when he compared operetta to opera
unfavorably, using the expression, "operetta is a prostitution of

art." Newspapers seized on this tidbit with glee, accusing Russell of calling the local girls "prostitutes."

The 1965 tour was in most ways a more formidable undertaking. Although it revolved around a single prima donna, this one was a dependable professional, ready (if not entirely willing) to sing three times a week for fourteen weeks, and to spread this tremendous effort over five roles. As could be expected, the problem would be to sell out the nights when Sutherland was not singing. These would include not only two additional operas, *Eugene Onegin* and *L'Elisir d'Amore*, but several of her own *Traviatas*, *Lucias*, *Fausts*, and *Sonnambulas*, when a "second" singer would step into the leading role. Her fifth opera, *Semiramide*, could be shared with no one: it was a feat no other soprano cared to contemplate.

Richard would, of course, conduct all his wife's performances; but, for the others, another conductor was engaged. Where Melba's company had suffered prima donna explosions, Sutherland's ran into conductor trouble. Even before his first assignment, John Matheson let it be known that he was returning to England because of a dispute with Richard. Bonynge was, after all, artistic boss. Whatever the trouble, no one ever divulged it. It passed as an "artistic disagreement," but the headlines caused by Matheson's accusations of "confusion," and his statement that "wild horses would not drag anything more out of me," cast a temporary shadow over the venture that had opened sensationally two nights before. The chorus-master, Gerald Krug, took over some performances, and a young man who came along as repetiteur, William Weible, was appointed by Williamson's to fill the vacancy. (He later turned up at the Metropolitan.) Still another potential conductor, Georg Tintner, was put out of action when a car hit the bicycle he was riding, damaged it not a bit, but left him with a broken leg.

With their customary generosity to young singers, the Bonynges had assembled a troupe of twenty-one principals of considerable merit. Among them were a few nuggets that would become pure gold. Two of these, young tenors, aroused particular comment: the American John Alexander and the Italian Luciano Pavarotti. Alexander would sing the opening-night *Lucia* and later would share the roles of Edgardo and Alfredo with Pavarotti; he would also do the leads in *Onegin* and *Faust*. Pavarotti was down for *Elisir* and *Sonnambula*. Completely unknown to this public, the rotund tenor almost immediately began to emerge as a potential world star. This was his first real exposure and the beginning of a long and affectionate association with the Bonynges.

Others in the first-night *Lucia* were the young American Dorothy Cole as Alisa; the Canadian baritone Cornelis Opthof as Enrico, and the Australian Clifford Grant (who was to make a reputation in England and America before returning to Australia) as Raimondo.

That Margreta Elkins should be in the company was a foregone conclusion. The tall, handsome Australian had partnered Joan in many ventures. Elkins would sing the leads in *Onegin* and *Elisir* (departing from her previous mezzo range), and a lesser part in *Faust*. Another colleague of long standing was Monica Sinclair, who had as her chief allotment the companion role to Joan in *Semiramide*, where she sang effectively the part of Arsace. A Covent Garden luminary, the Australian contralto Laura Elms, to whom Joan insisted on giving larger roles than the local management had assigned her, also came into her own.

Many of the singers had appeared in one cast or another with Sutherland; most were new to Australia. Elizabeth Harwood, the pretty soprano known in Glyndebourne and at Sadler's Wells, was slated chiefly for Adina in *Elisir*, and added three *Lucias* and two *Sonnambulas* on Joan's off nights. Doris Yarick, a young American, found congenial chores in three operas. André Montal sang several tenor roles.

Others from England were Joseph Ward and Alberto Remedios; Richard Cross and Spiro Malas had American reputations; Joseph Rouleau and André Montal were Canadians. From Scotland came the tiny mezzo Morag Beaton.

Australians, native or adopted, filled out the roster nobly; Robert Allman, one of the most valuable of present Australian Opera regulars, and Robert McConaghie, still a favorite, and in addition, Joy Mannen, Ray Kearney, Tom McDonnell, and John Heffernan.

Among the baritones appeared Chester Carone, who had Italianized himself from Caronsky for operatic purposes. His cherubic countenance, cheerful disposition, and all-around talents attracted the Bonynges, who packed him up and took him along as their soon-to-be invaluable majordomo.

Norman Ayrton, in whom Joan still placed the confidence engendered in her early days at Covent Garden, came along as stage director for five operas (Australians and the British call the post "producer"). Martin Scheepers, a choreographer for the Dutch opera, produced and danced in *Faust* and produced *Elisir*. Another member of the troupe was unofficial: Randolph Mickelson, who went along to keep up the work he had been doing on assistance in ornamentation and other arcane versions of scores Bonynge had in hand. The chorus numbered thirty-six local singers; the ballet, twelve. A local orchestra of forty-four had been carefully chosen by Bonynge.

Tonina Dorati had been chosen as designer for the seven operas. The daughter of conductor Antal Dorati, she had been born in Melbourne in 1938, when her father was leading Colonel de Basil's Covent Garden Ballet Company. Sets for several operas were designed in London and manufactured in the Firm's workshops. *Semiramide* barely made it under the wire, so difficult was its construction. The Elizabethan Theater Trust took over in the emergency and constructed *Faust* and *Sonnambula* in Sydney.

Meanwhile, Barbara Matera in New York had been slaving over Joan's costumes for weeks. Other costumes were Australian-made. For six weeks the company rehearsed. Tension began to build up, as one newspaper after another called attention to the promised glories, and printed "intimate" disclosures of the stars' lives and foibles, even revealing the suburban hideout that the Bonynges, who had been joined by Adam, had hoped to keep secret. Joan was nervous, although carrying on professionally as ever at rehearsals. After the "dress," she was heard to chide Moffatt Oxenbauld in gentle banter for not having changed the sets for that night's performance. Moffatt, then a stage manager, rose to a high administrative position with the Australian Opera after the new house had opened.

Then came the momentous July 10. That opening night went down in history as something the Australians had never experienced before (the nearest competition anyone could remember was the visit of Queen Elizabeth in 1954)—the glitter of gowns (at a conservative estimate, at least six hundred new ones) under brilliant lights (even in "the gods," or as Americans would say, the "peanut gallery," many wore evening dress, which was unheard of in Australia), the festive air of the theater, the mounting excitement of the performance, the tumultuous aftermath.

It went a little tentatively at first, as far as the audience was concerned. Only one shout of "Bravo!" rent the air after the first act, and the brash fellow who had uttered it was looked at very curiously. But it was, so to speak, the first olive out of the bottle. When Lucia came out in her bloodstained nightdress after the Mad Scene, there was such shouting and stamping that it might just have been a soccer game! It took seven minutes for the curtain calls. Unheard of! Joan stepped back, almost fell through a back-drop, and laughed. When the curtain fell, it knocked all the flowers askew. Joan came out and righted them, picked out one red rose for her own (of course, she had the customary flower, brought from the garden of the elder Bonynges, set before the Madrid madonna in her dressing room.) Then she waved at the cheering crowd. Many of the elaborately gowned ladies were even standing on their chair-seats in an unaccustomed display of enthusiasm. Never had there been such a night, everyone marveled.

Every dignitary Melbourne could summon up was there in Her Majesty's Theatre in all his—and his wife's—glory. At the head was the Administrator of the Commonwealth, Sir Henry Abel Smith, and his wife, Lady May, who were accompanied by Lady May's mother, Princess Alice of Athlone, a granddaughter of Queen Victoria.

Writing of that night in her book, *A Family of Brothers* (Melbourne: Heinemann), Lady (Viola) Tait, pretty and vivacious, herself a former Gilbert and Sullivan and musical comedy star, recalls that it was "a triumph and a history-making event. It fulfilled a dream for Frank [her husband, Sir Frank Tait] and for Joan: her long-cherished ambition to sing *Lucia* in her native land had been realized." Lady Tait had been one of the adjudicators in the contest that Joan had won, in what seemed like so many years before, the contest that sent her on her travels.

Even at ten guineas a seat, remarked one writer, the show was worth it. Everyone agreed that, since Melba's time, no such thunderous ovations had been vouchsafed a singer, and, if the opening night seemed tumultuous, it was mild in comparison with closing night.

This time it was *Sonnambula*, with Pavarotti, Harwood, and Malas backing up Joan. The tenor had already won favorable comparison with Björling. They sang to the rafters, and the rafters responded with the wildest ringing yet. The curtain did not fall. The stage remained motionless for an appreciable second; the viewers silent. Then the audience found its release and in a twinkling the stage was massed with flowers—white roses and purple violets—tossed by stalwart arms, and a shower of brilliant confetti. Ribbon after ribbon filled the space between and fell softly upon the line of bewitched singers at the footlights.

Finally, an upright piano was pushed on stage. Bonynge sat down to accompany the prima donna in "Home Sweet Home," entrancing the listeners and recalling to the historically minded the similar postopera bouquet of Adelina Patti.

Long afterward, Bonynge and Joan and Oxenbauld would remember this evening with a touch of awe.

· · ·

It had been a night of splendor, of utter triumph—and of crushing fatigue. Only two days intervened before the opening in Adelaide, where the Western Australian audiences would be treated to most of the repertoire.

At the beginning of the tour, matters had been handled with some firmness at their original landing in Sydney after a short vacation in Honolulu. A phalanx of protectors got them through the crowd that had been made ferocious by goodwill and curiosity. There was no real casualty, except for the loss of the family reunion that had been planned by the two remaining stepsisters, who were pushed and remained helpless on the outer fringes of the mob. The travelers made the local plane to Melbourne with only a few ruffled feathers, but were considerably shaken from the experience. Richard particularly was affected. Joan felt aggrieved that, instead of a dignified welcome, one paper had quoted her involuntary exclamation: "Crikey, it's cold!" as she scurried across the tarmac to the waiting limousine. She had, after all, retained many of these homely expressions of her Aussie girlhood; it was one of her most endearing traits.

In Adelaide, they learned, to their shock and sorrow, of Sir Frank's death. The final Melbourne *Sonnambula* performance had marked his last visit to the theater. He had looked pale and tired, but had insisted on escorting Joan through the cheering crowd to her car after the show. Then he and Lady Tait had gone off for a few days' rest. He had died on August 23.

The Bonynges sent Lady Tait their tribute to this great man of the theater: "He contributed more to Australian culture than anyone we know. His death is a terrible blow and the only consoling thought is that he lived to see in Melbourne, his home ground, the big success of this opera season."

It was in Adelaide that Pavarotti first tasted the real sweetmeat of success—singing an encore. The clamor after "Una furtiva lagrima" in *L'Elisir d'amore* was so fierce and demanding that Bonynge yielded and let the victorious tenor sing it again. Unbelievably, the racket did not let up. So, for one of the few times in recent operatic history, a tenor sang an aria three times before he was let go. Bonynge commented in Pavarotti's biography that Luciano from then on was a trifle miffed if they didn't ask to repeat the aria at least once.

Without Sir Frank's active personal domination, things went slightly awry. Sir Frank had promised there would be no incidents in Sydney. But his death had the effect of releasing some of the restraint in that city. Now the frustration of the press raveners, denied their prey on the former occasion, burst out in fury.

Joan didn't even put on her makeup. And when the plane door was opened, her dismay can be imagined at the surge of reporters and cameramen up the steps, virtually stopping her descent for the moment.

It might have daunted stouter—and more experienced—hearts, and Richard's reaction was impassioned. Some hot words were exchanged, and the Bonynges eventually escaped, but the incident rankled with both camps.

The first few days in Sydney were a bit strained, as the press pursued its "victims." Richard did not exactly pour balm on the wounds by walking out of a press conference and calling the interrogators "orangutangs." The appellation was gleefully picked up by the scribes, one of whom persisted in signing himself "Martin Orang-utang Collins" in the *Australian*.

The crowning bit of nonsense was a cartoon by "Rigby" in the *Daily News* that showed a timorous Joan in the wings being counseled by an official: "You'd better be good tonight—the Gentlemen of the Press are out front!" In the front row and in the pit, brandishing a banana at a dowager, hanging from the chandelier, and even walking the rail between pit and stalls—the waiting simians. This broke the ice. The Bonynges could not help but be amused, and eventually secured the original cartoon as a keepsake.

Joan herself did not escape the barrage. She, too, had departed the press conference in the restaurant, The Four Corners, and was only persuaded to relent from her huff by the grandiloquent gesture of the restaurant proprietor, Peter van Brunk, who fell to his knees, kissed her hand, and begged her to return. It was at least high camp, if not exactly good theater.

One paper chided her for not handling with dignity and charm "the little imbroglios excited Press and public create when she appears," and for reproving those who had, after all, helped her achieve stardom. One paper published "before and after" shots of her face in reaction to flashbulbs and film cameras.

Indeed she was not lacking in a display of pique. At a reception in the town hall, the lights and cameras shone hot in her face, and the cameras were so noisy that she snapped, in the middle of an attempted speech: "Stop that—I can't hear myself think, much less speak." This time, Richard showed composure, but Joan's temper grew more and more heated, until the Lord Mayor Jansen had all he could do to stop her from walking out. Some of those near her reported that she declared it was a marvelous idea to support opera production, but not to pour all their money into that great "effigy" (the new Opera House). She was heard to add that she had hoped to return to Australia one day, perhaps in 1980, but now she might never come back. It seems odd that the couple had not learned to take their lumps and smile through the adversity of press attacks, as they later managed to do with fair competence. But this was their home territory; they had expected better and felt aggrieved. A certain wariness and cynicism marked their attitude toward public acclamation long afterward. The public, caught in between, did not seem to care, and went blithely in droves to hear the prima donna—she who had been one of them.

All the while, Joan was reviving old memories and meeting old friends, especially in Sydney. Those who "knew her when" tried to draw closer, and were warmly received whenever time permitted. This was truly a Cinderella transformed, yet never having lost her original simplicity and frankness. "She has no side," Australians said wonderingly. The threats never to return that had been quoted by reporters had vanished, and now the Bonynges were eager to try out the new opera house that was being built. This was not to happen for nearly a decade.

· · ·

The Cinderella image was complete when Joan appeared in a full-length chinchilla coat. (She had also brought along a mink that was reserved for ordinary occasions.) Her wardrobe proved a fascinating subject for the magazines, especially the mammoth *Women's Day*, whose Sally Baker went into elaborate detail. First, it seemed, Richard had to approve everything she put on her back. Her dresses were more or less straight-lined, with buttons down the front and a little collar. Probably because she spent so much time on stage laced up tightly into bodices or corsets and laden down by heavy skirts, her daytime clothes were simple, loose, and lightweight. Also, because in the theater she had to wear such a lot of makeup, in private she was a soap-and-water girl. "I never had a facial in my life." For evening, she liked an occasional full skirt. Her skirts were mostly A-line; that is, sloping outward from the waist.

Pants? Never! "I look dreadful in slacks." (Later, when the

fashion of jumpsuits, which combined long flowing trousers with a blouse, arrived, she would adopt it gleefully.) She fancied chiffons with floating panels, figured patterns, vivid, yet soft colors. Green or bronze were ideal with her hair. She bought designer dresses occasionally from Hardy Amies in London and Arnold Scaasi in the United States. Barbara Matera had begun to make most of her daytime clothes, as well as her costumes. One favorite outfit at this time was a white corded silk coat trimmed with white fur. Joan would wear it over a black dress for cocktail parties. Another favorite was a flowered silk lined in apricot. Because she was traveling so much, she had settled for black and occasional beige accessories—shoes, hats, and such.

The "news" writers also got out their purple inkpots. "The flash of diamonds, the swish of mink, and the soaring voice of Joan Sutherland" brought the "most expensive opening of the city's history. The local girl who sailed away to become the greatest opera singer at last came home, exactly fourteen years, four months, and ten days since she had last sung in Sydney Town Hall," was how one meticulous writer put it.

All this hullabaloo was apart from the serious business of music criticism, which went on more or less serenely. It could be counted as nothing less than an absolute triumph for the prima donna, but Richard also gained some highly complimentary comment on his newly developed skill as a conductor.

Joan did win over some of the most ardent detractors. After opening night, Ron Saw, one of the most violent, made his amends in the *Daily Mirror*: "There she stood, head high, chin jutting, no longer the petulant prima donna, but proud, regal, defiant, every inch the splendid woman we had come to see—La Stupenda. She can call me an orangutang any time she wants." Frank Harris, music critic in the same paper, added: "Going mad with Joan Sutherland is one of the sweetest and most blessed experiences I can recall." Not even the most tactless tantrum of her husband could spoil her triumph, he thought.

Still, Sydney's welcome was a shade more subdued than had been Melbourne's. Perhaps a trace of jealousy of the southern city remained in the bustling metropolis. After all, the homing pigeon had nested there first, instead of in her birthplace. Through the five weeks in Sydney, audiences remained consistently warm and appreciative, although standing ovations were few.

Lucia opened each city's stand—an inevitable hit. Sutherland nights remained sellouts. Of the other two operas, *Elisir* and

Onegin, the former proved an elixir indeed with its complement of fine singers—Harwood, Pavarotti, and Malas. *Onegin* never did catch on; it was too somber, and the casting did not exactly illuminate the dark, passionate score. Elkins, it was remembered, had been a mezzo, and the higher part of Tatyana did not suit her.

True to Australian predilection, Joan's achievement in *Semiramide*, uninhibitedly amazing, was compared to sports: "In effect a performance of master acrobats, magicians, tennis players, and high jumpers." Then, reverting to another art, the critic explained that Joan "kept every tuck and fold of the elaborately pleated music in place." Monica Sinclair, too, was "death-defying . . . heroic."

After the five weeks in Sydney came another stretch. The final trials awaited the company in Brisbane, where, it was said, requests from all over Queensland were pouring in for tickets. The excitement in that northern city had risen to a feverish pitch because Brisbane had fewer opportunities for such galas. "Stupendous" was the word for it, and the season itself had to be counted utterly splendid. "If I could hit a high C like Sutherland, I would put my cry of approval on the same plane," asserted Frank Harris in the *Mirror*.

· · ·

It is interesting in light of later costs to break down the expenditures of this company as released by John McCallum, a longtime executive of the Firm. The figures (in pounds) are: physical mounting of operas, 150,000; payments to singers, 187,000; overseas singers' fares, 30,000; internal fares and freight, 20,000; lighting, cleaning, etc., 37,000; holiday pay, taxes, insurance, 14,000; advance publicity, printing, 24,000; music scores collated and duplicated, 12,000; orchestra rehearsals, 10,000; orchestra performing salaries, 31,000; ballet and supers, 22,000; front of house, 28,000.

Sir Frank had counted on the dropping off of attendance on non-Sutherland nights, but he had hoped that Sutherland nights would make up for it. Australia was not used to a subscription deal, and there were grumblings about having to see no-Sutherland in order to see Sutherland. Some even called it blackmail.

One acknowledged mistake was hiking the prices for opening nights. It scared off a lot of people. Some students were even threatening to picket the regular performances.

Was it all worth it—the £570,000 it had cost the Firm? Deficit was certain—about £24,000 as it turned out—but the Elizabethan Trust had promised £12,000 and the Firm's balance was righted in the next two years. Sir Frank thought it was every bit worth the time and trouble and expense. He said: "There has never been anything approaching it!"

CHAPTER
15

Diva as Tomboy—
Bonynge at Met

✳ IT DID NOT TAKE MUCH PERSUASION TO DRAW SUTH-
erland into her next exploit. After all, she had given the "loony
ladies" a good run and would never totally forsake them; but a
little vacation from madness and the vapors would not hurt a healthy,
strapping prima donna. She agreed to tackle Marie in Donizetti's
La Fille du régiment for Covent Garden in June 1966. Having
endured the rigors of a *Don Giovanni* at La Scala on April 30 (where
her colleagues were Pilar Lorengar, Mirelli Freni, Luigi Alva, and
Nicolai Ghiaurov, with Lorin Maazel conducting), no doubt it was
easier to turn on the spigot for a little froth.

Sandro Sequi, who had been a part of the ill-fated *Sonnambula*
in Venice, and who had encountered the Bonynges again in Rome
in 1962, was assigned to produce. He had already done the London
Turandot, which had gained some notoriety for its Cecil Beaton
designs. This would be a complete change of scene for him, as well
as for Sutherland—a comedy.

"Rather, I thought of *Fille* as an operetta," Sequi told me.
"Not at all sentimental. It would show a new side of Joan, who is
so marvelously full of humor as a person. She accepted my idea,
although she doubted she could do it—she was always full of self-
doubts before a new thing. I wanted to do a complete send-up of
the prima donna image."

Joan, of course, was always making fun of herself anyway.
Always conscious of her size, she was reluctant to wear the pants
that Marie sports in her regimental life. But the dubious garments
turned out to be rather full "bloomers," and, tucked into high boots,
not at all unbecoming or awkward. From the first day of rehearsal,
Covent Garden was enveloped in a curtain of merriment. Richard

loved the whole thing; the others joined in with a will. (Although will was not enough to direct the bulbous Pavarotti into spontaneous capering. His comedic talent did not blossom until the Metropolitan showing of the opera some years later.) The chorus laughed like mad, Sequi remembers.

Monica Sinclair showed a marvelously funny streak as the Marquise who snobbishly looks down at the girl brought up under the regiment's eye, until she realizes that Marie is really her daughter. She takes the girl in as a niece, but does not reveal the true relationship until the last.

Spiro Malas used his extensive comic gifts as the gruff Sergeant Sulpice, the only father (except for the whole regiment) Marie had ever known. All of them sang brilliantly. It was Pavarotti's first real triumph. The nine high Cs belted out so securely and beautifully struck the bell that was to resound from then on.

Edith Coates's superb comic sense was evident; when she made her extravagant entrance in the last act as the Duchess of Crakentorp, she stopped the show. But the show was essentially Joan's. London was more than surprised—shocked would be a fitting word. They did not know what to make of their Lucia, Amina, Violetta—a hoyden, yet! Many tut-tutted, while the reaction of the critics was even harsher. In the first place, they did not relish this lighthearted Donizetti. Donizetti was for tragedy, for madness (entirely ignoring his *L'Elisir d'amore* and *Don Pasquale*). As for Sutherland, the Queen had stepped down off the throne and was cavorting ridiculously, smirking and uttering foolish words.

Philip Hope-Wallace in the *Guardian* joined the stone-throwers. "We must ask Sutherland to do *Annie Get Your Gun*," he suggested meanly. He commented on the "acres of nasty scenery" (by Anna Anni), and relished only about ten minutes of catchy music.

The Times was a little kinder, but Frank Granville Barker in *Music and Musicians* perhaps excelled for pure bile. "The whole inglorious affair . . . embarrassing," he called it. Sequi's direction was at best unsubtle, and the visual jokes corny. It was a saddening experience to witness a distinguished prima donna grimacing and galumphing about the stage (her singing was of course exquisite), but what a pity she decided to appear in the piece instead of just recording it, he thought. Giving Pavarotti more credit than he perhaps deserved, Barker thought he seemed reluctant to take any part in the dramatic action. His only honeyed words were for Bonynge, "who conducted with flair and affection that made it clear what Donizetti wanted, even if no one else did."

Joan had only to whisper and get any role she wanted, sighed one observer. He wished she had whispered in another direction. Bonynge retorted that it was not their function to educate, but to entertain. The usually sympathetic Noël Goodwin waspishly opined that the production veered from sentimentality to slapstick, and the handling of the soldiers' chorus was acutely embarrassing. Andrew Porter, too, was disgusted. Sequi, he said, gave up any idea of Donizetti's terms. Sutherland was bound to look like a guy. She stomped and strutted and swaggered and made hideous grimaces. But her high spirits bubbled over—this was undoubtedly the least inhibited performance of her career. She almost brought it off.

A critic's contempt for the score itself was nothing compared to the contempt shown by Sequi, the critic thought. Bad French from everybody was counted as part of the fun.

In sum, the exquisites were displeased, as one more perceptive critic noted with amusement. Felix Aprahamian, writing in *Opera News*, gave his confreres a few gentle nudges and went on to express his utter capitulation. Joan could be seen and heard as a jollier if no less unusual human being. Vocally, there was no surrender—the voice was flawless, meltingly beautiful in quiet legato, effortlessly brilliant in *fioriture*. French diction in song remained problematical, but her dialogue proved more than passable.

"The unexpected delight of her performance was her hilarious acting; her rubber-faced, outsized regimented tomboy made a complete contrast to her posturing, cooing, and lunatic Lucia," Aprahamian concluded.

The pundits deplored what they called Sequi's "vulgarity"; Aprahamian thought it healthy and consistent. Bonynge and his forces entered wholly into the fun.

It was, of course, very amusing and gratifying to insiders that, for once, Joan was able to show publicly some of the marvelous grimaces that always contorted her famous face when she was dissatisfied with something she had done in rehearsal. After a command performance of the Donizetti opera, she showed her delight, telling Queen Elizabeth that she had never had so much fun on the stage. It was obvious she would want to repeat the experience.

Joan's stunning turnabout was not to be truly appreciated, however, until the Metropolitan's series of performances in 1972.

. . .

A *Puritani* was mounted in San Francisco in 1966—considered to be the first time there for the Bellini opera ("the sort of opera that made Gilbert and Sullivan possible—Songbird and Puppetland," wrote Arthur Bloomfield in his history of the San Francisco Opera.) There were local debuts by Alfredo Kraus and Nicola Ghiuselev, the former's Arturo winning high acclaim, but the latter proving less effective as Giorgio. Clifford Grant, the Australian, was the Walton. Dorothy Cole, remembered from her Australian appearances with the Bonynges in 1965, as well as for other occasions as a member of their cast "family," was credited in *Opera News* with an opulent voice by Anthony Boucher, whose reputation as a writer of superb mysteries ranked even higher than his occasional music criticism. As for Joan, he proclaimed, she should be declared an international natural resource and placed under the protection of the United Nations. She had never appeared to better advantage. The heroine, Elvira, suited her gift for simple poignancy, and the music she embellished exquisitely. The unending chain of Bellini melodies was lovingly conducted by Bonynge.

A great deal of flurry surrounded Mrs. Lyndon B. Johnson and her inevitable Secret Service agents. But the evening belonged rightfully to the prima donna instead of the First Lady. This was San Francisco's opening of the season, on September 20.

Philadelphia saw its first Sutherland *Lucia* on December 1, with the heroine backed by Michele Molese as Edgardo and Anselmo Colzani as Enrico. There was nothing special, except for Joan's vocal fireworks.

Yet 1966 had a very special meaning for Joan in other ways. That was the year she brought out the album of Noël Coward songs; the prima donna descended quite gracefully to the melodies and manners of the musical comedy stage. Coward's compositions really transcend this level, for their sophistication and quirkiness, as well as genuinely beautiful melodies.

The Bonynges had met the English entertainer on a boat trip to New York several years previously. Coward visited Joan backstage after a *Traviata* performance in Philadelphia and said gleefully: "Imagine the shock for all the fuddy-duddies! And imagine my feelings, hearing my songs sung by the purest, greatest voice in the world! I'm as merry as a grig!"

The Bonynges visited Coward's retreat at Blue Harbour in Jamaica to select and rehearse the songs. During their stay, many hilarious moments came naturally to the trio, plus Coward's devoted friends (among them his biographer, Cole Lesley), and at least one rather dramatic turn. Lesley describes it in his affectionate memoir of Coward, *Remembered Laughter*, published after the great theater artist's death.

They had had a frightful argument about religious intolerance and the theory that men are descended from the apes.

Noël started again on the killer apes . . . to which I said: "But that's so long ago, it sounds like the beginning of the Bible" . . . Noël banged his fist on the table, making a horrible clatter, and jumped to his feet. "If that is all you have to say, I shall say goodnight." He stormed out. Joan and Richard went to bed, but soon after, the jeep drove up and there was the sound of someone at the verandah door. I opened it, and there in the half-light stood God the Father, avenging arms outstretched, booming: "I am on my way up to Noël and I'm going to frighten the hell out of him." It was Joan, draped in a sheet and with a long, cotton-wool beard.

Laughter came as a blessed relief. Coward's reactions are not noted.

. . .

The climax of 1966 was a matter of serious import—Richard's debut at the Metropolitan. *Lucia* was thought to be safest to launch this unknown quantity—unknown, that is, to the Metropolitan. Come weal or woe, in the past few years, Sutherland had invariably been able to look into the orchestra pit every time she walked on stage and see the reassuring face of her husband, his upraised arm ready to give her the cue to begin. Through long and grueling rehearsals and home coaching, she had found his inspiration and unremitting critical faculty her guiding force. It had taken five years to get him to this particular and crucial spot.

Rudolf Bing later expressed himself rather forcefully to me about the presence of married couples in his company. In principle, he was against it. "If you have a row with one, you have it with two." But Bonynge's accession went off smoothly enough. "There was never any serious problem," said Bing. Both the Bonynges, thorough professionals that they are, gave him no trouble. As for repertoire, he may have had suggestions, but the upshot, Bing insisted, was that "she told me what she wants to sing and she sang it. He is a remarkably good musical influence. I remember no feelings of unpleasantness." He added that, although the following remark was attributed to Bonynge, he himself originated it: "Mr. Bing, anytime you say anything, it's worth missing." It does smack of the general manager's brand of wry wit.

For Richard, the big night was December 12, 1966. His was a generous share of the applause that welcomed Joan after a year's absence—another of those ten-minute frenzies after the Mad Scene. Even those who professed to scorn the opera itself (and they still persisted) found much to admire. Richard got high marks from William Bender in the *World-Journal-Tribune*, who noted Bonynge's specialization in this music and thought his performance quite refreshing in its snappiness, intelligent deference to the singers, and precise rapport between stage and pit. Even Schonberg had begun to melt. He noted that the two Bonynges worked as a smooth team, understanding each other's ideas about tempo and phrasing, operating with split-second precision. Still he held back a little, believing that Bonynge was not yet the complete conductor. "He tends to rush tempos at times, has not learned to shape a phrase with authority. But what he does know is the tradition of the *bel canto* style—a knowledge as comprehensive as any conductor before the public—perhaps more so."

This went far toward vindication, and Richard was the first to acknowledge what the *Times* added: that all he needed was more experience. Perhaps he even admitted another need: "more psychic power over the orchestra."

As for Joan, little but rapture. She was, as the *Daily News* put it, cheered all the way. It was generally seen that she had added much to her previous characterization, had acted more convincingly.

She had always acted with her voice, as old Philip Hale of the Boston *Herald* liked to say in the days when bodies moved about the stage with little pretense of dramatic evocation. She could take a phrase with the purity and authority of a great violinist, and the little rubatos and interpolations that had previously sounded somewhat calculated were now an integral part of the line. She had obviously been working hard to correct the swooping into notes and the mushy vowel sounds that had bothered so many observers.

If only Chicago could have agreed that she was an artist and incomparable singer! Thomas Willis came all the way to New York and admitted in the *Tribune* that he liked her a little better than in 1961, but he had no good words for Richard. It would take a while.

Nobody cared much for the production, which had been new in 1964. Attilio Colonello's lugubrious scenery and Margherita Wallmann's "unmoving, posey direction" cast a pall. The Sextet seemed lifeless. Winthrop Sargeant in *The New Yorker* confessed that he longed to hear a robust, rhythmic, and rousing Sextet, with swords drawn and fury and dismay all over the place, but this limp approximation was not it. This happened to be the most expensive-looking *Lucia* ever seen, but deficient as a background for the unsettled lady. There was not even a staircase for her to descend crazily, and you would have thought Raimondo's announcement about the murder merely an absentminded observation about the weather. Nevertheless, the Bonynges could go home to their little rented Greenwich Village duplex happy in a twin achievement.

An interview with Bonynge in *Opera News* just before the broadcast of *Lucia* on December 31 revealed that the young man had indeed been nervous—still was. He gained confidence with later performances, even conducting *Lucia* for sopranos other than his wife, who had turned her attention and energies into another channel—Mozart instead of Donizetti.

On January 4 she sang her first Donna Anna at the Met. It was the fifth performance, conducted by Karl Böhm, and retaining the handsome Cesare Siepi as the Don and Justino Diaz as the Commendatore. Fresh assignments were Pilar Lorengar as Donna Elvira, Laurel Hurley as Zerlina, Alfredo Kraus as Ottavio, Ezio Flagello as Leporello, and William Walker as Masetto. "The finest hour of her New York career to date" is how Irving Kolodin saw her Donna Anna. (It must be remembered that he had given her the first American review in 1958, and for this same role, when she had sung it in Vancouver.) Not only was it Joan's triumph, but the best *Don Giovanni* of the year, perhaps in years, thanks to the exacting standard set by Sutherland and the competitive response aroused in a cast well disciplined by Böhm. It was a heady experience for Joan to be surrounded by a half-dozen who could and did rise to a challenge. Kolodin noted that the pride in her profession and the respect for her colleagues led her to be a "member of the wedding, even if not the bride" this time.

Others agreed heartily. "One of the most remarkable vocal achievements not only of the season, but also of many years," said Miles Kastendieck in the *World-Journal-Telegram*. The ease of "Or sai chi l'onore" was the miracle of the performance, and her voice was stunning in ensembles as well. Harriett Johnson in the *Post* noted that Joan dominated the stage as an actress, with new powers of projection and intensity. Only Conrad Osborne, writing for the London *Musical Times*, remained somewhat cool. Apparently, one did not feel inclined to let any American achievement succeed too well, even though the protagonist remained a London favorite (or perhaps it was because of that fact).

Shortly after her last Met Donna Anna on January 11, 1967, Boston welcomed the same role on February 6, 8, and 15, when Sutherland was a "marvel of Mozartean eloquence." Justino Diaz played the Don Giovanni and Donald Gramm showed his flair for comedy as Leporello, benefiting from Bonynge's understanding approach to buffo roles. Joan's old pal Margreta Elkins came out of the mezzo realm for Elvira, and a mezzo destined to become part of the Bonynge "family" was the Zerlina—the attractive Canadian Huguette Tourangeau. Loren Driscoll sang Ottavio, and Robert Trehy, Masetto. Sarah Caldwell was the director, as expected, and held over the stunning designs by Oliver Smith from the previous season.

• • •

Joan's first glimpse of the new house at Lincoln Center had been during this season—a visit for a photograph session at the behest of the NBC Bell Telephone Hour, which planned to put four prima donnas on the air in one program. To get the quartet together at one time proved impossible—only Joan and Renata Tebaldi showed up at the early December photo call. Joan wore a black suit with pearls, Tebaldi wore green without pearls, as reporter Joan Crosby noted in an article for the Almeida (California) *Times-Star*.

The two prima donnas gossiped about tenors, theaters, and performances, clowning their way through the session. Joan kicked off her shoes and arranged herself in exaggerated poses; Tebaldi practiced an imitation of the raucous laugh of Phyllis Diller, the TV comedienne. Joan cautioned the photographer: "Do try to get one picture of me with me mouth closed, won't you?"

They were standing on a level that brought the lobby ceiling just above their eyes, and they noted that the paint was peeling already. Shoddy workmanship, they called it. Joan had bemoaned the loss of the old house when she first sang her Lucia there, and now she wondered how the new one would be for singing.

Tebaldi assured her it was good. "But the old house I have in my heart," she added.

Never yielding in her belief that the new structure was more like an ornate movie palace than an opera house, Joan did discover its acoustic felicities and agree that singers had reason to be happy in Lincoln Center, at least while they were on stage.

Curiously enough, Joan was singing her fourth *Don Giovanni* on January 17, 1967, the very date that the wrecker's ball first hit the old "Yellow Brick Brewery" on Thirty-ninth Street and Broadway, so revered and so doomed.

CHAPTER

16

New Horizons

⁜ NOW THE ESTABLISHED PATTERN REMAINED VIRTU-
ally unbroken. Joan and Richard grew accustomed to jet travel,
although they were hardly ever comfortable with it, for Joan's back
(her "weird" back, as she wryly calls it) made it difficult for her to
sit for hours in one position.

Packing and unpacking numerous bags was also a chore she
did not care for. "I think I'll scream if I ever see another suitcase!"
she wailed at one hectic moment. Richard usually needed the
preponderance of luggage, what with his scores and bulky dress
clothes, and Joan's share was not inconsiderable. Particular costumes could be shipped separately, but it was not uncommon to
see the handsome Bonynges surrounded by a pile of a dozen or so
handsome russet leather cases at any airport.

"One-night stands" were avoided whenever possible and accepted only when it meant a few days away from a central resting
point, such as a date in Philadelphia away from their New York
base. Wherever their engagement needed more time, they would
inevitably seek out a private retreat—some friend's house or apartment loaned or rented—to which they could flee swiftly after the
usual ritual of greeting friends and fans backstage.

Occasionally, they could be lured out to a gala supper, but
not often. In fact, they were prone to walk out of parties where
the crush seemed overwhelming and the food not forthcoming, to
make a beeline for "home," where Chester (whom they had re-
cruited in Australia and who was now a fixture in their entourage)
would prepare their supper and where they could take their shoes
off and enjoy their own company.

In 1969, several definitive moves changed the picture. The Bonynges finally abandoned London as a residence and chose Switzerland, where previously they had fled only for summers. Now, in a mountaintop chalet next door to Noël Coward (who found the property for them), they established the Chalet Monet in Les Avants, near Montreux, overlooking Lake Geneva. It was soon enlarged, modified, and crammed with Richard's booty from all over the world.

At the same time they found a permanent perch in New York—or rather in Brooklyn—renting the top two floors of a rambling house owned by Martin Landron, an actor-teacher and superfan. He soon became a virtual majordomo for all their Metropolitan appearances, and many times on the road. The Bonynges get back and forth from the outlying borough by hired car.

To the two *pieds-à-terre* was to be added a third—Sydney. The soprano and conductor were to decide to give much of their time to their native country. But that came later, after 1976.

In the meantime, there were new peaks to scale and older territory to retain. Each year saw two or three new roles for Joan (which were recorded in summer sessions), and there was always someplace that wanted her Lucia for the first time. A six-performance run in Vancouver in March of 1967 elicited from an *Opera News* reporter the opinion that this was a gilt-edged sample of what money, when wisely spent, can do for opera. A large part of the $51,000 given to the Vancouver Opera to help celebrate Canada's one hundredth birthday was thought to have gone toward the impressive sets for *Lucia* by Jean-Claude Rinfret. It was the most handsome production ever seen in Vancouver. (If only a spirit of lavishness had persisted in Vancouver's cultural pretensions, a different scenario might have evolved. But that story must wait a while.)

Sutherland's magnificent voice together with Bonynge's impeccable conducting positively electrified the Vancouver audience. Old favorites John Alexander as Edgardo and Dorothy Cole as Alisa were joined by Dominic Cossa as Enrico and John West as Raimondo.

A little Oriental spice was not amiss just now, provided by Delibes's *Lakmé*, a French bon-bon in Hindu wrappings that Joan undertook in Seattle for the first time in 1967. Familiar mostly for its tinkling, elaborate "Bell Song," the opera has had few adherents in the United States, although it had been an early favorite of Lily

Pons, whose costume scandalized New York at the time, with its waistband ten degrees below the belly button. Joan's fanciful veilings were more circumspect, although not less alluring. It was a sweetly beautiful setting for her pure, limpid voice and air of innocent involvement in a forbidden love. Seattle heard the opera five times beginning April 10. Some new friends joined Tourangeau (Mallika) and Opthof (Frédéric): Joshua Hecht as Lakmé's fanatic father Nilikantha; Frank Porretta as her lover Gérald; Marina Kleinman (Mrs. Spiro Malas) as Ellen, and Lowell W. Palmerston as Hadji. Joan got full marks for melodious and flexible singing, but fell below in acting in the eyes of Frank J. Warnke, who let it be known in *Opera News* that he still was not convinced of her dramatic prowess. Perhaps he was looking for a little too much dramatic fervor in this rather stereotyped version of the Oriental lass betrayed by a white lover. *Lakmé* is no *Madama Butterfly*. At any rate, a more dazzling "Bell Song" has seldom, if ever, been heard, and is perpetuated by the usual Bonynge recording.

Glynn Ross, who was to be voted the impresario *in excelsis* for bringing to Seattle, some years later, the Wagner *Ring* in both German and English, fell below standard in the critics' eyes for a lifeless production of *Lakmé*.

Another role for Joan in 1967 was in Haydn's *Orfeo ed Euridice*, an opera that got lost when the composer went to London and was caught in a quarrel between the King and the Prince of Wales. Found again and produced by Rudolf Hartmann for the opening of the Vienna Festival in 1967, it drew a crowd of locals and tourists to the Theater an der Wien (that same little house whose first director was Emanuel Schikaneder, librettist of Mozart's *Magic Flute* and himself a character in the opera). The theater had a distinguished history from the first—Beethoven's *Fidelio* was given its premiere there, and the Staatsoper found a home in the theater after the war.

The whole of Vienna was *en fête* on the night of May 21, and not the least of the jubilation was caused by Sutherland and Nicolai Gedda, who sang the Haydn title roles with great élan. Bonynge won praise as a sensitive conductor as well. Spiro Malas sang the part of Creonte; with the other two, he was part of the cast at Glyndebourne and Edinburgh, and later with the American Opera Company's concert performance in New York. But where Vienna had admired Gedda extravagantly, a New York critic called his Orfeo one of the casting mistakes of the century. Gedda, so revered for his sense of style and expertise in languages, was put down on this occasion as a pusher, a belter, a forcer. This acid pen wrote that Haydn's wig would have uncurled had he encountered this travesty. Other judgments were not so severe. Still, the opera did not persist in Sutherland's cupboard; after all, it had not been her best vehicle either.

More to the point was the gala *Fille du régiment* that Covent Garden mounted for her before the Queen in June 1967. By now, after a year's absence, the opera seemed more palatable, and London's favorite prima donna's grimaces and caperings seemed just right for the gamine role. She won more hearts with her Rat-a-Plan and her exquisitely funny music-lesson scene.

A concert performance of Meyerbeer's *Les Huguenots* on January 7, 1968, brought London the first all-star lineup for this opera in forty years—a galaxy that entranced a Royal Albert Hall gathering. All six artists joining Sutherland were new to London: Martina Arroyo, who astounded with her golden singing of Valentine; Anastasios Vrenios, the Raoul; Dominic Cossa; Huguette Tourangeau; Nicola Ghiuselev; and Robert El Hage. Joan provided the glittering pinwheels as Marguerite de Valois, and Richard conducted masterfully.

In a *Traviata* in Boston on March 11, something happened that at first seemed unfortunate, but that turned into an addition to Joan's conception of the role. In the third act, Alfredo is supposed to fling his gambling winnings at Violetta's feet to shame her. Instead, the tenor, Vrenios, waxed overexcited and hurled the banknotes directly into Violetta's face. Not expecting this shower of money, Joan was caught off balance and fell to her knees. Not quite certain what to do, she remained a moment, stricken. Martin Waldron, standing in the wings, whispered violently: "Use it! Make it a part of the action! Pretend!" So Joan added a note of verisimilitude to the anguish of the scorned heroine.

May of 1968 found Joan in Florence for the Maggio Musicale. The opera was *Semiramide*, which, with its heavy pageantry and stagy ritual, suited the Florentines very well. They adored Joan in her extravagant Peter Hall costumes, and were polite to most of the remainder of the cast (including Renato Cioni as Assur), but found fault with Monica Sinclair as Arsace. The mezzo, who had been a Covent Garden regular and a member of the Sutherland-Williamson tour, seemed perfectly acceptable as Arsace in several Australian performances, but did not suit Florentines, who became rather vociferous about it. At supper afterward, Sinclair said wonderingly: "These Florentines—what do they want! They booed Joan!"

Joan, sitting queenlike across the table from the director Sandro Sequi, gave him a quizzical look but said nothing to disturb Sinclair's false assumption. Sinclair had been a perfect Marquise in *Fille du régiment*, observed Sequi, but Arsace was just not her meat.

Sonnambula regained its place at the Met in 1968–69. Joan's tenors were George Shirley and John Alexander (who kept taking over in Act III). The basses were Bonaldo Giaiotti and Justino Diaz. Bonynge presided firmly in the pit, and the bridge Amina had to walk in her sleep seemed as high as ever.

The soprano's first (and only, to date) trip to South America took up much of middle 1969. *Norma* and *Traviata* were her operas (each considered at more length elsewhere).

· · ·

Hamburg proved an interesting port of call in these years. Tito Capobianco and Ming Cho Lee repeated their New York City Opera production of Handel's *Giulio Cesare* on December 9, 1969, with Joan experiencing the power of the dynamic director over her Cleopatra. Others in the large cast included Tourangeau as Caesar, Lucia Popp as Sesto, and Tom Krause as Achilles. In 1971, *Caesar* was to be repeated, and Hamburg to mount a new *Lucia* for the soprano, directed by Peter Beauvais. At that time, the German city expressed shock, not at the soprano or her obvious superiority in the role she knew so well, but in the fact that there was more to Donizetti's opera than hardly anyone to that date had realized. Bonynge had opened practically all of the cuts; the Wolf Crag scene after the Sextet was restored, in which Enrico seeks out Edgardo and challenges him to a duel. This accounts for the hero's presence on the Lammermoor premises in the last act, when he kills himself on learning of his sweetheart's death. Another crucial scene, between Raimondo and Lucia, shows the seemingly kind pastor and tutor advising Lucia to marry Arturo and accept the inevitable. It is this pressure, coupled with her brother's insistence, that sends the unstable girl over the brink after she is rejected by the returning Edgardo in the midst of her wedding preparations. A smaller restoration, but quite vital, is an exchange among Enrico, Raimondo, and Normanno in the midst of the Mad Scene, giving the coloratura a chance to catch her breath and gird her talents for the spectacular conclusion. Most of this remained in whatever *Lucia* the Bonynges performed after the Hamburg revelation, and appears in the re-

recording they made the summer after Hamburg. (*Rigoletto* was also re-recorded, a vast improvement over an earlier album.)

Now the Bonynges were well launched into a new decade, firmly entrenched in the admiration of the operatic world, and ready for new opportunities.

CHAPTER

17

A New Priestess and Some More Queens

NORMA RUNS LIKE A BRILLIANT SCARLET THREAD through the tapestry of Sutherland's career. The diva and her husband were quietly polishing the supreme role for testing in that most important house, the Met, in March 1970. Rudolf Bing had advanced the idea of the Bellini opera in 1964, had even let it be announced; but the Bonynges remained cautious, and *Lucia* was repeated instead.

Joan had said that a soprano should be thirty-five before she tackled Norma. She let it run a few years beyond that point when she first ventured the role in Vancouver in 1963. There were still other "tryouts," although one hesitates to put Covent Garden in that category. Still, her performance there in December 1967 remained somewhat tentative.

Its designer, Pier Luigi Pizzi, fancied the Druids as pre-Christian nuns in heavy robes and cowls that too often obscured their faces. Director Sandro Sequi struggled against these odds. Joan and Richard suffered some of the critics' thorns, while Marilyn Horne, in her London debut, received a full complement of roses. It was beginning to be globally noticed that the voices of these two women constituted a very special blend. One more attempt at Norma, the North American first for Joan, came in Philadelphia on March 26, 1968, with Margreta Elkins, Spiro Malas, and a noncompetitive tenor, Bernabe Martì (incidentally the husband of Montserrat Caballé). Max de Schauensee in the *Bulletin* expressed surprise at Joan's dramatic effectiveness, not only in singing, but in acting. Donal Henahan went down from New York and wrote in the *Times* about the peerless Bellini artist.

Then Buenos Aires performances in June 1969 brought Joan's Norma total to forty. At the Colon Theater, the Adalgisa was Fiorenza Cossotto, the Pollione Charles Craig, the Oroveso Ivo Vinco. Sequi staged both this and the *Traviata* that formed the South American repertoire.

With such a success behind them, the Bonynges went on to the Met with some assurance. The first of nine performances in the house took place on March 3, 1970. It had been an abbreviated season because of an orchestra strike; nothing stirred until December 29, 1969, so *Norma* provided reason for a display of celebrative high spirits. It was the hottest ticket at Lincoln Center. That was quite a night—a Guild benefit, with a very dressy, but also knowledgeable, crowd from top to bottom of the house.

The curtain went up on Desmond Heeley's idea of ancient Gaul, an affair of huge steles and rocky promontories, which could twirl around on the newly working turntable (out of order since the opening opera's heavy scenery had disabled it) to form different craggy shapes.

Everyone waited until the High Priest, Oroveso (Cesare Siepi), had led the Druids and warriors in a prayer for vengeance against the occupying Romans. Breaths grew shorter as the Roman Proconsul, Pollione (Carlo Bergonzi), confessed to his friend Flavio (Rod MacWherter) that he loved the young priestess Adalgisa and cared no longer for Norma. Then, at last, the electricity crackled as Norma herself—Sutherland—appeared in a sweeping silver blue-gray robe, her hair piled high. She cut the holy mistletoe, then invoked the goddess of the moon. This is the moment of moments—the "Casta Diva." Its long, pure, seemingly endless line is the true test, followed by a brilliant cabaletta that leaves hardly a chink for breath, and all in the original key, G, instead of the usual F. There is usually applause between the aria and the pendant (making something of an anticlimax at the end of the scena), because a march begins immediately. But Bonynge discovered an 1840 ending for the cabaletta that gave clapping space, so to speak, before the advent of the march.

The house exploded, then exploded again, after Marilyn Horne's marvelous chiming with Joan in the "Mira, o Norma." And again . . . and again. This kind of performance in the opera world can polarize the fans. They are all too apt to choose up sides. Some Horne partisans argued that Joan was a known quantity, while Jackie (as Horne has always been called) came on the scene like a fresh new rocket. At any rate, the "girls" had a triumph, and each let the other know that she thought highly of her partner.

There remained no equivocation in the press reception. Schonberg capitulated; Sargeant glowed; Kolodin used the words "almost divine" to describe the singing of some of the most divinely beautiful music ever written; Johnson tagged Sutherland "ravishing," Horne "spectacular." It was all that any two prima donnas could have wished. One or two scribes deplored the lack of drama, and spared Bonynge floral tributes. In the conductor's favor, Speight Jenkins in *Music and Musicians* contended that "All of his bad press has overlooked the ease, the grace, the buoyancy of his approach. He has developed from the original Bellini score, stressed pre-Verdian lyricism." His feeling for singers' breathing patterns stands unique among Metropolitan conductors, the writer thought.

Callas, whose memory was still overriding in London, retreated to her place in history in New York (which, after all, had experienced less of her notable achievement).

Joan, however, recalled Callas very well. The "tigress" had always been her inspiration, ever since 1952, when the younger woman appeared as Clotilde with her idol in this same opera. At first, she had practiced imitation, then realized she would have to do it her own way.

Sutherland had now reached another pinnacle—the most difficult role of all. Even the challenge of *Traviata*, severe in its way, did not compare. (It is interesting to note that she took on both in South America, where the Norma was highly favored, but the Violetta thought to be not quite "Italian" enough.) It was Lilli Lehmann who said she would rather sing all three Brünnhildes than one Norma. The Bonynges spoke of these problems in an interview with Francis Rizzo in *Opera News* before the broadcast on April 4.

"It's incredible how Norma builds and builds," said Richard. "When you get to the end, that last half hour, it's simply terrific." And Joan added, laughing, "You don't really get much chance to rest, you know. Lord, she never stops singing!"

Nor did Joan stop singing Norma. To the nine performances in the house were added seven on tour—Boston, Cleveland, Atlanta, Memphis, Dallas, Minneapolis, and Detroit. There were male cast changes: Bonaldo Giaiotti or John Macurdy or Ivo Vinco as Oroveso; Renato Cioni or John Alexander as Pollione; but Horne was faithful, and the two women created swaths of excitement and trailed clouds of glory through seven states. Joan further participated in *Lucia* with Placido Domingo twice in the following June season in New York, rounding out a full and happy schedule.

•   •   •

The team of Sutherland and Horne inspired discussions of voices —their problems, joys, and the circumstances that shape their possessors. A number of interviews appeared in the press, purporting to reveal the secrets of this marvelous pair, Joan and Jackie. The most extensive was from Cleveland, where Richard Meryman wrote a piece entitled "A Tour of Two Great Throats" for *Life* magazine. The twin stars seriously got down to certain principles; Horne occasionally shot out a wisecrack, and Joan reacted with pretended shock. It was Joan who thought that a singer had to be strong as a horse; Jackie who used the comparison of a baseball pitcher. They even named some names: Callas had lessened the strength of her voice by slimming; Moffo had a solid figure; Kirsten showed no excess fat, but "was really built to go a few rounds." (The sports allusions are all Horne's.)

They bemoaned the necessity for getting into crowds where germs lurk, where people are smoking, and where "you have to talk loud." Joan insisted she was against wrapping herself up in scarves and antiseptics, but on another occasion she had exclaimed vehemently that she could kill those who came up and kissed her, but that it was a risk one had to take. Horne confessed that she was superstitious about colds and lived on vitamin C. Joan said thoughtfully, "There is not a moment when one is not aware of the next performance."

Then Joan held forth on the principle that she had expounded previously and that Pavarotti had found so helpful, "that it all goes back to support."

"The chest cavity should be," she said, "as large as possible, and one should breathe only with the diaphragm, keeping the chest and shoulders motionless. You should feel as if you were holding up this long column of air on which the voice is resting—like one of those Ping-Pong balls on a fountain."

Horne put in her bit: "You get these terrific muscles in the diaphragm and in the back—and in the derrière. Your legs are planted like an athlete's. You hold and measure out the air, let the perfect amount of air pass over the vocal cords. The reserve of air goes clear around me like a tire—maybe that's why we all have spare tires."

Joan: "Please!"

Vocal cords—the perennial question. Joan had said on another occasion, "I don't know, I've never seen mine;" Richard added hastily, "I don't know that I want to."

It seems that singers can never hear themselves as they really sound. Or each other. The sound goes out in a fan shape from their mouths. (The nearest thing to hearing oneself, Joan told Dick Cavett in a TV interview, is to listen to a recording through earphones. "You get the sensation in your own head . . . You need someone to keep an eye [or an ear] on you and correct you.")

Marilyn made a joke that passed without comment when there was talk of "placing" notes.

"Some singers place notes on the teeth," she said. "The Italian teachers will say: 'Right on the teets.' "

Both ladies agreed that singing high notes often made for dizziness, and Joan remarked that when they were singing together, a kind of oscillation occurred, like ringing glass. It hurts the ears. Both agreed that it was like walking a tightrope to keep their concentration—anything could break it: long dresses, lopsided stage, an uneven stage, uneven scenery, friends in the front row, people running in and out of boxes, *and* backstage noise.

"In Italy the backstage noise is murderous," and made worse by the assistant director yelling at everybody to shut up.

Horne was rapturous over her Met debut, "surrounded by love from colleagues, friends, family, and people backstage, and the audience."

And when Joan said to her at curtain calls: "It's all yours, dearie," tears came into her eyes.

Joan confessed to goosebumps when singing with Marilyn. They could go on forever, until they drop.

They did go on, for a spell, and then Marilyn broke away to follow her own path, also to be as much as possible with her own conductor-husband, Henry Lewis. Joan was sorry, but understood. The two peerless ladies were to get together again before too long.

. . .

More skyrockets lit up the sky when Chicago opened its 1971 season on September 27 with *Semiramide*. Carol Fox was betting on a sure thing, even though many doubted that Rossini's opera could show up as spectacularly as promised. Still, the canny Danny Newman, who had press-agented and touted the Lyric Opera into unprecedented success at the box office and in the subscription rolls, boasted that either Sutherland or Horne could sell out a house and that together, larger than life, they were dynamite.

To the surprise of many, he was right. The production was

probably more sumptuous than any on stage that season. Sandro Sequi described the settings by Pier Luigi Samaritani as in the style of La Scala drawings of the eighteenth century. The costumes were by Peter Hall, the lighting by John Harvey was awesome, and Sequi staged masterfully. Of course, the two ladies were lauded to the roof. Joan was in splendid voice, and, as for Horne, many thought her the sparkling diamond of the show. Chicago critics always keep their quivers of arrows full; some were launched at this superproduction, but most blunted before they could hurt the targets. A few did get through, however, notably a correspondent for *Opera Canada*, who ridiculed scenery, costumes, and direction. But the overpowering virtues of the two women singers at last melted all reserve. Spiro Malas made his Lyric debut as Assur, and a young black bass, Simon Estes, had a small role.

San Francisco then boasted a new Sutherland role, Maria Stuarda. Not only was it a first time for the soprano, but, strange as it seems, it was the first staged performance in the United States of the Donizetti opera. There had been a 1967 concert performance in New York with Montserrat Caballé, but now San Francisco rented some rather skimpy sets by Pier Luigi Pizzi from Florence and managed a grand style. The opera, which represents a historically incorrect confrontation between Elizabeth I and Mary Stuart, gives Elizabeth far greater dramatic range and actual time of appearance than Mary. Huguette Tourangeau made the most of her opportunities as the English Queen, and, although she seemed deficient in commanding presence (Sutherland towered over her, of course), she made up for it with extravagant gestures, lustered pearls, and a chalk-white face and red wig that reminded Arthur Bloomfield (author of *Fifty Years of the San Francisco Opera*) of Bette Davis.

It was not altogether a happy bit of casting, although it persisted throughout subsequent performances in other houses. Dramatic sopranos have sung it with great effect—Pauline Tinsley for one—but Tourangeau's frequent use of the chest voice seemed incongruous. Tito Capobianco was probably responsible for most of Elizabeth's exaggeration. Joan, who did not appear until the second act, sang the long and lovely prayer just before Mary goes to the block. Bonynge conducted the score that he had prepared from the 1835 original, Robert Commanday commented in the *Chronicle*. The critic added that the conductor achieved a very satisfying totality in stylistic grasp, pace, and in the finesse of the ensembles. Familiar in the Bonynge train were Stuart Burrows as Leicester and Cornelis Opthof as Talbot. Ara Berberian sang Cecil.

．　．　．

At last, Joan was permitted to show New York her comic sense when the Met mounted *La Fille du régiment* on February 17, 1972. Luciano Pavarotti again partnered her in the high jinks, and Fernando Corena played the fat Sulpice to a turn, with Regina Resnik the capricious Marquise.

A real *coup de théâtre* was secured by hiring Ljuba Welitsch to make a brief and hilarious appearance as the Duchess of Crakentorp. The former sensuous Salomé and flamboyant Donna Anna (not to mention Musetta) had the audience roaring for a minute or two. The less tinselly honors went to the singers, who strutted in high good form and humor. The antics that London had deplored were received in New York with a proper appreciation of their validity. Sandro Sequi's direction, one critic remarked, "helped make Sutherland so uninhibited, charming, and so good-natured in self-parody," and had to be credited with "coaxing almost nimble deportment out of the super-portly Signor Pavarotti, not to mention the admirable restraint which helps focus Corena's bonhomie and Resnik's silly-goosemanship." This was Martin Bernheimer, who came all the way from Los Angeles to observe that almost everything about the production was wonderful.

The sprightly opera was a welcome visitor in all the tour cities that spring. Six performances in the 1972–73 season gave Joan further confidence about her comedic talent.

Before she could give way to merriment, however, there was to be a *Rodelinda* at the Holland Festival in Schweningen on June 25. Joan brought to the Handel role her matchless technique for long ornamental trills, but was also impressive in the radiantly expressive music of passion and sorrow. *Opera News* also praised Tourangeau as Bertarido, and congratulated Capobianco on his enlivement of the static baroque opera. Varona's elaborate decor recalled in silver and gold the fanciful etchings of the eighteenth century.

Joan's success with the saucy Marie of Donizetti's caper persuaded her that she might dip a little deeper into comedy—even into operetta itself. In San Francisco in the fall of 1973 she was given the chance with her first *Fledermaus*. Her Rosalinda was all that could be asked for—beautiful, flirtatious, soulful in the Czardas, playfully revengeful to her straying husband.

What the audience did not know was that the heroine was almost unable to stand through the performance, let alone execute the few spirited dance steps she managed. Just before leaving Switzerland, the Bonynges had held a party in Chalet Monet. It was very festive, with paper Japenese lanterns bobbing about in the garden. Suddenly, a storm blew up, bringing sheets of rain. Joan, fearful that the wind might blow the lanterns about and cause a fire, hurried down the porch steps to extinguish the candles. The railing had become slippery with rain; she lost her hold and fell, twisting her ankle. It was bound up, of course, but still painful when she reached San Francisco, where a doctor gave her an injection of cortisone. She was able to go on.

·   ·   ·

All this while, the Met had been annually putting forth one of those galas that showed off the superstars and persuaded hundreds of dollars out of loyal patrons' pockets for the good of the company. Such a one was dated April 11, 1970, when Richard Tucker stood at the center of a jubilee that celebrated his twenty-fifth year with the company. Three prima donnas honored him: Sutherland, singing with him in the first act of *La Traviata*; Renata Tebaldi in Act II of *La Gioconda*; and Leontyne Price in Act III of *Aida*. Bonynge conducted for Joan's segment, which she did not feel was exactly the best "Sempre libera" she had ever done. She came off stage and ran into John Gutman, Rudolf Bing's right hand.

"Ow, wasn't that last note awful!" she cried.

Gutman smiled his best continental smile, and, bowing slightly, answered: "Who am I to contradict a lady?"

At the curtain call, a touching scene was enacted. Joan accomplished her best curtsey before the tenor, then kissed his hand. Long after the tenor's tragic death, Tucker's widow recalled that incident as one of the highlights of his career.

Sutherland was, of course, called upon to join the parade in honor of Bing's departure in 1972. The Authentic Event, as it was styled in the *Times*, went on until one-thirty in the morning. Joan's portion was a scene from *Lucia* to be sung with Pavarotti. Richard conducted it, as well as a ballet, Strauss's "Acceleration Waltz." Hardly a famous face was absent; hardly an illustrious voice not heard. The anecdote of the occasion: Bing had promised Birgit Nilsson that, if she would sing Salomé, he would render his head on a salver. She did sing—the final selection—and when Bing went back to her dressing room, there was the head—a plaster cast of the bust of Sir Rudolf by Virginia Page—on a silver salver.

Joan and Nilsson had another thing in common besides their superstardom: the salaries that Bing was prepared to pay. It had long been rumored that Sutherland received the highest salary of any at the Met; this was confirmed by Alan Rich's revelation in a

New York magazine article some years later. (The feisty reporter-critic had found a leak in the Met's roster who supplied him with what he called Metropolitan Opera Papers.) An interesting letter from Bing to Sutherland's manager, dated August 28, 1968, stated (according to Rich): "This is to assure you that Sutherland's fee will automatically go up regardless of what the contract says." The top fee in 1968 was $4,000, Rich noted; others who got this amount were Tucker, Corelli (always Bing's idol, no matter how shabbily they treated each other), Tebaldi, Price, Rysanek, Nilsson, and others. Yet Sutherland was always to receive an extra $2,000 for travel expenses.

Indeed, Joan was making top money and would continue to do so. There was not an opera management in the world that did not think she was worth it.

CHAPTER

18

Vancouver Venture

✳ THE VANCOUVER EXPERIMENT BEGAN AS A DREAM ✳ and ended somewhere in nightmare country. It seemed such a splendid idea for Bonynge to lead a company as artistic director, and Vancouver seemed just the spot—fairly well developed musically, but with plenty of room for refinement and growth. The company had ambled along to apparent satisfaction, if not always triumph, since 1959. Its repertoire relied on the tried and true, with an occasional splurge for an artist such as Sutherland. Richard was keen to freshen its repertoire; to groom new singers; to widen the British Columbia viewpoint.

For Joan the venture carried an element of pure sentiment. After all, Vancouver had been the scene of her North American debut, and her Donna Anna in *Don Giovanni*, undertaken in the most trying conditions, had been an accomplishment indeed. Also, she had returned several times, giving Vancouver her first *Faust*, her first *Norma*, and *Lucrezia Borgia* (and singing *Lucia* as well).

That this burgeoning metropolis, rather on the outskirts of the opera merry-go-round, had seemed an ideal place for her to try out new roles did not bother Vancouver until later, when more serious troubles brought up every possible grievance and the city entertained mixed feelings about the whole operatic scene.

Richard was appointed to the new post in 1975. Irving Guttman, who had long produced for the company, quietly disappeared and later surfaced in other Canadian cities.

The final season, 1973–74, before Richard took over showed a characteristic range—*Carmen, Don Carlos*, and *Traviata*. Richard enlarged the number of operas by one, the number of performances by three, and spread the season out more widely. His

144

choices were *Lucia*, Piccinni's *La buona figliuola* (a lighthearted satirical comedy by Gluck's rival that Bonynge revived and was very fond of), Handel's *Rodelinda*, and *Rigoletto*, together with a "workshop" workout of *Die Walküre*. (This workshop constituted a group of eight young singers whom Bonynge hoped to train in the manner of a baseball farm team or the apprentice system favored in other companies; eventually it faltered and died.) This was the general mix: two favorites and two unknowns (comparatively speaking, that is).

Bonynge stretched it a little the next season, with only one staunch standby, *Faust*, while the dazzling *Semiramide* of Rossini (a Canadian premiere), the gloomy *Queen of Spades* of Tchaikovsky (new to Vancouver), and the flighty *Merry Widow* (touted as a world premiere in Bonynge's new version) gave West Canadians a bit more novelty than they were accustomed to. *Bohème* and *Fledermaus* held the fort in 1976–77, while Thomas's *Mignon* lit no fire of real excitement, and Meyerbeer's *Les Huguenots* did not manage the full complement of the seven stars the opera requires. Neither of the latter had been heard in Vancouver before. The season of 1977–78 showed Bonynge in a still more adventurous mood, with the production that finally broke the back of the new regime, Massenet's *Le Roi de Lahore*.

The Vancouver enterprise had started off bravely enough, with banners flying. Bonynge quite naturally wanted his own people around him; any new broom wants a clean sweep. He hired as manager Barry W. Thompson, the handsome and soft-spoken husband of Huguette Tourangeau, who was the Bonynges' favorite mezzo of the time. Barry had been the general director of the Edmonton Opera (where Guttman had presided as artistic director), giving up the job in 1972 to run a ticket agency. He had also held an administrative position in a hospital. Good training for an opera company, Barry thought; the prima donnas are the same in the operating room, and the boards of directors show certain similarities.

At the time, Vancouver's opera board was headed by W. R. Steen, who later gave way to Jack Perles. An opera guild was in the process of forming. Up to 1976, the opera had been using the Vancouver Symphony, which was an arrangement not to the advantage of either body. Bonynge formed his own opera orchestra, and the Symphony moved to a movie palace for its concerts, thereby making the Queen Elizabeth Theater more accessible to the opera company.

The company paid $1,000 per night to rent the theater, but

got it back from the city as a grant. It really was not a question of theater cost that made the arrangement problematic but of the other limiting facilities that result from using a theater that remains multipurpose, Barry Thompson thought.

About a hundred chorus members could be counted on, part-time professionals, and, although no ballet company existed, very young pickup dancers could be pressed into ad hoc service. The roster also inevitably changed character under Bonynge, who brought in singers from many places, trying to keep a balance with native talent, but in the long run not succeeding, in the opinion of certain chauvinists. In his second season, however, newcomers numbered ten Canadians (three of them making company debuts); seven came from the United States (four debuts); one from Yugoslavia; one from the Netherlands (debut); and one from Australia (Joan).

In his third season, the balance had shifted slightly: five Canadians (one debut); five Americans (four debuts); four Australians (three debuts); two from the United Kingdom (one debut); and one debut from New Zealand. All these new faces might have delighted Vancouver, but chauvinistic criticism remained outspoken.

Highlights among these new encounters constituted a fairly respectable showing: the soprano Marvelee Carriaga as Semiramide; James Morris in *Semiramide* and later *Don Giovanni*; Samuel Ramey as Count Tomsky in *The Queen of Spades*, with Regina Resnik directing and playing the Countess; Heather Thompson as Marguérite in *Faust*; Jan Rubes making his Vancouver Opera debut in *The Merry Widow*; John Brecknock from England as Raoul in *Les Huguenots*, which also featured Margreta Elkins as Valentine and Noelle Rogers in Sutherland's old part, Marguerite of Valois; Mary Costa and Costanza Cuccaro in *Fledermaus*; Tourangeau quite naturally as Arsace in *Semiramide*, Pauline in *Queen of Spades*, and Urbain in *Huguenots*. Add to the list Clifford Grant, an old Australian buddy from *Esclarmonde*; Clarice Carlson, Don Garrard, Barbara Shuttleworth (Canadians all); and New Zealand's Heather Begg; plus Vinson Cole, the rising young American tenor, and you have a fairly respectable, if not always entirely brilliant, set of components for a provincial opera company—not to mention, of course, La Stupenda herself! How they fused in individual casts is, of course, another matter.

Joan had not sung in Richard's first season ("They couldn't afford her," he said wryly), but she was to light up the skies as the Merry Widow in April 1976. This pilgrim flew out for the occasion, but nothing seemed easily accomplished; the Bonynges were too strained with the new production (and the growing problems of the company) to talk; sight-seeing was discouraged by weather; and only a few interviews were gained. Everyone in the production seemed a little uptight, although Jan Rubes, the delightful troubadour and radio star, provided a cheerful half hour of reminiscences and humor. He played the baron in the show and was a comedian of the first rank, the kingpin upon which the somewhat outworn humor of the plot rested. Margreta Elkins had been persuaded to sing the Maxim girl Fo-Fo. She had just moved back to Australia from England, and had halfway intended to retire. The other half eventually prevailed, however, and her name still appears in many Australian casts. Joan is always comfortable when Margreta is close.

Richard had, of course, suggested that Joan do the Merry Widow, and had talked her into it for 1976. She had managed to overcome her tall-tree syndrome in *Daughter of the Regiment* and *Fledermaus*, so she yielded rather less cautiously to Anna Glawary (as Richard's new version named her. This adaptation caused a good many ripples later, and even in Vancouver some remarks were made about its "authenticity," whatever that may mean in relation to an extremely dated piece of froth.) Richard had augmented it: some ballets and an aria from another Lehár piece for Joan in the last act—"otherwise I'd just sit around at a table and do nothing," she justified it.

The press received the show with the expected mixture of scorn and rapture: scorn that it had been done at all and that a prima donna had stepped down from her pedestal; rapture at its verve and excitement. The audience ate it up. The opera house seemed, in fact, one place where the people of Vancouver could loosen up their rather prim and reserved attitudes and let go their emotions, a useful outlet for a city that was still feeling its way toward cultural enlightenment, and consequently putting on a shield of sophistication and cosmopolitanism very shallow indeed. *Merry Widow* was good for them whether they realized it or not.

As for the performance, let me quote my own review in *Musical America*, which touches on several aspects not locally noted:

It seemed that instead of [Sutherland] being too monumental, the others were too small—all except the statuesque Margreta Elkins, who flounced seductively as Maxim's girl Fo-Fo. One comment had it that "never were there so many feathers and so much costume concealing so little." It was that kind of show: elaborate art-nouveau settings and costumes by José Varona (the hats were spectacular), spirited direction by Lotfi Mansouri that dipped occasionally into pure camp, and a lot, quite a lot, of interpolated ballet in the Maxim setting, danced by Vancouver lads and lasses quite zestily to choreography by Martin Scheepers and music from six other Lehár operettas ferreted out by Bonynge and arranged by Douglas Gamley. Bonynge conducted the sparkling score with sweep and lightness.

The comedy . . . in its English adaptation by Christopher Hassall, had chief exponents in the insouciant Canadian veteran Jan Rubes as the Baron Zeta, the elfin Australian Graeme Ewer as Njegus, and a sprightly pair, Gordon Wilcock and Phil Stark. The sub-plot lovers Valencienne and Camille were sung and acted prettily by Barbara Shuttleworth and Graham Clark. No one matched Sutherland in the vocal department of course. Her "Vilia" carried enchantment, and a particularly lovely song had been plucked from Lehár's *Paganini* for her.

The Dutch Danilo (Peter van der Stalk) proved the biggest disappointment, lacking in voice and panache. He waltzed the Widow around quite handily in the first act, but could barely get his arms around the stunning avalanche of silvery-grey ruffles of her last-act costume. It occurred to me that this is probably the only role in which La Stupenda has enjoyed a young and eager male entourage such as, say, Shirley MacLaine plays to regularly. What's more, which bel canto opera offers the opportunity for a real kiss? Most of the Vancouver press begrudged Sutherland her fun, but the public rose to it wildly—for Vancouver.

The ominous rumblings that had already begun were owed to finances more than to artistic shortcomings, although rooted partially in the latter. Richard seemed too extravagant, was how it was summed up. The deficits mounted and were never met. The 1977–78 season saw the debacle, with Massenet's *Le Roi de Lahore* singled out as the main culprit. An extravagant production it was ($75,000 was the figure bruited about), and not enough to the popular taste to arouse great championship. Richard had secured his new orchestra, and, though the theater problems lightened, others took their place.

Le Roi de Lahore, redolent with Massenet's sweetness, and demanding lush, exotic scenery and costumes, rather fazed Vancouver. Surprisingly, in view of his general animosity toward the company, Ray Chatelin gave it a generally good review in *Province*, saying that it had been too long overlooked by North America and calling its production a "progressive step towards fulfilling some of the ambitious plans this season has brought with it." The production registered "a high degree of vocal and emotional intensity throughout," and the cast showed "a balance between vast amounts of unrefined energy and lyricism."

He praised Sutherland's voice as a "soaring power of seemingly limitless boundaries, while at the same time possessing the controlled lyricism needed in some of the opera's more delicate moments." Other attractions included "the dark, rich voices of bass-baritone James Morris as Timur, baritone Cornelis Opthof as Scindia, and bass-baritone Spiro Malas as the god Indra"; there was also Tourangeau as Kaled, a young officer. The Australian tenor, Ron Stevens, as the hero who is joined in death by his loved one, Sita, proved the least attractive of the lineup. Another reviewer gushed slightly more freely, concluding that *Le Roi de Lahore* "is French opera's answer to *Desert Song*—with Elephants."

Also bringing animals into the picture was the review of a visiting Toronto critic, William Littler: "Not only do they not write operas like this anymore, but they very rarely stage them, except in places like Vancouver where a steak and potatoes city is being fed turkey stuffed with truffles."

Seattle was a trifle kinder when the opera was taken there, but that can probably be attributed to the fact that Seattle's own Symphony Orchestra, opera chorus, and ballet officiated there.

The Daughter of the Regiment, with Pierre Charbonneau, Constanze Cucaro, and Graham Clark, salved everyone's feelings for a time. Also welcomed was Joan's appearance as Donna Anna (her original role in Vancouver), with James Morris as Don Giovanni, Spiro Malas as Leporello (virtually "stealing the show," according to Ray Chatelin), and Marvellee Cariaga (one of Bonynge's discoveries), who seemed miscast as Elvira. Cesar Antonio Suarez was Ottavio, and Tourangeau sang Zerlina. Norman Ayrton was director, a role he assumed with increasing frequency, continuing his early friendship and tutelage of Sutherland.

But the money was not there. A deficit of about a quarter-million was bruited. It was announced on January 19, 1978, that the later performances projected of Thomas's *Hamlet* (revived so successfully by Tito Capobianco in San Diego) and Gluck's *Orfeo ed Euridice* would have to be canceled.

Exchanges with the Seattle Opera (which had taken *Lahore* to the Washington city) had included a *Magic Flute* in the spring of 1978. To this were added some conventional old favorites, *Butterfly* and *The Barber of Seville*, to form a little Spring Season.

Richard filled out his contract as artistic manager for this appended season, but Vancouver was finished for him.

"They promised me the moon," he said sadly. "But they didn't deliver. And my manager blamed me for everything." Barry himself resigned soon after.

The dream had ended. Whose fault was it? The blame cannot be precisely placed, but it seems clear that the board, inexperienced and perhaps dazzled by Bonynge's plans, remained confused and divided throughout. This was the aftermath conclusion of Ruby Mercer, the experienced editor of the magazine *Opera Canada*. Instead of making a concerted attempt to raise money, they sold the Muir Street office, which had been their one certain base (the second sacrifice of real property to meet deficits, leaving the company with only a costume warehouse).

And recriminations continued. Ray Chatelin of *The Province*, who had twisted his knife before, wrote a venomous attack on Bonynge in *Musical America*, holding him responsible for the debacle. The writer also castigated the "buddy" system that Bonynge employed in hiring friends—manager, singers, and others. Not so noticeable was a reply in the same magazine by Andrew P. Swanson, President of Community Services Consultants, Ltd., who charged that Chatelin had allowed the board of VOC "to escape the blame that is clearly theirs alone." He went on: "In any organization the board of directors is solely responsible for the carrying out of the organization's purpose, for the determination of policy, and for the hiring and supervision of the artistic or executive director. While the artistic or executive director must play a principal, if not leading, role in the formulation of policy, the determination of policy is the responsibility of the board of directors alone. Whatever the details, it is apparent that the board of the VOC abdicated their responsibilities—an all too common occurrence among performing arts organizations—and the inevitable disaster ensued."

TWO

CHAPTER

19

"Operation Hoffmann" —Backstage

✻ WE ARE ALL A TRIFLE EDGY. IT IS SATURDAY MORN-
ing, November 10, 1973, and the suspense has been building
up. It is early in the Metropolitan Opera rehearsal period for *Les
Contes d'Hoffmann*, the opera starring Joan Sutherland that I had
been assigned by *Opera News* to cover during its production buildup.
We are waiting for the prima donna. All the others have gone
through days of rehearsals—music with various coaches, blocking
(learning their positions and action) with the stage director, Bliss
Hebert.

Now the queen-pin is ready for her entrance. She has had a
day's private blocking with Bliss—Bonynge has warned me that
she wants no one around in those first stages. "She forgets everything between times." I remember that she has been called a slow
learner.

We all stand around in the big rehearsal room on C level, the
Met's busy basement. Huguette Tourangeau, the luscious Canadian mezzo who will sing Niklausse, takes off her blond mink hat,
and Placido Domingo, clowning, tries it on and mugs. He is our
Hoffmann. Andrea Velis, the buffo tenor who sings four "servant"
roles, grumbles that another weekend is shot. It is chronic with
him. Greetings fly around in three languages. Martin Rich, the
authoritative, bustling little man, is fussing around at the piano.
He, with Gildo di Nunzio, a harried but sweet-tempered small
Italian, will be credited with the "musical preparation," which
means they exchange seats on the piano bench till the orchestra
takes over. Christopher Beach, Hebert's assistant, is taking notes
for Bliss, who is still fiddling, as he has done for days, with chorus

placement. Allen Klein, the scene and costume designer, pops in to mention white flowers being added to something or other. The rehearsal lineup is quivering with anticipation.

There she is: Sutherland at last! Pink-cheeked from the cold and obviously keyed up; the adrenaline is high to meet this always excruciating moment: confrontation of a new team in a new situation. First she embraces Huguette: "Hi, gorgeous!"

Her exuberance is just a tiny bit forced. "Sorry I'm late"— looking around. "Isn't my naughty husband here yet?" They've had a long drive from Brooklyn, but it turns out that Richard Bonynge is congenitally late. Furthermore, he has stopped on the way through the house to greet someone.

"Look at these hideous slippers," Sutherland chatters on. (They are turquoise kid flats.) "The only ones I could find to toddle around in [as Olympia, the doll]. What do you know! I'm down to 219 pounds! [from what? 220?] These skinny people!" Enviously, to Bliss.

She has shed her coat (a tweed, not fur) and trotted out to sit on Olympia's couch, carrying her ever-present needlepoint. It is a kind of security blanket.

She has cut her hair! Gone is the yard-long mane she used to wind around her head, swooping down over one eyebrow. (I haven't seen her since a chance meeting or two during the past two years). Now it is just above her shoulders, with a nice wave —very becoming. When I question her later, she admits to its convenience. "Do it meself in the shower, dear!" And much easier under a wig. Ricky has never become quite reconciled, however.

Now the delinquent husband-conductor finally slips in and takes command. He thinks Velis is hamming a bit: "Don't go overselling; just a light suggestion." All the way through, one feels Bonynge is trying to tone down this experienced, even somewhat blasé, artist who has had his own way as the leading comprimario for a long time and grown famous in "secondary" parts.

At a pause to allow Bliss to adjust some persons and things, Ricky (we are all on first-name basis by now) turns to Marie Cosindas, our distinguished photographer who will illustrate my *Opera News* article. She has been pointing her Leica here and there. "When you photograph Joan, she'll probably give you a dirty look from time to time, but that's habitual."

Joan chooses that moment to recognize me from where she is standing in the scene. She gives me a rather startled "Hi!" and a comment on the Scottish tartan I'm wearing. She's still tense when I approach her in a quiet moment. "Didn't Ricky tell you I was doing this?" I ask. Maybe he had, but she isn't too keen on it. My heart sinks. I murmur something about not embarrassing her, and slink back to be as inconspicuous as possible, considering my bright red plaid.

A question arises about the possibility of amplifying the dialogue. Bliss is doubtful, but Ricky recoils in complete horror. "Positively no!" Someone mentions that the critics get diarrhea at the very mention of amplification. Ricky's comment is censored. Then he makes the first of many complaints about the heaviness of the air. The singers cannot stand air-conditioning, so he must bear with this. Bruno Ferro, the downstairs prop man, opens the side doors now and then to catch a false breeze.

Now we are really into the music, with Olympia's brilliant air: "Les oiseaux dans la charmille, dans les cieux l'astre du jour." Ricky and Joan engage in a duel that seems very acrimonious. He's so rough on her that I quail inwardly, but she takes it, obviously accustomed to such treatment. She says later: "We're always harder on each other than anyone else could be."

Richard: "Don't press on the trill. It gets a rattle in. Like to do it again?"

Joan: "No, but I will." (With a big sigh. She reaches up and pulls something out of the air—an old-fashioned toilet chain? Everyone laughs.)

Richard: "What *are* you doing there?"

Joan: "I was thinking of "Les cieux l'astre du jour." (There is a discussion of taking an entire phrase in one breath. She can do it, of course.)

Richard: "Don't pull faces at me—just go."

Joan: "Faster?"

Richard: "Just sing, exclamation point! Don't take a breath *there*. And try to head off applause [at the end of the first verse]."

Joan: "Are we having a prompt?"

Richard: "Sure to, in this house."

Joan goes into the bit where the doll runs down mechanically and sings: "Ah-ah-ah-ah-ah-aaah. . ."

Richard: (exasperated) "How many are you *doing*?" (She has sung full-voice up to now, but omits the final high note this time.)

I walk out for a moment's respite and run into one of those conducted tours of the house, a group clustering outside the door and in a little anteroom in which a large window looks in on the rehearsal chamber.

"Why, it's Joan Sutherland!" exclaims one female. "I'd know that jaw anywhere." Already partisan, I want to slap her.

When they have gone, I slip back in. Allen Klein arrives in a loud plaid jacket, and Ricky comments, referring to my tartan: "Ha, a meeting of the clans." Ricky is my most appreciative audience for the variety of hats I wear every day to amuse him. It seems that Joan used to have a passion for mad hats, but never wears them nowadays.

Joan has to have her shoes specially made, with low heels designed to appear as high as possible. Right now she is wearing the hastily bought blue slippers for the waltzing doll. Bliss says it need not really be a waltz, there's nothing more tiring. Joan finds it easier to simulate the steps, only she cannot get around fast enough. Bliss will go over this with her alone. "The footwork won't show under your long skirt, but you must be in the right place at the right time."

Joan repeats the coloratura passages with Ricky.

Richard: "Don't watch me for the tempo."

Joan: (little girl voice) "I get screamed at if I don't watch."

Richard: "Just don't watch *here*. Look at me before you go off."

Joan tries again, and at the top, cackles. She's always making funny noises, doesn't seem to take herself seriously. It is one of those endearing traits that makes devotees of her colleagues. There's a click of her tongue that cracks like a whip, and when she starts Giulietta's second-act duet, "Malheureuse," etc., it becomes "Mal. . . mal. . . miaow!"

She discovers a joint in the great mirror that takes inches off her figure and stands fascinated and rapturous, gazing at it. Ricky takes advantage: "That's right, look in the mirror, watch. . . watch. . . that's what it's for." She sighs for the lost illusion and goes back to drill.

Richard: "You're pulling faces all the time. Watch what you're doing!" Bliss shows her the path she must take to exit—it will be through a crowd of choristers—but she goes out too soon and gets a general laugh.

What a long day! I have an interim discussion with Ricky about his version of *Hoffmann*. For one thing, he has substituted spoken dialogue for the recitatives (composed by Ernest Guiraud in completing the opera Offenbach left unfinished at his death); he has also reinserted the Muse in the Prologue and Epilogue to show that she takes care of her poet by becoming Niklausse (the poet's constant companion through his three adventures in love); and he has made a major change in the second act. This act, set in Venice, was omitted at the very first performance and has been a subject of controversy ever since. There was a septet at the end (possibly inserted by Guiraud) that Bonynge has transferred as a quartet into the Epilogue.

Hoffmann has always suffered from versionitis; Bonynge's ideas seem no worse than some others, and better than many. The spoken dialogue certainly provides the big stumbling block for this cast, which contains only one native French-speaker.

· · ·

It is an afternoon round table with Danielle Valin, the diction coach. And it's about time! They read through the Act II dialogue. Placido has suffered through numerous corrections; his native Spanish accent doesn't fit the French. Aggrievedly he plucks the strings of the harp all singers play when diction is in question—tessitura. " 'Offmann is so 'igh!" It's his hardest role, he later confesses— high, dramatic, and he is on stage practically every minute in a long opera.

Joan stumbles over a particularly tricky passage and keeps stumbling, until, with her usual determination, she masters it. But it is sticky; when Giulietta apologizes to Hoffmann for her "bouffon" Pitticchinaccio (Velis), she says: "Il a ici son franc parler, et il faut que vous en passiez par ses compliments." Even after she has got it, the stress is not quite perfect.

Later Joan cries longingly: "Oh, what it is to be French! Or," glancing at Huguette, "French-Canadian. I'm ashamed. Studied five years, too." I ask if she had had a good teacher, and she exclaims: "No! Not for pronunciation!" The English rattle off French without a care for pronunciation subtleties, and I wonder if the Australians are not the same. *That* accent does have a tendency to pervade.

There will be another session with Valin at four-thirty. Meanwhile, back to blocking. Joan is on Giulietta's sofa, Andy at her feet. Ricky worries about Placido singing his aria twice full-voice, then holding up for the Antonia trio. Placido says charmingly: "It's hard, but once I've sung it I might as well do it twice." Joan, on her same old track, insists he's just trying to take off a few pounds. Ricky comments that the heavy orchestration is what makes the difference for the tenor in this aria.

The afternoon drags on. Joan and Placido maneuver with the fatal mirror that will steal Hoffmann's reflection; Joan practices the tricky French passage. Joan and Huguette run over the Barcarolle twice, lightly.

At the break, Placido sits at the piano playing his own accompaniment to a snatch of *Hoffmann,* then *Rigoletto,* then Antonia's aria, and Joan joins in: "Elle a fui, la tourterelle." Placido finishes with the crashing chords from *Tosca* that delineate the sinister Scarpia.

Placido is a big boy with a sunny temperament. His career will take off like a rocket from here on. Marie has fallen in love with him and photographs him at every possible moment. She and I note that singers are invariably "on"—such stamina, outgoing force. We congratulate ourselves on being with this particular team. (Joan seems reconciled to the outsiders, and quite friendly, thank God!)

A discussion arises about Schlémil's body, and who should carry it out. The cast-off lover of Giulietta is killed in a rigged duel with Hoffmann. Joan quips: "No body in my act, please." The rest of the afternoon alternates between blocking and musical sections. Placido is in full voice, quite overwhelming. Joan jests with him and embraces him fondly. Everybody is a little frazzled. Ricky asks the whereabouts of Thomas Stewart, the baritone who will sing the four villains. He has worked on previous days, but we need him now. He may be rehearsing for a concert with his wife, Evelyn Lear. He has sent a message asking if he may transpose the Venetian villain Dapertutto's Diamond aria down a tone—the top G-sharp is worrisome. It is often done his way. Many times a different singer is allotted to Dapertutto—the other three villains stay lower in the register. (This aria is suspect, by the way, and subject to some controversy that has recently arisen over the entire subject of *Hoffmann*'s "original" version. However, we are paying no attention to that. Ricky has kept this aria in its accustomed place.) Ricky is not pleased, but agrees to Tom's request.

Joan is forgetting her words now, and Martin Rich's offer to help is met by an unusually curt "No." She wonders how she can lie on the sofa with her great headdress—it turns out to be a sweeping hat, and Placido once knocks it slightly askew in the passionate love duet. The solution is to give her cushions to half-recline against; otherwise, she cannot hold herself up when she leans back.

Ricky insists on another go-round: "It's really very poor."

Joan: "Musically?"

Richard: "Both, music and action."

Placido is moving uncertainly, and Ricky is prompting almost every sentence of Joan's. She apologizes: "I have it all somewhere in the back of my mind. It'll come back, I know."

Finally they stop, only to confer about the shuffling of schedules. Ricky is indignant at the paucity of music rehearsals and issues a command to get Tom Stewart for sure on Monday *and* Tuesday, before the *Sitzprobe*. I perk up my ears at that ugly word. It means just what its German syllables say: a *Probe* (rehearsal) sitting down. This will be a complete musical run-through with the entire cast, orchestra, and some technicians, and is a watershed in the proceedings. It will take place on Wednesday. Seems to be rushing on us fearfully fast.

There is a final dispute about rehearsing the "covers" (those singers who stand by for each role, getting called in only in case of illness, unless, of course, they have been scheduled for later replacements). It appears that etiquette forbids taking the second cover before the first. In this case, they discuss the Mother's role, which Cynthia Munzer will sing. Jean Kraft and Batyah Godfrey are covers. I am not sure who is first, but they have to get one for Munzer, who is extremely busy just now with other roles. They hope for Kraft, who is "family" and intimately associated with the Bonynges (as are Huguette, Placido, and the other tenor, John Alexander).

Finally we separate. It has been everybody's most grueling day. Thank God for a Sunday!

      •   •   •

We have had several intensive sessions before. For me, the adventure really begins on a cold, rainy, blustery Monday morning, October 29. Bonynge has flown in from Chicago for orchestra rehearsal, and will return immediately to conduct *La Fille du régiment*. I penetrate for the first time of any importance into the lower regions of this mammoth music factory, needing a page for a guide.

At ten-thirty sharp, Bonynge strides into the great chamber, where the orchestra is already assembled. He receives welcoming applause, exchanges cordial, brief greetings, then raises his baton to begin the Prelude to *Les Contes d'Hoffmann*.

He seems taller than I remember. Around his slender, pointed face, he has let his hair grow to a wider, very becoming frame; it is very curly and a trifle grizzled at the temples. To me it is much more pleasing than the close crop that had made his head seem too small and gave him the look of a boy—inappropriate beside his luxuriantly built wife. How old was he now? Fortyish; four years younger than Joan. With long, supple legs, he moves with quick, small steps and a certain air of eager nervousness.

At first there is an expectable roughness in rapid, exposed passages. "Fifth bar after letter C," says Bonynge—a problem with a trumpet entrance. A tricky syncopated duel between horn and trumpet comes off neatly. When Bonynge raps for a stop, a squeak from a wind instrument (probably a clarinet) provokes laughter and the kind of witticism common to orchestra players.

After twenty minutes, Bliss Hebert and Allen Klein slip in. They have partnered each other many times as director and de-signer, officiating at the Seattle birth of this production in 1971. Bliss and Allen are old-timers. I have witnessed their Santa Fe operas for several seasons and was briefed the previous summer on this *Hoffmann*. Not having seen each other for at least two months, we embrace affectionately. (I note that even a few hours' absence in the opera house brings on fresh "Hi's" and even kisses. Opera houses resound with kisses, seldom full on the lips, but constant tokens offside into the air or on one or both cheeks, or on a woman's hand by certain unregenerate Europeans. It depends somewhat on nationality.) You may take the busses for granted in this narrative.

The rehearsal ends suddenly, almost in midmelody—union time. Bonynge is detained by this one and that one; he finally sees me and smiles warmly. I praise him for the buoyant, successful session.

"This is such a fabulous orchestra," he compliments. "They are used to playing under many conductors—adapt easily."

Bonynge takes off, but I linger in the conference between Bliss, Allen, and Clemente D'Alessio, assistant to technical director Michael Bronson and assigned to this project. Undercurrents of unease and dissatisfaction break into speech. The rehearsal sched-ule has been juggled—fouled up is more like it. Two new pro-ductions come before *Hoffmann*, and one of them is the fearful colossus *Les Troyens*, the impossibly large show of Hector Berlioz that is being attempted for the first time at the Met. "Everything is behind *Trojans!*" has become the battle cry. Not only is the time for *Hoffmann* being cramped, but so is the production immediately preceding it, Rossini's *L'Italiana in Algeri*, which is a tricky piece to be produced in his debut by Jean-Pierre Ponnelle, who is apt to come up with oddities. *Italiana*, in addition to normal impos-sibilities, has been swept by a prima donna high wind. This is the way the grapevine has it: A maestro of inconsiderable stature and achievements (in some opinions) has been assigned to this brilliant piece, over the objections of the star, the effulgent mezzo Marilyn Horne. Jackie, as she is known universally, wanted her own husband, Henry Lewis. (Later, she got him.)

Put up with the assigned man she did not. Unsuitable ornamentation of her arias, tempi, general ambience, or whatever found them at variance up to the shouting point. Jackie walked out (or so I'm told), and was not pacified for a week. Then, just about to return to the fold, she caught cold and had to extend hooky time a couple of days. This put *Italiana* far behind, and had Frank Paola, the veteran rehearsal scheduler (now retired), climbing the walls.

Today's worries are a direct result. "We must set up a day's work before Thursday," Bliss frets. The production, rather scanty in actual scenery and props for a big show, nevertheless needs special lighting. It has been rented from Seattle, but partly rebuilt and repainted in the Met's shops.

Richard L. Abrams is added to the conference. He is at that time the house assistant director, advising with typical cynicism never to make any first draft of anything on the typewriter because it is bound to be changed.

On the second floor, in rehearsal room 205, Catherine Rice Parsons of Santa Fe, credited as choreographer, is trying out a children's ballet group, who are all pretty well trained and "not like the little hellions in the children's chorus," says Abrams sotto voce.

That afternoon I spend some useful time with Allen Klein and Charles Caine, the staff costume coordinator. Charlie is tall and slender and moves quickly. His head is topped with reddish curls. How many curly types there are in this crew! Allen belongs, but his curls are dark, and his body is short and compact. With a mobile, expressive face and great dark eyes. They call him the Brooklyn Elf.

I soon observe that a price tag is firmly attached to all processes. This production has to be brought in cheaply, and it shows in the last-detail caution of the department. The more they "find" the less they have to "make." So we go on listing "find" or "make" through several hours.

Bliss begins blocking with Thomas Stewart on November 5. It is a long, tedious process to convey position, motivation, and gestures to sometimes recalcitrant, occasionally merely (shall we say) dumb, and, more often than you might expect, intelligent and receptive human beings who happen to be singers and (God willing) actors to boot.

Tom is the only important cog new to this wheel. The four *Hoffmann* villains are a first for him. In fact, the French repertoire is just opening up to him.

Now it is November 6, Election Day. After voting, I sit in on the rehearsal from two-thirty to five. Tom and Bliss are going over and over Coppélius's entrance in Act I, where the supplier of the doll's eyes is seeking payment from her creator, Spalanzani. Encountering Hoffmann, who has come to gaze at the beauty he takes to be real, Coppélius will sell the poet rose-colored spectacles that will preserve his illusion.

"I'm a sucker for a role that can be really acted," Tom confesses. He has proved it many times, and will again. And it will be his French diction that is singled out for praise above all others but Tourangeau's.

At four o'clock we are still working on the first act, with John Alexander in for Domingo, who sings *Traviata* tonight. Alexander has been Joan's tenor many times and is scheduled for six *Hoffmanns* here.

We also have a different repetiteur. Jan Behr is jolly, competent, agreeable. He gives a pat on the long black hair of Tourangeau. This is the sexiest lady in the opera house. No man can resist the current, even the canteen operator who sells her an apple, and the stagehands who don't get very close. There is an electricity in her aura as old as Eve. She knows it and uses it. It is like breathing––she cannot turn it off, but she can regulate it. She lets us know she is happily married to a "gorgeous" man (footnote: he *is* attractive). She has luxurious furs out of Canada; it is cold up there. Blond mink one day; ranch mink the next. Huguette was a real discovery of the Bonynges, and has shared their public and, to an extent, their private, lives ever since Marilyn Horne went off to sing with her own husband.

One prop has appeared—the huge key that the servant Cochenille will twist in the doll's back to wind her up. Bruno has cleverly inserted a rachet that fairly screams when the key is turned. Andy tries it on everyone. We indulge in a lot of laughter at Andy's comical stuttering as Cochenille, as the scene is taken from the top. And once again . . . and again.

Wednesday, November 7: Hoffmann has been going on down below, but I'm up in the auditorium, watching the dress rehearsal of *Italiana*. Very stylized, very stylish. One thing strikes me as odd: long stretches where only the orchestra plays and the principals merely stand around. This is not like Rossini. Then it dawns on me—the chorus is missing. And where is it? On C level, rehearsing *Hoffmann*. So far has the schedule been snarled. Unprecedented, I think to myself.

In a short break below, David Stivender, who rose to chorusmaster after being assistant to Kurt Adler, exudes unhappy vibrations. He has a wracking cold, and the chorus has had absolutely no music run-through since August.

I watch curiously. This aggregation is almost impossible to whip into any stylized shape. They simply are not used to much more than getting their bodies on and off stage. Youth is spotted only in the first row; the rest are veterans. Twenty-eight couples are involved. "There ought to be someone in back to catch mistakes," someone suggests. The answer comes quickly, cynically, and, one suspects, truthfully: "Mistakes in back don't count." It is like a disorganized gym class. Won't the costumes help? I wonder. With time comes the answer: "No!"

The ballet is on hand, too. Not very inspiring at this juncture. And replete with male clowns.

Thursday, November 8: Bliss works with the third-act gentlemen, Crespel, Antonia's father, and the evil Doctor Miracle. Crespel is James Morris; very tall, very handsome American-style, with dark eyes and, yes, curly hair. He will achieve stardom very quickly.

The rest of the day labors on: Huguette fearfully contemplates the high elevation from which she will sing the Barcarolle. Clifford Harvuot, the Schlémil, undergoes a stiff lesson in swordplay from George Kolombatovich (who, with his father, Oscar, own a weapons factory on Long Island. They supervise the lot of bloody derring-do that opera seems to call for). Tom tries out the huge "diamond," which, with an electronic flash, will blind Schlémil and enable Hoffmann to run him through, and will also entice Giulietta into stealing Hoffmann's reflection. Placido bounces in, grabs George's sword, and stamps, shouts, swashes and buckles all over the place before settling down to business.

Friday, November 7: The most tiresome and mysterious shenanigans of all for a layman—a technical rehearsal. Nothing seems to happen in the darkened auditorium except endless shouts from Rudolph Kuntner, head electrician, in arcane jargon: "Bring up [or down] Special No. 2 [or 3 or 4 or 5 or 8] one point [or two]." A super lolls in (presumably) Tom's place on a high balcony. I am as bored as he looks.

Bonynge is in for orchestra rehearsal. This is where the real grind begins, but we are all still in second gear. John Grande, the cheerful librarian, pays me extravagant compliments on my two "Opera Production" handbooks. Meanwhile, Bliss is working the Prologue with the male chorus. It is controlled pandemonium, with stamping feet on wood floors, mugs on tables, noisy tin trays in the tavern. Charles Anthony and Russell Christopher, playing Hoffmann's buddies, Nathaniel and Hermann, stand atop a table. God! What a noise! It only gets better regulated; never less in decibels.

In the afternoon, Bonynge enters, staging rehearsals for the first time, evoking a ripple of applause. Musicians show this courtesy to each other; warm greetings at first go-round, a certain *politesse* to the top stars, and always some cordial acknowledgment each day.

Now the lineup is virtually complete in two rows of chairs facing the "stage" space. I try to keep a low profile at the back, but occasionally move up to consult someone.

We run through the Epilogue, which takes the same set. Edmund Karlsrud, who plays the innkeeper, Luther, questions the air plaintively: "Isn't there some music here somewhere?" No, there isn't. His part has been reduced to a tinier bit and only dialogue. All the comprimarios are grousing at this.

We take it from the top. It is extremely tiring, but exhilarating. Bonynge has a word afterward, apparently not too taken with the chorus. "They must understand that it's not heavy German although laid in Nuremberg, but light French—Offenbach. The only thing German is the beer."

And so ends the day.

CHAPTER
20

"Operation Hoffmann" —On Stage

ON WEDNESDAY, NOVEMBER 12, THE WHOLE AMBI-ence has changed. We are on stage for the first time. The intimacy of C level has dissipated as we experience the machine gearing up to work, irrevocably turning, turning—and we are caught in it. Instead of the friendly mirror, there is an awesome view of the half-lit auditorium, stretching away and up in its deep redness. The very size of the stage is intimidating—huge itself and dupli-cated exactly at both sides and to the back. We will be on stage almost every working day from now on, with periodical revisits below for the continuing process of "brushing up."

A few new characters emerge. First is the tall, lean fellow who seems to be everywhere at once. He is Chris Mahan, executive stage director, who will play the most important part in my back-stage life, finding me out-of-the way nooks to perch in, explaining procedures. His cohort, Stanley Levine, the stage manager, is an old friend from Thirty-ninth Street, full of reminiscences and slightly off-color stories. Clemente D'Alessio, assistant technical director, who will have charge of this show, is a curly-headed, happy chap who loves every instant of his job; there are all too few like him. Last but not least, there is Rudy Kuntner, the veteran master of lighting. During one of these crazy days that follow, I manage to get in a few words with Chris Mahan, the man who makes the wheels go round. He has been with the Chicago Opera, too, and likes the cross-fertilization possible in a smaller company. At the Met, everything is compartmentalized, and he does not attend rehearsals until they reach the stage.

Life is suddenly more serious. Even the jesting of the motley chorus is subdued. One middle-aged woman mumbles: "Things in my body are moving that never moved before." The first couple in front seem never to keep step or feel rhythm. Bliss Hebert indulges in the understatement of the year, sotto voce: "I think they need a little more training."

Joan is still unflappable, and occasionally pipes up with something that causes a swell of laughter, relieving the strain. Her own laughter rises freely again and again—a very special sound. Huguette, too, takes minds off troubles in a very different way. Joan notes the attention paid the little Canadian in her short-sleeved black sweater spangled with brilliants, and twits her: "The only woman I could ever fall in love with, especially in pants," and chucks her under the bosom. Men gasp in envy at this indecorous gesture. Andrea Velis comments: "Don't think the orchestra doesn't notice her, too, and Martin Rich plays wrong notes every time she walks by."

It is always a relief to get back down to C level after one of these trying stage sessions. I watch Joan entering, burdened by a great handbag, score, needlepoint bag. Martin Rich insists on kissing her hand, forcing her to put down handbag, etc. She is not much for this continental *politesse* anyway, especially in working hours.

Cynthia Munzer is in for the first time and is introduced as Joan's (Antonia's) "mother." Everybody breaks into a rash of "Sua madre?" "Sua madre!" from the *Marriage of Figaro* scene in which the former housekeeper claims Figaro as her son and releases him from a contract of marriage. It strikes us all as terribly funny. In fact, no one is quite ready for work yet.

The men—Placido, Tom Stewart, and Jim Morris—cluster around the piano like an old-time "sing," and go through the Act III Trio for Hoffmann, Dr. Miracle, and Crespel. At close range, the impact of these powerful voices is fierce and wonderful. The trained opera voice can twang nerves and sensibilities to the breaking point, whether or not it shatters glass. To cap these three great ones, Joan comes in on cue with the trill on high A and the ascent to D, followed by the downward chromatic run of two octaves that transfixes me every time.

When Ricky mentions that Munzer sings from the pit, she clouds up. She won't be seen and is afraid she won't be heard, either. "No amplification—some sort of megaphone?" she pleads. But Ricky is adamant. He soothes her by explaining that she will be standing right up near the conductor's podium, singing out into the hall. "They'll hear you all right!" (Sure enough they did, so vividly that, ironically, Harold Schonberg in the *Times* was sure she had been amplified.)

Now to work. At Ricky's instruction to someone "not to hurry," Joan interjects: "He never thinks anything is too long—it takes all your breath." Of course, she is the one who can handle it.

In a short break, there is acrid comment on changed schedules. Placido, playing "My Hero" on the piano, lures Joan into singing it. It happens to be one of her favorite encore pieces for concerts. I think she sings it to Ricky.

Then, as Antonia, Joan sings beautifully. "I die so much," she sighs, asking for a canvas on the floor to protect her dress. Her broken dying thread of song she considers very dangerous, because it is tricky to sustain the breath all the way through.

Joan hits a high note and something bangs backstage. Much laughter.

All the comprimario singers are still unhappy about the cuts in Richard's version. Even Velis (who has a truly star part as the four servants) grouses, but this is his style as a privileged veteran. David Stivender, the young chorus master, admonishes Andy Velis at one point: "Be sure you're noticed here." (Funny, *that* to *him!*) "I'll wear my green tongue," he promises.

Back on C level for "notes," the theatrical name for corrections. Placido is worrying about the violin that is Dr. Miracle's prop. He plays it now like a country fiddler with the instrument on his knee, then like a cello. A tired Joan sits for the musical repetitions, going through the finale perfectly, trill on F and all. She, Huguette, Placido, and Tom then sing the final quartet that Richard has inserted in the Epilogue, replacing the Septet in the Venetian scene. It is thrilling, whether "orthodox" or not, with its high E-flats for Joan.

I have a small conversation with the weary prima donna. "There's very little socializing in times like these," she admits, pointing up the unglamorous side of the opera star's life, often ignored by the public. "I wear old clothes because I have to mop up the floor so much. We're going home for Christmas, thank goodness!" She has shown snapshots of the Bonynges' chalet in Switzerland and of their son, Adam, who is eighteen at this time and "bigger than Richard." He likes skiing better than opera or ballet, and speaks three languages, she says proudly. It is for him that she is making needlepoint slippers.

Ricky talks about Australia. They are taking *Hoffmann* there, too, with both scenery and costumes by José Varona, who is admired for his work with the New York City Opera. I discover that it is he who has designed Joan's costumes for this show, causing some heartburn on Allen's part, which takes all of Joan's tact to soothe.

The drill goes on doggedly, lightened by a mention of *Il Trovatore*, which inspires Joan to cackle an elaborate passage—another of her spontaneous gestures that breaks the tension. She persists through this session, even though Ricky demands in capital letters: "HOW MUCH MORE CAN YOU TAKE?" She says stubbornly: "I like to know where I am with the music." Ricky prompts, as she tires. At the climax, she and Tom are saving their voices. Bliss says tiredly: "I love technical rehearsals . . . you just sit there."

· · ·

In the midst of this alternation between chaos on stage and repairs on C level comes the *Sitzprobe*. Everybody is in the orchestra rehearsal room, the instrumentalists on the floor, the singers perched on bleachers behind them. For the first time, Millard Altman, who will be in the prompter's box, shows up for an entire session. It is exclusively music—no dialogue, and goes splendidly, with applause in the right places.

Next day, on stage, at the end of Act I, Tom is throwing bits of the mechanical doll over the balcony railing. He pitches them toward the lower stage-left corner so as not to hit anyone who rushes in to scavenge. Placido complains: "You throw me only a leg." Joan is worried about mounting the steep backstage stairs leading to the balcony, so narrow for her voluminous skirts. It is much higher than Seattle's. "Not that I find them hard to climb, dearie," she protests. "It's only, will I get there on time?" Olympia must show herself before being dragged back by Tom and presumably dismembered.

Fumbles and stumbles are the watchword today. The French diction, which has constantly worried the pretty French coach, Danielle Valin, slips out of control, even with Tom, who has shown up pretty well in this department. Joan repeats her speech: "Je n'ai qu'un mot à dire pour qu'il soit à mes pieds!" and comments: "Soit? All these *swats*—someone's going around with a flyswatter." This important word can mean a simple "will be" or "so be it!" as uttered by Don José in his renunciation of Carmen: "Eh, bien, soit! Adieu!"—a chilling moment.

Bliss fumes, but quietly. Everything, everything, has to be refined. Another understatement.

. . .

Now we anticipate another trying day—the first with costumes on stage. All is placid upstairs—Charlie Caine and Maureen Ting Klein (head costumer) have long ago sent costumes down, and Nina Lawson is calm among her wigs. It is time to renew old acquaintances in the dressing-room section: Rose Calamari, costume supervisor (whom the Met was to lose not long afterward), and John Casamassa, head dresser for the men, both veterans of the old house and eager to talk about dear departed Jennie and Angelo, their predecessors. I meet James Pinto, head makeup artist, and Victor Callegari, his assistant, as well as David Winter, men's dresser.

The whole dressing-room section seems such an improvement over the old house, where there was but one shower for the men (and that on the third floor), and the warrens were rabbity indeed. Here there are rows of fair-sized cubicles, each with its own bath, on either side of a corridor, which is at right angles to the passage to the stage.

Suddenly the place comes alive. Joan breezes in. Gears are shifting into high. Still, everyone seems a little fatigued, nerved up. It reminds me of the skylab launching that very morning. Only the trials lie ahead for this crew.

The rehearsal begins badly. The snake dance of the students into Luther's tavern is too fast and ragged; the chorus too slow, clumsy on its feet. The men in the Olympia act appear rather ridiculous in tight pink costumes. Ribald comments fly like swallows through the corridors about the white plastic bosoms sewn to the chorus and ballet girls' front facades. Allen meant these to stand out startlingly against dark costumes and to echo the dead white faces and gloves of the women. Body paint at $7 per face per performance is a no-no, so the "boobs" have to go, too. "Biggest mastectomy in history!" moans Allen.

Next morning is for the sillies. Andy is not the only one who is reluctant to accept Saturday work. John Alexander, who replaces Placido (he will sing half of the performances), tells Polish jokes. Most of them evaporate into silence. Joan and Ricky are late. It is now eleven-thirty. "My husband lost our call sheet," she apologizes. I say: "It's from ten till unconscious." Old sally, but gets a laugh. I add: "Marie [our photographer] is absent—probably feels she's done this enough." Joan giggles: "So have we. But we shouldn't knock it."

"Is there such a thing as overtraining?" I ask.

"Not really," she answers. "Still, it could be. Felsenstein [the late Walter of East Berlin] trains all spontaneity out."

Joan looks like a doll herself this morning: family size, to be sure, but pretty in a green jumper with lighter blouse and wide belt. Her hair is concealed under a clever wig Nina has made to look like the real thing: short, curled at the ends, with a blue band across the front.

The family feeling is showing. Joan calls Alexander "a dear boy." He was a member of the company that toured Australia in 1965, and is often in their casts. I ask: "How many in this cast did you pick?" Joan laughs deprecatingly. "We can suggest, not pick." I reserve an opinion on this.

Ricky asks suddenly: "Is it lorgnon or lorgnette?"

Joan: "Monocle."

I: "Duocle."

Laugh; my third in a row.

Bliss gives a long sigh. Joan and Andy in duet: "Me, too!"

Joan adds flatly: "Moi aussi." Saturday is done for.

· · · ·

Monday is reserved mostly for rehearsing "covers," those singers who will step in in case of mishap to one of the principals. They all work hard, but few will make it to the footlights. Only Paul Franke (Spalanzani) and David Holloway (Schlémil) are scheduled for regular performances. Colette Boky, a tiny French girl, will come in for Joan at the last moment on the only occasion she has ever canceled a performance at the Met, and Harry Theyard will jump in for Alexander one night. Otherwise, the cast stays together.

On the stage, Placido seems dispirited for the first time. It is the shadow of a premonition. The Sunday rest has let everyone down. Ricky is fuming because it is his once-a-year bad day. He gives wrong cues, loses his temper. Joan never seems to get these megrims, he says, recalling the time in Palermo when her abscessed ears did not keep her from singing gloriously, even after the abscesses broke and let blood stream down her face.

Afterward, Bliss gives Joan pointers about falling and keeping her full skirts properly down. Crinolines and other voluminous trappings can cause embarrassment, as many an actress and singer can testify. Down you go at a certain angle and whoops! Up come your hoops in front. Joan is worried that her Giulietta costume will catch in the sinking platform where she and Huguette are resting in a gondola for the Barcarolle. Bliss kids her: "A hand will come up and help." A certain amount of ribaldry breezes through the room.

Chris Beach, Bliss's assistant, asks Joan if she would like a "cuppa." She immediately sits up straight, hands raised like the paws of a begging puppy.

Velis is working on Franz, the garrulous, hard-of-hearing servant in Act III. His little song about how he pleases himself by singing and dancing when no one is home is always a hit. At the end of the first verse, when he vocalizes too strenuously, he is supposed to "crack"—the voice breaks ludicrously. Andy finds it difficult. The entire group concentrates on the problem, each with a contribution.

Bliss: "Can't you do just a *little* one?"

Placido: "I did a big one when I was young. Every time in *Faust* when I came to the high note in 'Je t'aime,' I'd crack. Five performances in a row! In the sixth, I just held on to that damned note until it came clear."

Joan: "Je suis la Duchesse de Crack-entorp." (the comic lady in *Daughter of the Regiment*).

Someone: "Let's give lessons in crack."

Ricky: "Get Don Julio!" General laughter. They refuse to reveal that "craqueur's" identity.

Andy: "I'm going home and practice my crack."

Joan: (parting shot) "Don't wear it out, luv!"

.   .   .

On Friday, the tension is high voltage. It is piano dress, the last rehearsal before the final dress, with piano only. It is crisis time, all right. Seems all sixes and sevens. Murphy's Law applies: if anything can go wrong, it will. Hardly a bar of music or bit of stage action is not halted for correction. It is the stop-and-go session.

I find out that this is completely traditional; everyone expects it, and the stage director is particularly grateful for it; it is his last chance to firm up all details. But it is very trying for the conductor and an untried spectator.

As luck would have it, this rehearsal is the one Kirk Browning, TV director, chose to film and time as reference for the actual live televising of the second performance. (This is the pilot experiment that led to the series *Live from Lincoln Center*. It was not to be shown to the public.) Browning, experienced to his fingertips in these TV matters, had not realized the difference in priorities in stage rehearsals.

Minor catastrophes follow each other in quick succession. Mahan is everywhere, his long legs scissoring like a sandpiper, his beaky nose way ahead of himself, sniffing trouble.

Most disturbing of all, Placido is singing roughly, looking very uncomfortable, one hand pressing against his abdomen. Before long, he disappears, and John Alexander is in. Rumors spread immediately, carrying wisps of panic. We do not learn till afterward that he has suffered a hernia attack and will eventually need an operation. But—thank God!—he has been fitted with a truss and can sing the dress, at least. But how far can he go? There are some bad moments. (Eventually, he sings his entire stint and goes on and on, seemingly never pausing for repairs.)

· · ·

Now comes Monday, November 26. DRESS REHEARSAL! This is the real show. After it, the performances—even opening night, which brings built-in nervousness—will find the opera in everyone's bones. The excitement level is high once again, but lacking the undercurrent of hysteria. Dressing rooms are abuzz with spouses, secretaries, intimate friends, managers, press agents, and favored hangers-on, wishing everyone luck in three languages. It is supposed to be bad luck to say "good luck" right out, but I notice a few Americans doing it. Most others say the German "Hals und beinbruch" ("Break your neck and leg"), or the Italian "In bocca al lupo" ("In the mouth of a wolf"). The Polish custom is "Toi-toi," signifying spitting on the favored one. The Swedes deliver a hearty kick in the rear. But the French is best: the scatological "Merde!" Charlie Riecker, assistant artistic administrator and French expert, magnifies this to "Merde au treizième degré!"

In this highly charged atmosphere, I feel the professional energy of the dozens of talents all converging on this one spot, this one hour.

I have decided to watch the entire show from backstage, to see the wheels go round. I will be out front opening night, time enough to catch the spectacle along with everyone else. But this is my own private affair: I want to see the pieces put together, the patchwork finally completed. I choose stage left for the beginning and ending, stage right, behind Chris's switchboard, for Act II. The latter is not especially felicitous, because one cannot see the stage from behind the tall switchboard, a drawback that bothers Chris considerably. Everything is seen on monitor; even the curtain has a little screen all its own, showing how far up it is.

On the other side, it is quiet after the Prelude. At various strategic points, monitors show Bonynge in the pit, the modern way to relay his beat to the assistants, who will get the singers on stage at the right moment or lead a backstage band, and to the chorus-master for offstage performers. There is also a monitor in the prompter's box.

In the dusky cavern, reminiscent of Wagner's Nibelheim, shadowy figures move about or stand slouching. Stagehands await the warning light and buzzer that will summon them to action. A long table is set with dozens of small props—goblets, steins, Lindorf's cane, the two swords, the "diamonds," and other oddments. Schlémil's breakaway key to Giulietta's chamber, which will be snatched by Hoffmann from his dead body, is already attached to Harvuot's handsome black-and-silver costume. A plump gnome, Mike, peeks into Giulietta's mirror and makes a horrid face. Wardrobe man John Casamassa sits in a black-cloth cubicle just at the edge of the set where Stewart, Velis, and Nico Castel (Spalanzani) will effect quick changes. The steep stairs to Spalanzani's balcony rise into obscurity. Assistants stand ready to give a hand to Stewart and Joan, particularly to the latter with her big skirts. The two do make it in time, but Bonynge wants a repeat—some musical cue has slipped. Joan, by now already in her dressing room and with her outer costume removed, returns hastily in a black wrapper over petticoats. It is the only stop all day, a tribute to the team.

If stage left is the motor center, stage right is the nerve center of the organization. Chris is in complete command, with Stanley Levine at his right. Just as Chris is about to lift a long finger to cue the electrician, who will manipulate a lever that controls the rheostat that raises the curtain (a house that Jack built), comes an SOS. A table has tipped over on the scene. Chris sandpipers around the corner of his barrier and rights the table. Only seconds have been lost. (The Met prides itself on "Curtain at 8" on the dot.)

Once launched, the show is directed from here. Rudy Kuntner is warned of light cues coming up, all of which have been entered on Chris's score during rehearsals. (Some will emanate from the big board in its booth at the back of the orchestra seats, especially the follow spots that have to hit the performer "on the nose.") Chris pushes buttons to alert dressing and rehearsal rooms, supplementing calls over the loudspeaker by Levine. Red lights show up on the switchboard, and the "callee" must push his own button to cancel his light; otherwise, a posse will be sent out. All this mechanism replaces the legs and lungs of the old "call boy."

Half of today's switchboard is for stage operations. A separate board handles drop scenery. Chris presides coolly over this maze. He has, he says, "learned everyone's language—artists, technicians, electricians, directors."

Back on the prop side for Act III, it is largely a matter of peering out from the darkness of the wings to the slit of light on the stage. Magic dwells there. And true magic comes to us for a moment: Joan's incomparable voice trilling, running its two octaves from high to low D-flat, and at such close range that one's body vibrates with its vibrations. Antonia is singing her death warrant in glory.

At the end, everyone is in the clouds. The relief is almost devastating. Velis has invited us all to a party in his dressing room and soon the jollity spills over into the corridor, which is awash with champagne and congratulations and back-slapping and embraces and kisses and gladness and bubbles. This has been the real test, and they have passed it triumphantly.

The only sour note comes from George Kolombatovich. Schlémil's sword has unaccountably broken in half—a flaw in the blade. It would never do for Hoffmann to win by default.

Now the creators of the Met's new *Tales of Hoffmann* have two days for relaxation and soul-searching.

·   ·   ·

The actual first-night performance came not exactly as an anticlimax, but more as an expectation realized; no surprises, no serious mishaps. Everyone looked flushed and happy at the Opera Guild party that honored the cast afterward on the Grand Tier at the house. Joan loomed especially regal in a low-cut black gown.

Nor did any letdown appear next day, when the important newspaper reviews looked favorably on most of the proceedings. Harold Schonberg in the *Times*, who had gradually warmed to Bonynge, conceded that he had begun to develop as a technician —or, at least, seemed to have begun. There was no qualification in his admiration of Joan: she was nothing short of magnificent, with championship singing, and when she and Placido blended in duets, "the house was filled with a kind of controlled, forward-projected sound rare in this day and age." Everyone else came in for a pat: Stewart as one of the evening's gems; Velis a genius at characterization; Tourangeau, splendid. Adding to Bonynge's meed: he conducted with taste and knowledge and only one or two awkward moments.

Only the production bothered Schonberg, who cursed the darkness without mentioning the one lighted candle on the tavern table. This practice of leaving the tavern visible at one side to emphasize the dreamlike nature of Hoffmann's adventures has been employed many times, but here it did not please anyone (Martin

Mayer in *Musical America* called it a disaster) except Speight Jenkins of the *Post*. He also approved Bonynge's version, commenting on the final Quartet as a musical bang of cosmic proportions to end the show.

. . .

Here I need to say a word about versions. Misconceptions about this score have prevailed for generations; its unfinished state at the composer's death left many many loose ends and uncertainties. Did Offenbach intend spoken dialogue in the tradition of the Paris Opéra-Comique where *Hoffmann* had its premiere in 1881? Or were there original recitatives? And wasn't it true that Offenbach's friend Ernest Guiraud wrote those recitatives to replace that dialogue, as he had done for a Vienna performance of Bizet's *Carmen*? And which act came last—Antonia or Giulietta? Giulietta had been left out of the premiere and only restored later, improperly in the middle, as musicologists have since argued.

The ins and outs of this debate, almost a century old, have no place here, except for one observation. At about this time a French conductor and *Hoffmann* expert, Antonio de Almeida, made public his discovery in the hands of Offenbach's descendants more than a thousand pages of original manuscript. These show that the composer himself had composed recitatives and had fully intended them to be used. This utterly routs claims of "restoration of original dialogue." But Bonynge's version is no worse, and is considerably better, than dozens of others who have practiced mayhem upon the helpless score, investing it with diverse horrors, for he is to be credited with firmly establishing that the Muse is Hoffmann's ultimate love and his protector in the form of Niklausse. This is shown in the Prologue and Epilogue, which all too often are omitted or truncated in other productions.

Thus we were stuck with this version, so to speak, and vulnerable to what slings and arrows the critics might fling. Not to be taken seriously was *Women's Wear Daily*, which thought "the soporific evening much too expensive a substitute for choral hydrate."

The weeklies came out with seldom an encouraging word. Alan Rich in *New York* magazine spewed the most virulence. Bonynge came in for "half-baked musicology of a piece with his conducting." The production was "a distorted torso draped in flabby flesh, a clutter and mess."

A ray of light came from *The New Yorker*, where the visiting English critic, Desmond Shawe-Taylor, was accustomed to writing about Joan and Richard and looked beneath the surface. The production and direction and costumes deserved to be called ingenious and fanciful; the costumes were even handsome (though he may have credited Klein with Joan's Varona-created gowns along with the others.) Mistakenly (although he did not know it at the time), he called the recitatives spurious, but deplored the fact that the talk was in a language unfamiliar to actors and audience. Bonynge, at his best in French music, conducted with spirit and considerable skill.

Martin Mayer shared the misplaced praise for the restoration of dialogue and condemnation of its execution ("De Gaulle would have bombed the opera house"). He rather grudgingly admitted that "Bonynge loves, deeply understands, and dammit can *conduct* the score!" Joan, though she worked hard at the dramaturgy, was not convincing.

To this day the tall soprano still has to bear on her shapely shoulders the accusation of nonacting. With a review such as this, one sighs: "Here we go again!" Oddly enough, it was Schonberg, usually so severe in this department, who applied some balm. She continues to grow, he wrote, moving more gracefully and acting with infinitely more assurance, with a great amount of convincing detail. He credited her with working out an amusing routine as Olympia (no medal here for the director), as being extremely touching as Antonia, and handling herself with dignity and assurance as Giulietta.

There we might perhaps leave the New York *Hoffmann*, except for a delicious detail that the audience hardly noticed. It happened during the second performance and, consequently, was captured by the TV cameras. In the second act, Placido, in too exuberant an embrace, knocked askew the large hat that Joan had worried about all along. She righted it quickly, but later, when Ricky and I saw the mishap in the screening room at the Lincoln Center television office, we hooted. Perhaps it is just as well that the TV experimental version will never reach the public. Varona later designed an untippable headdress for Australia, where all our thoughts turned next.

All this time I had been in contact with the Australian Information Service, inspired with the idea of following the stars to the faraway continent and observing them in the familiar opera under unfamiliar circumstances. So it was as a "cultural emissary," accredited by the Australian government, that I next saw Offenbach's opera. On the first page of my article in *Opera News* (which had started the whole thing), Ricky's autograph reads: "See you in Aussie!"

CHAPTER

21

Intermission: Very Fine Feathers

✣ BARBARA MATERA'S ATELIER FORMERLY PERCHED
atop a ten-story building on West Forty-third Street in New
York City. It is there that Joan spends a good many of her waking
hours while in New York, in that most tiresome of occupations,
trying on clothes. One hour standing on one's feet or revolving
slowly equals about six hours of active rehearsal. The prima donna
takes it stoically. "It's me job," she answers absentmindedly to a
wondering query about her stamina.

There she was one morning, trying, and approving, the three
elaborate dresses and one great cloak she would wear for the Australian *Tales of Hoffmann*. She had enjoyed only a brief night's
rest after flying back from an engagement in Portugal, and would
leave within twenty-four hours for the Met tour. Yet she stood
patiently for a punishing three and a half hours, sitting down only
when a headdress or hat had to be positioned. She had rolled up
her red hair into pincurls revealing a nobly shaped head, to facilitate
fitting the headpieces. This is also her procedure at performances
in order to accommodate the inevitable wig. It is much simpler
now that she has cut her Mélisande-like tresses.

Barbara supervised the entire fitting, assisted by Courtney
Davis (quite a gifted draper on her own) and Connie Peterson,
with Woody Shelp bringing headdresses in and out.

First to consider was the long, frilly, rose-sprinkled organdy
fichu for the ill-fated Antonia, which had to be draped over the
shoulders and caught in two panels at the waist. The 1830s gown
was pale blue taffeta, with its sweeping skirt held out by layers of
petticoats. There were no dangerous hoops, for which Joan was
grateful.

At one moment, the singer's face, while looking at Antonia in the mirror, perhaps reflected that thwarted prima donna's unhappiness, but perhaps it was only her own concentration and growing fatigue.

Over this costume, as it would hastily be thrown in the opera for Stella's final entrance, Barbara placed the swirling violet silk cape, with its heavily embroidered collar and front panels—all handwork. Woody brought in the felt shape that would blossom into Stella's huge black velvet hat (or was it deep purple?) tipped over one eye, loaded with flowers. It was a beauty, but I still coveted José Varona's Met picture hat for Stella—a flatter and more becoming shape, elaborately trimmed with feathers.

Next, several girls carefully carried in a confection of froth and frills that resolved itself into the entrancing costume for Olympia, in which Joan would skitter briskly around the stage as the mechanical doll. It presented a picture of delicate grace, breathtaking for its exquisite workmanship and myriad detail. A V-shaped bodice joined a wide apron edged with silver lace. Three scalloped tiers of fine lace underlined as many rows of dainty rosebuds, each with its spray of green leaves—and all handmade by one of Barbara's experienced and talented European workers. At the neck, a narrow white chiffon collar joined Joan's own skin to resemble the porcelain of the doll. Varona, whose detailed sketches lay scattered on a nearby table, dropped by to give approval. He suggested mittens, instead of Olympia's Met gloves of white silk, thus allowing her fingers freedom to make doll-like gestures. He dispensed with the gauzy little bird that had been wired to her left wrist, a fanciful touch, but not effective.

The headpiece, which ended up as a great white ornamented wig topped with a curling ostrich plume, instead of the Met's tiny tricornered hat, was only rudimentary at the moment.

"It's too short here for my long face, but mustn't be too long in back," cautioned Joan, as professionally careful of detail as all the workers who clustered anxiously around.

I had glimpsed a long greenish-blue heap of chiffon, gold embroidery, and beads stretched out on a bench, and now came the time to try it. It was Giulietta's alluring costume. I caught my breath in admiration as Joan appeared in its sea-green folds. A long, subtly curved body, finely embroidered bosom seductively visible through layers of sheer chiffon, great wings for sleeves, iridescent with green and blue beads—the very spirit of the Adriatic temptress. This had to be the most slimming and sexy costume Joan had ever worn. How refreshing, and revelatory, to banish the really unnecessary hiding of the hipline by the bouffant skirts she constantly demanded. Seen in this well-designed covering, Joan is well proportioned, graceful, and even sinuous. But she continues to apologize for her "figger."

It is true that the figure is rather heavy-hipped, but it is the spacious rib cage that is truly astonishing—the housing for those lungs that furnish the phenomenal breath on which floats the glorious voice.

Barbara has contrived a way of fastening her bodices that secures a perfect fit, yet allows flexibility for any changes that may occur between wearings. She laces them up exactly like old-time corsets, with eyelets and soft, strong cords of a fabric that matches the costume.

After a few moments of rest came the comparatively less taxing try-ons of daytime clothes—another aspect of Barbara's expertise. She makes almost all of Joan's personal wardrobe. Otherwise, favored occasionally are Hardie Amies and one or two others.

Later, when I talked to Barbara alone, I discovered that the two women met when Joan made her first Boston appearance in 1964 as Elvira in *I Puritani*. Born in Kent, Barbara had worked in various London theaters, including Sadler's Wells and the Old Vic, as well as at Stratford-on-Avon. She then headed her own business for seven years. She came to America in 1961, associating first with Van Horn in Philadelphia. After they merged with the more famous Brooks establishment, she stayed there. At last she branched out for herself. It had been Brooks who sent her to Boston. She had heard Joan in *Lucia* and the Carnegie Hall *Beatrice di Tenda* in 1961, as well as a New Jersey recital in some big gymnasiumlike hall. Properly awed, the young costumer went to call on Joan in the Bonynges' little apartment on Ninety-fourth Street. She found the singer easy enough to get along with, very businesslike, but still a bit wary at first. In Boston, they had only one fitting. Sarah Caldwell's gifted and eccentric way with the Opera Company of Boston then, as later, consisted of equal parts of genius and uncertainty, with regular processes of opera-giving fitted in somehow, anyhow.

The two women and their husbands became warm friends, one of the few personal anchors Joan has been able to put down in the sea of fluctuating operatic life.

Then the 1965 Australian tour came up, with five whole operas to do. Fortunately, one of them, Rossini's *Semiramide*, was already in the bag, so to speak. But Barbara was still at Brooks, and had to work at home nights on the gargantuan task. Joan would come evenings to the Matera house for fittings. It took from December to May. Barbara made the costumes all by herself, with only a few women to help now and then. It was not as if she had fifty women to help, such as she often employs now.

"I certainly couldn't do it again!" she exclaimed. There were four costumes each for *Traviata*, *Lucia*, and *Faust*; three for *Sonnambula*, added to the five for *Semiramide* already done. A Brooks man helped with the packing of the many boxes. She had them weighed; the cost of shipping came to $1,500! Barbara almost fainted.

"I called Joan, and could hardly breathe as I told her. Quite matter-of-factly, she said: 'Well, if that's what it's got to be . . .' and paid. Those costumes don't owe her a penny."

Barbara did not have to work on the other operas of the Australian tour in which Joan did not sing, but the five were quite enough.

For the current Australian assignment, a separate set had to be made for the second cast that would sing in English—hardly a one would be used from the original set. Matera shipped fabrics, all identical to the originals, except the chiffons, which don't travel well. Off went the material for the little roses as well, and I wondered how it would all turn out from Australian shops. At least they were expert in making scenery, Varona testified. The cost to the company, Barbara figured, was almost as much as the originals. She thought they would put *those* under glass.

After having made sixty or more creations for Joan, and even with their deep friendship, Barbara confesses that she still gets more nervous with this prima donna than with anyone else. There is so much to do for her, and she is so intensely interested, cares so much, is such a perfectionist.

Barbara at the moment was rooting around through great shelves and in drawers under the many breast-high cutting tables in her huge loft. She was searching for a sleeve pattern she had made for a Sutherland concert dress. At last she found it—a great wing of thin, tough paper—and proceeded to slash into delicate white chiffon with what seemed to be reckless abandon. The shaped result went to the dyer on the premises, who presently came back to show its shades of green.

"Oh, fine, but it should be a little deeper . . . just dip it, don't dye," instructed Barbara.

The "wing" would be one of two sleeves, expertly pleated in

a manner comparable to the lost secret of the famous designer Fortuny, then beaded in exquisite patterns. (This is a technique for which Matera is noted, as her colleague and rival Ray Diffen attested when he dropped in to order work on a *Salomé* costume for Maralyn Niska at the New York City Opera.)

Joan was to wear this dress for two concert appearances. The color, most becoming to the titian hair and fair skin, would distinguish her concert in Sydney.

Barbara had to whiz that one together, she confided, to replace a similar gown in white that was stolen off a rack in the anteroom and never traced. But the green was even more striking.

Shortly after witnessing the lady herself graced by these creations, we came to photograph them without her, she having left. My friend, the gifted fashion reporter and photographer Bill Cunningham, a most charming and persuasive gentleman, soon had the shop working with him and loving it. At the end of a busy hour of snapping, he called out: "Let's get everyone who worked on the Doll's costume together." To our astonishment, every woman in the shop put down what she was doing and came forward. Each one had added her touch to the marvelous whole. The result appeared in a stunning full-page color reproduction in the Australian *Women's Weekly*, for which I wrote a piece about this fascinating encounter.

CHAPTER

22

Australia Once More

BIG, BOLD, AND BEAUTIFUL, SHE CAME OUT OF THE house and advanced, smiling her wide smile, to meet the three or four press photographers who had been tipped off to catch this end of her first official visit to Sydney's Opera House. She had no words for them, only a friendly wave of the hand. Her titian hair gleamed above the luxurious red fox collar of the brown wool coat that trimly hugged her figure. In the car, she remained silent, storing up confidence for the ordeal ahead. When we approached the Opera House and started to penetrate the gloomy tunnel of the Concourse entrance, she spoke up: "Why not stay outside in the light, so the photographers won't have to fuss?"

This was typical: a thoughtful as well as practical suggestion for getting the business done in the best possible way.

She alighted from the car, which drew up to the edge of the water line, and was immediately surrounded by the insistent reporters with their umbilically attached cameramen. They pushed back to the retaining wall, and could easily have crowded her into Sydney Harbour. The questions came thick and fast, many of them defensive, reflecting uncertainty; a few aggressive, even defiant.

Do you still feel Australian? Would you like to live here? How long will you go on singing? Wasn't your last trip here not very happy for you personally? How do you like the Opera House?

She fielded them all with, as one reporter put it, "more ease and sophistication than you would have thought, and quite assured. At forty-eight, every inch a prima donna *assoluta.*"

The prima donna laughed in the sunshine, and quite earnestly tried to answer each question for its own worth. She was never able to parry, evade, or toss out a pert quip.

182

Certainly, she felt Australian. She had, after all, been born right here in Sydney. She thought she would not want to live here permanently, however. Her real home was in Switzerland, and, of course, she traveled a lot.

"My husband says I'll still be singing at seventy, but I do feel a bit long in the tooth." (It's hard to imagine another diva so candid.)

"What do you mean? Our last visit was unhappy? We were all rather tired when we arrived." (There was no further reference in the reputable papers about the chaotic 1965 entrance into Sydney.)

The Opera House looked fine. She was aware of some deficiencies, but had not had a chance to explore it. After all, this was only her second visit to the new house, and like the first, it would be spent mostly below decks, rehearsing assiduously.

Well!

La Stupenda was home again! Joan Sutherland had come back, her international reputation and domination of the opera world assured. The headlines blared, and the lady interviewers filled their columns with her graciousness, lack of "side," craving for sweet and fattening delicacies, difficulties in carrying out the role of a proper mother, and all the usual tidbits that the sisterhood and their readers find absorbing.

Note was taken—it could hardly have been avoided—of the absence from the scene of the husband-conductor. He had not shown up for this first press crush; nor did he accompany his wife at any others. Not until later would he be personally quizzed, and only in one-to-one encounters. This had been a conscious decision, probably a wise one. Memories still rasped about Richard Bonynge's collision with the Sydney journalists he considered uncivilized. Fear of a similar incident had dictated their secretive entrance into the home country. With only one or two higher-ups in the Opera management in the know, Joan and Richard and Huguette Tourangeau had arrived on Saturday by plane from the Fiji Islands, where they had soaked blissfully in the sun—and nary a soul wiser. (Perhaps this was not altogether to Huguette's satisfaction, Joan hinted later. A prima donna hullabaloo would have suited the pretty Canadian, who knew exactly how to handle one.)

The sneak entrance ruined my plans for reporting and photographing their touchdown on native soil after nine years. But the extra days ahead of the big event were useful indeed. Hours were spent touring the fabulous Opera House with the blessing of Frank Barnes, the general manager, and the guidance of Ava Hubble, the attentive and congenial press girl. I met the public relations officers of both the House and the Opera Company—two Davids; Brown for the House, Colville for the Company, both tall as basketball centers.

Unlike other opera companies that owned their buildings, it seemed that this one merely rented, and, with its own staff, occupied an office downtown. The situation of the Symphony Orchestra and other groups that played in the Concert Hall and other spaces in the House was parallel. It was an arrangement that caused considerable contention and heartburn, inefficiency and budgetary horrors.

Moffatt Oxenbould, the affable assistant to the general manager, had arranged for me to be in the car that took Joan for her first meeting. No less helpful and friendly were David Colville's two lieutenants, Gai Murray and Glen Lehman. David Brown, stiltlike, obligingly took my camera and held it high for a shot of Joan's smiling face peeping through the crowd of interrogators. All of these attractive and accommodating people were to be constant in their assistance to a visitor.

Once inside the House, after the press ordeal, Joan stood tight-lipped and wary beside the smiling José Varona, scene and costume designer, waiting for the next trial—her first rehearsal with most of the *Hoffmann* cast. The day before had been comparatively secluded, chiefly a welcome from general manager John Winther, and consultation with Tito Capobianco, an old friend and confidant. Today she would meet the rest of the cast, all new to her except Huguette, who had been brought along to sing Niklausse. Any outsider was discouraged.

· · ·

The building in which we spent most of our waking hours from then on may be the most photogenic in the world, a masculine counterpart to the delicate Taj Mahal. For all its 125,000 tons of concrete, 6,000 tons of steel, and 28,000 tons of roof weight, it seems to float fragilely on the Bennelong Point that thrusts out into Sydney Harbour, belying its strength and solidity. It has inspired reams of poetic comparisons: inescapable are the images of a flock of doves, a panoply of white sails. Yet these visions are perceptible only from the air or a distant approach across the water. To stroll around the spacious granite "broadwalk" that surrounds the buildings, to glance up at the dizzying shells in their odd, asymmetrical placement, never quite to be sorted out and identified except by recourse to a map, is to be overwhelmed by their massive and all-too-solid magnificence. The figures that underlie this splendor are all the more subduing. The million or more Swedish ceramic tiles that cover the roofs gleam in the sun; the 16,000 square feet of French glass filling the mouths of the shell roofs glitter with their underlying topaz tint.

A silhouette so individual and unmistakable has become a symbol, a decoration for countless baubles and souvenirs, perhaps destined to replace the familiar kangaroo as the nation's emblem.

Intimidating indeed is the mammoth flight of stairs one must climb to reach the interior; they spread wide and steep, and are at this time missing handrails (which were later installed). My legs and blood pressure are grateful that I never had to toil up, and only came down them once. As privileged as the "aged or infirm" by virtue of an ID card that marked me as part of "the Sutherland party," I could use the one lift, virtually hidden in the underground passage that leads from the Concourse motor entrance. It goes only as high as the stalls (orchestra level to Americans). Woe to the slow or "infirm" who occupied Circle seats. That meant scrambling up a flight of spiral, slick, marble steps with no handrail—and no breath at the top—to avoid being shut out at curtain time. This is but one of the inconveniences locked in by architects insensitive to human needs. Lacking in loos is the alliterative way to describe another— the dearth of comfort retreats. One quickly learned their hidden locations and triumphed if there was no long waiting line. (I've since learned one possible origin of the word "loo." With their passion for wordplay, often unintelligible to strangers, the English Cockneys may have derived it from "Waterloo.")

But these are minor flaws when compared to the lamentable blunder perpetrated by political shortsightedness. The surrealistic history of the project has often been recounted, along with the remarkable fact that the eventual cost of $102 million was absorbed by public lottery. The 1957 prize-winning Danish architect Jörn Utzon had stayed with his futuristic and seemingly impracticable design through its initial difficulties, but gave up in despair in 1966 during the construction of the shell roofs, with their heretofore unheard-of innovations in the engineering and building trades. Four Australian architects took over and managed to complete the exterior. When the interior of the shells came to be constructed, the story goes that the ABC (Australia's Broadcasting Corporation), all-powerful in the public concert life as well as radio (and now television), was asked—or volunteered—to decide whether the larger of the two main shells, originally thought of as housing the Opera, should remain so, or whether it should be allocated to concert activities.

The question was at once posed: Which brings in the most

revenue? The opera company at the time struggled for its very existence and had not yet found a firm foundation for its limited activities. On the other hand, each of the six Australian states boasted its own Symphony Orchestra (funded mainly by ABC, partially by the government), and ABC imported most of the foreign musical soloists and ensembles, gradually exceeding even the famed J. C. Williamson enterprise (which sadly expired from attrition just at the time of this writer's visit).

The answer was writ plain: Use the large hall for concerts; the smaller for opera.

Not only did this wrench the building itself out of proper function (it prevented the opera's use of the huge chamber under the large hall for scenery storage and movement and made installation of scenery possible only by painful hoisting from a shallow restricted space under the small hall), but it provided an opera house of only fifteen hundred seats, leaving the 2,700-seat auditorium for concerts. On the surface, that seemed proper: a smaller house is good for opera, and concerts always draw large audiences. But the sightlines in the smaller hall are not all desirable, the acoustics are tricky, and, worse, the limited intake from tickets, even at steep prices (as much as $37.50 for galas such as Sutherland nights) prohibits the opera company from coming anywhere near its budget through box office.

Perhaps the gravest indignity suffered by the lyric troupe in performance is the nonexistent space backstage and the excruciatingly small orchestra pit. All of this had become apparent with the opera's first season in the new house the year previously—the ambitious mounting of Prokofiev's *War and Peace*, on September 28, 1973. The Russian composer's score calls for a huge orchestra, a full chorus, and scenery of some magnitude to fit the "war" episodes.

Those who witnessed the show marveled at the results. Edward Downes (Joan's onetime detractor turned friend), who conducted, remarked afterward that it seemed a miracle, worth everyone's impossibly hard work. The comparatively shallow stage was used to the hilt; the panorama spread wide instead of deep. The orchestra crowded in somehow, reduced to such proportions that barely skimmed disaster. Backstage, they still remember the ordered chaos with horror.

The orchestra pit, which could hold thirtyish players comfortably, fiftyish uncomfortably, barely got by on seventy-five for this one. (The average orchestra numbers from eighty to 105.) Of course, no big Wagner or Strauss works should be done—still, *Tannhäuser* and *Rosenkavalier* were, and successfully, it seemed.

Every possibility had been explored toward enlarging that hellish cavity, where violin bows hit the ceiling on an upstroke, and wind players at the back were threatened with decapitation if the turntable above should rotate. (That adjunct to modern staging had since been abandoned; if a turnaround is needed, it is constructed atop the stage floor and not allowed to protrude over the apron.)

When enlargement to the sides was contemplated, they discovered that the inside wall could not be touched because of intrusion on other functioning chambers, while the outside wall contained the entire electrical cable system of the building. It seemed hopeless. However, after struggling with the problem for several years, in 1978 they accomplished a modest enlargement, retreating still farther under the stage.

The sides of the stage were meant for single artists or ensembles in single file, presumably, as an entrance. They seemed no wider than six or eight feet. On one side, the lighting console has to crowd in. There is no back stage to speak of, and to reach this commodious playing ground, the stars have one small elevator from dressing-room level; the others must straggle up steep, narrow, concrete-bound-and-stepped stairs, so constricted that big costumes have to climb sideways.

Producing is, therefore, not exactly easy, and playing not exactly fun, but they manage somehow to put on excellent shows and with staunchly good spirit.

Recently, still another remedy has been found: to produce opera in the large hall, where it was meant to be in the first place. About seven hundred seats are removed in front to make room for the orchestra below the rather high stage level. The affordable spectacle is what grand opera was meant to be. *Aida* and *Salome* were sensational successes in the larger frame. *The Merry Widow*, with Joan in the title role, was rapturously received in the Concert Hall in 1978.

One amenity sets the Sydney Opera House apart from many others: a king-size Green Room. Originating in the Paris Opéra as a rendezvous for the sportive Jockey Club members and their chosen ballerinas, this backstage retreat has undergone mutations in the opera houses and concert halls of the world and has become vestigial in many. Nonexistent in, for example, the old Metropolitan, a chilly, inhospitable corridor in the Philadelphia Academy of Music, an impersonally furnished cube—not too spacious—in the new Metropolitan, the Green Room should serve as a neutral meeting ground for the artists and their friends.

Sydney's may be unique. It is set between the Opera and Concert Hall complexes, so that one may encounter at some time or another all the opera personnel as well as symphony players, soloists, technicians, and a dignitary or two. At one end of its enormity is a cafeteria, serving moderately priced and moderately tasty food. Tables of various sizes fill that half of the room. The other half contains a bar (a glass of mildly exhilarating native champagne was 45 cents at my visit), and is red-carpeted, with great overstuffed chairs.

Monitor screens told us what was going on in the two halls. One night it turned out rather confusing to hear simultaneously the great choral movement of Beethoven's Ninth from the concert side while on the opera screen Joan was singing some *Hoffmann* roulades. Here Marge Helmore, the wardrobe mistress, worked at her needlepoint; chorister Faye Delmaine busily embroidered a huge tablecloth; supers stood around in their slave costumes; a chess game managed to keep aloof from the bustle. In neutral ground, between the two service areas, a bridge game could be said to be permanent. At every free moment, the four would neatly cover a square table and begin to shuffle. They seemed to keep fixed positions: Norman Parker, technical director, at North; Jim Paine, a scenery flyman, at West; Ian Audsley, of the mechanical staff, at South; and Peter Webb, prop maker, at East. Nothing could disturb them, but they suffered their pictures to be taken. After all, it did not interrupt play.

It was the place for a convivial glass hoisted with chorusmaster Geoffrey Arnold, or with Elizabeth Connell, the incandescent mezzo who lit up the *Jenufa* stage as the fierce Kostelnicka; or to get press releases from Gai Murray or Glen Lehman; or to tease Tony Everingham, stage director (stage manager, in American terms), or to rendezvous with Jennifer Bermingham, the little treasure who became my guide and companion throughout rehearsal time (she would sing Niklausse in the English performances that followed the French series); or to interview John Copley, the impish stage director; or to watch him spin out some naughty tales to the spontaneous combustion of laughter from Caroline Lill, one of the gifted repetiteurs, and a couple of other gals, and, joining them, manage to capture a few wicked ones on tape. The Green Room, in short, is the heart and nerve center of the great complex. Very adult, as Ricky put it.

.   .   .

There can be no doubt that the set of *Hoffmann* performances, which brought together significant personages from the big world outside and the native nucleus of performers and technicians, reinforced the pride of Australians in their opera company and provided a foundation for an even prouder future.

The opera itself was a resounding success. None of the tributes paid by the press was forced or shammed. The public, many of whose members would have paid $500 for a ticket, loved the whole thing, even if most of them could not get in. The very idea excited them. It seemed to certify Australia as one of the great companies, sister to the most illustrious, taking the sharp edge off the isolation that still is both bane and blessing.

As evidence of this, the event, thought David Geiger of the *Australian*, was more exciting for what it revealed about the opera development of Australia than for what it revealed about Joan Sutherland. What Joan did on these occasions was not spectacularly more than what she had done when she was last here in 1965. Even with her astonishing change in dramatic credibility, the infiltration of these world-class artists into the "outlander" company proved that the resident talent could rise to the occasion—even excel itself. The great personal local triumph was scored by Raymond Myers as the four villains, his black bass and devilish malice bringing some magnificent moments. Henri Wilden, the Belgian tenor, made a handsome and ardent hero, and his French, added to Tourangeau's, gave that extra *soupçon* of class. Vocally, he veered between acceptable and stunning, Geiger thought. Graeme Ewer won the right to a spot among the world's celebrated character tenors with his four comic servants. Various others had their time in the spotlight—the sort of collaboration that makes stardom take on real meaning, commented Roger Covell in the *Herald*.

But, of course, that spotlight never got very far away from the heroine. To hear Joan in four such varied roles was the opportunity of a lifetime. Her trio with Myers and Elizabeth Connell (as the Mother, in the pit as at the Met) proved her the complete dramatic soprano, while in the doll scene she demonstrated something very like sporting prowess, according to Covell, who, as a true Australian, could be counted on to drag in sport somehow. "The tempos were fast, the variations and cadenzas were dazzling, and there were impeccably proportioned echo effects, diamond-cut staccato passages, and fearless excursions into the D-flat and E-flat area of soprano summitry," he wrote.

Bonynge was equal partner in the appraisals. He was in vital command of the singing, of the pace as a whole, and of the Elizabethan Trust Orchestra. In holding firm control over the ensemble, he proved to be worth his weight in gold.

Varona's sets were exquisite, glittering in what one writer called "the cogwheeled aerial jewelry of Spalanzani's laboratory," and with a cunning gilt cage to hold Olympia until she was ready to appear. The Venetian scene dripped glittering stalactites into the greenish blue dusk, and Antonia's chaste salon boasted a dainty harpsichord that lit up malignantly green when Dr. Miracle wrought his sinister magic. The sides of the tavern were let stay throughout in the traditional way. Among Varona's costumes Giulietta's caused a sensation, and there was a concerted gasp from the audience when Joan was thought to be topless.

Tito Capobianco and his wife, Elena ("Gigi") Denda, almost stole the show from Joan, thought Maria Prerauer. Capobianco created an uncanny, nightmarish atmosphere, piling horror on horror all through the macabre story. The slow motion of the Venetian duel under weird green light made a specially vivid impression.

It was a night to go down in Australian history, no doubt the sort of marvelous event for which the Sydney Opera House was conceived. When the two distinguished visitors accepted from John Winther a certificate of honorary membership in the company, the augur was plain: they intended to return. The fact became known in a few days. Come back Joan and Richard would; he as music director of the company, and to conduct *Carmen* with Tourangeau, *Lakmé* with his wife. But not until July 1976. Before that, other adventures called.

CHAPTER
23

Aussie Episodes from My Notebook

✳ JOAN AND RICKY IN AUSTRALIA IN 1974 REMAIN IN
my memory as a series of vignettes, apart from my own adventures as a "cultural emissary" from the United States, the first,
I believe, to be sent out by the Australian Information Service.
Captivated by the idea of an American journalist traipsing after the
Bonynges and getting to know their world in the opera house in
their own home town, that congenial ex-newspaperman, John Cole-
man, had the AIS lay on the amenities from here to there and
back. My calendar shows trips to Melbourne, Canberra, and Adelaide, visits to the theater, interviews with government and artistic
officials, and a warmhearted reception from all those generous
people. One tends to think of Australians as very much like pioneer
Americans, and this is partly true. But because so much of my
experience lay outside the Bonynge ambience, it does not belong
in this narrative.

· · ·

On the way from the Sydney airport, my AIS mentor, Stewart
F. O. Wallace, drove past the house the Bonynges would occupy,
and I was lucky enough to catch the landlady coming out of the
door. She gave me the Bonynges' phone number. My early arrival
enabled me to settle in at a convenient motel, the Cosmopolitan,
in a section known as Double Bay ("Double Bay, double pay!" was
the chant I heard many times afterward, and appreciated from the
start). It was about halfway between the Opera House and the
Bonynges. As usual, there was no way to be close to both.

Once the rehearsal grind began, I saw Joan and Ricky almost
every day. It was a rehearsal situation almost identical in character

to those in other opera houses and needs no elaboration here. The other times with Joan and Ricky, more intimate and relaxed, rightfully belong in this narrative.

. . .

When Joan gets that withdrawn look, it is best not to approach her. She has obviously gone within to ponder something that concerns her deeply. Once later, at the dinner table in Switzerland, the look appeared, and to Ricky's question, she came back to reality with the apology that she had been thinking of a recent tragedy to some children that had been in the news.

This day in the Green Room she sat at the head of one of the long tables, plying knife and fork busily to the purpose of demolishing a large plate of veal and potatoes. Thinking her preoccupation was only with the viands (which, to be truthful, did not deserve such religious attention), I asked her a question. Receiving no reply, I turned to Chester for conversation. Suddenly, she came back to us and said: "I was thinking about Antonia." Capobianco had given her several bits of business she had not used before, notably the "rising from the dead," which she did not altogether relish.

Several of the performances I witnessed from the Green Room, because there were no tickets to be had. That comparatively tiny house was sold out to its gills, and I was lucky to be out front four times. I would pay a fleeting call to Joan, possibly Huguette, and occasionally to Ricky in their dressing rooms, to wish toi-toi, then station myself at one vantage point or another. A favorite perch was just outside Joan's dressing room, next to a tall double stack of wig boxes, where I could talk to her dresser, Sandra Siddall, a pretty girl. John Lauder, the men's dresser, and Caroline Turner, who performed the same service for Huguette, would occasionally wander over to gossip. They all seemed very young for the job; I compared them with the veterans at the Met, but their experience was mounting fast, to match their enthusiasm.

One night just as the Prologue ended, I watched Joan emerge from her room and glide to the elevator that would take her to the stage. She was in the doll's costume, holding the long, cumbersome skirt up a trifle; her eyes were fixed straight ahead, the "veil" down over her face—that mask of concentration that falls on the performer as a shield before the actual moment of going on. It affects all performers differently, but, with the dedicated ones, you can always see it. Some of the heartier men, usually baritones or basses, rollick in the wings until the moment of their entrance, as if they hadn't a care in the world. Tenors are apt to be tight-lipped, except when uttering strangled sounds of throat clearing. Sopranos vary, but Joan is always in that self-contained, hermetically sealed but invisible package, which miraculously disappears the moment she is "on." She may speak cordially or even sweetly to a well-wisher, but with mind absent and forces gathered within. It is a fearful moment, that one just before the assistant conductor gives a sign, or says: "Go!"

. . .

One night, Joan is dressed for the street before Ricky. It is not necessarily that the process is faster; she is almost always ready before he is, no matter what. After dress rehearsal, waiting in the central space that separates two wings of dressing rooms, holding a "floral tribute" some old friend brought her, she responds wearily to Chester's query about supper. "See what Sir would like," she says.

I have noticed her use of the title for Ricky several times and finally question her. She is, rather surprisingly, embarrassed.

"Oh, Quaintance, do I still do that?" she asks. "I didn't even realize it. It all started when Paul Garner came to us as secretary. We were so close to Noël Coward. And his friends, Cole Lesley and Graham Pine, invariably referred to Noël as 'Master.' So Paul got to calling Ricky 'Sir,' and we all did. I must stop it."

But is she appositely "Madame?" I think not. "Sir" seems a half-serious, half-jesting tribute to Ricky's head-of-household status.

That afternoon they drive me home. It is too late to ask for one of the government cars the AIS so lavishly supplied me with. As we come out of the tunnel, where parking is allowed a few privileged characters, under the building, past the stage-door entrance, a little knot of fans and TV cameramen still patiently wait. They begin to cheer and crowd up to the car's front window, only to draw back, disconcerted and disappointed when confronted by a strange face under a squashy blue beret, instead of the classic features crowned by glowing locks. Joan has chosen the middle of the back seat, and is practically hidden by the flowers.

. . .

Opening night, July 13, is *très gala*. There is to be a formal party in the board-room at intermission. Luckily, someone knows I am invited and admits me to the crowded elevator that carries dressed-up dignitaries and no outsiders. We parade through several corridors and find the room in which a long table is spread with hundreds of delicacies and waiters struggle through with glasses of champagne (French). There is a receiving line, of all things, in that crowded space. I am at the end, and am presented to the Governor General, a tall, sloping man, and his cheery wife. Among the luminaries are Charles Berg, the new opera board chairman, and the beautiful and powerful Lady Fairfax, owner of the *Herald*. I have established contact only with the *Australian*, Rupert Murdoch's "respectable" paper, which has reprinted my *Opera News* article with smeary black-and-white reproductions of Marie Cosinda's color slides. But intermission is soon over, and we hurry back to our seats. In the broad corridor outside, an American can be seen to slide rapidly along the side, trying to reach an upstairs Circle seat. Suddenly, with a panicky look over the shoulder, she discovers that sure enough, there is the Governor General, ambling three paces behind. The brash American has committed a faux pas in a country not yet democratic enough to approve a commoner trying to get ahead of Her Majesty's representative.

. . .

The Opera Company commanded the services of a very good young photographer, John Walsh. It is to him I entrust the mission of shooting Joan in her dressing room doing needlepoint for an article in *Opera News*. I thought it would be amusing to show her working away at her homely task decked out in her doll's extravagant costume. We arrange to do it in the middle of the Prologue, when she will be dressed, but still minutes before her call for the first act. She is sitting with her shoes off, a luxury she snatches at every possible moment, and, though we insist that her feet won't show, she hastily puts on shoes. The photo is charming, and duly appears in the magazine.

While we are there, I steal the opportunity for a picture I covet: me touching Olympia's shoulder to make her speak, as Spalanzani does, and her response with a sidewise smile that always breaks me up. So we do that, and I treasure the slide. All the more reason to hoard it is that I look comparatively tiny beside her in her bouffant costume, big wig, and tall plume.

. . .

It is not often I ask the favor of a ride. My faithful drivers are usually johnny-on-the-spot. On opening night, the crowding backstage to congratulate and embrace and chatter is not to be missed. I land at the stage door at about one A.M., with no transportation. The driver has given me up, this on the one evening I have promised a lift to Ava Hubble's friend, Mrs. Masson, a gentle lady who has run the Metropolitan's auditions here. The considerate stage doorman phones for a cab, but none can be roused. At last, a taxi draws up, but just as we two women are about to climb in, it is claimed by a company functionary, Stephen Hall, accompanied by his mother, a queenly dame whose dignity is sharpened by asperity. Some sort of surface politeness prevails, and they grudgingly allow us to share. The atmosphere remains frigid, however, and Stephen and his mother alight at their hotel with the barest of grace and no intention of sharing the fare. Then Mrs. Masson will not take my money and insists on dropping me at the Cosmopolitan.

Still, I pay in another way, dropping from my camera the electronic flash without which I am lost. Happy ending to this, though. The taxi company finds it, and one of my most congenial drivers takes me out the long way to the taxi office to retrieve it. Meanwhile, however, I have to buy a new one from my little camera shop in Double Bay.

I have been misled in New York by information that the Opera's general manager is this same Stephen Hall. Indeed, he has filled the position temporarily, but is now known as "artistic director." The boss is John Winther. Hall is down for a production of *Tosca*, but his vocation is decidedly not stage direction, for this *Tosca* is a limp business indeed. Rather, with his ingratiating manners and gallant way with the dignified ladies of the budding Friends of the Opera, he belongs in a promotional job.

· · ·

After a performance, Joan is ready to go home, but a little crowd outside the ladies' chorus dressing room causes her to halt. It is a birthday celebration for five choristers at once, and we join the jollity for a few moments, sampling cake and wine. Betty Allen, of course, is there, and so is Pauline Garrick, the buxom "Polly," who I discover is the daughter of Ralph Errolle, a tenor we had all known in earlier days. Polly is a delightful lady, full of energy and anecdotes. The crowd gives room to Joan, at the same time displaying perfect ease and friendliness. She is "just one of us," it is plain to see. Her slim Olympia "cover," who will sing the later performances in English, is Norelle Davidson, ready to hand her a glass reverently, and watching with more awe than most of the others. We leave a wave of noisy conviviality behind.

Quite another kind of party is at the home of Charles Berg. The house is "moderne," with rather heavy furniture and some paintings that we have little chance to inspect. Mrs. Berg, who wears her hair in an extraordinary pagodalike twist atop her head, has concocted every morsel of the feast herself—three different cakes and fancy salads and other delectable mysteries.

This is the first time I have had any chance to talk to John Winther, the general manager, a big, shaggy sort, quietly genial. His soft Danish accent is charming, and his eyes crinkle pleasantly as he speaks. His wife, Lone Koppel Winther, is one of the leading sopranos, and is singing the Jenufa in the fine production of Janáček's opera. Her sister is with them, newly arrived from Denmark. Moffatt Oxenbould, Graeme Ewer, the Bergs' daughter, and the Bonynges, Adam included, are the only other guests. Moffatt is called "personal assistant" to the general manager (and is later promoted to artistic administrator), and Graeme is the company's buffo tenor, one of those priceless artists whom any opera house is lucky to have. He sings the four servant roles in *Hoffmann*, of course.

Joan delights everyone by her informality, and makes the most of the delicious food, digging into a great slice of cake. She will have to watch her diet for a few days. Whenever she is feeling specially relaxed and merry, she puts something outrageous on her head and looks like a mischievous little girl.

The Bergs are agreeable hosts. They take me along one night to a chamber concert in Chalwin Castle, owned by an eccentric philanthropist.

Another party after the premiere of *Jenufa* is more formal. It has been a splendid performance, and everyone is keyed up. John Copley is very happy at his sensitive production and the way it was received, and the conductor, Edward Downes, positively beams. He has given a searching and exciting analysis of the opera in a seminar of the Friends, and has created a burning desire to hear the piece. A rather shy man, he promises me an interview only because the talk is to be about Joan. I learn a great deal about him, too. His eyes are so bad that he shuns camera flashes fearfully, because one would blind him for a half hour. The opera's music director at the time, he later turns over the job to Richard himself, and plans only guest engagements in Australia. Joan, of course, remembers him fondly, and is an old friend of his wife's. They seldom meet nowadays—this party, in fact was their only chance to chat. "When we are on different productions, we merely pass each other in the halls once in a while and wave," Downes explains.

· · ·

One night Joan comes into the Green Room still in her Antonia costume, covered by Stella's lavender folds and crowned with that magnificent hat. She leans wearily against the back of a big chair and says she has promised to meet a group of blind children who have been brought to the performance. Presently they arrive, shepherded by their teacher. They crowd around Joan, asking timid questions and proffering little slips of paper or programs for her autograph. Sweetly, she answers and scribbles. One little boy, advancing until he is practically under her nose and unknowingly placing one foot on the hem of her cloak, simply stands there. I manage to move him off the cloak and get him a scrap of paper to hold out for her signature. Pretty soon, Joan realizes that there is no point in showing her outer costume. She strips off the cloak and doffs the hat, finishing the rather sad little ceremony in comparative comfort.

Back in the dressing-room area, Graeme Ewer, still in his disguise as the deaf servant Frantz, is also signing autographs. José Varona has devised a comical costume for him that includes a built-in ear trumpet that extends a foot or so from Graeme's head, wobbling like a great painted morning glory as he moves.

. . .

"A Great Occasion" and "Low-key Sutherland" are the opposing newspaper views of the gala concert, the first of two, that Joan and Richard give in the big Concert Hall on July 6, anticipating the *Hoffmann* opening by a week. The timing is not exactly the best, but inevitable. I believe that neither of the two relishes concerts very much, although Ricky enjoys digging up bits of old repertoire and also undoubtedly welcomes the feel of his hands on the keyboard in public. Both newspaper critics have a point. It *is* a great occasion: the stunning enclosure of native wood paneling, with its baylike boxes and vaulted ceiling, packed to the brim with her fellow countrymen panting and eager to see their idol, if only in the comparatively tepid atmosphere of a sedate song recital. Hundreds of them will never get into the opera house—the fifteen hundred seats have long ago been snapped up for all eight performances. An extra concert may console a couple of thousand.

So here we are, breathlessly waiting. At last, out she comes, a vision in apple-green chiffon, bordered with silver, its flowing angel sleeves fluttering gracefully in the slight breeze she makes as she glides toward the piano, where handsome Ricky now takes his place.

Perhaps it might be most appropriate to let Maria Prerauer have the first word. This *grande dame* of the critical world writes reams for the *Daily Telegraph*, and is a potent blend of sob sister, acid critic, and den mother. She turns up everywhere, knows everything, and tells it pungently. Her account of the concert is headed with the expected superlatives: "Our Joan's a knockout: La Stupenda was quite stupendous," and there is a subhead: "Superb!" In one-sentence paragraphs, she elaborates:

"She has a dozen voices rolled into one.

"There's never been anything quite like it in this century.

"And made in Australia too."

The quality of the program arouses another critic's disquiet. David Geiger writes in the *Australian*: "Much of it was almost perversely low-key—pretty little songs which she sang very well, but no better than dozens of others far less talented could have done." He bewails the brevity of real operatic material that the singer could get her teeth into, so to speak.

In contrast to his inevitable praise, Roger Covell, a more restrained critic writing in the *Herald*, also is quizzical about the program, saying that "Anyone who automatically exclaims, 'How divine!' when confronted with the bric-a-brac of a Victorian drawing room would have fallen in love at first sight with the program . . . It was a decorator's collection of minor *trouvailles*, picked out by a discerning eye in a cluttered salesroom and made to appear significant in splendid new surroundings."

But this is the way of Sutherland-Bonynge concerts, and the reason for a good many unflattering comments similar to Sydney's. San Francisco, for example (or was it Los Angeles?), gave Joan a booby prize for that inconsequential programming and called it insulting that the list had been practically repeated from a previous recital.

But never mind. Here we are in Sydney, and no one can resist the glowing red hair, the sparkling eyes, the wood-nymph creation of a gown, the heavenly voice (no matter what it sings), and the "dropping kisses and red roses of her exit," in Prerauer's phrase.

From her first entrance, I notice that Joan is walking very carefully, almost sliding along, not lifting her feet an inch. She is wearing silver pumps, and I wonder if they are pinching.

"Lord, no!" she exclaims. "It was that bloody slippery floor. I was scared to death I'd fall flat on whatever!"

Do not let that down-to-earth aftermath spoil the impression of "a great occasion."

.   .   .

Joan does not forget her old friends, and to a man, or woman, they remember her, of course. One day at lunch in the Green Room,

Chester describes his encounter with several of the "girls" who used to play on the basketball team with Joan. He calls their names, and Joan ticks off every one. This happens over and over. They come backstage with their individual memories, and Joan reinforces them.

One lovely day, I snatch the opportunity to take the boat ride around Sydney Harbour, several hours of cruising near the beautiful wooded shores of the dozens of inlets. Often they are dressed up with pretty villas and more modest dwellings, all in light colors, none unsightly. As we pass some point of interest, a hefty baritone voice booms over a loudspeaker, calling it to our attention. I discover the source: a tiny cubicle on the lower deck, where a corpulent figure matches the bullfrog voice. We have some conversation, and he learns my mission.

"I played accompaniments for her," he says, to my astonishment. Sure enough, he is George Brown, ex-navy man, ex-pianist, who played at least once for Joan's "I Know Where I'm Going" and "Green Hills of Home" at the Burwood Bowling Club in her earlier quest for fame. I later came across his name in the scrapbooks.

"Our Joan" indeed.

24

Kaleidoscope: Evening at the Bonynges

✳ JOAN, PROFOUNDLY TOUCHED BY THE WARMTH OF her reception from the Australian public and her old friends, chatted over the inevitable needlepoint one evening in her daintily furnished bedroom, before the informal dinner to which I had been invited. "You really forget just how marvelous Sydney is. It's gone ahead so much, and so well. Some people think they've ruined the city, but it's splendid."

And then, an unsuspected prophecy: "How tragic if somebody put their foot down and said the opera company couldn't spend so much money!" (The inflation and economic distress that would soon follow was apparent even then in spots.)

It was heartening to her to see the members of the opera company so interested in bringing themselves up to international level. "I know we had that conviction much earlier—Goossens made us believe it. One felt not quite good enough, and so we had to work extra hard. Now it's the same. I'm so impressed at rehearsals by the way they've worked on that dialogue—they're not French-speaking at all. Fantastic." For herself it had been a sticky point, so she appreciated their effort all the more.

"There are always some problems. Some nights are better than others. That's just human nature. It doesn't matter how well you know your technique and your language. Some nights you think you are no good. Then you seem to sing better than ever, even if you didn't expect to."

I had heard six performances of *Hoffmann*, a couple from the Green Room, not the most favorable way, to be sure. I told her that no matter how she felt, when she came on the monitor screen, everyone stopped knitting or playing chess or whatever to listen."

"Oh, come on!"

"The only thing that didn't stop was the bridge game," I teased. "But as far as the company goes, they're all inspired by you. One chorus woman asked: 'Is she always like that? So easy to work with, always on time, working so hard?' "

Joan characteristically turned aside the compliment. "When rehearsals keep going until midnight, I get so tired. I hate to break my regular routine: go to bed at a reasonable hour, seldom after midnight. Then I'm usually awake early; otherwise, you don't get things done. After a performance or a special evening, it's a bore to wake at seven or seven-fifteen. Sometimes Chester brings me breakfast in bed, especially on the day of a performance."

At this time, Frank Sinatra, visiting "down under," was undergoing a furious hassle with the press, flaying them for intrusion into his privacy, stalking out of engagements, putting on his bad-boy act.

"So what do *you* have for breakfast?" I played inquisitive reporter. She was amused, then thoughtful at the suggestion that Ol' Blue Eyes's antics had drawn the attention of the sensational element of the press away from her and Ricky. Chester, coming in at that moment, referred to it as "a blessing in disguise."

Joan: "No disguise. Just plain blessing."

Then she talked about their unfortunate arrival in 1965.

"We had worked so hard to get that season going. Doing seven operas! As for me, I had been singing three times a week, *every* week. We'd had seven weeks in Melbourne, two in Adelaide, then on to Sydney. One was terribly eager and anxious to do well in one's home town. And Frank Tait, so good and conscientious, had worked himself to death. He was under such strain. Other 'international' companies hadn't lived up to contract; they'd walk out before they'd finished their promised weeks, so he was determined to succeed. And then he died, just before Sydney."

"How few realize your sense of humor about yourself," I commented, remembering the cartoon of orangutangs in the Sydney newspaper.

Joan giggled. "You should have seen the one from Covent Garden when they gave Schoenberg's *Moses and Aaron*. It was audience participation time. Everyone wanted to get up on the stage and join in the orgy."

"By the way, speaking of humor, not orgies, did you see the interview headed: 'Not Quite Pope Joan'?"

"Garbled, wasn't it?"

One critic, recalling his famous colleague, Neville Cardus (who had graced Sydney for many years, then gone back to Britain to stay almost too long in a post at the Manchester *Guardian*), playfully discussed Cardus's wish to be Pope, and wondered whether Sutherland was ready to be mitred as pope of the world's diva-level songstresses. His headline told his premature conclusion: he hadn't heard her *Hoffmann*, only the preceding concert.

The conversation turned to family matters. They had, of course, seen Ricky's parents. There had been a big party at half brother Jim's, with his six children who ranged from twenty-four years down to nine. Jim, now the secretary of a big steamship line, is eight to ten years older than Joan, and, at the time, was very unhappy "because shipping has gone to hell." She had not had much chance to talk to him. One of her half sisters, Nancy, with husband and son and daughter-in-law, had been there. And another half sister, Ailsa, had come backstage after the opening performance. Ailsa was a radiologist, and had married for the second time "one of my mother's cousin's inlaws," Joan said. "They had been attracted to each other, so she told me, when she was eighteen. But then everyone thought he was too old for her. So they married very late, and he has since died."

Joan and Ailsa had never been very close. One of Ailsa's traits that bothered Joan: "She tends to enlarge on things. Always. She spent some time with us in Les Avants in Switzerland before we went back to Australia in 1965, and when we got here, Jim's wife amazed me by asking: 'Do you really have forty rooms in your chalet?' Ailsa had told her that, and all about the old masters hanging on our walls. She just likes to romance. You have to divide by at least half everything she says."

Aside from a picnic or two, the Bonynges' only real excursion had been spelunking. They crawled through caves in the northern part of the state, "wonderful colorings from iron deposits, practically pure limestone, beautifully lighted. Chester was fascinated by the collection of quartzes—he has quite a lot himself: paperweights and so on. Oh, that bending over! All we tall people! When I think of my back . . ."

The room grew cool. Joan supplied a pretty afghan, saying that the English Olympia, Norelle Davidson, had made it for her. (Norelle, tall, slim, rather self-conscious, was constantly posing—she had been a model, it seems, and had not yet ripened into stageworthiness.)

"Such a present-giving lot—they're always handing me cakes," she moaned. "Great whopping Pavlovas. I have a terrible reputation for loving sweet desserts. What are Pavlovas? Huge, round confections of the sweetest possible ingredients. Norman Ayrton's secretary, Evelyn Kopfer, presented me with one—sponge cake with strawberry filling and frosting. And Pauline Garrick—you know her, Polly—made me a mammoth boiled fruit cake. Oh, I never ate so much! Wish I didn't, but it's there. Like Mt. Everest. I must have gained."

"Do you look at the scales?"

"Haven't any. But, oh . . . when I get to a certain point, I stop. I can be good if I really try. I have a feeling that I've got more, a little bit here, a little bit there, more of Joan than we really want."

"Do you swim?"

"When I can. It's marvelous exercise—good for my arthritis, too. I wanted to put a swimming pool at Les Avants in Switzerland, but it was so expensive and we get there so little in the summer. You can't just dig a hole and let the snow fall in. It's hard enough to keep the grounds nice, to get flowers to grow, besides pulling the house together.

"I have to walk, too. If I don't, I go bonkers."

Chester poked his head in again. We were summoned to drinks.

Waiting for other guests, Ricky took up the subject of their current reception in Sydney. "I was slightly scared—had misgivings—but it's been wonderful," he said. The press had shown skepticism, speculating that they might not return to Australia, but Ricky now told me in confidence (it was publicly announced some days later) that it had been decided: Yes, they would come back, and he would be musical director of the company beginning in the season of 1976.

His enthusiasm for the company had grown mightily. Their youth and enthusiasm, their desire to become fully professional, had fired him. Also, the standard already reached—he had noted it in the production of *Jenufa*—astonished him.

"I had heard that opera many times in Europe, and went only dutifully to one performance, but I'd go back if I could. I got so much more out of it here. All the virtues just shone out."

"So you do think there's a future here?"

"They could have one of the best operas in the world."

With the *Jenufa*, the *Hoffmann* also offered a case in point.

Of course, imported talent had a lot to do with it—Varona's scenery and costumes and Capobianco's production.

I brought up a point about Tito's direction—he invariably makes singers kneel at some point or other. Or even lie flat. Had he a floor fetish?

"Ooh, you didn't see his *Norma*," Joan laughed. "Up and down, down and up."

As in the earlier Covent Garden *Hoffmann* Venetian scene, Giulietta had been asked to throw herself down on a pile of pillows.

"Looked as if copulating in the middle of the street," Ricky interjected indelicately. This brought to mind that the streets in Venice would be water, and that streetwalkers had better swim, and led to further ribald comment from Chester, just out of range.

Joan brought us back to sobriety.

"Tito is great. He gives you such confidence and finds something for everyone to do. Everybody loves to work with him."

But Ricky shared my heated objection to Antonia's final scene. Tito insisted that the dead singer rise and glide back to disappear behind the portrait of her mother. A most poetic touch, the singer-daughter dissolving into the singer-mother, but not convincing as stage business. Joan dies so beautifully, in one of those collapses Norman Ayrton taught her, and to get up again is an anticlimax. Then it leaves her father staring blankly at space, and Hoffmann crying his beloved's name to the audience. Ricky admitted that he had tried to get Tito to change it, but was always put off by that wily Argentinian's soothing: "Let's wait and try it out, and maybe . . ." But he had no intention of giving up the bit. He had done it before, too, in his New York City Opera production, so it was a fixed conviction.

"Laugh at me," Joan added, "disappearing in a puff of dry ice."

"A specially large puff," teased Ricky. "And those bubbles floating down during the introduction—one hit my baton right on the beat. And the orchestra got a bath."

A smoke effect, too, had caused problems. One might say it did not go off. It was a paraffin spread, Chester explained. Made such an awful smell.

Joan had brought out her needlepoint, an elaborate design for an English church that had begged a favor. She had said before that her grandest achievement to date had been chair and couch tapestry covers for a set of imposing Spanish furniture the Bonynges had bought with currency they were not allowed to take out from

Spain on their first visit to Barcelona. They had shipped it home to Switzerland. I asked her now how she had got started on the hobby, which seemed to be almost an obsession.

It was during their 1965 visit to Australia, she said. "I had to be careful what I did between performances . . ."

"You can't go running about," Ricky interrupted.

It was suggested that there were other possibilities we need not investigate too deeply.

"Now, darling, don't put any more ideas in her head. She's got enough already," Ricky protested. "I'm a terrible old-fashioned male chauvinist pig, and believe that thing about women's place —now don't *you* slap me. Joan's used to me."

He laughed at a memory, and trotted it out:

"One time a real women's libber came to interview Joan in New York, and babbled on about being 'liberated.' Joan looked her dead in the eye and declared: 'Women's place is in the home!' "

"I really meant it," Joan contributed earnestly, leaning forward to emphasize her conviction. "But *he* went into hysterics. Of course, I could have said something about a career being enough."

Then, somewhat confusedly changing the emphasis, she went on vehemently: "One could get up on one's high horse and declaim: 'Try to do it as well, and see what a prima donna's life is like!' "

It was the only time I have heard her make that defiant defense of her own capabilities and of the difficulties she had overcome.

Ricky exploded: "Liberation! All women have been bloody liberated for fifty years—a damn sight too liberated."

"But what about the women's vote?"

"Ask the Australian women who voted for Whitlam [then Prime Minister] just because he's so handsome. That's how women vote."

Speaking of women in public life, I had been quite impressed with the ability and charm of Jean Battersby, the executive director of the Australian Arts Commission, and mentioned this.

"No politics in our house," asserted the head of it. "We can't be bothered—just do our job and that's all."

Joan added that she thought it was bad for artists to mix in politics. "Just let them support us!" she cried, half laughing, half serious.

Ricky closed the subject: "I will not lobby or try to cope with the 'right' people. If they want me, okay."

I thought it better not to assert that politics, in fact, did have a great deal to do with them, whether they willed it or not, as is always the case with the arts in our democratic society (and as later events proved). I choked on this thought, and Ricky offered:

"Sit forward and I'll give you a whack on the back."

Huguette came into the room at this moment, and thought this was funny. She screamed with laughter.

Could anyone make sensible conversation after that, particularly about acoustics in the Concert Hall? Nevertheless, I tried. These acoustics seemed rather strange—good from one spot, really distorted from another, when a violinist was playing with the orchestra on stage. Just wait till he conducted a concert there, I told Ricky, and he could say what it is like from his point of view.

"That'll be a long time, dear," Ricky replied. "I don't care anything about concerts."

Huguette interposed: "Unless it is a concert with all those lovely things he dug out." For Huguette, as well as for Joan, the indefatigable researcher had often found obscure gems, and, indeed, loved to play their accompaniments. He went over to the piano and gave us a song from Meyerbeer's *L'Étoile du Nord*. Joan joined in for a few bars.

"I gather you don't dislike operetta, then," I ventured, and related the experience of Henry Russell, the English impresario who had run an opera company in Boston for five years and, through his friendship for Melba, had brought a troupe to Australia in 1924. We have seen that he was almost run out of the country for allegedly calling musical comedy stars "prostitutes." The scandal filled the newspapers for days.

Ricky proved his devotion to this kind of lyric stage not so long afterward, with *The Merry Widow* in Vancouver. Indeed he had preceded this with a San Francisco *Fledermaus*. In both, Joan enjoyed a romp.

We reverted to the Opera House amenities. The Bonynges showed enthusiasm for the Green Room, though Joan wondered if it wouldn't be a mistake for the performers to patronize the bar too freely, especially before going on.

"But there was a time in the Williamson company when all alcohol was banned backstage," Chester recalled.

"It's a very pleasant room," Ricky decided.

I recalled that once, in intermission, sitting outside Joan's dressing room, I had noticed Ricky dashing in and out.

"Powdering your nose?" I asked now.

"Absolutely—it was the closest," he answered. "But did you see the little boy who brings me a glass of ice water from the bar without being asked? Everyone's been so considerate."

Photo: Branca Gaica.

An unaccustomed kind of role, the vituperous Elettra in Mozart's *Idomeneo* with the Australian Opera.

Proud Mummy, holding Baby Adam, born 1956.

The revengeful Lucrezia Borgia reaps a tragic harvest, mourning the son she has inadvertantly poisoned. Ron Stevens is the dead Gennaro in the Australian production.

Photo: Bernsen's International Press Service.

At home in Cornwell Gardens, early sixties. Richard's burgeoning collection of operatic posters and prints plainly visible.

Early happy collaboration.

In Venice, in 1962, surrounding the deus ex machina Franco Zeffirelli.

Photograph: Eleanor Morrison.

Divas Resnik, Sutherland and Nilsson and Ballerina Danilova at a New York soiree in the 60s.

Joan and Renata Tebaldi grace the lobby of the new Metropolitan in a publicity junket.

Photo courtesy Robert Tuggle.

Lord Harewood, one of Joan's early mentors, in his office in 1970.

Photo by the author.

Flushed and happy after the 1975 London *Traviata*, with the young producer, Michael Rennison.

Photo by the author.

Photo by the author.

Backstage after the 1975 London *Traviata* with Morag Beaton, the Scottish singer who had been with the company in the 1965 Australian tour. Joan is wearing the splendid turquoise necklace, Richard's Christmas gift.

Chester on the road to Montreux at Christmas time.

Photo by the author.

Photograph by the author.

The music room in Chalet Monet, Les Avants, with the famous needle-point chairs, all Joan's handiwork, displayed before the cabinet of prized figurines, a few of Richard's trophies.

Ready to depart from Les Avants for London after the 1974 Christmas holiday. The prima donna dominates the front row, with Ruthli (holding Rachel) and Moffatt Oxenbauld to her left; the author to her right. At back, Gertie Stelzel and Graeme Ewer. Chester took the photograph, and the Maestro was still in his bath.

"Big, bold and beautiful," she goes for her first press conference at the Australian Opera in 1974.

Photo by the author.

Cornered by the importunate Australian press, she peeps quizically over the barricade at the camera held high by six-foot David Brown, Sydney Opera House press officer.

At a party with Charles Berg, the Australian Opera's powerful chairman.

Photo by the author.

Longtime friend Terry McEwen (now general director of the San Francisco Opera) flew out to Sydney for the television "This Is Your Life" surprise for Joan.

The happy family. Son Adam with Richard and Joan at the surprise television show, "This Is Your Life," produced by Helen and Bill Lovelock in Sydney.

Sandro Sequi rehearses Joan as Elvira and James Morris as Sir George for the Met's *I Puritani.*

Photo: Gerald Fitzgerald.

Making up for *La Fille du Regiment* at the Met. The "military" jacket hangs ready to be donned; the inevitable single rose casts its benign spell.

Photo: Erika Davidson, courtesy Opera News.

Barbara Matera, Joan's trusted costumier, with one of the prima donna's old costumes.

Maestro Bonynge in command.

A recent portrait.

"There's been a lot of laughter"...

I had noticed Adam performing that duty one night, very proud to be of service to his dad.

"Some bugger pinched my sign!" Ricky exclaimed suddenly. The three visiting "stars"—Joan, Huguette, and Ricky—had been favored by a veteran doorman named Tom, who painted, decorated, and hand-lettered attractive wood plaques to identify their dressing rooms. Joan's and Huguette's remained safe.

Now Caroline Lill, the pretty repetiteur and an old friend of Joan's, arrived, followed by Jani Strasser, who brought memories of early Glyndebourne days. He was in Sydney as a "guest consultant for voice and interpretation," which is a euphemism for coach. Joan had undergone his fierce discipline from her first *Figaro* Countess, and at succeeding Glyndebourne engagements. ("All right for coaching recitatives, especially, but he *would* try to give one voice lessons," she had said of him once.)

After a brief argument to untangle the order of Joan's Glyndebourne stints (all Mozart except the Bellini *Puritani*), Strasser reminisced: "I was in Glyndebourne a year before the festival started. John Christie had asked me to work with his wife, Audrey Mildmay."

Ricky recalled a thorny point: "Remember when Joan auditioned for Constanza [in *The Abduction from the Seraglio*]?"

"They turned me down, said I was too big. *I* don't think I was," said that aggrieved lady. It is one Mozart role she had never sung, and so always wanted to.

Her memories of Glyndebourne were tinged with wry humor.

"Christie went around turning the lights off. As soon as the last busload of audience had gone, off went the lights. And we'd still be dressing."

"Was it economy?" I asked, thinking of the lavishness laid on in that glorious estate.

"Probably not," answered Strasser. "One time a dresser left an electric iron on, and it burned through the board and nearly caused a bad fire."

Conversation got contrapuntal here, with bits emerging: Strasser imitating the croak of a singing teacher with a false larynx and commenting on mutual musical acquaintances; soprano and contralto obbligatos from Caroline and Huguette; Joan murmuring aside that she had been trying to get Adam to come in, but that he had been playing tennis with the governor and was now sulking. Didn't yet know the result of his college exam . . .

Chester: "The meat is getting cold . . ."

Strasser: "Yes, I know [Sir Rudolf] Bing. Very forceful. Beyond that, nobody knows him . . ."

Joan: "I get so confused between 'director' and 'producer.' "

Chorus: "Don't we all! . . ."

Joan finally: "Darlings, would it be outrageous if we all sat up to the table?" And we did.

25

Fairy Tale West, Fairy Tale East

RICHARD'S CHOICE OF SAN FRANCISCO TO LAUNCH Joan in a new role, backed by a spectacular production of Massenet's *Esclarmonde* in 1974, could be said to be apt from several points of view, one of which was the couple's own history. "Out-of-town tryouts" had been their practice, whether deliberate or merely coincidental. Sutherland's appearance as Donna Anna in the comparative obscurity of Vancouver had been her first on the North American continent. She also chose the British Columbia city for her first *Norma*, for Marguerite in *Faust* (1963), and for *Lucrezia Borgia* (1972). Seattle heard her *Lakmé* first in 1967. All these had caused comparatively little national or international splash.

San Francisco has a reputation as an operatic cynosure: almost anything performed there attracts attention.

For Kurt Herbert Adler was without question master of all he surveyed, and what he surveyed (until a few years later) was the operatic life of San Francisco. Absolute monarchy was the rule in the City on the Bay, as it was with Chicago's late Carol Fox. Opera companies seem best served by despots, benevolent or not. With Adler, the duties of management were matched with frequent invasions of the pit, conducting when he felt the urge. Did the old firebrand mellow in later years? Reporters one time found him gracious instead of defensive at fielding awkward questions, and "joking about his not-so-endearing way of bellowing about the office, referring to himself as a 'bitcher' . . . Was this the old super-actor, whose stage was the whole opera house, assuming for the occasion one of his more sympathetic roles?"

Adler saw to it that new singers, fresh productions, and even occasionally a brand-new opera took off into the uncertain blue from the Golden Gate. In 1971, Sutherland and Bonynge had given Adler their first *Maria Stuarda* (one of Donizetti's three "Queens" revived in another operatic sector as well), and had reaped hilarious results with *Fledermaus* in 1973. *Esclarmonde* was a chancier matter, completely unfamiliar and consequently subjected to a good deal of pretrial ridicule by critics, some of whom are inclined to believe that if they don't know a piece it can't be very good.

Esclarmonde was one of three operas Jules Massenet wrote for the petite Sybil Sanderson, the California girl to whom he had temporarily lost his heart. Of the other two, *Le Mage* has been completely submerged, but *Thaïs* has survived with a fair measure of health. Sanderson's assets included a fresh beauty and svelte figure, as well as a clear voice that climbed to seemingly impossible heights. Alfred Bruneau, himself a noted composer who is credited with introducing realistic drama on the French musical stage, wrote of her voice as "accurate, flexible, wide-ranging, and notable for crystalline limpidity and voluptuous tenderness." Massenet was bewitched.

"Quelle voix prestigieuse (What a fantastic voice)!" he gushed to his publisher, Hartmann. "J'étais émerveillé, stupéfait, subjugé." He marveled that the voice went from lower to upper G— three octaves.

Does Sutherland sing these notes? "Not on your life!" Bonynge exclaimed when we spoke of it. "Hers was a freak voice; those notes sound like a steam calliope. I believe Massenet never wrote them, although they show up in the score he gave to Sanderson, inserted, perhaps, by her hand." She may have been the exception to the "steam-whistle" school, for Paris raved about her "Tour Eiffel" notes. (The famous tower had made its first appearance at the Exposition the same year as Sybil's debut.)

But she also impressed Massenet as "an intelligence, an inspiration, a personality," and she continued to be the rage in Paris, attracting princes and at least one wealthy husband. *Esclarmonde* had one hundred performances at the Opéra after its premiere on May 14, 1889. The worldly Camille Saint-Saëns, not to be outdone in homage to a reigning love goddess, wrote *Phryné* for her in 1893, and she continued to sing entirely worthy Gildas and Juliettes, although her visits to America in 1894–95 and 1901–02 with Grau's barnstormers from the Met were fiascos. For flamboyance and romantic appeal to the public, she had few equals. A protégée of hers, Mary Garden, no less, did her proud. Still, they don't make prima donnas like that anymore. Maria Callas was probably the last of the breed. But then, few princes, grand dukes, and no tsars are around these days to provide a glittering milieu.

Despite Richard's enthusiasm, Joan resisted *Esclarmonde* at first. Perhaps she felt it too unrewarding to warrant the work it would take. When Ricky finally persuaded her, she realized *Esclarmonde* would be a new theatrical experience.

Esclarmonde is Massenet's tribute to Wagner, and indeed the importance of the orchestra takes it into the realm of music drama. Another sign of the composer's confession of faith to the Master of Bayreuth is the use of motifs, those little musical tags of identification. Still, the French stamp, the Massenet individuality, are unmistakable. Joan would find much musical satisfaction in mastering its difficulties.

During the *Esclarmonde* period, in San Francisco, it would have been impossible to be close to Joan and Ricky. They stay in Sausalito, across the Golden Gate Bridge in Marin County. It is a delirious scramble of tiny and not-so-tiny shops and dwellings up the sides of the steep hills. Jack Sheldon and his partner, also a Jack, own a large, quiet house with a swimming pool. Jack Sheldon is a gourmet king of the Bay Area, writer, broadcaster, bon vivant. "The Jacks," as everyone calls them, cherish the Bonynges as friends and guests. This is the couple's preferred procedure in any extended stay: to rent an apartment or part of a friend's house so that their hours away from work can be as homelike as possible. Brooklyn is a case in point for their New York stand. In London, they find a flat. It's only in the short spells that they resort to hotels.

San Francisco had not yet gotten around to building appropriate facilities for the opera company apart from the outmoded opera house itself, although plans toward this end were burgeoning. So blocking rehearsals were farmed out to the rented Annex, which looked like a decrepit TV studio, its only possible virtue a floor approximating the size of the opera stage.

There was a heat wave in San Francisco that October. *Esclarmonde* developed under a stifling roof and windows that let in the merciless sun for hours each day.

The rehearsal "lineup" was headed by Bliss Johnston. The pretty, blond, snub-nosed pianist, conscientious to a fault, devoted to Ricky through work in Vancouver, and as close to indispensable as any individual can be, was at the decrepit piano. Brian Gray, staff stage director, Susan Webb, prompter, Ralph Clifford, stage manager, and Matthew Ferrugio, company coordinator, completed the working crew.

Out on the floor, Lotfi Mansouri was positioning Joan and

Huguette Tourangeau, who would sing Esclarmonde's sister, Parséis. The bouncing Persian had become known as a stage director in Zurich and Geneva and France, then had come to Washington and Wolf Trap. I had seen and admired his *Anna Bolena* and *Don Carlos* in Santa Fe, where he often directed, as well as in San Francisco and numerous European centers. A jolly soul, he is undaunted by prima donnas or stiff tenors, and has since become director of the Toronto Opera.

Our hero was Giacomo Aragall, with sultry Spanish good looks and little animation, but given to picturesque poses, the effect spoiled by perspiration-dark patches on his blue shirt. He had not bothered to learn English and chattered in French only when he felt like it, and then mostly to tell jokes that had the ladies laughing naughtily. Huguette was his likeliest target. "That Aragall!" she shrieked. "He telling how pederasts do carroty." We tried to figure out the vegetable connection; then she demonstrated with a slash of the hand. Oh, karate. Aragall hadn't bothered to study all of his part and learned by doing, then professed not to remember what it was all about when the New York performance came along.

Tenors, tenors! Their vagaries trouble the strict professionals, who, however, can do little about it but exhort, cajole, flatter, exercise patience—and, privately, curse. Aragall was apparently worth all the trouble, for both public and press liked him. He had made his mark as a lyric tenor; I had heard him as Edgardo in a London *Lucia* and thought his voice strong and brilliant, but without velvet or a great deal of nuance and sensitivity (I still thought so), and he left no personal stamp, no sense of identification with a character.

Not that Roland in *Esclarmonde* has much to identify with. Because the heroine takes all the initiative, spiriting him off to an enchanted island and rather aggressively making love to him, how does this square with the vaunted Spanish *machismo*? I asked later. He paused hardly a moment before answering: "Happens all the time." (Ladies indeed are rather susceptible to his stage attractiveness, and this obviously lingers offstage, although he does not seem to go out of his way to bring it on.)

Clifford Grant, the Australian who had sung a great deal with the English National Opera (formerly Sadler's Wells) and was marking his eighth season in San Francisco, provided a temperamental contrast. He stood at the piano in an interval, picking out with two fingers Bartolo's buffo patter song in *Le Nozze di Figaro*, showing either where his heart or his next assignment lay. He was to be the abdicating Emperor Phorcas, Esclarmonde's father. "Weather-Phorcas" was his brand of jest. After making his Metropolitan debut in the same role, he would head back home to become a regular member of the Australian Opera.

William Harness, the young tenor who had won his way to the big opera by auditions, was ready and willing to play Énéas, the lover of Parséis (Tourangeau). "I hate every minute of it!" he grinned. Philip Booth, an experienced bass, singing the King of France, would turn up at the Met as Joan's father in *I Puritani*. Robert Kerns, who had made his baritone career mostly in Europe, was in San Francisco for the first time, appearing as the stern Bishop of Blois.

Joan stood in the middle of the large floor, singing in full, superb voice the aria that extols the knight with whom she has fallen in love. The music was so tricky she could not do with any distraction. She had spent a good portion of the past days in a state of abstraction, digesting the difficult music and coordinating with Huguette and Aragall in duets. At the end of the scene they were then going over, the really startling moment of the score erupted. Esclarmonde summoned spirits of air, water, and fire to transport her lover to the enchanted island. It was a birdlike "Ho-jo-to-ho," replete with odd intervals and swiftly repeated notes at the very top of high tessitura, a trill, and a long glissando downward—Rima the Birdwoman, with Wagnerian overtones. The spirits she summoned huddled in a little group at the side of the hall—ballet dancers in a world of their own. Sharp-faced youths in jeans or tight pants rolled up fiercely at the waist to make their little buttocks as tight and shapely as possible; pretty, languorous, long-haired girls with smiles generous and sweet and innocent.

They played with their gossamer costumes, one throwing his into the air and trying to get under and into it as it came down, all looking somewhat incongruous in fluttery gauze over work clothes as they mimed menace by an up-and-down motion of their arms, protectiveness by down and up. It seemed hopeless and boring; later, the Canadian choreographer Norbert Vesak (who was to be conscripted by the Met) pulled it together for moments of enchantment under lights.

The San Francisco rehearsal schedule was a jumble. Even the Met's hectic juggling seemed rigidly regular compared to these hours; they were in the house only some afternoons and dark nights.

At one of the sessions in the house, Ricky threw a tantrum, apparently disgusted with the lack of time, the impossibility of

hearing anything from the stage, and other accumulated griev-
ances.

"Why should I conduct this opera? Let somebody else!" he
shouted, throwing down his baton and rushing up the aisle right
past Adler. The general manager had not a word to say. (He had
been noted to possess a streak of Puritanism, however. When Frank
Corsaro, the outspoken stage director, spoke out in four-letter
words, Adler scolded him, saying: "We don't like that sort of language here!")

Ricky had his regular run-ins with Adler. Joan never complained, but the maestro twice came offstage fuming, both times
at the unseemly—and untimely, from an artistic point of view—
lowering of the final curtain, cutting off the graceful parade of
curtain calls. Joan hardly had a chance to bow after the *Esclarmonde*
premiere, with the house screaming for her. For a while, it seemed
as though the famous team was never to perform at the house again
and Adler could do with his next season's *Trovatore* what he wanted.
But the two men ended up having lunch together and making plans.
All was light, with a proper amount of sweetness. The first *Trovatore* would go on.

As for the abrupt curtailment of curtain calls, it was entirely
a question of economics, as at other houses. One minute past
midnight and union overtime sets in—the calamity to be avoided
at all other costs, even the prima donna's amour propre. The impresario gets the curtain up on time and expects it to go down
before the Cinderella curfew.

Dress rehearsal for *Esclarmonde* fell on a Sunday evening
before the premiere on October 23. We had been in the theater
several times, afternoon or evening, whichever fitted in. It was the
usual pandemonium unlimited, especially as the settings seemed
so controversial. Beni Montresor is a genius at the pointillist style
of scene painting and at lighting and projections, but the scrim—
or several scrims—have to be down and the lighting properly
imaginative or the effects are of splashes and spots of horrid color
indiscriminately flung from a wanton brush.

Performers loathe the scrim. They cannot see, conductor to
singer and vice versa, and feel, with some slight justification, that
the sound is muffled. The rehearsal of one act with the bare bones,
however, brought the unanimous shout: "Down with the scrim!"
and the illusion was restored.

A worse contretemps developed from the costumes. Contrary
to San Francisco's wishes and Joan's demands, Montresor, leaving
the building and painting of his scenery to an Italian firm, had sent

along the costume designs for execution. It is a shibboleth that Joan's costumes be made by Barbara Matera, no matter where the others are sewn. The Italian consignment arrived and the great god Pan took over. Everyone had been shrouded in shapeless sacks: "My dear, we looked like rice bags tied in the middle!" the prima donna moaned. The designs themselves had no doubt been pretty enough in their way, but from one-dimensional sketches to three-dimensional bodies is a gap to be entrusted only to gifted specialists.

Barbara was phoned, made up some costumes within little more than a week, then flew them out from New York, stitching, sewing on jewels and sequins, and fussing with Esclarmonde's veil all the way up until curtain time. Joan's Australian costume for Giulietta was used as a pattern, and consequently, no bouffant skirt appeared. Hoops don't seem to go with fairy empresses. The gowns for Joan, mostly form-fitting with softly concealing capes and veils, were among the most becoming she has ever worn and almost as sexy as Giulietta's. Her crown matched the description of Sybil's, but it was light and not too burdensome, though about a foot high. The veil caused more problems; in its fall over her face, it brushed her false eyelashes. What with the scrim and this additional barrier, she couldn't see much of what she was doing. But she looked as glamorous as a Fairy Empress should.

At dress rehearsal, problems still persisted. In Joan's dressing room as she was being made up, she protested about the eye makeup: "Not so big!"

"Darling, it's a big theater," assured Richard Holland, tying a soft cloth around her head to protect her skin against the wig, which he began to fit. "Don't you know girls' eyes are never too big?" And when the wig was on, her face looked thin and elflike, the enormous eyes beautiful and startling. He tucked her hair up. But Ricky, dashing in at the moment, said, "Leave it down, it's a better line for her jaw."

She sat patiently through this, murmuring, "Mother isn't the one to complain," even though the headdress was hot and did slip.

"This production will go down as absolute chaos," Richard Holland proclaimed.

"So I'm not the only one," Joan said with a somewhat twisted smile.

Barbara meanwhile busied herself in a corner with last-minute stitching of sequins. The costumes hung from a tall rack, beautiful in their outspoken colors of red, gold, and blue. The air of haste, of improvisation, almost of panic hovered.

Huguette managed to arrange her costume becomingly, but

the chorus women remained shapeless. (They seemed far prettier in the Met's production, but Charles Caine, the wardrobe director, said it was merely superior lighting.)

At last, the show was ready for its premiere. San Francisco took lustily to the spectacle, cheering and stamping at every performance.

Montresor's sets enchanted by their rich and shifting colors and air of mystery.

One reviewer, Robert Commanday of the *Chronicle*, missed the point. (A malicious detractor claimed that Commanday alternated moods regularly: this performance good, that one unworthy. If that were so—and, of course, one does not take it very seriously—*Esclarmonde* fell on the dark side of Commanday's moon.) He thought it "hilarious" and "naive." He could not recall having such a laugh in opera, he wrote, as when the Empress was "swiftly borne skyward into the flies like a huge butterfly" to her tryst. This was indeed a whimsical invention, a sort of cardboard cutout resembling the prima donna, also suggesting one of the Valkyries. The Metropolitan retained it, to the amusement of those who caught its fleeting passage.

The other critics treated the opera more seriously, taking it "straight," as it was intended. Although surprised, Alexander Fried proclaimed it a major hit containing thrills in his *Examiner* review. Arthur Bloomfield, who also wrote for that paper, had his say in *Opera*, the British magazine, realizing that the opera was performed exactly at face value, as if everything happening on the stage were entirely plausible, including the flying Empress-magician, (He compared her to the Empress in Strauss's *Die Frau ohne Schatten* as not limited to normal forms of transport.) He added: "The main fascination is with the utter fantasy of the thing, a deadpan, heroical-magical children's story presented in never-never collagelike sets, half literal, half fanciful, which arrive in an inky, liquid, translucent parade of gold, yellow, red, and orange backdrops rising and falling slowly and inexorably before the audience's eyes. Sutherland sang with a combination of assets suggesting Alfred Bruneau's 1887 description of La Sanderson." All the other singers could add quotes to their scrapbooks as well.

· · ·

There had been several extracurricular sessions to lighten the three weeks. A merry dinner party at Bob Kerns's attractive rented house far out on Pacific Avenue, at which he cooked a gourmet dinner and we celebrated by some impromptu (and on Lotfi's part, wildly acrobatic) dancing to Ricky's piano essays of American show tunes. This is one field he has not yet put his mind to. Huguette helped by singing the lyrics in her lushest contralto, while Joan, sitting quietly for the nonce, suddenly turned pixie and took it into her head to wear a huge potted fern for a hat.

More formal bashes could be held nowhere but Trader Vic's. One, after a *Cenerentola* performance, had for hostess Mrs. Dewey Donnell, a lively matron warmly concerned with opera (sadly, she died a few years later). Another, on the heels of the *Esclarmonde* premiere, was given by Mrs. Rudolph Light, who, in the words of a program announcement, "made the production possible by a generous gift." This angel is the widow of the late J. Paul Getty. The Met, which borrowed the production, shared San Francisco's gratitude.

One afternoon could be considered a part of the travail for the Bonynges and Tourangeau. They spent three exhausting hours sitting at a table in the Odyssey music shop, autographing record albums and various and sundry bits of paper brought along by a constantly thickening stream of customers. It is a grueling part of the job. At one moment, when Joan's hand seemed to tire, Terry McEwen, old friend and at the time artists' representative for London Records (he was to succeed Adler as general manager of the opera in 1982), leaned over her shoulder and said slowly: "You spell it S-U-T-H-E-R-L-A-N-D."

The original star who inspired the whole *Esclarmonde* excitement was very much on Ricky's mind during these days in San Francisco. He came heavy-eyed into rehearsal one morning, but with a cat-versus-cream smile. Chester revealed the cause to me. Ricky had bid for and won at a Sotheby auction two unique Massenet scores—the very ones in which the composer had inscribed in his own handwriting his very personal directions to the lovely Sybil—*Thaïs* and *Esclarmonde*. What a prize! To my hesitant question came the answer—in pounds. Five figures apiece, the *Thaïs* twice as costly as the *Esclarmonde*. There went the *Esclarmonde* fees!

Monsieur may not have slept all night for the excitement, but it was worth it. Perhaps Madame was not so happy. Still, when she made up her mind to buy a new gown, it sometimes ran into four figures. Even so, she couldn't match him for spending. And why not? he reasoned. If you've got it . . . In more affectionate moments, she called him a "regular old magpie."

In the narrow-corridor crush backstage after one performance,

Schuyler Chapin, the new Met manager, waited patiently before Joan's door. When it opened, he called out: "Rehearsals November seventh!"

This confirmed what we already suspected—that the Met was taking the Massenet spectacle for Joan.

But that didn't happen for two years. And before then, Chapin had gone, ousted by an unsympathetic board of directors. So it was John Dexter (production director), and James Levine (musical director), who welcomed *Esclarmonde* in the fall of 1976.

CHAPTER
26

Intermission: A Conversation with Joan and Ricky

AFTER SEVERAL PERFORMANCES OF *ESCLARMONDE* in San Francisco had beeen safely put behind them, Joan and Ricky felt relaxed enough to talk over tea at the Jacks' one afternoon. Chester came for me, and we waited quite a while in front of my hotel for Ricky, who was at grips with Adler in the exclusive Cosmopolitan Club just at the head of the block on Post Street. Eventually he came striding buoyantly down the hill, apparently having patched up what differences had arisen over the manager's peremptory lowering of the curtain on the prima donna's bows.

"Adler's always getting in a state about something," said Ricky, "but it doesn't last long." I thought that Ricky himself had been in considerably more of a "state," but evidently that didn't last long either.

The conversation took place in their Sausalito hideaway. Watching them in the procession of rehearsals from bare walls and floors, with no costumes or scenery, into the fully panoplied stage with costumes and props and all set to go, I asked what made the difference in approach.

"Well, first of all, the difference between rehearsal and performance is the size of the theater—in the way you perform," said Ricky surprisingly.

"Difference to your tempo," added Joan, equally surprising to me.

"A tiny theater makes things move faster," Ricky amplified.

"Do you allow for that in rehearsals?"

"Yes, but you do rehearsals in all sorts of speeds. You don't take the same tempi even at different performances. Rigidity of that sort is ridiculous. Singers can be different, too. You have to allow for that. And the distance from the singers to the pit means a great deal. Mind you, we're all used to it."

The idea of distance warranted more exploration, but did not get it. I suppose it takes longer for signals to travel, and for the eye to pick them up. Joan switched to costuming.

"You mostly rehearse with no costumes; then, when you get them on, it is a completely new thing. [I remembered the struggle in the New York *Hoffmann* for the Doll to get through the chorus in her enormous bouffant skirt.] It's important to have plenty of rehearsals with costumes and props."

Ricky added: "When the singers are in costume and singing with full voice to the back of the theater, the tempi are affected. They tend to get faster. It's difficult to get any singer to give full voice, the way they would in the theater, when rehearsing in a small hall."

"That's another reason I sing out as much as I do," said Joan. "If I stop, I can't do anything at all to create intensity. I don't feel what I'm doing and I don't see how anybody can. One isn't projecting with the actual voice and getting the idea of what one will have to do eventually. It just doesn't show up. When you're consciously saving yourself, not singing out, not really giving your whole consciousness to doing the work in hand, you can't come up with it when you need to."

"Is it fair to the others, not to sing out?"

"Y-e-s-s . . . I think sometimes it's all right, when it's a part the others know very well and you do, too. As long as you give people their cues."

"You don't find out yourself how much you can sing if you don't give all at some point," Ricky added. "I know singers who save themselves in rehearsal and then can't sing at the performance."

"You have to pace yourself . . . ?"

"Certainly. The conductor absolutely; otherwise, he'll tire before the end. Sometimes you don't get the real pacing until after a performance or two."

"James King marked mostly through the *Otello* dress rehearsal," I remarked, having been dismayed at this loss of what the real performance might have been. In fact, there was a hint of the disability Ricky had mentioned, for when the tenor attempted to sing out in the last act, his voice was muffled, virtually untried.

"Corelli wouldn't give full voice for the *Huguenots* rehearsals at La Scala," Joan recalled. "The first night was incredible."

"If everyone else is going half-voice, how the hell can *you* know what will happen? How can you strike a balance?"

"Have a guess at it, use your instinct. Most important thing, instinct about what a performer is likely to do and is capable of. I usually know the singers," said Ricky.

"And if you don't?"

"Doesn't happen if I can help it."

"Joan only saves herself after the umpteenth repetition."

"One gets tired." She smiled. "We tried to get Giacomo [Aragall] to sing out, but he never would. He just didn't know enough to give full voice . . ."

"You mean he didn't know the role [in *Esclarmonde*]?"

"He learned it by opening night," interjected Ricky somewhat grimly. "Claimed we hadn't sent him the score till May. May, indeed. And this is September. Anyway, couldn't he have found one himself?"

"I started work on it this time last year," said Joan quietly.

"And I for several years," added Ricky.

"How do you begin to learn a role?"

"She sits down with the score. And I correct her. With piano."

"This one was awfully hard," explained Joan, "with its peculiar entrances. You simply have to pluck notes out of the air, and you know I don't have perfect pitch. [This recalled the "trick" Ricky had employed to stretch her voice higher and higher.] So in Brooklyn, Rick set down the whole score from the piano on tape, and cued my every entrance. This way I could work on it everywhere—in Bologna [where they had recorded *Maria Stuarda*], in Australia, and wherever I wanted. I'd wake up at five . . ."

"Good Lord!"

"The best time to work," affirmed Ricky. "Though, mind you, my best time is after a long plane journey when I wake up at three, study till eight, then go back to bed." He laughed.

"How do you manage to live through it?"

"True, I don't understand how singers can sing the next day after a flight. Even conductors have trouble . . . my dear, I flew from Switzerland to Vancouver, did a concert next night, and felt completely disoriented. But when the instrument is yourself, like a singer's, it's of course much harder. Still, even playing the piano, I don't feel in control soon after a flight."

"And it's hard to make big decisions," Joan said. This led to some discussions about the Secretaries of State who have to do just that.

"That's a world we just don't understand," proclaimed Ricky, reinforcing his blunt assertion in Sydney about politics. "Jet lag affects me," he resumed, "only in difficulty to sleep."

"We always allow ourselves enough time, and try to accept only 'block' bookings," added Joan. "I can't understand anybody being foolish enough to risk performing too soon after such travel. We always leave at least a day."

"Was *Esclarmonde* more strenuous?"

"Yes, it's tough," Ricky answered.

"Any new piece is," said Joan. (Remember her initial timidity in the face of untried ventures.)

"Did you have to do anything to the score?" I asked.

"Just what Massenet tells you to," he responded.

"Big score?"

"Very big. Big orchestration. But he doesn't drown singers, only puts the sound 'around' them—he knew what textures didn't overwhelm the voices."

"When you go back to an old work—one you know well—does it take as much work?"

"Not much," answered Joan.

Ricky hastened to add: "But if you have time enough, it always pays to restudy. I never stop. I learn something new about *Lucia* all the time."

"Have you done it uncut? They did at City Opera, restored all those little-bitty notes."

"Some little-bitty notes I could do without. But the Wolf Crag scene [where Edgardo confronts Lucia's brother and a duel is arranged] is wonderful. You have to have a strong baritone and tenor, though. We did it with Domingo and Krause in Hamburg, and with Molese and Opthorp in New Orleans."

"What about the scene where Raimondo [Lucia's tutor and mentor] persuades her to give up Edgardo and marry the man her brother wants?"

"Great!" responded Ricky. "Serafin did it at Covent Garden. And we included it in Hamburg. It's vitally important to the story."

"Don't you find the bass's cabaletta a trifle frivolous?" (like so many other of these rapid appendages to the more "singing" cavatinas in the *bel canto* and early Verdi operas).

"Not if it's well sung," insisted Ricky. Joan hummed a passage from the disputed piece. It sounded good from her.

Ricky said: "[James] Morris did it so well. We're fond of him [he had been Antonia's father Crespel in the Met's *Hoffmann*]. He has a big voice but can sing *piano*. He'll be doing *Semiramide* in Vancouver—not with Joan; we can't afford her—but with a young American, Marvellee Cariaga—with a great future, I think."

We drifted off into a discussion of our various difficulties with memory. I confessed to forgetting what I had written soon after writing it. and Ricky exploded:

"My dear, I forget what I conducted! I hear something on the radio and think, what charming music! Then the announcer says: "conducted by Richard Bonynge" and I can't even remember it. How about that?"

Joan tried to explain it by saying that one always had to go on to the next thing, even at the price of forgetting.

"Did you ever try hypnotism?" I ventured, pretty sure of the answer. I got it.

"If you can't force yourself to do something, don't do it," Ricky asserted. "Rubbish! Americans and psychiatrists! If you can't teach yourself right and wrong and put yourself right, God help you!"

Joan started to say that the subject was fascinating, but her husband interrupted her and she never completed the thought.

"We relax marvelously," insisted the head of the house when I suggested that hypnotism might be useful in that department.

I turned the topic. "Opera singers are such healthy beasts."

"They have to be."

Joan said, with a trace of irony: "We learn to breathe deeply," suiting the action to the word, and repeating several times. We all laughed.

The afternoon had gone all too quickly. As I expressed regret, Ricky said with a twinkle:

"We'll have plenty of time in Switzerland to talk about things."

"You mean . . ." I said, not quite believing.

"Yes, you must come for Christmas!"

And with this precious invitation clinging in the memory, I was driven by Chester back across the Golden Gate Bridge in the fog-rising twilight.

CHAPTER

27

No Carols in
Switzerland

THE SWISS DON'T CARE A CUCKOO CLOCK IF YOU'RE visiting their country to spend Christmas with the world's most illustrious prima donna and will probably write in glowing terms about their Christmas-card landscape. The idea of a complimentary trip for a musical journalist raised some Swiss eyebrows in San Francisco and New York consular offices. But I had to try, with passing thoughts on my budget, which had already been knocked lopsided by other jaunts. At least, my mission gained me an escort to the VIP lounge and thence to the plane. I learned that, without this pretty lady (she was not Swiss, but Turkish, I think) I should have had to open everything I carried for inspection by hand, even my nicely wrapped Christmas gifts openly displayed in a shopping bag. (The usual Geiger counter is not good enough for these extra-careful Swiss.)

About six A.M., hardly human after useless snatches of sleep, I crawled out into the airport at Geneva, staggering along an endless white-tiled corridor that made me think of what a bathroom in hell might look like, and finally reached the center of things—customs, passport, and luggage business. I had arranged with Ricky on the phone from San Diego to wait until after my arrival for Chester to drive over and fetch me, and anticipated a long, dreary two-hour wait. But, at the moment I was dragging my heaviest bag off the carousel, came a tap on my shoulder and a "Hi, monkey!" Chester had simply not gone to bed but had driven over early. Never was a sight more welcome than that beaming, cherubic face.

We climbed into a Rover-type vehicle and took off into the snowy landscape. Short of gas, we went the long way to Lausanne to find an open pump, then drove back the scenic route to Les Avants, through tiny towns where the road twisted so close to the shuttered, gabled houses that we nearly scraped the windowsills, so silent and slick and white that my breath came whistling and fearful and incredulous. Then vistas opened up to full view of the mountains, still, menacing, mist-crowned. We had the whole world to ourselves. Even the bustling Swiss were not up and about.

At last, we climbed a steep hill to the chalet that sat atop a fairy-tale castle, rosy and towered and secretive. This was Chalet Monet, the home of the couple known hereabouts as M. & Mme. Bonynge.

Stiff from exhaustion and cold, I was led into the garage level of the house and up to the first floor, and, because of urgent need, directed first to the small, elegant cabinetto thoughtfully placed nearby. Then Chester sat me down to coffee. Paul Garner, the saturnine secretary, was the first to appear, then Ricky; then Joan came to greet me with a kiss on both cheeks. Seeing my debilitated state, she put me to bed right away in a charming room called "Spanish" on the third floor.

"You'll have to make your own bed, dearie," she warned. "We don't have a retinue of servants. There's only Ruthli and me," and she departed, closing the door.

Grateful to have a bed to make, I tumbled into a nap after spreading the wine-red coverlet back to the posts at the foot, and wakened only at Joan's call to lunch.

Then down two flights of winding stairs to the dining room to join the company. At the head of the table sat Ricky. I was to sit honorably to his right, my back to the window that looked out on a snowy hill, thickly forested. Across from me were Adam and a friend. Next, Joan; then, when they came up the hill from the little chalet they occupied, two long-established friends. Then, as I remember, Paul Garner, the secretary. Round the bend of the table sat Ruthli, the housekeeper who had been with them since Adam was a baby. She was now supervising her own two-and-a-half-year-old, a charmer named Rachel (pronounced the French way, Rah-*shelle*). Next to her was Gertie Stelzel, the beloved wardrobe mistress at Covent Garden, who, I learned, had been forced by the age law to retire. She was bitterly missed, and she in turn missed her lifetime job as bitterly. (Gertie had been invited by the Bonynges to stay in a little cottage down the road as long as she pleased.) Then came Chester, next to me. The circle was complete until Christmas.

That day is still a blur, the hours from three-thirty to six-thirty relinquished to more sleep. In my ambiguous role as tactful guest and prying reporter, I had not counted on the enemy—the devilish jet lag. Not one night of the ensuing eleven did I sleep all through, but waked sharply at two, three, four, or five, and then was not able to get back to Morpheus. My inner clock never got on intimate terms with those Swiss watches. So the mornings became hellish —sleep at the wrong end. I remember very few breakfasts shared with anyone else. Usually, all places but mine had been cleared away, leaving only the single glass of acerb orange juice by the one lonely napkin ring; the bread to toast and the coffee kept hot in the kitchen.

I soon discovered that it would take hours to do any kind of thorough job on the huge scrapbooks, a prime investigative target. Trying to winnow through them on the circular table in the ante-room just above the great music room proved inconvenient. I was in the way of traffic and occupying space that Ricky needed for his current passion: clipping, in a sort of frenzy, dozens of photographs and memorabilia about Massenet and Offenbach from French magazines to put in his own neat scrapbooks. From my point of view, the lighting was inadequate there. So I formed the habit of toting one mammoth book at a time up to my room, or enlisting Paul as porter, and working there on a little desk where the light was somewhat better. Occasionally I spread one of the clumsy volumes out on the bed and leaned over it.

When I first arrived, I asked if the big double windows could be opened for some fresh air. Silly! Joan showed me how they opened, but it was such a production I never tried it again, and, in spite of the heated house, enough of that mountain air crept through those double panes to satisfy any but a fiend. Sitting close to the window, I even resorted to sweaters and blankets. No fiend I.

So went the days. I never seemed to get free from the bondage of the Bonynges' past, as recorded worldwide and in four languages, with real photographs pasted in among the newspaper reproductions, and everything neatly in order. Weenie had done it, they told me. (Weenie, or Anne Roughley, Richard's aunt, no longer traveled with them as secretary. She had retired and now lived in Germany.)

From my third-floor eyrie, tucked in around two bends of the corridor, I could hear little of the household stir. When not cutting Massenet paper dolls, Ricky immured himself in his basement quarters. Joan and Ruthli presumably indulged in a deliriously happy bout of domesticity. Though perhaps it was not quite that happy. I realized afterward that I had never heard Joan's voice raised in song "around the house," said to be a sure sign of felicity. She may have vocalized in Ricky's study, but no sound of it came up the stairs.

Perhaps Joan did not feel like competing with Adam's friend, who spent torturous hours each day—at least it seemed like hours—at the piano keyboard, fingering out the opening bars of Chopin's Minute Waltz. Halting and awkward, he came up to the identical mistake every time, gave up, and started all over again. Paul and I agonized daily. The music, if you could call it that, filtered even through closed doors. I never mentioned it to Joan or Ricky.

I felt I might lick the scrapbooks with diligence, but it allowed no daytime frivolity, and little else. I would cheerfully have skipped a couple of pasted-up years for more personal contact. Joan was easier to corral for taped interviews, but Ricky balked from the start at the sight of my "infernal machine." Vainly I protested that it enabled me to quote him correctly, that it made interchange of ideas freer and more relaxed. I wonder if he sometimes has second thoughts about what he has said, and wishes he hadn't said it. My pleas for trust fell on deaf ears. In Australia and in New York and San Francisco they had been agreeable, though after initial protests. Here my mechanical recorder, and, equally—perhaps even more so—my camera, were no-nos.

I have figured it out. As the Englishman's home is his castle, the Bonynges' castle is their home. So jealously do they guard every precious moment and all the perquisites of privacy, that they resent any intrusion. They had tried to forget, I am sure, that a guest in the house intended to write a book about them. It was evidence of my own dual personality—friend or observer—and I finally appealed to Chester to mediate. He told Ricky that they were not being fair, that, after all, their oldtime biographer Russell Braddon had spent months trailing them around most intimately. Ricky promised to give me some time—*sans* Sony.

Meanwhile, Ricky fell ill. He had been "sickening for it" for several days, and no doubt this accounted for his uncertain temper, altogether unlike him, I had thought. He went to bed for a day. Then Chester was victimized by a stomach bug and *hors de combat* another day. Adam, too, was down for a while. What with all the men ailing, the scribe and secretary perched disconsolately up above, while the boy took hours to dismember the Minute Waltz, Joan and Ruthli could well have "gone bonkers" (Joan's expression).

After everyone's bugs had been banished, Ricky gave me the interview. A formal one it was, yielding a few tidbits, which will appear in proper context, but nothing so free and outgoing as had happened previously or would later. I came to believe that, in a professional ambience, both of them give what is professionally necessary—not without grumbling, to be sure, but realizing the value of the fringe aspects of their work. Here in their dearly won home in the precious few hours allowed them, they instinctively close their lives.

The lunch and dinner table rarely offered serious thought or professional discussion, and quite rightly so. But since that was the only time I saw them together, I tried now and then. Adam and friend did not chatter much. Adam's future disturbed him and his parents as well. Perhaps too ambitiously he had tackled courses in three languages which involved, I believe, knowledge of each country's history, literature, art, and whatnot. Gifted as he is linguistically, he had undoubtedly taken on too much and failed one section. As a result, he seemed to have lost interest in further academic life. Joan and Richard found a solution, and a good one, but it came later.

When the old friends, Mr. and Mrs. T., or Edie and Sam, as I shall call them, came for lunch and/or dinner, as they almost always did, the decibel content at Edie's end of the table increased notably. Sam was quieter, occasionally breaking out a joke for Joan's ears alone, which convulsed that lady. Ruthli attended to Rachel, whose high-register speech no one but her mother could understand, although we all tried and felt rewarded when accorded a bedtime kiss. Ricky repeated: "Adorable child!" after each of her excursions around the table, bestowing favors on each in turn.

Gertie had little to say. Chester seemed his usual cheerful, talkative self, but was full of a project that had to be kept secret until the fateful day—a great doll's house for Rachel he was building in the garage. As for me, I merely went along with the currents, not being able to direct them, enjoying the chitchat, and seldom trying to start anything. There did not seem to be a chink in anyone's schedule, and I did not pursue my own interests persistently enough, I must admit. I should have looked at the color slides they have acquired by the thousands, but somehow there was never time to show me. Chester had been a professional photographer, a very useful art for his employers. Other professionals and friends had added their tributes.

Ricky asked Gertie to dust some shelves in the third-floor corridor, which held various mementos. Even standing on a chair, she could not reach the top shelf, so I came out of my retreat and helped, incidentally getting a very good color slide of this faithful, patient, dedicated woman. She had been at Covent Garden for about a quarter-century, and knew the place and use for every needle and spool of thread. Rather like a drill mistress, she ran the costume department. "Our workmanship was meticulous—you couldn't find a flaw," she stated proudly. Stage costumes were as perfectly fitted as couture gowns. She felt things were going downhill a bit now, a reaction natural enough for a perfectionist ruthlessly divorced from her life's work. She promised to show me Joan's costumes, which were coming to Les Avants after having been stored in Covent Garden. Now they too were being evacuated. But, alas! they arrived the very morning I had overslept. I dimly heard thumpings and muttered instructions outside my door, but couldn't move. And so the costumes arrived, were unpacked, stored in heavy plastic bags in an alcove in Joan's room, and the cartons hoisted up a ladder that descended from the attic storeroom to the corridor outside my door.

Joan and Ruthli ran the house by themselves, with Chester offside to execute any particular mission. The dining table was set for the next meal immediately after one had finished. Joan's china and silverware were all that their close friend in New York, Ania Dorfman, had promised they were, and each person had his own napkin ring. A huge bouquet of fresh "flahs" centered it all. A large carafe stood at each end of the table and held a deliciously dry white wine from nearby. "Buy Swiss" seemed to be the word, though indulging in that chauvinism could cost a packet. Edie came to the table periodically complaining of the soaring prices of even the simplest kitchen gadget. All her outrage was of course expressed to the shopkeepers in English. Like so many Americans and some Englishmen, she operated on the theory that the louder you talk, the more likely a stranger is to understand what you are talking about. It never works, and with the Swiss, it would be least effective. Self-containment is a polite word for these people. After all, it took courage and cleverness to remain neutral in the heart of a war-torn continent. Thrift and caution are deeply rooted ways of life, admirable or exasperating depending on how you look at it.

Ruthli is an exception, born in Basel and with roots still there. Warm, affectionate, impetuous, she has had her share of troubles and dismissed them.

Ruthli's cooking was both simple and rich. I remember a

delicious chicken, but Ruthli dressed it with huge slices of ham! Ham, that good Swiss viand, dominated many meals; a cheese board invariably rounded them off. My cross! Just before I left home, I'd been warned against those very delicacies plus eggs—the devils of high cholesterol. If only there had been enough time to get used to the idea and calmly break training now and then with a good conscience, I should not have refused, no matter how politely, those utterly desirable viands. Anyway, there were Ruthli's superb vegetables, the huge bowl of tasty salad, the delicious little Swiss cookies I relished so much that Gertie gave me a box for Christmas.

Evenings at Chalet Monet fell quickly into a pattern. After dinner on (I think) the second night, Ricky and Edie and Sam gathered at a card table in one of the two downstairs rooms. (The other is a small sitting room, crammed with Ricky's trophies: a corner enshrining Jenny Lind, a tall cabinet of mostly Staffordshire figurines, portraits of Catherine the Great and another dignitary, a wall of miniatures, and more). Joan immediately settled herself under a lamp with the obvious intention to work all evening at her most ambitious (and, at last hearing, still unfinished) needlepoint adventure, a mammoth rectangle in a wine-colored flower pattern to hang behind her bed.

I realized conversation was unwelcome, and wandered over to the bridge table, where a three-handed game was in progress. Ricky looked up and asked doubtfully: "Do you play?"

I answered with equal doubt: "Sometimes." There was no escape, as there never is for a missing fourth who turns up, I thought resignedly and joined in the cut for partners. We were fairly evenly matched—not expert, but competent, and so these games held some zest. Adam sat in one night, but gave up under the fire of advice from partner and opponents alike.

The alternate entertainment every other night was movies. Gathered in the darkened music room, we howled with laughter at a British film (somehow resurrected by Ricky) of a working-class family's squabbles and tribulations. Sometimes the dialect was so broad that I missed finer (or blunter) points, but there was no mistaking the burden of the acrimonious exchanges between two raucous women, vulgar and funny. To show the film has become a Bonynge Christmas treat. Other diversions were a tape of an Ed Sullivan show with Joan, a "home movie" (by Chester) of Les Avants in summer, flower-blanketed, green and lovely, with guests strolling about. There was also an excursion to Noël Coward's Caribbean retreat. "Here it comes!" somebody exclaimed. A candid rear view of two gentlemen who shall be unidentified, in the tanned buff, striding toward the surf. (Unidentified, that is, by me; although everyone else knew.)

Of more professional moment, the eight half-hour TV films of Joan's "Who's Afraid of Grand Opera?" were trotted out, two by two. I forget the coupling, but the operas were *Barber of Seville*, *Daughter of the Regiment*, *Périchole*, *Mignon*, *Rigoletto*, *Traviata*, *Lucia*, and *Faust*. Some rather fierce controversy had greeted their American career; the pros arguing for their light touch and the value of "bringing opera close to the public;" the cons objecting that masterpieces had been "desecrated." Particular loathing had been expressed for the intrusive puppets, whose ignorance and gaucherie alienated rather than ingratiated many viewers. I believe that, given the premise that opera needs a kind of mediator to reach the uninitiated, the puppet idea had merit, but their dialogue was a disaster. I am inclined to think the Bonynges secretly agree, but they would not come right out with it. Their aggressive press agent had thought up the idea and was listed as producer.

For days I had limited my wanderings through the house to the central territory. When they bought the property, acting on the advice of Noël Coward, who lived just next door, Joan and Richard immediately began remodeling the house, adding to it so cleverly that no distortion shows from the outside, and creating a diverting puzzle in the interior. I had become familiar with the three important rooms on the first floor, less so with the kitchen; knew the balcony anteroom and the vast music room, two-storied; and, of course, the third-floor domain. This began at the head of the stairs with Paul's office and bedroom; proceeded to a small guest room, now occupied by Adam's friend; to Ruthli's small suite; a bath; and around another bend Adam's congeries (dictionary definition: "A collection of particles, parts . . . into one mass; heap; aggregation"), a typical teenager's lair, with one unusual addition: a toy electric train under the heaps of discarded clothes. Next came my "Spanish" room, so called, I believe, because of a couple of framed portraits. At the end of the corridor was a study where one could watch television (in French).

The day after Ricky's recovery from his malaise, he gave me the grand tour. I had been cowed into leaving my camera behind, but tried to tote the infernal machine to record some details. No, he wasn't having any. With no aid to my by now enfeebled memory, the tour in retrospect reminds me of a time-exposure trail left by moving lights on a film—one long, beautiful blur: the first painting ever acquired at a flea market; the dozens bought since, many of musical figures, including a huge horror of Emmy Destinn (the opera singer who did not exactly enjoy a reputation for beauty), several of royalty or other celebrated persons, those of great ladies in the music room; framed programs, playbills, reproductions of opera houses, stage designs, posters, the Staffordshire and other porcelain figurines (the number was then above six hundred); the antique furniture culled from shops all over the world, a luxurious fur bed covering, clocks, bibelots, the "bits and pieces," as the host referred to dozens of treasures, in that bored voice that hides pride and glee. Have you ever heard an Englishman or a cultivated Australian utter, "bits and pieces"? It is to experience the ultimate in understatement.

Grand pianos are not lacking. There are two in the comfortable expanse of the music room, where four once gasped for keyboard space. Ania Dorfman had been responsible for relieving Chalet Monet of two of them (dating back to Queen Victoria, they were), to Joan's gratitude. Another is in Ricky's quarters, where the magnitude of books and music scores reaches astronomical proportions. (This element has overflowed into a storeroom on the third floor, packed with neatly catalogued orchestra parts for the music of all types that engages Ricky's unwasted time and energy.) We had reached the master's quarters by a short winding staircase leading down from the front hall, one that played a part in my one perilous adventure.

What a treasure house is this! Its wealth of cherished objects (all of Ricky's acquisition, not of Joan's), penetrates into almost every room, even my guest perch, which is tastefully furnished and with walls showing very few chinks between pictures. Ricky, one day checking on my progress with the scrapbooks, spied a small interstice between wall ornaments, and cried triumphantly: "There's a place to hang more pictures!" I photographed the wall, just to show how even that tiny spot would not be wasted. By now, I'm sure it's filled.

The guest room and bath that adjoin Joan's dressing room on the second floor bear their treasures: portraits, ornaments, charming beds and chairs. But Joan's room is her own—feminine, simple, uncluttered.

Ricky showed me a miniature he had been told was a portrait of Emma Eames. I demurred, having become completely familiar with photographs of that patrician countenance, either face-on or in profile, when I was researching my *Opera Caravan*, the history of the Met's tours. This round-faced, dark, curly-haired siren with the melting brown eyes was nothing like the American lady of the chilling blue gaze, the long, slender face, the firmly set mouth. I said as much, quite positively, then suggested that it might well be another Emma—Calvé. Later, I sent Ricky photographs of the sultry French diva and, I think, proved my point.

The most pleasant time of all was the tree trimming. I happened on it fortuitously, having been told that at that particular time I might photograph the needlepoint chairs for an article in *Opera News* about opera folks' needlepointing. Ricky had told me about them. When their first engagement in Spain left them with local currency they could not take out, he had bought a set of graceful chairs and massive sofa and had them shipped home. Joan had made needlepoint covers for all six chairs and the sofa, a beautiful dark blue background with a flower pattern. I was fussing about, getting angles and lighting, when Joan came into the music room. The tree had been set up, and heaps of boxes of trimmings covered the piano tops and tables. Evidently, I was not welcome, and Joan looked disturbed at my pursuit. Worse was yet to come. I think it was Paul or it may have been Chester, who ran down from the anteroom to bring the ukase that I was not to photograph at all. I had trouble keeping my temper at this point, for I had been promised this a long time ago. My distress must have been so obvious that, within a few minutes the word came back: "Go ahead and photograph." Joan relented too, rather *faute de mieux*, and helped me place the chairs to best advantage. In my haste and nervousness, however, I never got quite satisfactory pictures.

As I finished, I asked Joan, who had begun to trim the tree, if I might help. As if to make up for my previous discomfiture, she agreed. The next few hours were unsullied bliss. There is such a sweet ritual about trimming a Christmas tree. Everyone has his own favorite ornaments, cherished trifles from other years, loaded with sentiment; or bright new baubles to demand a place in the comfortable old pattern. Joan possessed many that were dear in association; these she placed lovingly at strategic points. I noticed the one deformity in the tree—a great gap between lower branches that spoiled the symmetry, and endeavored to minimize the fault. Joan took to the ladder for higher reaches, while I steadied it. The top angel is always a delicate balance problem.

Finally, there was a question: tinsel or no tinsel? We women were inclined to go without, but Joan said the men preferred it. We draped tinsel all over.

It was a lovely, peaceful, friendly afternoon. I learned afterward that I had been specially favored, for Joan always reserved the exclusive privilege of this ceremony.

Another gratifying incident that shines in memory enabled me to boast that I had "sung with Joan Sutherland." One night at the dinner table, we had gotten onto the subject of Massenet, and I remembered that long ago in boarding school I had given a short song recital, the nugget of which was Massenet's "Ouvre tes yeux bleus." Whether Ricky said to sing it or not, I began to, very softly. To my delight, from across the table, Joan joined in. It's odd how the memory holds certain bits, complete and untarnished. So it was with this song. We finished triumphantly with "Et le grand soleil qui nous brûle est dans mon coeur!" It was a duet that will never be recorded save in my rather bemused recollection.

The arrival of the Australian boys lightened the atmosphere somewhat. Midway in a long trip, they came from London for Christmas, then were to head away toward home. Moffatt Oxenbould and Graeme Ewer we have met before in Sydney. Moffatt, as the then assistant to the administrator of the Australian Opera (he has since been promoted), and his friend Graeme, a rather melancholy comedian at the moment, beset by a cold germ. With them in the house, the current ran operatically, and it was good to hear the gossip and the familiar shop talk. Ricky had much business to discuss with Moffatt, for his tenure as musical director was to begin the following season.

I saw them only at mealtimes, for I was still immured with my scrapbooks and beginning to panic at the idea of not finishing them. Note-taking became too cumbersome and time-consuming. I thought: If I can't use my infernal machine below stairs, at least it will help here, so I fell to talking to myself. This speeded up the process, and I finished cassette no. 9 just under the wire. This was the book devoted exclusively to concerts, in just about the right ratio to a dozen covering opera. The concert stage is not Joan's favorite platform, as I have noted before.

One afternoon I determined to test that glorious outdoors that lay beyond our windows. It was rather a grim decision, for I had not poked my nose out except once or twice to watch the clouds gathering over the mountains or a specially splendid sunset. The morning after I arrived, the sun had shone so brilliantly on the all-encompassing snow that Ruthli worried. When it blinds the eyes, she said, bad weather is sure to come. And she was right. We had rain before long; the snow became softer and mushier and eventually relaxed its white dominion.

I intended to walk at least down the steep driveway to the road, and perhaps get some shots of the exterior of the house. So I donned fur and boots and, from the front hall where my coat had hung, descended the wrong stairway. I discovered my mistake at the bottom, with a fleeting glimpse of a tanned fawn scampering across a far doorway. Ricky laughingly confirmed my fleeting vision, which I almost disbelieved.

I stumbled back up the stairs and then down the proper way to the great outdoors via the kitchen stairs. Once out, I enjoyed the short stroll and got a couple of rather nice pictures of the chateau and its tower. But an emissary once again dampened my spirits; I was not to photograph, please. The house did not look its best, was the excuse. This was beginning to look like unreasonable oppression.

By now, frustration at not being able to do the job I had been presumably asked to do was building up dangerously. I felt neither a good guest nor a competent reporter. Then, aided by several glasses of that excellent Swiss wine, both my manners and my competence shattered.

Edie, sitting to Ricky's left at dinner, was holding forth once again, not about her uncle or nephew or whatever, but on the subject of Schuyler Chapin, the then general manager of the Metropolitan. As the saying goes, Edie was entitled to her opinion, but it was her manner of voicing it, through a too-mobile mouth and in too fortissimo a tone, that finally lit my fuse.

I leaned across Ricky and spoke quietly but with conviction into that tirade.

"I don't like your face when you talk like that!" are the incredible words that issued from my own unrestrained lips.

"My God! What have I done?" was my first reaction. Hers was as childish as my own provocation.

"I don't like you either!" she spat. And she had the advantage of superior dynamics.

The momentary silence that followed could charitably be called awkward. Hastily, I looked across at Joan, and, into her frozen countenance began to babble something to the effect that weren't we awful, fishwife-brawling just like those two in the English movie—what was the name of the one who was so particularly dreadful? Joan supplied the name through stiff lips. Somehow the dinner ended. I apologized to Edie, of course, blaming the wine, and to my host and hostess for having overstepped the bounds of propriety. To insult a fellow guest! Unforgivable!

Many nights later I ran into Sam and Edie in Carnegie Hall, and we were at least polite. Edie inquired about the book, not suspecting, I imagine, that she would be in it.

My only other outing was to town, to Montreux, to investigate a shop that carried my favorite material, braids of silk and wool and metal threads, beautiful to look at and fascinating to work into whatever one's imagination can contrive. I had made for Joan a large bag of pink and silver for her needlepoint and had decorated an album of snapshots of *Esclarmonde* rehearsals for Ricky and a red velvet apron for Chester to wear while making *glögg*, that Swedish hot spiced wine (we never got around to it). I did manage to replenish my stock from the small shop.

One day when Joan was stretched out on her chaise longue and was gracious about talking, I had asked her if she had any braid. She went to a tall armoire and pulled out just what I needed—a strip about two inches wide. I told her it was for a present I wasn't altogether satisfied with—and indeed, it was her own. I had sewn the bag's sides together and cut off interior space. The added strips up the sides solved the problem. I sewed them on one night while watching TV with Paul and Gertie.

Christmas was almost upon us. Everyone made surreptitious trips to Joan's room where, spread out on the bed, were wrappings, seals, string, and labels in profusion. Down under the tree, the colorful cubes and rectangles began to pile up. The air became charged with that special emotion and anticipation.

We celebrated on Christmas Eve. What little order could be established soon vanished and everyone was left on his own to unwrap and marvel and try to get the attention of everyone else. The brilliance of the torn wrappings piled up higher and higher. Rachel, with her doll's house and myriad presents, remained a fixed star, but around her swirled a dozen celebrants, each intent on his own goodies, while called on to admire others'.

The amazingly thoughtful Joan had provided a drift of delightful gifts for her guests. Her own special present from Ricky was a squash-blossom necklace of fabulous turquoise that Ricky had bought in Phoenix, and which drove me, a longtime collector of American Indian jewelry, mad with envy. It was one of the most beautiful I'd ever seen, and looked magnificent on her shapely neck.

On Christmas Day, we trooped off down the hill and up another to Noël Coward's villa, left to his faithful friends Cole Lesley and Graham Pyne. It was a merry party, sunlit from without and champagne-lit from within. I had been warned about the drink they served—bubbly laced with brandy, the French 75, named after the famous French cannon—so nursed a single glass through the afternoon, watching some beautiful strangers and enjoying the cherished surroundings.

Next morning we were off. (It was Boxing Day, that first weekday after Christmas when British tradespeople and servants come round for gifts—their "boxes.")

I had hoped to stay on to be thorough about the scrapbooks, but the idea was greeted with horror. The house would be shut up, for Ruthli and Rachel were going to visit their family, Adam and friend had a skiing trek in mind, Chester was coming to London by car and Channel boat, and Paul, too, had to leave. This last was a blow both to the secretary and his employers. He had neglected to file at the proper time as an alien and get his work permit, so Switzerland closed its frontier to him. He would get a job in a London restaurant as a maître d'hôtel for a time, then find a place with Placido Domingo, to appear once more in the corridors of the Metropolitan and other world opera houses.

But leave-taking proved not so simple. The maestro was late. While we all gathered on the back porch and in the driveway, Ricky was still in his bath. We passed the time taking photographs. It amused me, if amused is quite the word, to note that when Joan was about to be back in harness, she did not object to posing. I got two prized views of her, one alone, bareheaded, in her luxurious mink coat, arms outflung as if in welcome, a radiant smile on her face; the other in front of, and dominating, a group of us. Chester must have taken that one with my camera.

Finally we scattered to our various destinations. Chester drove Joan and Ricky and me to Geneva, and we managed, with official help, to make the right plane. Our fourteen pieces of luggage (only two of them mine, I hasten to state), were not so fortunate. Officialdom had goofed, and in London, we waited weary hours till the laggard plane with the bags showed up. The hired car the Bonynges always requisition in London drove us and my two suitcases to town, and a taxi brought their twelve. In a somber drizzle, I was deposited at the Chesterfield Hotel, tucked away behind Berkeley Square and hard to find except that Joan remembered the neighborhood fairly well. We had passed close to their former home in Kensington, and I could detect a pang of nostalgia as Joan spoke of it. Now they would stay at the Savoy until a flat became available for their month of *Traviatas* at Covent Garden.

But that's another story. The Swiss Christmas was over. A

238 / SUTHERLAND AND BONYNGE

year later, in a Chicago interview taped without serious resistance to the infernal machine (it was for the Australian Information Service series of radio broadcasts in the U.S.), Joan referred to that holiday as "hectic."

A rather kind understatement on the whole, I thought happily.

CHAPTER
28

In Search of the Lost One

SUTHERLAND'S LAST PREVIOUS LONDON *LA TRA-*
viata had been twelve years before. Long memories ran back
to the first. In 1960, it had been not an altogether successful step
forward after the brilliant fireworks of the *Lucia*, but Joan had
faithfully pursued the fragile Violetta, seeking always to penetrate
more deeply into the proud, passionate character, as her vocal
mastery continued supreme.

It was a pity that a new production could not have been
devised for the 1975 occasion. Covent Garden had made one of
several resuscitations of the trappings originally produced by Lu-
chino Visconti in 1967, with Mirella Freni as the heroine. The stark
white stage designs by Nito Frescà now seemed dingy and frayed;
their small scale and fussy detail (with a rather tiny soprano in
mind) gave Joan trouble from the first. (They probably didn't faze
another early protagonist; Montserrat Caballé, who never bothers
to move around very much, and certainly fitted the latest previous
Violetta, the slender Ileana Cotrubas.)

Joan had put her foot down about going far into the suburbs
for earlier rehearsals, and got on stage very soon. The young director, Michael Rennison, who had succeeded John Copley (who
had succeeded Visconti), felt all the more eager to be helpful to
the reigning prima donna, who also had to walk in others' footprints.

The famous old market, which adjoined the Royal Opera House,
had faded from the scene. One no longer had to step on discarded
spinach leaves and dodge burly trucksters toting huge crates in
order to reach the front door by foot, and on leaving could walk
through the ghostly abandoned buildings right down the hill to the
Strand and the Savoy.

The opera house had at last sought to cope with its space problem by taking over a building across Floral Street from the stage entrance, and moving administration, press, and other departments there. It beats climbing secret stairs and crossing dangerous little bridges to get to the press room. The elevators didn't work very well, however, so there was a good deal of traffic on the stairs. A charming Miss Bell convoyed me from the new quarters to the stage door, across the street, where Mickey Clarke took over and led me backstage to attend a rehearsal. From there we followed a passage to the front of the house and a good vantage point in the upper circle.

It was chilly in the auditorium. Things got under way raggedly, with Mike Rennison here, there, and everywhere, darting about to position Joan, then interrupting Joan to put the Alfredo (Alfredo Kraus) in place, then hollering at the chorus, which seemed a trifle disorganized. Oh, well, Monday morning and early innings.

At a break, Ricky came over to chat, but was summoned for a conference with Joan—an emergency, she said hastily. Her face clouded as she talked. It seemed that the Australian government wanted her to fly out and give a concert on Saturday as a benefit for the cyclone-stricken city of Darwin, then fly back to open here on Monday. "I just can't do it!" she exclaimed in distress. "But they'll make a scandal out of it—just wait and see. Incredible!" (They compromised by organizing a benefit concert in London on January 25.)

Joan was patently unhappy with the spindly furniture (some chairs resembled old ice-cream-parlor affairs, with wire loops for backs.) A rickety armchair in the second act looked as if it would collapse when Joan was required to throw herself into it. They had given her a long yellow skirt with the hint of a train to flounce around, and it consistently knocked over a row of mangy potted flowers near the footlights. Finally, they did away with the minor obstruction. But the furniture was all in the wrong place, Joan kept complaining, not logical at all. It was a stop-and-go day, with little singing and not much of that in full voice.

I watched Kraus, wondering at the Londoners' adoration of this slim Spanish tenor. He showed no touch of expression in his long, mustached face, or in his bearing. ("He never smiles," someone said backstage. And someone else added: "He can't sing unless he's facing the footlights and as far forward as possible.") Joan had encountered him as long ago as her first repetition of the famous *Lucia*, and he had sung Elvino in her La Scala *Sonnambula* in 1962.

He seemed a rather stolid Alfredo for Joan to beat her wings against, but London thought otherwise: "The Rare Alfredo Kraus," they called him, and the magazine *Opera* came out with a long piece on his many virtues—a silky voice with a perfect line, aristocracy of mien, dignity, and so on. The accompanying photographs show him going through the motions, but never really involved (only one of them displays an actual smile, almost a grin, as he accepts congratulations from a festival director.) He had sung opposite Joan several times—even in the *Fille du régiment* in Chicago in 1973, when Pavarotti's image must have been evoked for any ears that had heard the big boy with the nine steady high Cs. Kraus had the high voice, too, had even sung Arturo in *I Puritani* (and would again), but it was for Werther, the Duke of Mantua, Edgardo, and so on that he was most acclaimed. (At this time, I was undoubtedly doing Kraus an injustice. Later, in a New York swimming club, I encountered him, tan and fit, and, yes, smiling as we chatted. His reserve also disappeared in later performances in *Daughter of the Regiment* and *Lucia*.)

One never saw him offstage. He disappeared as quietly as a shadow, still not smiling.

Never mind. We had Louis Quilico to provide the hearty moments. It was the Canadian baritone's London debut, and the London public press took to his Germont père very warmly.

Joan may still be thought of as "cold," but the aloofness of Kraus is seldom mentioned. Perhaps it is because he is Spanish. The attribution of coldness haunts possibly every singer outside the warm climates of Italy and Spain. Criticisms of Joan's acting almost invariably come from confirmed Italians, and from partisans of Albanese, Sayao, and Tebaldi.

Modern critics really gave up comparing Sutherland and Callas in the acting realm. There seemed to be room for two different worlds. But the reputation for coldness and reserve still lingers for Joan.

Early opinions of Joan as a somewhat gauche actress were not too long ago shared by the object of them. Joan, upon witnessing the early film of Sarah Bernhardt's *Camille*, with her lurchings and vast gestures, squealed (only in partial jest): "Gawd! That's me!"

Garbo's film was another matter. Richard confessed that he loves it and has seen it many times. Even Robert Taylor seemed good as Armand. Richard noted that Camille never lost her dignity even in the midst of the orgies that were common in her time and place. Dumas had always insisted on this quality in his original

Alphonsine Plessis, who became Marie Duplessis at the time when the younger Dumas fell in love with her. Then, after he enshrined her in his novel, *La Dame aux camélias*, it was only a short step to the Violetta Valéry of Verdi's opera. The quality of personal dignity remained.

Joan retains this delicate distinction in her Violetta, and the underlying and suddenly expressed passion appears without question in the voice. At the time of her latest recording, there are those who believe no finer Violetta exists—certainly not in the vocal realm.

Sandro Sequi has expressed the radical idea that Joan is best seen in a small theater, where she doesn't have to move around much and the subtlety of her facial expressions can be observed, matching the intricate and subtle beauties of voice. So far, this has been possible perhaps only in the fifteen-hundred-seat Sydney Opera House. Covent Garden is too vast a barn for such niceties; so is the Metropolitan. South America expressed its reservations about her Violetta, while giving full marks to Norma. So The Lost One continues to haunt Joan. It is pretty safe to say, she will pursue the elusive lady as long as her career endures.

One frustration remains. Franco Zeffirelli will probably never direct her in *La Traviata*, fervently as she has besought him. It seems that he is obsessed with the idea that a seemingly fragile creature must play the truly fragile Violetta. His experience with Callas in the role has apparently left an indelible partisanship. He was tackled on the subject after a lecture on his new *Bohème* production at the Met, and evaded a direct answer. When he learned that Joan's next appearance was as Leonora, he said: "Better *Trovatore* than *Traviata*."

. . .

One day between rehearsal periods in London, Joan took me to a pleasant lunch at the Nag's Head pub, a great favorite with opera folk, down the street from the stage door. Over a Scotch egg (new to me—it is a hard-boiled egg embedded in chopped meat cloaked in bread crumbs), she exchanged greetings with a half-dozen old friends. Among them was Frank Edgerton, who had grown a beard because Edward Downes thought him too young to sing the monk Missail in *Boris Godunov*. Then Joseph Rouleau came over, an early Covent Garden colleague indeed. He kidded Edgerton, jeering that the baritones never get the girl, but sometimes the bass does. (Name three?) He had just been singing Arkel in the Garden's *Pelléas et Mélisande* and observed that the American baritone,

Richard Stilwell, as Pelléas had been well liked. Chorus men approached diffidently and invited Joan to a party.

Then for a while we were left alone and Joan talked about previous *Traviata*s. She remembered how she had run to Norman Ayrton after rehearsals for her first Violetta and told him what the director had said he wanted. Norman tried to show her how to do it. It was a very patchy, unsatisfactory method, and Joan, working feverishly nine to twelve hours a day and in great emotional stress, developed tracheitis and muffed the first performance. This had been Joan's first brush with Nello Santi, the conductor who was to cause her so much trouble in Venice later. And as for the director (he was and remained nameless): "He never gave an inkling of the character or motivation to make Violetta a human being," she declared, still passionate about the injustice of it. "And Norman never got a line of credit." But his training stood by her when she did the Boston *Traviata* in 1964.

"I'm afraid it was the last of Sarah [Caldwell] for me. She wouldn't show up for all the rehearsals, only certain days, for she was out raising money. She may be a genius, but so disorganized." Many times she would just stand around, generating an idea, while the singers stood around, too, generating boredom, according to Joan.

I interjected that, of course, there is the opposite method, the daily, weekly, monthly drilling of Walter Felsenstein, also labeled "genius," whose productions in East Berlin were hailed worldwide.

"I couldn't work like that either," Joan said thoughtfully. "I would get so bored. How can you keep any freshness with so much rehearsal?

"Now, this *Traviata*, the costumes are beautiful. White and deep aubergine. They fit me well, with a little fullness in the back and a small train."

Sure enough, the gowns of the *belle époque* into which Visconti had translated the story from the usual 1840s (originally it had been shown as in the 1700s to avoid seeming too contemporary for the mid-nineteenth-century stage), suited Joan very well, except for the too matronly dress in the second act. The gowns were close-fitting in the waist, with becoming low necklines and large sleeves, deep purple trimming on the white gown, white on the dark one. The last act showed her in a frilly white nightdress, over which she threw a simple robe.

We talked about the physical productions. In several *Travia-*

tas (notably at the Met and in the *Lucias*), enormous staircases are designers' delights. "I don't mind them if I have the time to get used to them," she said. "But it's terrible when you have to be thinking all the time of where you're going to put your feet instead of what you're singing and the character who's singing it."

The first rehearsal with costumes came on January 3, when Flora's ball (as scene 2 of Act II) startled all with the vivid hues of the costumes—the only real splash of color in the opera. Crowded on a stage cluttered with a Moorish pavilion and sundry pouffes and stools, it lacked cohesion and focus. The full dress rehearsal came on Saturday, the fourth.

Meanwhile, I had spent hours away from the Opera House in London's favorite pastime—the theater—and at movies, and one endless evening at the English National Opera's *Die Meister-singer* at the Coliseum. Frequent companions on the Covent Garden rounds were two youths, Richard Goldstein, one of the chief supers at the Met, whom I had encountered many times during the *Hoffmann* siege, and Tony Freyberg. We watched rehearsals together and lunched in the crowded little commissary deep in the house, reached by labyrinthine white-walled narrow passages—far more diverse and puzzling than the Met's and without the amenities of elevators. One could so easily get lost; a guide was imperative. Tony said that whenever he felt surprised he made a "Joan" face —mouth open, lower lip drawn in. She caught him at it once, but said nothing.

Joan had named a favorite restaurant, the Imperia, just up from the Strand on Charing Cross Road, and we lunched there one day. I discovered my next-table neighbor to be Louis Quilico, who introduced me to calamari (little doughnut-shaped pieces of squid). Not unpleasant, but rather tough and tasteless.

It rained, of course, and was never more threatening than on New Year's Day, when I went to lunch with the Bonynges in their suite at the Savoy. Joan and I had intended to visit the Turner exhibition at the Tate Gallery, but the murk outside the windows persuaded us to stay inside and watch two Marx Brothers films on TV. Of course, one of them was *A Night at the Opera*. The other, not quite in the same class, but pretty funny, was *The Big Store*. Richard and I engaged in some hearty knee-slapping to accompany the laughter, while Joan smiled over her needlepoint and at one juncture went into another room to give an interview to a local newshound.

I looked forward to renewing acquaintance with John Copley,

the leprechaun of the Australian Opera, but he was suffering from a horrible cold and kept his distance at a *Rosenkavalier* rehearsal. This was an ENO production, starring as Octavian Josephine Barstow (later to be met at Santa Fe as a splendid Salomé), Anne Evans as the Marschallin, Valierie Mostyn as Sophie, and Neil Warren Smith as Ochs. Charles Mackerras, the jovial Australian, was conducting.

One afternoon, I took the opportunity to observe Richard at one of his recording sessions for London Records. I strolled along the wide thoroughfare, Kingsway, trying to find the address Richard had given me for the recording studio. Puzzled at seeing nothing that remotely resembled a studio near the address, I accosted a man carrying a violin case. He pointed to the entrance where I was standing—a church! I should have realized, for there had been a lot of talk about this old place, apparently so excellent in acoustics for recording that everyone went there. Rather hesitantly, I penetrated beyond the lobby filled with appurtenances peculiar to the building, and through a door into the "auditorium" proper.

It was so dimly lit that one could not read or take photographs. Gradually I moved forward a few pews until Ricky saw me and invited me to the control room, down a few steps and into a low-ceilinged, crowded rabbit hole. Here the lords of the manor were Douglas Gamley (a colleague who later returned to his native Australia to conduct some performances) and Michael Woolcock.

It might be: "More crescendo on the horn," or "Don't hear the winds here," or some such criticism. Ricky would listen, then go topside and do another take, come down and listen to the playback, go up again, come down again. That was the way recordings are made. However picky and time-consuming, *Les Patineurs* and *Le Cid* ballet and some other snippets came through nobly. Everyone paused at times to partake of bitter tea and Auntie Olive's cake.

Opening night, January 6, came, and the Gamleys were my hosts in their box. We sipped wine in the box during the first interval and I wandered through the Crush Bar in the second. They are longish periods because, as Tony explained, it takes so long to get the scenery in: fifteen or twenty men must practically build it on stage.

It always is a stunning experience to witness a fully realized product from the bits and pieces of rehearsal, and this *Traviata* was no exception. In spite of the frayed scenery and not always expert lighting, the show went off brilliantly. Joan and her Alfredo were in top form, and Quilico got a lion's share of praise. All of Mike's fussing with detail paid off, and Joan died touchingly.

Next day, John Tooley, General Administrator who had succeeded David Webster, was good enough to give me a half hour in the new offices. He had joined the company about the same time as Joan, and was pleased by and proud of her spectacular rise, delighted by her lack of pretension. "She feels at home here," he declared, quite rightly. Her next venture at Covent Garden would be *Maria Stuarda* in 1977, and Tourangeau was to sing Elizabeth again. I was a little apprehensive about that, but as it turned out, Huguette won some raves from the London critics.

Meanwhile, the obliging press girls promised to send me the cuttings on *Traviata*, so I learned later that Kraus was still in highest favor as this, his first Covent Garden Alfredo. John Higgins of *The Times* thought that the first act was a blend of bland and brilliant, and the last showed the first signs of the vulnerable, almost childlike nature of Violetta. Martin Cooper in the *Daily Telegraph* struck his usual sour-note refrain where Joan and Richard were concerned. Knowing how they had both developed since early days, I felt Cooper needed a new pair of ears.

But Philip Hope-Wallace went all out in the *Guardian*, making amends.

I never thought to hear Joan Sutherland so good as Verdi's "Strayed One." Twelve years ago she used to vocalize the role with great brilliance, but had not found her way into an effective interpretation. Last night, with the sympathetic and finely judged conducting of her husband, Richard Bonynge—forget the nervous, tense first act—who gave the soprano and indeed all the characters the really understanding support they needed, the Australian diva pulled off a most loving and memorable last act, with a gentle swell of pathos in "prendi quest' immagine" which went straight to the heart like the phrase "Alfin son tua" in her *Lucia di Lammermoor* in which she conquered us years ago.

Then he backtracked a little.

I don't honestly think Verdi's *Traviata* is a natural assignment for her: she is too big and healthy, too strong and vivid, not sad and delicate enough for some of the scenes, but her big second-act duet with the splendid Quilico, a magnificent baritone too long absent, and a grand stage presence, were most effective.

Joan carried on through the next four performances in a rising curve, then in the last, on January 27, the old affliction struck. She had been in some pain intermittently. One sign of trouble had been seen after our arrival in London from Switzerland, when saying good-bye from the back seat of the car in which they drove me to the hotel, I thoughtlessly pulled her head back a trifle to kiss her on the cheek. She winced and cried out in pain. But she had seemed in fair health through the run of performances. Then, on January 27, while she was singing her high-flying "Sempre libera" in the first act, her right arm—held high with a champagne glass in her hand—stiffened and she could not bring it down. She had enough presence of mind to dance over to the wings, where someone relieved her of the glass. The arm gradually lowered, but it was a portent.

The doctor grounded her for several weeks for a thorough rest and treatment. Regretfully, she canceled some concerts in America with Pavarotti (though they later turned up in full glory). The wheels began to turn again in April, and for me it meant our next encounter—*Lucrezia Borgia* in Houston.

CHAPTER
29

Further Encounters with the Diva

✲ VANCOUVER HAD HAD THE HONOR OF THE FIRST
Lucrezia in 1972. David Gockley's up-and-coming company
in the Texas metropolis of Houston was the second to assign Sutherland to motherhood—seemingly an unlikely role for either demented damsel or tomboy. She recalled only two other operas in
which she displayed maternal feelings: Mozart's *Magic Flute*, where
the Queen of the Night is a mean mamma indeed; and Puccini's
Suor Angelica, a convent novice whose motherhood has shamed
her. "I suppose you wouldn't count the Mother Superior in Poulenc's *Dialogues of the Carmelites*," she joked.

Lucrezia proved a splendid role—mature, yet with a spontaneous flow of passion that embraced both maternal love and
fierce, chilling revenge. Her Houston colleagues were excellent:
John Brecknock, the English tenor, as Gennaro, her long-lost son;
Michael Devlin, a New York City Opera star, as her husband, the
Duke of Ferrara; and Huguette Tourangeau as Orsini, whose Brin-
disi, calling for merriment in the face of a terrible death, always
brings down the house. Old friends set the stage: Lotfi Mansouri
as director and José Varona as designer. The opening scene in
Venice had particular shimmering charm. Bonynge, in the pit,
offered a superb lesson, thought Ann Holmes in the *Chronicle*.
The orchestra was in perfect control, brilliantly keyed to and guiding every move and breath on stage. Joan's voice was termed a
glory. After the performances she signed autographs with a right
hand still in pain.

Lucrezia would get a new production at Covent Garden in
1980, with John Copley, Michael Stennett, and John Pascoe heading the production team for performances in March and April. Ann

Howell was the London Orsini, while Afredo Kraus sang Gennaro, and Stafford Dean, Alfonso d'Este. Then Rome borrowed the production, and these roles were taken respectively by Elena Zilio, Piero Visconti, and Luigi Roni.

A very different proposition was Joan's first Leonora in *Il Trovatore*, in September 1975, an experiment sanctioned by Kurt Herbert Adler in San Francisco. This was the soprano's first plunge into weightier Verdi. She had sung Gilda previously, and in almost another incarnation, the Covent Garden Amelia and Aida, as well as Desdemona. *La Traviata*, as we have seen, posed a different set of problems. Rumors flew all over the place: "Sutherland is going in for heavier stuff!" Edward Downes, now back in England, would have been delighted, as he had always thought she should have been the greatest of Verdi singers. Others were not so sure. With possibly the only concession to insecurity about the part, Joan had studied, she confessed to me, the records of Zinka Milanov, one of the greatest near-contemporary Leonoras.

When the big night came, not much really could be settled. For several days, Joan had been victimized once more by her treacherous sinuses and teeth, and her mouth had swelled to balloon size. Emergency antibiotic treatment reduced the swelling, but her lips were still stiff when I caught the only possible personal glimpse of her: as she sat under the hair dryer in a beauty salon the day before the opening. She smiled gallantly, spoke little (one could not put her to the trouble of answering questions), and hoped for the best.

While it is true that some stiffness remained, hampering her usual freedom of enunciation and causing her to react more cautiously than she wanted to, little evidence of her indisposition remained. Still, it was enough to dim the luster of the opening night. Elena Obraztsova was in splendid health and plangent voice for Azucena and, understandably, stole the show. Subsequent performances, I am told, went far better. Shirley Verrett sang a later Azucena.

Another venturer upon unknown waters in a very slender barque (not physically speaking, but vocally), was Luciano Pavarotti in his first Manrico.

The tentative approach of hero and heroine made its effect on the press, if not the audience, which responded warmly throughout. (It was, after all, the fifty-third opening night of a San Francisco season, and it was attended by all the glitter and pomp that the Bay City can command.)

Robert Commanday in the *Chronicle* appeared puzzled at the

lethargy of the opening acts, attributing it to Bonynge. Sutherland's voice could not be mistaken, but "it was not yet warmed to the occasion." Pavarotti's "bold commanding tenor was not yet in command." It took the advent of the fervent Ingmar Wixell as Count di Luna to bring the show to life.

When the soprano, tenor, and baritone recorded the opera later, bringing Marilyn Horne into the fold as Azucena, some of the original complaints were registered by John W. Freeman in *Opera News*, who added a few on his own. It amounted to the deficiency of a festival of stars attempting an ensemble opera, where all should pull together in one style. His funniest comment concerned Horne, who sailed up to a high C in a cadenza "with the freedom of a wildcat in a tree."

Nothing daunted, Sutherland later scheduled a *Trovatore* for Covent Garden in December of 1981.

• • • •

There were no reservations from any source when *I Puritani* became the star opera of the Met's 1975–76 season, at last bringing to the New York stage the opera that Joan and Richard love so dearly and that she had sung in many other corners of the globe. This was a production of quiet loveliness, with sets by Ming Cho Lee, costumes by Peter Hall, and direction by Sandro Sequi. The jeweled constellation of singers called forth comparisons with the original quartet who launched the opera in Paris in 1835: Giulia Grisi, Giovanni Battista Rubini, Antonio Tamburini, and Luigi Lablache. No one had actually heard *them*, of course; but it is a source of amusement to call up the past in comparison with the present. Usually the "golden age" syndrome prevails, and the past wins; but not in this case.

Joan's three men were Pavarotti, Sherrill Milnes, and James Morris. Perhaps Milnes is better at Verdi than Bellini, but his quality and volume as the spiteful Riccardo could not be faulted. Morris revealed new depths, vocally and characterfully, as Sir Georgio. Pavarotti sang Lord Arturo Talbot with his high Ds intact, and a beautiful spinning legato for such airs as "A te, o cara."

Tastefully costumed, looking youthful and beset, Joan portrayed the vagaries of the slightly unsound Elvira with tenderness and fervor, showing the girlish fears that give way to delight when she is told she may marry Arturo, the man of her choice; then the ecstasy of contemplating the wedding in "Son vergine vezzosa," the sudden plunge into mild dementia when she thinks Arturo has betrayed her, and her pitiful utterance, "Lasciatemi morir," just before she comes on stage to sing the famous "Qui la voce." Another point of high tension, the martial duet between Riccardo and Giorgio, "Suoni la tromba," was splendidly sonorous. The rapturous reunion of the two lovers provided a deeply satisfying musical experience, even though the drama that has preceded it seems a bit shaky and contrived. The performances gave mounting delight. A sag occurred only when the two deeper male voices were replaced by Cornelis Opthof and Ezio Flagello.

The opening night had been scheduled as a benefit for the Opera Guild on February 25, 1976, and went off with all the accustomed éclat, electrifying the house. No pair of operatic singers of the age could match Sutherland and Pavarotti, the *Times* opined. In a criticism that contained hardly a shadow, the writer thought that the lady "sang a beautifully controlled performance, trying to evoke music rather than pure technique. That big, colorful voice of hers had no trouble with the tessitura; her diction was much better than it used to be [a real concession], there is far less portamento, and she phrased with extreme sensitivity. Long line followed long line, and then, when technique was needed, Miss Sutherland was mistress of liquid trills, and carelessly tossed-off roulades."

Pavarotti came in for equally fervent words, and James Morris was singled out for his Giorgio: "Full-voiced, colorful, smooth in delivery."

As for the direction, Sequi had the good sense to require these Very Large Persons to move at a minimum.

Among other critics, it was amusing to see George Movshon in *Musical America* climb down from a violent anti-Bellini position to complete capitulation for "singing and conducting of a quality to make a bold case for [Bellini's] particular style of writing."

This had not been the easiest production to pull together, I had noticed. Stage rehearsals had seemed rather scrappy and more confused than is customary. Sequi had trouble up to the last minute to get the chorus women to show a little spontaneity—"Move, move! Go, go!" he was constantly exhorting the sluggish ladies. A scrim was raised and lowered, raised and lowered, never quite acceptable.

A week before the opening, the rehearsal was without costumes, and Joan was unhappy. "I can't judge my movements until I know the size of the costume," she complained. This was a reminder of the conversation in San Francisco, when the soprano had laid great stress on this point. Usually burdened with wide, heavy skirts, she could unwittingly knock over furniture or find herself hedged in unless she could be prepared.

Time after time, Joan fiddled with the skimpy bunch of flowers she was given to hold in the first act. Even when their stems were shortened, they seemed a shabby bouquet for a bride.

When at last the costumes were assumed, the second-act dress for Elvira nearly sank the prima donna.

"Oh, it's heavy! How they ever wore these things!" she exclaimed fretfully.

The assistant stage director, Patrick Tavernia, an old friend, confessed to me that Sequi's secretary, Hugo, would turn out to be his cross—at his elbow every minute, with trouble. My old mentor from *Tales of Hoffmann* days, Chris Mahan, was everywhere at once in his function as executive stage manager, soothing frayed nerves, solving problems.

One incongruity in the casting concerned the mezzo chosen for Enrichetta, the Stuart Queen whom Arturo smuggled out of Puritan bondage by placing Elvira's wedding veil on her head and passing her off as his bride. This was Cynthia Munzer, who had sung so unhappily (but beautifully) from the pit as Antonia's mother in *Les Contes d'Hoffmann*. No fault could be found with her performance, but her stature, considerably under Joan's, made it highly unlikely that she could be taken for Elvira under the all-too-skimpy veil provided by the costumer. Never mind; these incongruities are only part of the game. It would take a mezzo the size of Margreta Elkins (who, indeed, has sung the part with Joan) to make the substitution plausible.

The real problem here was Pavarotti's tardiness. His excuses were meant to be charming—the wife, the bambini, home, whatnot. This time, he had undergone a hair-raising escape from a plane crash in Milan at Christmas, in which he was described by a fellow passenger in the tenor's "autobiography" as a hero, rescuing many, especially children. That had been two months before, however. At any rate, he showed up the day after his arrival for an interview along with Sutherland and Bonynge, ". . . a six-foot butterball, with bubbling spirits, his hair thinning, his cherubic features partially camouflaged by a mustache and a trim beard," wrote the ensorceled *Post* interviewer. There was comment on his rather motley attire, including red socks, which he said Joan liked. She giggled and said he belonged to the Red Sox, and he added, "If you cannot be well known for elegance like Ricky, then you must be well known for inelegance." After more of this persiflage, the interview got down to some serious matters, mostly biographical review, which need not detain us. Of more import was the conversation I had with Joan after Pavarotti's first appearance at rehearsal. Her patience had, for once, worn thin.

His absence from the *Maria Stuarda* recordings in Bologna in 1974 still troubled her. He never arrived, and an entire crew had to be reassembled the next year to fit him in. That's why this album is dated 1974–75.

Now, in Joan's dressing room, where she busied herself with needlepoint, Pavarotti strolled nonchalantly in. Grinning, and with a "Hello, pussycat," he began making suggestions about the action in one scene, which, of course, he had missed when the director originally set it.

Joan quietly advised him to let the director settle the matter.

"We must have a beautiful day together—otherwise is no good," he offered. And, "I am really a brigand," he confessed in a little-boy way of admitting fault only in order to be forgiven. After an exchange of the usual "Ciao, pussycat," he departed.

Joan said with a certain amount of indignation: "He really is a brigand . . . . He's always late. Ricky had to reprimand him in front of everybody. Too bad Ricky had to be the one to do it, but Luciano needs it. The recording bit was inexcusable."

We turned to happier matters.

"We had a wonderful vacation in Switzerland. When I woke up and realized I really didn't have to do anything but a couple of hours work a day I really learned a role quite quickly without pressure. One can really get overtrained with too much rehearsal." (A reminder of her doubts about Walter Felsenstein's methods, expressed in London.)

Adam is always a good subject of conversation. The Bonynges' son had seemingly settled all his problems by attending the Switzerland school for hoteliers, a plan that has worked out very nicely, and eventuated in an excellent position in Sydney.

· · ·

All backstage tribulations out of the way, the series of performances went on to be one of the prime achievements of the Met's season. Let Harriett Johnson of the *Post* have the last word (quoting Confucius): " 'The demands that a gentleman makes are upon himself; those that a small man makes are upon others.' Last night there were only great men about." *And* a great lady.

During the *Puritani* radio broadcast intermission interview, Richard told William Weaver of his long attraction to Bellini, and emphasized the likenesses between the Italian composer and Chopin. "Sometimes I think Bellini is the greatest of composers, wonderful to perform; he starts marvelously and never lets down. *Norma* has greater tragedy and drama, and starts more slowly. I don't always enjoy the first act, but get involved in the second and third. *Sonnambula* is the most extraordinary, and perhaps the most perfect ever written. I would love to do it again, but have great trouble with my wife. She loves to sing it, but not to perform it on stage." (After all, there is that high-wire act, pretty difficult for a prima donna.)

"Bellini is different from others," he continued. "With that long melodic line—heavenly length—and his attention to the word is extraordinary. The librettos are not as bad as people make out. He elevates simple words so that they become absolutely sublime.

"And in spite of what some people say, the music for each character is individual—Amina, Elvira, Norma, Giulietta, all are conceived differently."

And how well Bellini composed for the voice! the conductor claimed. "Verdi in his early years was not so careful, with extreme jumps that could break a voice. Strauss, too—too much high, too much low. The line should be based on the middle, wherever it is placed by nature, and the composer who understands writes that way and everything comes out of it—high and low. Handel wrote well for the voice, but today he is played higher. Massenet understood the voice. Bellini is not easy, but if one understands, there is more chance of lasting if one sings Bellini rather than Verdi or Strauss."

· · ·

The morning of the dress rehearsal, Richard got a phone call from his mother in Sydney, saying that his father had died. It was a shocking blow for someone who had to go on stage with a premiere in a few days, reminiscent of Joan's similar plight at the threshold of *Beatrice di Tenda* years before. Richard and Martin Waldron did not tell Joan till after the rehearsal, for fear of unnerving her. At this crisis, Joan deputized Martin to sound out Ricky about the possibility of his flying home for the funeral. It was quickly decided that nothing would be served by this exhausting flight and quick return, for he would be too late for the ceremony anyway. So hearts were heavy for that especially entrancing production.

CHAPTER 30

Met Two–Covent Garden One

❊ *ESCLARMONDE* IN THE FALL OF 1976 DREW EX-actly the same response in New York as it had in San Francisco. The public loved it and the critics diverged widely.

Opera News had given me the assignment to write its "cast page" for the *Esclarmonde* issue, a short piece about each of the principals, with a practically impossible deadline. To meet it, I made the tactical error of showing up at the first rehearsal on Election Day, November 2.

Even though I explained my predicament, a decided coolness hung in the air. Joan took refuge in remarking on my hat; Ricky was rather gruff. Fortunately, I had been able to glean some bits about Clifford Grant, who was repeating the Phorcas, and to make a date with Giacomo Aragall before the others arrived. Tourangeau and Louis Quilico, who sang the Bishop in place of Kerns, talked on the phone. So I met the deadline, but without talking to either Joan or Richard. Fortunately, there was enough material from previous encounters. The Met made objections, however. Someone had squawked—I think it was a new rehearsal scheduler to whom I was a stranger—and I had to apologize to the press office the next day. It left me a little damp, and I didn't pursue rehearsals with my usual zest. Peter Allen, the gentlemanly successor to Milton Cross, and an entirely successful new "Mr. Opera," invited me to sit in the broadcast booth for a late rehearsal. One couldn't see as much as in the open theater, and heard through microphones, but could comment freely. Peter was interested in my San Francisco experience and I was fascinated by the glimpse into this secret place, tucked away on the Grand Tier.

After the dress rehearsal on November 16, I went backstage to see Joan, and gossiped a little about Adam, who had found his way at last into a school for hotel training, which could lead to the top in management.

"He thinks his mummy and daddy are pretty smart for finding it," Joan said proudly.

It was interesting to see Harold C. Schonberg's right-about-face toward Bonynge. Up to and through the previous season's *I Puritani*, Ricky could do hardly anything right in the *Times*. Now Schonberg wrote: "This was one of the memorable performances. He led *Esclarmonde* with style and spirit, and with a firm rhythmic base not always encountered in his work in the past. ["Limp rhythm" and those accented upbeats had seemed to haunt the *Times* critic.] Mr. Bonynge was very careful to work with the singers [a quality other reviewers had long ago discovered], holding the orchestra to a level over which the voices could penetrate. Yet he did not neglect the scoring, and the orchestra sounded firm, sonorous, and—most important—sensuous. It was a most satisfactory evening, and it well could spark a look at some other virtually forgotten Massenet operas." (Richard could have suggested a few, I'm sure.)

This capitulation on the part of Schonberg extended, with a little "nitpicking," to Joan, emphasizing that "the big soaring line was there, the golden sound remains unparalleled, and there was some radiant singing. Miss Sutherland's instrument is still unique."

He thought the production lovely, and amplified on this opinion, which found some contradictory reverberations in Alan Rich's *New York* column. That brash critic suffered a hate-love relationship with *Esclarmonde*, calling the music awful, but in an enchanting sort of way; its "gorgeous" staging drawn on the best of France's bad painters from Massenet's own time—Puvis de Chavannes and Gustave Doré—for a wonder of a setting. "If you take the whole thing as a parody of opera at its most extravagant [which was not at all the intention], you won't go far wrong, but it has been wonderfully managed," he continued. "It's a little like a child's dream of what opera ought to be and, alas, seldom is." So, though it came close to "disaster" as musical and dramatic art, Rich thought the production an "illustrious hoot . . . the absolute embodiment of its period."

If there was plenty of alternate chuckling and tooth-gnashing to be derived from that, nothing but smiles could have greeted Harriett Johnson's happy review in the *Post*. "Forget the 'Arabian Nights,' 'Zoroaster,' 'Camelot,' and all the rest of the fairy tales and magicians," she crowed. The effect of the production is "alternately dazzling, dreamy, mysterious, or muted flamboyance [how do you mute flamboyance?]. As one wag put it [I suspect herself], 'You go out humming the scenery.' "

Schonberg's review was so warm that John Rockwell's in the *Times* a few days later came as a cold shower. He raked the opera and performance over spiked nail beds, lacerating everyone concerned. One wonders about the impact of these second, contradictory reviews on readers. Eventually it comes down to agreeing with the critic who agrees with you, I suppose. At any rate, *Esclarmonde* came and went in a sort of rosy cloud, and remains for posterity on the recording made by the Met principals. Several days before the premiere, the Metropolitan Opera Guild treated a considerable audience to a panel discussion conducted by the engaging and knowledgeable Robert Sherman, host of several attractive programs on the radio station WQXR. He quizzed Sutherland, Bonynge, Lotfi Mansouri, and Beni Montresor, eliciting from them a great deal of lively chatter and information. Bonynge was allowed his paean to Massenet, but when he mentioned the need for a Wagnerian voice for this opera, his wife interjected: "Not so much emphasis on Wagner, please!"

Mansouri confessed that at first the prospect of doing the piece scared him. It was so very different from anything he had encountered. He went ahead to emphasize the imaginative, the colorful, the fairy-tale elements, aided enormously by the colorful genius of Montresor. Treating the characters as human, while throwing around them the fantasy and magic, was the central problem. The fantastic lighting "was like a trip," he volunteered, to appreciative laughter.

The Metropolitan offered better technical facilities, especially lighting (with Gil Wechsler in charge) than San Francisco had, and Joan thought also that the acoustical conditions were more favorable—San Francisco had seemed a bit dry.

The recording of the opera between the performances on West and East coasts had deepened everyone's love for the piece. Bonynge stated that, as between the two processes, it was much easier in the pit, where you had something beautiful to look at. He was directly affected by the stage picture.

In response to a question, Mansouri declared that moving people around the stage was easy or not, depending on the kind of people you had to move.

"At La Scala, for instance, they expect the women to be stage left, the men stage right, and to get them to change at all requires at least eight extra measures of music."

Dwelling on the more difficult aspects of her role, Joan stated that she felt the way Melba must have felt when she tried to sing Wagner.

Esclarmonde, as we have seen, has its Wagnerian ambience, and, in fact, was supposed to be Massenet's tribute to the Master of Bayreuth. To a few more searching questions, Bonynge replied: "Come and see the piece!"

· · ·

Sutherland chose Donizetti's *Maria Stuarda* to celebrate a very special occasion in 1977, her Silver Jubilee as a Covent Garden singer. Earlier in the year, this opera had been the choice of Amsterdam, Rotterdam, and The Hague, with Tourangeau, the tenor Vittorio Terranova, and the baritone John Bröcheler. The role of the Scottish Queen had been close to Joan since her first assumption in San Francisco in 1971, and a visit to Philadelphia in 1974. On this latter occasion, one of my first pilgrimages in my chronicling of Joan and Richard, the City of Brotherly Love shamed its reputation by booing the young tenor, John Sandor, who had heroically undertaken the role of Leicester as a last-minute replacement for John Alexander. Sandor had sung the minor role of Arturo in *Lucia* in Miami with the Bonynges, and was available for the thankless task. It cannot be said that he was impeccable in the role, but that supposedly gentlemanly audience showed a ferocious temper. All the brotherly love was saved for the heroine, with cries of "Joan, Joan!" megaphoned through many pairs of cupped hands, and floral tributes (contravening a house law) hurled at the curtain calls. Bonynge, in fine form, proved the hero of the evening. Tourangeau needed more vinegar and power in upper tones—I do not remember an Elizabeth with such tremendous chest force. Tito Capobianco directed the simple production in sets by Pierre Luigi Pizzi, borrowed from San Francisco.

At supper afterward in their hotel suite, Joan and Ricky relaxed in warm comradeship stimulated by a very little white wine. "I can't drink much," the lady confessed. "It gets me tiddly." Supper was sent up from the hotel's restaurant, and afterward, Joan entertained with a version of a former London teacher, who, with an enormous bosom, used to thrust it out like a great shelf and swing a long rope of beads around like a hoop. It was reminiscent of Bea Lillie's marvelous acrobatic circles with a necklace. We parted that evening with Joan's laughing injunction: "Don't forget to water your flowers!" My hat was a green pot on which sprouted a shower of nasturtiums. It had been a jolly and memorable postlude to a musical evening of mixed blessings.

No such intimacy occurred in the 1976 London *Stuarda* experience. The Bonynges had taken Douglas Gamley's flat, which was quite a distance out of the center of town, and could be reached only by phone in my limited stay. On the night set for *Stuarda*, I had a seat fairly forward, and, as Ricky came into the pit, and in the spotlight turned to acknowledge the applause, I gasped, and cried, too loudly, I am afraid: "Ricky's dyed his hair!"

It was a shock to see that distinguished head, which had been graced by the rather wide spread at the temples with a silver streak, now close-curled to the pate and a dusty all-over black.

A telephone conversation with Chester confirmed the horrid truth and elicited the additional information that Joan and he, Chester, kidded the maestro mercilessly about it. In fact, they hated the transformation. By the time I saw him face to face, Ricky had had the grace to let the black soften to brown, but it was still minus the silver. Only later, in Australia, did I learn his reason for the step—so casual a proceeding for a woman, so drastic for a man.

The Australian Opera had held a gala one night, in which many takeoffs and jokes were perpetrated. At one juncture, an electrician came out to take the conductor's position. He sported a head of wiry hair filigreed with tiny electric lights that flashed on and off. The next day, Ricky appeared with his new dusky top.

The condition of the conductor's outer mien did not impair the excellence of the performance that London night; nor the warmth of the British public's appreciation and love for its most celebrated artistic citizen. Joan was not only Queen of the Scots, but of the entire nation (saving Her Majesty, Elizabeth II) in those evenings celebrating her Silver Jubilee. The critics responded nobly as well, allowing a certain amount of nostalgia to creep into their appraisal of present-day accomplishments. "Amazing" was a word frequently heard and read. William Mann remarked in *The Times* that Joan looked far more handsome than in her days of girlish promise, and that she sang "with a wide range of vocal color and expression, enunciating clearly."

Schonberg was in London for the *Stuarda* and wrote home to *The New York Times* that "Sutherland remains one of the vocal miracles of our times."

Tourangeau as Elizabeth caught the fancy of the London press. Mann found the mezzo "a villainess of riveting malevolence . . . spiteful, eyes ablaze, lip arched in scorn . . . with smirks and head-tossings, her orange hat raked frivolously, her attitude carelessly autocratic, her riding whip ever poised . . . It is a tremendous performance . . . [she] has the voice, as well as the physical personality, to carry this terrific characterization, the cavernous alto register synchronized to a bright, easy, rasping top." Schonberg liked her, too, calling her "a perfect dramatic and musical foil for Miss Sutherland."

Stuart Burrows had often sung with the Bonynges; now he was at his best as Leicester, while David Ward sang Talbot, Richard Van Allen was Cecil, and Heather Begg sang Anna. Desmond Healey's sets, borrowed from the Coliseum production, seemed shrunken and inadequate on the big sister's stage, but John Copley's production remained in good state.

It was amusing to note that the Covent Garden program printed an advertisement for Decca Records showing Bonynge still with his silver wings. As a tribute, there were also photographs of Joan in fifteen other roles for Covent Garden, and photographs of some long-ago singers and productions.

· · ·

No one could know that Joan's Donna Anna in 1978, my next encounter with the prima donna, was to be the last role she would sing at the Metropolitan until 1982. It had not been planned that way, but an all-too-well publicized conflict between artists and managers arose in 1979, which would banish La Stupenda from the sacred citadel for four seasons.

Meanwhile, *Don Giovanni*, first performed on March 10, 1978 (and in the old Eugene Berman sets that were triumphantly saved after a financial flurry had proscribed a planned new investiture), drew a contradictory storm of reviews, split almost down the middle between high and low estimates. Oddly enough, we find Schonberg saying a vehement "Yes!" while Andrew Porter uttered a stringent "No!" departing from his usual favorable attitude and confessing that he had "very seldom been bored as he was by this Met *Giovanni*." Bill Zakariasen of the *Daily News* ranked himself along with the yea-sayers; Speight Jenkins in the *Post* had little good to say except for Joan, whose performance was "supreme."

Porter is always interesting, no matter where his sympathies fall, and particularly if one can get past his inevitable prelude of almost more historical data than one wants. After he came down to particulars, his words could not have aroused delight in any performer's breast, except for the Masetto, Allan Monk, who seemed "the best of the men." That indicates the general tone of the piece. Joan could not have relished his comparison with her 1960 Glyndebourne Anna, which showed "more than spitfire heroics." He added that "a touch of this inner quality remained, but little of the quick, realistic intensity with which she used to observe, and in gesture, inflection, and accent, react to the murderous drama around her. Her voice sounded large and shrouded in timbre—which suits some of the music, not those passages where it should flash out like a sword."

Contrast Schonberg: "Sutherland is in very good voice these days. The sound is as golden as ever, and firmer than it was several seasons back. It is hard to think of any living soprano who could have projected 'Or sai che l'onore' with equal command and color. Miss Sutherland's scooping days and poor vowel shape are long gone. In a few held notes of 'Non mi dir' there was a slight beat, but otherwise the singing was sheer magnificence and the coloratura went with signal generator accuracy."

Equal divergence of opinion greeted the others: James Morris as Don Giovanni; Julia Varady in her debut as Donna Elvira; Huguette Tourangeau as Zerlina; Gabriel Bacquier as Leporello; John Brecknock in his debut as Ottavio (whom we heard as Gennaro in the Houston *Lucrezia*), John McCurdy as the Commendatore, and the aforementioned Allan Monk as Masetto. Bonynge's contribution both glowed and suffered, depending on whom you read.

Joan's costumes—one of black, one of vibrant ruby red velvet—came in for some comment. They seemed to overburden her, and indeed were most sumptuous, bejeweled—and heavy. They stood out conspicuously in an otherwise shopworn production.

A more trying ordeal than the performances must have been the television interview, seen on closed circuit throughout the nation, when Joan and Ricky sat facing the camera with Francis Robinson by their side, he reading questions received from curious critics from many cities. Francis allowed me to witness it on a house TV set. Both stars showed some discomfort, but tried earnestly (Joan always does) to answer truthfully and painstakingly. Richard has to a degree learned his lesson, but Joan has never mastered the art of turning a question aside in favor of something she would rather say, of taking things lightly and easily. It is thoroughly commendable, but does not always work to her advantage.

Certainly this was a problem when the rift with the Metropolitan occurred the next year.

CHAPTER
31

Australia Rediscovered —L'Affaire Hemmings

❋ THE YEAR 1976 MARKED A DECISIVE TURN IN THE Bonynges' lives and careers. It was the first year of Richard's new post as Music Director of the Australian Opera, and consequently a great chunk of his calendar had to be carved out for the new responsibilities. Eventually, the couple would spend almost half the year in their original home, settling in with the comfortable assurance that they were very welcome. Later ructions would roil the calm, but not appreciably diminish the strength of the affection that both felt for the country, the people, and the opera company that soaked up the greater part of their lives.

They found this company pretty much the same as it had been on their 1974 visit. Charles Berg still held the reins as Chairman of the Board, a man of fierce energy and dedication, who closed his perception to hostile winds and championed the new "settlers" against the inevitable backlash that followed the initial rapturous welcome, particularly on the part of the press. John Winther, the big Dane, with whom Bonynge got along admirably, still held his title as general manager. Bonynge would have a great deal to say about repertoire and casting, particularly where it concerned his wife, but the two men seemed amicable enough partners in harness.

Moffatt Oxenbould had advanced to the post of artistic administrator in the eleven years since he had steered Joan around the stage in the 1965 supershows. Always jolly, unflappable in the face of trials that would unsettle a less serene soul, he provided an anchor amidst the boiling seas that occasionally overwhelm an opera company, especially one that is, to most intents and purposes, isolated from the mainstream of the world's opera currents (and consequently prone to internal upheavals). Anthony Everingham was now technical administrator; called production director then, he had been a backstage mentor during the *Tales of Hoffmann* adventure. The press department was well in place, headed by David Colville and with able and charming lieutenants in Glen Lehman and (at first) Gai Murray, who would soon depart to marry and start a family, but would later return as Gai Burns. Meanwhile, another charmer, Carole McPhee, joined the group with a cheerful assistant, Robyn Simms.

Other familiar faces abounded, among them guest and resident conductors, the repetiteurs (including the good friend Caroline Lill), and, of course, the singers. Heading the alphabetical list of choristers was old chum Elizabeth Allen.

So the stage was set; the curtain ready to rise on the new regime.

Richard chose *Lakmé* as a first foray for Joan. Delibes's fragile opera, with its Oriental color, lilting melodies, and much more listenable music than merely the famous "Bell Song," was an unknown brand of champagne to launch the new ship. The public, which yearned to see Joan in anything at all, made the ten performances immediate sellouts—no matter that the gala premiere on July 10 required a top price of $40 per ticket and subsequent performances reduced the price by only $10. Aficionados always seem to have at the ready the cash to outlay for "Our Joan." Among the critics, the concern was with whether the opera was "worthy" of the heroine, a plaint that arose at the slightest departure from a routine expectation of what a prima donna should sing. This was to be a bone of contention all the way through, as Bonynge sought to loosen up the conventional repertoire.

Some of the gloss of the opening night was dulled because of an unfortunate incident that delayed the performance by forty minutes. Twelve musicians had been dismissed from the Elizabethan Theater Trust orchestra in Sydney and a like number from Melbourne's orchestra, presumably for reasons of economy. Whatever the merits, the Union held meetings almost until curtain time, then prepared a statement that John Winther was asked to read, so that the public might know of their grievance. This was not the most impressive way to accomplish a mission, and the long delay, coupled with the dressy audience's desire to get on with the proceedings, produced "boos and brays," as one scribe put it. At last the performance got under way.

The substance of the vote after Delibes's opera had run its course was that *Lakmé* was indeed worthy of La Stupenda, although the rest of the cast, except for Clifford Grant as the stern Nilakantha, was relegated to the shadows. These included the important role of Gérald, the English soldier who strays from propriety into the arms of the alluring Lakmé. Henri Wilden, the Hoffmann of other years, took the part—valiantly, but without the necessary romantic appearance or sound. Huguette Tourangeau as Mallika sang the melodious duets with Lakmé, and other singers were Isobel Buchanan and John Pringle.

Norman Ayrton reverted to opera (he had been the chief producer in the 1965 tour and had been involved in many a theatrical production in America and England since) to produce his first show with the Australian Opera. One amusing comment came from Brian Hoad: "There is only one dramatic flaw in the plot, and that is the manner in which Lakmé dies, committing suicide by eating a flower of the Datura or Angel's Trumpet tree, which (as any Sydney gardener would know) should not be attempted upon the stage because the blossoms are so large. It would be like eating a cabbage. Director Norman Ayrton has therefore advised his Lakmé merely to sniff at the flower before falling dead—an unsatisfactory solution, since the Datura has a beautiful perfume, designed to be sniffed at."

Designer Desmond Digby came in for some digs, for as Hoad said, he apparently was seduced by the exotic side of the piece and managed to hide the more serious aspects "under countless swags of plastic flowers more reminiscent of the Western Suburbs than the flower-loving land of the Hindus. In general, the designs serve to emphasize *Lakmé* as a quaint museum piece, despite the very workable plot and the often glorious music drawn from the orchestra by Richard Bonynge."

One novelty for the audience was the presence for the first time of a prompt box, which broke the smooth line of the stage edge and caused some acrid, some indulgent, comment about Joan's feeble memory power.

During the preparation of *Lakmé*, a film showing how backstage life and snatches of the music and plot had been made diverted many audiences. It was the first of such celluloid documentaries that would bring the prima donna into the consciousness of any who might not see her on stage, providing color and human interest.

The operatic peace did not last long. Rumors began to creep

through channels, and finally broke into print. John Winther was resigning—or being fired. The position of general manager has always been a tricky one in Australia: before Winther, Stephen Hall had tried to fill the gap created by the loss of Donald McDonald (accompanied by the accustomed torrent of newspaper pros and cons). But Hall was no administrator; in fact, he was the weakest possible reed in such a job. The word had it that as a public "front" he had all the charm necessary, but with nothing solid to back it up. The 1974 experience I witnessed had shown that he possessed no stage directorial expertise either.

Winther had seemed a very capable fellow, also showing a wry sense of humor that was engaging. He had described to me in an interview in New York his method of getting things done, which reflected this.

"It is an autocratic job, but not in the sense of being despotic. Your opinion is *your* opinion. You should not set out to say 'I want this, do it this way.' I don't think that works in a modern society, not even in an opera house. You don't get the best work out of people.

"You should listen to everyone, and form an objective opinion gradually. You don't start with a positive view. Then you make up your mind and we do it that way.

"And of course," he added ruefully, "it pleases nobody."

But his departure was apparently not the result of any fault in his capabilities (although a wave of dissent had greeted his earlier production of a rock opera, considered to be an extravagance wildly misplaced) but rather of personal troubles that had threatened to become scandal. No one wanted to talk about it, but the hints were enough to show that the personable Dane had spread his affections too far and too indiscriminately. His wife, the soprano Lone Köppel-Winther, sadly returned to Denmark. Winther remained in Sydney, where he was still giving piano recitals occasionally, this being his forte before he donned the administrative hat. He had accompanied two of the opera singers in excellent lieder recitals (one of which I attended) in 1974, a sensitive and thoughtful musician.

He had joked: "Singers are eager to be accompanied by the boss—for different reasons."

Now, in 1977, he was out.

And who was in? Peter Hemmings, whose experience had included a few years with the Sadler's Wells Opera (now English National Opera), then doubling in this role with administration of the new Scottish Opera. In 1966 he gave full time to Glasgow. He, his wife Jane, and five children arrived in Sydney to considerable fanfare. All would now be smooth sailing.

And so it appeared for a while. A man of great persuasiveness, with the ability to elicit personal support from many quarters, his administrative qualities were not called into question until tales began to leak out, as they always did. "They" said: he didn't get along with Bonynge; he didn't get along with the board; he wanted to do things that were progressive and presumably good for the company, but cost too much: the same tales that any opera company is subject to, and Australia more so than many.

Still, as Moffatt Oxenbould remarked: "A new general manager can do no wrong."

The honeymoon was brief. Difficulties were taken up (as banners) by the press, certain elements of which in Sydney operate in a way that would elsewhere be frankly called "yellow." Salvos of accusation, directed toward the company, Bonynge, and the board, met with less rebuttal from the board than might have been expected. So vehement was the press in championing Hemmings that anyone looking at the matter impartially could sense scandal-making out of very thin cloth. Starved for hard news, the eager beavers concocted "news" where none existed, or blew up to distressing proportions the scraps they managed to ferret out from a too-silent "establishment." At least, so it seemed to one investigating from as many viewpoints as possible.

There was a *Rashomon* quality about it. (*Rashomon* is the Japanese film that showed the same incident from different points of view.) Four "sides" appeared. First of all, the British Hemmings himself, suave and long-suffering; then, Richard Bonynge and Joan Sutherland, sometimes linked as a formidable team in the columns of the dailies, or separated as individual targets; then the board of directors, headed by Charles Berg, reticent, somewhat controversial, yet obviously single-minded where the opera was concerned; and finally, the government, which was constantly involved in the subsidy of the opera, but whose own voice was never publicly heard.

The press itself practically constituted a separate viewpoint. A constant of their barrage was a complaint that the taxpayers should have more say in a government-supported institution—what were these elitists doing with good Australian money anyway? This is a litany familiar in Europe, but as yet only a potential threat in the United States.

Hemmings went out to Sydney with some grandiose ideas, and, it is probable, no very clear understanding of the local situation. Whether or not his exact duties were spelled out in his contract it is impossible to say, although the informed sense is that it was a hastily executed document and more word-of-mouth understanding than written and signed outline of responsibility. However, it seemed certain to close observers that he cherished the strong impression that he had an overriding power. After it had all blown over and Hemmings had left in October 1979, he made available to me his ideas on the duties of a general manager. If he had submitted these to Berg in the first place, there might have been more give and take. Certainly there would have had to be a good deal of give on his part. In two pages solidly packed with single-spaced typing, Hemmings set forth a credo that reeked of pure authoritarianism. It reminded an old opera-watcher of Rudolf Bing's early dictum: "I am responsible for every detail in the opera down to the buttons on the costume of the third Orphan in *Der Rosenkavalier*."

Many of the positions Hemmings outlined as his responsibility to fill were already occupied—notably that of music director in the person of Richard Bonynge. It seemed clear that the Australian Opera was not about to subordinate the importance of Sutherland to the company's well-being and reputation.

Moffatt Oxenbould showed me in 1980 a balanced view of the situation.

"When Richard came out in 1976, we had known him as a guest conductor, and John Winther and I had established a relationship with him that worked well and was fairly clear, so that there wasn't obviously a need for definitions to be spelled out."

In that year, Bonynge had become an integral part of the opera's mechanism, conducting other performances than those in which Joan sang, coaching young singers (at which he is considered an expert), taking a vital interest in the entire roster, and choosing portions of the repertoire. (The latter became a press target, for, whenever things got dull, one or another of Richard's choices would be hauled out and ridiculed. Sarcasm was especially loaded onto the frail but resilient structure of that little-known comedy, Piccinni's *La buona figliuola*.)

In late 1978, Brian Hoad, a constant opera observer, published an article in *The Bulletin* that created some stir. Chiefly dealing with the strange doings of an opera board member who, having made trouble in many directions, was at last disposed of, the piece went on to investigate the board for "dithering," and to quote Bonynge at some length.

The conductor had frequently disavowed any interest in politics, and claimed that he "stayed outside" such things. Now they touched him directly, and, worse, affected his wife. He expressed himself thus:

"The trouble has been that the board has been telling me one thing while telling Hemmings another. In those circumstances, obviously, we must improve our own communications. I have absolutely nothing against Hemmings. But . . . the board should have laid down what our individual functions were from the start. They did not. Instead, there has been all this namby-pamby pussyfooting about." He added the observation that had also occurred to others, that board members regarded their activity as a kind of hobby.

"As far as I am concerned," he continued, "Hemmings's function involves finance, fund-raising, image-making, and politics. He is one of the finest politicians I have ever met, but he is not a musician. It's my job to sit down with the company's musical staff and work out repertoire and casting . . . I do not expect unnecessary interference in the musical side of the company. I'm quite prepared to bend over backward to achieve agreement in this matter; but I am not prepared to compromise again to the extent which we compromised over the next Sydney season . . . A preponderance of works from the German/Viennese schools makes it all seem rather heavy-going—a trifle dull. But opera is above all about the excitement of theater."

Maybe it had only *seemed* heavy and Germanic. In actuality, the repertoire in 1979 (January and February) contained *Die Meistersinger* (but done in English) and *Fidelio*; and two other operas in English: *Merry Widow* and *Albert Herring*, both light. There was only one Italian, *Don Giovanni*. In the "winter" season (July –August), two German: *Entführung aus dem Serail* (which ought to have been in English, although a poll taken around this time showed that Australians by now were sophisticated enough to prefer original languages), and *Salomé*. Three were in English: *Queen of Spades*, *Falstaff*, and *Jenufa*; Italian rated two: *Idomeneo* and *Simon Boccanegra*.

Perhaps the real lack of "excitement" stemmed from what was considered a strange choice of roles for Sutherland—a repeat of *Merry Widow* and the short and uncharacteristic part of Elettra in *Idomeneo*. ("At least, she'll get a lot of needlepoint done in her dressing room," her husband remarked.)

In the same season she sang Donna Anna in *Don Giovanni* and *La Traviata* in Melbourne. (This may or may not have revealed an inkling of Hemmings' growing bias toward the Victorian city. In fact, it was sensed as an evangelism of decentralization.)

Hemmings's first suggestions for Sutherland did not sit well with either her or Bonynge. Britten's *Gloriana* (well, it is a worthy and even beautiful opera, but Joan had already sung a part in it as long ago as 1954, and didn't relish resuscitating it, even for the major role). And Janáček's *Makropoulos Case*? Not even considering the current revivals of the Czech master's operas justified this casting, which involves little lyrical singing and much flamboyant acting. Furthermore, both operas depict ladies of many more years than Joan, even with her usual honesty, cares to admit to. Elena Makropoulos indeed had achieved 342 birthdays!

The situation worsened, each day bringing a fresh onslaught from the press. One newspaper aggravated the excitement with a daily column headed "Concern for Opera," in which readers aired their ill-informed opinions, demanding that the board be fired, that Bonynge be reprimanded, that Sutherland's fee be investigated— all in all, that Hemmings be supported.

"We are tired of Sutherland and Bonynge and want to hear others of equal calibre." This is laughable, considering how many "others of equal calibre" there are in the world.

Dame Joan Hammond, a venerated prima donna, formerly of Covent Garden, got into the act in a public excoriation of the board; when the other Joan was blamed for it by mistake, she wrote a rather sad letter championing the opera. (It was rumored about this time that Sutherland had left a letter with her solicitors to be made public in case she left the opera.)

A tenor, Ronald Dowd, put in his oar, complaining that he had had no work for twelve months. (His complaint was later dismissed as unjustified by a report from a commission charged with clarifying the mess.)

One excellent accomplishment of Hemmings was the institution of the subscription system so brilliantly executed by the dynamic Danny Newman in many opera centers. The general manager, after a favorable experience with Newman in Scotland, brought him out to shepherd the mechanics, with the result that the opera could advertise: "You can hear Joan Sutherland for as little as $5 or so at a subscription performance."

It is true that the income from subscription made up $3,333,500 of the 1978 expenditure, and that the government subsidy amounted to three million plus. But just now an unexpected disaster darkened the opera skies. A computer ticket company went broke in February 1978 with the Australian Opera its chief victim—to the tune of more than a quarter million. Another blow: the destruction in a warehouse fire of half of the sixty productions of the Opera, including the scenery for the new *Merry Widow*. Insurance covered this substantially, but the reconstruction of the many properties proved a nightmare.

Peter Hemmings had broached a tour to Edinburgh, as well as a complete *Ring* cycle. Both were washed out. The first project seemed impractical on the face of it; perhaps a more modest circle of Far Eastern ports would have had an effect and certainly would have cost less. But for now, neither was possible.

The *Ring* remained a bone of controversy for months. Supposedly there are in Australia a good many Wagner fans; they were cited as yearning for Wotan and Company. Hemmings commissioned designs from Bill Dudley on his own and costumes from B. Bjornsen. He would enlist the team that had made *Mastersingers* such a success. Incidentally, Bonynge commented afterward, that it would have been far more economical to build the *Mastersingers* sets locally instead of importing them from Scotland, and they could have then been used for fifteen years afterward.

Moffatt Oxenbould described what producing the *Ring* would have entailed. "Because of the length of the works, what can we rehearse the day after? Each counts as two calls for orchestra and chorus and is, therefore, twice as expensive. Also, we projected a rather light income. And to get the proper singers—where are the Wagnerian singers today anyway? We would have had to import at least a Brünnhilde and a Siegfried, probably Sieglinde. And this would cut deeply into the six 'imports' we are allowed by Equity each season, not to mention the technical equipment necessary. Perhaps as a festival arrangement sometime . . ."

Indeed, plans for 1981 included a series of concert performances of the operas. This was a temporary solution.

The venue poses great problems—the Opera House is out of the question, although *Mastersingers* did sound well there even with a reduced orchestra for it (the enlarged pit will accommodate at most seventy players, depending on the number of percussionists). The Concert Hall has its own limitations, chiefly that no scenery can be hung and flown. "A spectacle with a few pieces of scenery and lots of people is better," said Moffatt. The operas given there at this writing include *Aida*, *Salome*, *Merry Widow*, *Nabucco*, *Fidelio*, and *Lucia*.

Hemmings, in the 1980 interview in New York, when I asked where he would have put the *Ring*, answered, with an expansive gesture, "Melbourne!"

It was to Melbourne he seemed to turn, lobbying quietly for his prospects there. The new center there was scheduled, after years of problem-solving, for a 1983 opening.

It was in Melbourne that Hemmings got his notice. (Not, as the Sydney newspapers initially accused, by a memorandum posted on the bulletin board of the Sydney Opera House for all to see.) Patrick Veitch, Hemmings's successor, told me the story, from a viewpoint not entirely disinterested, but, considering the natures of the two men, likely to be as authentic as any. (As a matter of fact, Veitch himself brought out the concept of *Rashomon* to describe the muddled situation. "There is no *one* truth," he concluded.)

Veitch had been out to Australia as a consultant to various groups. He had been invited by Ian Campbell, manager of the South Australian Opera, the most important of the regional companies, who had visited New York.

"On my second trip, in July 1979," related Veitch, "I was in Melbourne coincidentally with the visit of the Australian Opera, and a board meeting was held at which they decided not to renew Hemmings's contract. There in the hotel lounge, it was like a Feydeau farce—little groups of people gossiping and running from table to table.

"I had planned to have dinner with Hemmings that same evening, but when he came down about five o'clock after learning the bad news, I thought he might want to renege. Besides, I was reluctant to involve myself in the business affairs of the company. But Peter said, no, he wanted company. We had quite a few drinks. Yes, he seemed bitter. There's no denying he is one of the fine professional managers in the arts, with a distinguished Scottish career, but it just didn't work out. With Bonynge and Hemmings, it was a shotgun marriage.

"One scenario I totally reject is that Richard is some sort of Machiavellian out to do Hemmings in. One has only to meet him to know he is not devious, not a conniver. He's 1) a very nice fellow, and 2) a serious musician who just wants to get on with his job."

But the stream of vitriol from the press, ejected chiefly by Maria Prerauer in Rupert Murdoch's *Australian*, didn't let up. This lady, it was suggested, is a singer manqué, bent on, as one observer close to the opera scene whispered, destroying Sutherland. As she dared not send her shafts directly to the superstar's heart, she took it out on Bonynge, with sideswipes at the opera board and an occasional thinly disguised dart at the diva.

Hemmings, considered to be an "enemy" of her targets, became the object of her partisanship. Sly little paragraphs appeared constantly, but the main barrage came on November 12, 1979, in the weekend magazine of the *Australian*, a full page and carryover headed: "What's Gone Wrong at the Opera?" Accompanying it was a photo montage showing Bonynge and Sutherland looming hugely at either side of the distinctive Opera House silhouette.

What was wrong? Everything: the "monstrosities" dug up by Bonynge; the lack of authority granted Hemmings by the board; the revision of that board to throw out the only Hemmings supporters (she said there were two; a later report narrowed this down to one woman); the size of Sutherland's fees, and the remark that she was supposed to get less than the Australian $10,000 elsewhere, which is diametrically opposed to the truth; equally the enormous sum paid Bonynge (she estimated $40,000 salary and extra fees for each time he conducted). "There is nowhere else they could have it so good," she concluded. Her spleen spilled over time and time again, in remarks about the dependence of Joan upon Richard and vice versa. She dragged in Sir Rudolf Bing's remarks about hiring husband and wife together. The sharpness of his tongue in his memoirs had been modified in later years, but it suited this pamphleteer very well.

Called as witnesses to the sad state of affairs were disaffected members of the company, which they termed a "Sutherland Circus." It was hinted that additional resignations were in the wind. The Vancouver experience also provided grist for this murderous mill. And on and on until the final summing up: "Unless decisive action is taken soon, the curtain could come down over the Australian Opera and stay there."

It is possible that these assaults might have constituted some help in pressing the button for an ultimate debacle.

At last, a commission was set up by the Australian Industrial Council to investigate and report. This organization had taken a lordly position over the arts in the past. The members of the new commission were six respected citizens, among them the music critic for the *Herald*, Roger Covell. Their report riled the board still further, and that body "rejected" the criticism of Charles Berg implicit in its language. It concluded that the hiring of Hemmings had been hasty and not barricaded with clauses and safeguards (not a new and startling revelation); that the confusion between Hemmings's and Bonynge's responsibilities had not been cleared up (also self-evident); that the board neither confirmed nor rejected Hemmings's overambitious plans for the *Ring* and Edinburgh.

Its determination held the board responsible for the loss of confidence in the public image of the company, but also cited Hemmings's attitude as in opposition to the board, and thought that the change for Hemmings from "a smaller company in which he had grown up to a bigger, more complex company in the Australian setting had not been smooth." (This was the point that stuck in Hemmings's craw, as he revealed in the 1980 interview. He resented the slight to the Scottish Opera.)

There was a good deal more of this presumably judicious summing up, which one official of the opera company thought had been reached without sufficient evidence. The whole affair was messy and inconclusive, and a real danger of dissolution appeared possible as the newspaper barrage continued.

One stopgap attempted by the board was the appointment among its members of a "repertoire" committee, which should have pleased no one but those members. It persisted into 1980, when Bonynge professed to get along nicely with it.

The morale of the company was undoubtedly affected, for what starts at the top trickles down. To counter newspaper reports of this disaffection, two dozen of the principal singers signed their names to a public letter disavowing loss of morale, but the air was heavy with doubt and worry.

One subject that never came to light concerned Hemmings's alleged indifference to the actual workings and personnel of the company. It seemed that he had not won the confidence of many performers, nor even become acquainted with the ins and outs of the technical staff; and, it was said by another source who must remain nameless, he had no real grasp of the finances in general and the opera's situation in particular. These are rather damning faults for a general manager who declares himself to be the overall head of a great company. Whether the accusations were entirely accurate will probably never be known, but one of his claims that the board had never given him a promised house, a plaint that was widely circulated in the press, turned out to be a "shoe on the other foot" detail. He and his wife had apparently turned down several offers as not being good enough.

A further comment on the impact of the Hemmings family on Australian society is enlightening. At dinner one night in the home of one of Sydney's illustrious educators, Jane Hemmings is said to have remarked airily that she felt obliged to send her children back to England to school. Little undercurrents such as this ran beneath the public fracas.

In the emergency situation, the board appointed Ken Tribe as "caretaker," while they advertised for a new general manager. Tribe, a retired lawyer who had devoted his life to the arts and was active in many fields, including the Australian Commission, held the pieces together; low key in style, not a public figure, but trusted by all sides.

In response to the advertisement, two promising candidates showed up. The first choice was Patrick Veitch, whom we have already met. That young man had a job as marketing director for the Metropolitan Opera, and enjoyed it, as well as the confidence and respect of Anthony Bliss, who himself was at the time in a kind of "caretaker" position at the Met (although he later assumed the title of general manager). Veitch had to have a decision by October of 1980, for then he was due back at the Met. The board dithered once more, and the deadline passed. Veitch returned to New York, and Ardis Krainik was given the nod. This estimable lady had been with the Lyric Opera of Chicago since its inauguration under the dynamic Carol Fox and had risen to become Miss Fox's assistant. Then came the startling news of Miss Fox's sudden death, and Ardis was summoned home to take the top job there.

Australia was back to square one. Various Australians sent out an SOS to Veitch, who began to reconsider, although he protested that he had not been officially invited. That lack was remedied when Charles Berg telephoned him in mid-January 1981. Pat and his wife Kathleen flew out later that month. Pat signed a contract for five years as general manager on January 19. They found a house in Darling Point, ten minutes from the Opera House, and Kathleen and their eighteen-month-old daughter "Princess" Alexandra followed Pat for a new life.

It seems never to be in the nature of a general manager to think highly of his successor. Edward Johnson expressed to me some bitter sentiments (after the fact) about Sir Rudolf Bing, and Sir Rudolf in turn delivered himself of the opinion that Schuyler Chapin should never have gotten the job anyway. Peter Hemmings, as far as I could ascertain, maintained a discreet attitude toward Patrick Veitch.

As for Bonynge, he told Jill Sykes of the Sydney *Morning Herald* that if he let it all get to him, he would be out of this profession. "I am relaxed about it and I love my work. I am a Libra; we are well balanced; we take things as they come." The reporter thought that his professed lack of worry was a little too aggressive to believe it came naturally. "But as an acquisition it is a valuable asset to a career of public performance—perhaps an essential one."

The claim to balance is interesting; it is justified, in a sense, for Richard's volatility takes him to sometimes instantaneous heights and immediate lows, which soon settle into the midway path of "getting on with the job." This faculty has been noted in most of his contacts with other elements of opera production. This time in Sydney there is no doubt that he emerged victor of the situation. His valedictory for the *Herald* interview was a passionate defense of the Australian Opera as an ensemble.

"It is very precious. There are very few in the world, and it must be kept at all costs. At all costs. It is essential that these people be on contract all year around, that we keep certain older members of the company for their experience, and introduce younger singers. I think people lose sight of the fact that Australia is a country far away from the rest of the world. We depend on the quality of the ensemble and new productions to keep an audience coming back."

CHAPTER
32

Sydney Settles Down

HOW DID ALL THIS *STURM UND DRANG* AFFECT THE central heroine of the plot? We have seen that Joan's distress at some of the more strident accusations against the company and the board had prompted her to write the public letter previously mentioned. Before and after that, she kept silent, going about her usual round of work and snatching recreation at the flat in Potts Point, with its spectacular view of the harbor, and at a new retreat at Whale Beach, a northernmost suburb on a slender point of land exposed to the ocean on three sides. She met any reference to L'Affaire Hemmings with a raised eyebrow and a firm set of the formidable jaw, breaking the silence only once, as she talked to me during the San Diego *Fledermaus* period in October 1980. She put forward a vehement defense of Charles Berg.

"That man has absolutely sacrificed himself for the opera!" she exclaimed, leaning forward to emphasize her words, her beautiful eyes gleaming, her face alight with emotion.

"His business turned against him [he was a respected accountant], and he has spent his money entirely for the opera's good. I will not hear a word against him!"

Berg himself has never "gone public" with his point of view. There developed a growing sentiment that he was badly judged by, chiefly, the press. His board was reorganized with some of the more controversial and lightweight elements absent, and a new spirit seemed to have entered the company after the advent of Patrick Veitch.

Joan's typical reaction was that what concerned her most was the attitude of the public. She did not want to—could not afford to—follow every convolution of the antic press. Her appearances invariably called for an outpouring of love and money—no dearth of either, as far as "Our Joanie" was concerned. "They have always been wonderful to me," she affirmed. "That's what matters."

To return to the opera schedule, after *Lakmé*, the next assignment was *Lucrezia Borgia*, chosen to open the 1977 season. The festive audience reacted passionately, heaping applause on the heroine. Her villainous husband was played by Robert Allman (who had powerfully increased his vocal and acting abilities since 1974), and Margreta Elkins had the trouser role of Orsini, with her lilting ballad in the face of death. A half-dozen critics were quite happy with the new production, its lavish costumes, and the singing of at least these three principals. "Profound professionalism and opulent beauty of the title role" was Nadine Amadio's estimate in the *Financial Review*; a second hearing confirmed and heightened the impression. One or two writers thought Lucrezia was the best thing Sutherland had yet done in Australia. Most complimented Bonynge on his choice of opera and conducting; Roger Covell believed the opera needs stronger, less decorative handling by a producer (in this case George Ogilvie) and designer (Kristian Fredrikson) "if it is to communicate the dramatic excitement implicit in its story of Lucrezia's legendary (and apparently unfounded) reputation as a poisoner." Ron Stevens as Gennaro, Lucrezia's lost-and-found-again son, did not come off so well, his voice appearing too light, although his acting seemed apposite enough. The fact that the opera concerns poison gave the cue to the detractors. The *Daily Telegraph* man shied away from Donizetti's music, which to some might appear luscious, but to others had a prevalent taste of poison.

Distaste for Donizetti also animated Maria Prerauer, for, although she laid the praise on rather thickly for the heroine (adding the usual bit that contained the bite by calling La Stupenda "Cinderella incarnate"), she claimed that "We will even suffer her in some flabby poor man's *Rigoletto* like *Lucrezia Borgia* or whatever half-forgotten opera Richard Bonynge chooses to dig up instead of *Traviata* or Donna Anna or [heaven help us!] the Queen of the Night." Her review was headed with a built-in sting: "Magnificent Freak."

The year 1977 also saw Joan as the pitiable outcast in Puccini's *Suor Angelica*, a role she had never sung before. She later recorded it. This, in fact, is the only Puccini opera she has ever sung professionally and on stage. Her voice, after all, is not considered a Puccini voice. One has to go back to 1952 to find her earliest attempt: the Giorgietta in *Il Tabarro* at the Royal College of Music, which so aroused the interest of Joan Ingpen's husband. The recording of *Turandot* in 1973 is the only other foray into Puccini territory.

When it comes to *The Merry Widow* (and come it did to Australia), Joan explained to me that she had always loved operetta. "It was all we had," she recalled. "We heard *Katinka, The Merry Widow*, and so on. Gladys Moncrieff, the absolute star of operetta in Australia, was my great favorite. I saw her just the other day, and she's still the same grand old gal."

First persuaded to show her comic gifts in *La Fille du régiment* and then to convey the lilt of Rosalinda's music in *Die Fledermaus*, Joan found the next step to *The Merry Widow* not too formidable. It seemed natural that the Bonynges should bring their production of the Lehár classic to Australia. Their experience in Vancouver had convinced them that it was a viable, amusing piece, and deserved to be mounted wherever possible. The Sydney Opera Concert Hall was chosen as a venue, offering space for the extravanganza that Bonynge, the choreographer, designer, and director had created.

The much-touted Lehár-cum-Bonynge-cum-Lotfi Mansouri confection opened the season on January 19, 1978. As was to be expected, the critics were sharply divided into two camps. Frank Harris of the *Daily Mirror* thought Joan lived up vividly to the frequent claims that she is a natural comedienne. Nadine Amadio of the *Financial Review* called Joan's acting elegant, her singing alluring, and Bonynge's conducting of the full-strength orchestra superb. It was four hours of magic for Leslie Walford in the *Sunday Herald*, and the new version could well be the most lavish in the history of "this light bit of froth."

"Froth" was also the description by Brian Hoad in the *Bulletin*, "but what superb froth!" He thought that Sutherland's jolly and somewhat matronly version could well fit into the slim plot, and particularly liked the idea that this was a robust country bumpkin who had innocently caught the eye of the local banker and so found fame and fortune. "It is just that mixture of the banal and the sublime, the gawky girl and the grande dame, which lies at the heart of Sutherland's theatrical magic."

Roger Covell in the *Herald* called Joan's singing the great asset, and, less predictably, her stage presence. "She is enchanting, utterly at ease with the part, wholly lovable, and genuinely merry."

Other pro critics plucked at the same strings, and all, even the cons, marveled at the gorgeous settings and extravagant costumes. The negative contingent, with its accustomed leader, included a headline in *The National Times* that suggested spiders: "The Deadly Widow." The nugget of adverse opinion held that the prima donna should not step off a pedestal into a playful posture. Joan herself remains quite serene about the matter: she enjoys it. The chance at such a romp is one of the great reliefs from the thousand deaths she has died on stage—and will continue to die.

The cast surrounding her, both at this earlier series and at a revival in February 1979, could not quite live up to her stellar status. Her Danilo, first Ron Stevens (handsome and debonair) and later Peter van der Stolk (who had made so little impression in Vancouver), remained in shadow. The couple of young lovers, played first by Isobel Buchanan and Anson Austin, were charming enough. The Valencienne was later taken by Beryl Furlan, and the comedy provided by Gordon Wilcock as Baron Zeta and the impish Graeme Ewer as Njegus carried over from one series to another.

Norma in July 1978 brought the deepest satisfaction for both audiences and performers, while only a few critics remained Bellini-haters. Joan was happy in the comradeship of Margreta Elkins as Adalgisa, and the two tall beauties, as they had so often done, dovetailed their talents perfectly. At rehearsals, they provided a constant flow of merriment and lightheartedness, encouraged by Sandro Sequi. He had produced for Joan so often by now that he was virtually a family member. Bonynge conducted with his usual dedication to this particular composer. In April of 1979, Brisbane welcomed the opera with joy, not having heard it for more than sixty years, and laid on a genuine extravaganza welcome for Sutherland, whose first appearance there it was in fourteen years.

CHAPTER

33

Intermission: The Met Fracas

✳ IN EARLY 1979, THREE THINGS HAPPENED THAT
✳ shook the operatic world one way or another. The first concerned Sutherland alone. In the Queen's Honors List at New Year's,
the soprano was made a Dame of the British Empire. It has been
pointed out that this distinction is lower in protocol than the Companion of the Order of Australia that was bestowed upon her in
1975, but, in worldwide recognition, it ranks higher. Before this,
only Nellie Melba and Joan Hammond from Down Under had won
the honor, and the latter, after all, is of New Zealand birth. Joan
was singing *Norma* in Amsterdam at the time and so could not
accept the investiture in person, but Australia made up for it in a
later ceremony. She had possessed her CBE for almost twenty
years, and Richard had received a similar decoration in 1977, so
the Bonynges' household felt doubly honored. Joan, secretly proud,
let it be known occasionally that she adored being called "Dame,"
but with her usual modesty, laughed in embarrassment when I
ventured to curtsey, just to see how she would take it. Still, it was
an acknowledgment of her golden worth to the British Empire, as
well as to the more encompassing world of opera—one that many
thought was overdue but all greeted with warmth and affection.
Henceforth, it was "Dame Joan"—publicly, at least.

Not so welcome was the news later in January. It broke just
before Sutherland and Pavarotti were to embark on the first of the
fabled series of concerts as centerpieces of a Great Performers series
in Lincoln Center, New York. An unhappy announcement indeed.

The Metropolitan Opera and the Bonynges had suffered a
breach of relations!

280

The news was launched in a *Daily News* bulletin by Bill Zakariasen, who had a pipeline (not always reliable) into the Lincoln Center opera houses by reason of having acted as chorister some years before. His scare story predicted a complete break between artists and opera management.

Speight Jenkins in the New York *Post* followed up the same day, his story gained from an interview with the principals after a rehearsal for the forthcoming gala concert. It seemed that the hiatus was to be for three years. This was bad enough news.

Others of the press picked it up, and their glee, sometimes too obvious, in targeting a hitherto almost invulnerable idol, blew the affair up into a near *scandale*. Everyone got into the act, including a soprano of long and honorable tenure at the Met, who was quoted as somewhat piously averring that *she* would never act like that.

It became, in several righteous views, a question of who should run the opera house—management or singers. This has been a sore point in many such conflicts and is not easily resolved. One school of thought believes that the opera boss should rule absolutely. Another would allow for some leeway. What seems certain is that the few superstars can pretty well decide what they want to sing, and only a very tactful individual can persuade them to give way even a little.

Certainly there had been no tact displayed by the Metropolitan management. On the contrary. It became plain that Anthony Bliss and the board were averse to the Bonynges' projected *Merry Widow* for the season of 1980–81. Apparently, they had agreed to it only, in their view, as one segment of a threefold "package deal," bracketed by Mozart's *Abduction from the Seraglio* in 1979–80 and Rossini's *Semiramide* in 1981–82.

The announcement that Miss Sutherland had withdrawn from the Mozart work, because it was no longer suitable for her voice, afforded the Met the excuse, given the "package" understanding, to drop the *Widow and Semiramide*. There is more behind this than was brought out in the thrashing accounts at the time. While it is clear that Mozart and Lehár were sacrificed with various aspects of regret and recrimination, one mystery remained—what happened to *Semiramide*? Taking into account the Met's position that it was a package deal, the loss of the Rossini is understandable, if regrettable. But the Bonynges disclaimed the package excuse when it came right down to it. This three-or-nothing rationalization was the Met's way out of what it considered an embarrassing situation.

For the moment, let it rest there while we look at the first two sacrifices.

Joan had always wanted to sing Constanza in *Abduction*. It was one of those roles that seemed to elude her. She spoke wistfully about it many times. What had chafed her memory was the Glyndebourne decision in 1960, when she was just coming into the starlight.

"She is too big for Constanza!" the Glyndebourne oracle had pronounced. She has always been sensitive about her size, a tender condition she has managed to ameliorate but never quite to cure. This blunt proscription of *Abduction* remained with her, so that when James Levine offered it to launch a Mozart cycle in a gala way, Joan was delighted.

The decision was made, according to Speight Jenkins, at a private luncheon with Levine, during which the entire scheme was discussed. It boiled down to the Bonynges' wanting the *Widow*, the Met suggesting the other two. Everything was amicably agreed upon; whether the Bonynges considered it a package or not became moot.

Joan took the Mozart home to Switzerland and began to work on it in earnest. How deeply she regretted her decision to abandon it—costing her a few shreds of pride along with the sorrow of an unfulfilled wish—it was a brave act, an unprecedented one. She gave the Met the news thirteen months in advance—in October 1978—certainly long enough, one would think, for them to secure another soprano (as they promptly did). Bonynge explained that the difficulties lay not in the top Ds, which Joan handles expertly, but in the general tessitura, which was uncomfortably high for her voice at this time.

One additional speculation remained. So accustomed has Joan become to singing only with Bonynge that there might have been the faintest chance that she was reluctant to "submit" to anyone else—especially at the Met. She has done so at other places since, but this was a special case. However, at the meeting with Levine, the question was brought up, and the Bonynges are said to have declared that it presented no problem.

The Met had quivered under the prospect of the *Merry Widow* all along. Their opposition was somewhat understandable, even if stuffily presented, and with excuses that did not go quite to the heart of the matter. Operetta had had a few flings on its august stage: the early *Fledermaus* and *Gypsy Baron* of Heinrich Conried, the sensational *Fledermaus* and less attractive *Gypsy Baron* and *Périchole* of Rudolf Bing all had set precedents. But the Lehár

version as concocted by Bonynge and Lotfi Mansouri and seen
hitherto only in Vancouver seemed strange and alien territory. Mr.
Bliss stated rather stiffly in a *Times* interview: "The board was
unhappy at having to do *The Merry Widow* in a version that might
be marvelous with Miss Sutherland, but would not be adaptable
for other sopranos." This is faintly ridiculous, for a version does
not invalidate the capability of any soprano equipped to sing the
Lehár operetta anyway. He added: "Besides, we do not feel the
Lehár work has a place in the house until we are ready for a full-
fledged commitment to light opera." These excuses were made
after the fact; if they had obtained previously and in force, the
Widow should never have been even tentatively accepted. However, it seemed the quid pro quo in the negotiations. There was
also a subtle frisson of feeling on the part of the Met that such
adventures might well be left to their neighbor, the New York City
Opera, which has indeed tried them out for several years, with
variable results.

The newspapers blew this all up like a whirlwind in a brown
bag. Australia put in its word with a screaming headline: "Our Joan
Sacked!" Along with aggrieved comments from Sutherland that the
Met was undervaluing great singers came the insistent motive:
"Who's boss?" The Met won its points and lost the diva for three
seasons. The name for that sort of victory: Pyrrhic.

And here the question still pricks: What happened to *Semiramide*? This had been scheduled for 1981–82 with Sutherland and
Marilyn Horne once more in the partnership that had brought
other audiences to a point of delirium. Its loss was passed over
rather lightly, as the package idea seemed to prevail. But what if
that were a rationalization of the Met's position *post facto*, and the
fact seemed to be a case of gross negligence on somebody's part?
At Jenkins's interview, Bonynge stated only—somewhat vaguely
—that "dates had been messed up." Met officials were not very
approachable on the subject. One who did talk freely apparently
had not been present at the time of the upheaval, and was quoting
colleagues who had. Quoted in good faith, no doubt, but reliable?

The story went like this: When it came time to smooth over
the *Abduction* and *Widow* imbroglio and get on with the *Semiramide*, it was discovered that Bonynge had not left the time for
this opera in his datebooks for 1981–82. Incredible as it may seem,
considering the meticulous accounts Joan and Richard and their
management keep of their doings, this had to be taken as gospel
until proved otherwise.

When I confronted him in 1980 with the accusation, Bonynge

responded indignantly: "It was not my oversight, but that of so-and-so at the Met!" That official left the company soon after the incident, and was not available for questioning. (Another official stuck to the Met point of view as late as 1986.) So the gap remained. No *Abduction*; therefore no *Merry Widow*, no *Semiramide*. The Met hinted that *Puritani* had been offered instead of the Mozart and rejected, but Joan denied this. One reason for sorrow persists in all of this: New York will undoubtedly never hear the great *Semiramide* with the two flaming stars; it will be too late for Joan, as she would be the first to acknowledge.

They patched it up, of course, and for Joan's return after the hiatus, *Lucia* was thought to be appropriate. She remarked thoughtfully to me that she sometimes feared that singing these "demented dames" at this time was a bit precarious, but "they keep on asking for it," and she can pretty much judge and control Lucia's abandoned flights—it is a question of cadenzas and ornamentation. This Bride of Lammermoor was set for 1982–83, and the following season, the Met's one hundredth, would be graced by the tomboyish *Daughter of the Regiment* (this time with Alfredo Kraus instead of Pavarotti.)

It was all very sad, and seemingly unnecessary.

Joan went on to the third event that was to mark 1979 with some kind of special star—the Concert of the Century.

CHAPTER
34

Concerts of the Century —and Others

✹ THE EVENT COINCIDING WITH THE METROPOLITAN BROU-
haha was called "Concert of the Century," perhaps a trifle
presumptuously for those whose memory went back to Lotte Lehmann's farewell, or the historically minded who could cite the likes
of Chaliapin, Caruso, and Sembrich. Nevertheless, it and the two
that followed were the most splendid, the most extravagant of
events—one more glamorous and exciting than the other, it seemed.
The acknowledged three greatest voices in the world came together
in varied combinations: first, Joan Sutherland (now "Dame Joan")
and Luciano Pavarotti; next, Sutherland and Marilyn Horne; third,
all three—together.

New York went wild, to be sure, but the excitement was not
confined to a single metropolis, for Public Television exhibited all
three events throughout several hundred stations. So the world
looked in on Avery Fisher Hall and on intermission features where
the stars became themselves in candid, often hilarious, inter-
changes.

From the first row on January 22, 1979, the view was intimate
and dizzying. Dame Joan swept out from the wings right above
me, regal in a softly flowing gown and cape of green with touches
of purple, her smile warm, if a bit nervous. Pavarotti followed, his
hand clutching the inevitable white silk handkerchief like a security
blanket; Richard Bonynge brought up in the rear and took his stand
on the podium before a full-sized orchestra. He had started the
evening off with the Overture to Mozart's *Le Nozze di Figaro*, but
the audience seemed to be holding its breath. The first of innu-
merable waves of applausive sound broke out at the appearance of

the imposing singers. Duets followed solos, each wildly cheered. Perhaps the highlights were Dame Joan's ecstatic Mad Scene from Thomas's *Hamlet*, which one reviewer compared to a cool cascade sparked by sunlight, and Pavarotti's deeply felt "Pourquoi me reveiller?" from Massenet's *Werther*; but the duets from *Traviata*, *Rigoletto*, and *Lucia* should not be faulted, and it was satisfying to hear both in excerpts from operas they have eschewed to date— for Joan, *Ernani* and *Gioconda*, for Pavarotti, *Macbeth*, *Fedora*, *Africana*.

In the interval, Joan was seen modestly claiming that she was merely "a very ordinary human being who has been given a rather wonderful voice." She also observed that singers are "a nice family of crazy people."

After intermission, the soprano appeared in a white, glittering confection created by Barbara Matera, as were all her concert costumes. The cheering audience would not let their idols go until they had sung four encores. As for the television public, it was a revelation of what a musical event could be—faultlessly expert in technique, thoroughly professional, and unbelievably glamorous in content. As one commentator remarked, it was difficult to believe the singers were human.

Human they were—a combined five hundred pounds of human flesh, as pointed out by the *Daily News* man. But, he added, their sincere romantic appeal remained amazing.

The crush backstage was insupportable after the last note had resounded. It was almost impossible to struggle through the tenor's coagulated horde of fans to reach the soprano's dressing room. Marilyn Horne made it, even beat Joan's dresser, and helped the evening's star change into mufti. The great mezzo would be the next attraction alongside her old chum. Sutherland and Horne were booked into the same spot for another of the Great Performers at Lincoln Center for October 15, 1979, when the hullabaloo was repeated.

In London, some nervousness had showed itself in a pre-concert interview, when the reporters made perhaps too much of the prolonged lack of togetherness of the two stars. It had been seven years since Sutherland and Horne had appeared on the same stage. Both prima donnas, in the event, were their marvelous selves, and no doubt remained that this is truly a wonder team. Both took the opportunity to change costumes midway, adding to the glitter of the night. Joan's first gown was what Matera called a pink butterfly, with sweeping sleeves, lavishly trimmed with pearls. Her after-intermission garb was green and crystal.

This time, Bonynge conducted the New York Philharmonic, opening with the Overture to Bellini's *I Capuleti ed i Montecchi*, and the girls sang their famous duets from *Norma*, *Semiramide*, and *Lakmé*. Then each provided an individual Roman candle. It was not all fireworks, however; Horne stirred the pulses with her quiet "Jeanie with the Light Brown Hair," to harp accompaniment, and Joan showed the Metropolitan Opera functionaries present what they had lost, by singing the *Merry Widow*'s "Vilia."

The clowning in intermission was largely Horne's—she wrestled a double bass with some glee and announced that it was not so difficult to play. Fans of both ladies cheered for their favorite individually but proved generous to both.

The next very large evening would be the combination of the three superstars. On March 20, 1981, came the grand climax, not a whit less exalted for being the third in a row and possibly the last of its kind (although Sutherland and Pavarotti planned to give Australia the benefit of their concert partnership in January 1983). Quite simply, it provided a vocal feast for opera aficionados who thrived best on a star diet. Bonynge had the New York City Opera Orchestra this time. At first glance, it might have seemed difficult to find enough trios for these voices, but they drew on *Norma*, *Gioconda*, and, with Jake Gardner as the baritone, the final scene from *Trovatore*. One oddity showed up: the trio from *Ernani*, in which Horne sang the bass part transposed upward—strange, but intriguing. Each had an aria. Pavarotti's was his pet from *Bohème*; Joan's a lesser-known excerpt from Verdi's *I Masnadieri*; and Horne's from Rossini's *La Donna del Lago*. Also, three duets gave each a chance to sing with one another. There seemed no end to the pandemonium at the close, and the television viewers missed some of the final joyride. If one watched TV in color, Joan's first-act dress was especially handsome—of burgundy chiffon—while the change showed her in a lavender handpainted "butterfly," with great, soft pleated wings.

One truth was obvious, as reported by Harold Schonberg in the *Times* after the first of these concerts: This is what it's all about: "a maximum of voice coupled to musical taste, and it is given to very few singers of any generation to have it. There have been reports that an official of the Metropolitan has said that the house could do without stars of the Sutherland-Pavarotti type. If that is a true statement, the man who said it is out of his ever-loving mind."

.   .   .

Standing on a concert stage with no help from costumes and scenery, no flamboyant or suffering character to portray, and the immediate presence of an audience practically under her nose has never been Joan's ideal of performance. "Concerts terrify me," she has confessed. "You have to change mood so often." Nevertheless, she enjoys the exploration of rare veins of song that Richard mines for her, even though it means learning new material in the midst of a busy season. And, of course, she likes the rapturous attention and acclamation of an audience that has come expressly for her and not for the trappings and other characters and involved plots of the operas she sings.

Still, concerts remain something of an ordeal. The very fact that her opera routine is interrupted has something to do with it; her innate shyness, supposedly long overcome, but still lingering, may also operate. Yet concerts are necessary for several reasons.

Many cities in America, north and south, cannot welcome La Stupenda in opera, for, quite simply, there is no opera house and no backup organization. A public clamors for celebrities just the same, and concert series or symphony orchestras bring the best they can afford. There is hardly a corner of North America that Joan has not graced either in recital or as soloist with a local orchestra. Concert series no longer flourish as abundantly as they once did, before the nights when the "public" stayed home in front of a small screen. Still, there remain plenty of enterprising impresarios. For example, Joan and Richard played concert dates in the Far East in 1978—an adventurous trek that was recorded for television by an English-Australian, Brian Adams (who was understandably inspired to write a book about La Stupenda, published in Australia).

Joan gave her very first recital in the United States at Winthrop College, Rockhill, South Carolina, on February 2, 1961. Exactly twenty years later, she and Richard went back to Winthrop to celebrate the anniversary. (Joan was given an honorary degree, one among many she has received.) While the earlier occasion was a recital with Richard at the piano, the anniversary called for the Charlotte Symphony, whose conductor, Leo Driehuys, led part of the program. He then gave way to Richard for the prima donna's selections: "Tornami a vagheggiar" from Handel's *Alcina*; the Liebestod from *Tristan und Isolde* (preceded by the Prelude); "Tu del mio Carlo al sesto" from *I Masnadieri*, and the *Lucia* Mad Scene.

The first concert had contained samplings of Handel, Paisiello, Bianchi, Pergolesi, Bellini, Balfe, Offenbach, and Thomas (the *Hamlet* Mad Scene)—a variegated nosegay, further complemented by five songs. The revisit proved touching and thrilling on both sides of the footlights.

One earlier concert had not been so rapturously received. Joan has always been apologetic about her faulty memory, and learning "bits and pieces" for concerts in the middle of a long operatic stretch can be quite trying. On this occasion, she dashed into Washington for a solo platform appearance, and "read her way through 23 songs and four arias," chided the *Post*. "Turning pages during Annie Laurie! One of the highest priced singers! Just about threw away her right to claim her greatness." Fuming, the writer thought the singer had deadened the whole thing by her disdain of the universal niceties of communication with the audience.

Her encores, "standing away from that damned music stand, were exhilarating, really thrilling, with her looking one straight in the eye, she tossed off the waltz song from Ricci's *Crispino e le comare*." She could do it if she had to; and, when her programs are almost uniform during a season, she manages to dispense with constant use of the offending word book—not an unknown adjunct to a good many singers, it might be added.

Many times Joan shared the responsibilities and applause with other artists, and usually a good time was had by all: winging duets with Marilyn Horne in Los Angeles or New Jersey; with Placido Domingo in Philadelphia for Eugene Ormandy's birthday; singing a concert version of *Les Huguenots* in London's Royal Albert Hall with Ryland Davies, Anastasios Vrenios, and Nicolai Ghiuselev; joining in a crazy-quilt evening of rarities for CBC in Toronto. This last entailed the participation of Huguette Tourangeau, Cornelis Opthof, Pat Brooks, and Pierre Duval in a merry-go-round of excerpts from a dozen operas under the blanket (and misapplied) title of "The Age of Bel Canto."

The generosity of Joan and Richard in giving their services for various benefits must not be overlooked. They have responded with fair frequency, although there are times when acceptance is impossible.

The problem of Joan's diction rarely arises in concerts (although there are complaints from those who hear her on radio in television broadcasts simulcast, so that they do not see her expressive face). Perhaps this is because she is in closer communication with the audience (Washington critic to the contrary), without the distraction of moving around the stage and the effort of cutting through a great symphonic body of sound. At any rate, the subject was discussed by Max de Schauensee, the thoughtful and experienced critic for the Philadelphia *Bulletin*, who proclaimed one recital "immaculate." In songs by Rossini, Gretchaninoff, and Cui, and in exquisitely sung German and French songs, everything was crystal clear, with rare refinement. The ordinary complaint about diction disturbed him not a jot. "Galli-Curci's diction was slurred," he contended. "Melba and Garden were faulty, nor were even the first two divas noted for psychological probing. When it is a voice of this caliber [Sutherland's], if we have any sense, we'd better settle for that."

· · ·

Joan has always made records with comparative composure (although no less dedication), for in the recording studio she can kick her shoes off, make faces, relieve tensions by a bit of wry or homely humor, and let herself go vocally as well. But the same microphones in a radio studio, not to mention the lights and cameras in television territory, are something else. Even more than concerts, they terrify her.

When she had to face her first Telephone Hour telecast (the TV incarnation of a very popular radio series), she shook with trepidation. "I never fancied myself as a movie star, and, after all, that's about what it turns out to be," she remarked. Many of these ordeals followed, but the tension did not lessen appreciably.

One of the least fortunate of grab-bag television affairs was an appearance with Howard Cosell, the sports announcer who was a favorite butt of jokes, but persisted in his idiosyncratic ways. Joan was booked into his television hour by her press agent, and it cannot be said that the encounter added many laurels to her already well-crowned head. Appearing near the end of the mishmash, following such other "celebs" as basketball's O. J. Simpson and Lee Majors (the "Bionic Man"), the regal Sutherland in her showy green gown changed the prevailing tone for the better, but not for long.

Nibbling off a delicatessen sandwich between lengthy waits and equally lengthy rehearsals, she worked calmly at needlepoint squares in her dressing room and discussed with me Adam's latest encounters with his schooling. Her patience and professionalism operated as usual; they deserved a better showcase.

· · ·

Australian experience seems to have partially overcome her reluctance to face cameras and lights: the *Lakmé* film and a surprise appearance on the "This Is Your Life" series, as well as Brian Adams's film, are evidence of this growing ease. "This Is Your Life" was initiated by Helen and Bill Lovelock, whom I had introduced to the Bonynges during the 1974 run of *Contes d'Hoffmann*, and who had quietly persisted in securing this prize for their series.

The format followed closely that of the old Ralph Edwards show, introducing one personality after another who had been instrumental in the prima donna's life and career, and arousing from her gasps of surprise and amusement. Keeping it a secret had, of course, been a trial for Richard, but it was cleverly managed with some excuse about attending a reception. Joan looked very dashing in a multicolored, flower-patterned silk jumper suit, and her delight at the succession of tributes was registered in rainbow shades of emotion. School chums she hadn't seen for thirty years, Elizabeth Allen, Margreta Elkins, Norman Ayrton, Lady Viola Tait, Sister Marie Bernard (who made dolls of all of Joan's roles), all brought anecdotes of early days. Marilyn Horne was seen from America, as was Franco Zeffirelli, who recalled the mutual embarrassment of their first meeting when his embrace made her blush ("She's come a long way—hasn't blushed since," he said mischievously, adding "except to show her enormous pleasure at some success").

The most spontaneous laughter was reserved for Luciano Pavarotti, who twinkled "Ciao, pussycat!" from London and recalled the incredible experiences of 1965, "and my hand exploring your diaphragm" to learn about breathing, naturally. "I send you an enormous kiss from my bottom—of the heart, I mean," he concluded.

"He doesn't change," Joan commented through her laughter. "He knows perfectly well what he did."

The producers had gone so far as to import Terence McEwen from New York, Ruthli and her baby from Switzerland, and Russell Braddon, Joan's first biographer, from London. Adam was present, vastly enjoying the proceedings from a seat between his mother and father.

Asked by Master of Ceremonies Roger Climpson for her reactions, Joan summoned up enough courage to say with her usual modesty that she hoped she didn't take all this for granted. "I think of it as a partnership," she continued, "not just one person. We've had everything we wanted" was her tremulous conclusion.

CHAPTER 35

New Roles for Dame Joan

✻ AFTER THE REPEAT OF *THE MERRY WIDOW* IN FEB-
ruary and March of 1979, the new Australian experiment for
Sutherland was indeed novel, and more of an experiment than
could have been imagined: the torrential Elettra in Mozart's *Idomeneo*. La Stupenda in a rage was a true curiosity. A fury of action
and singing in a relatively brief span was what was needed.

The production was borrowed from the Victoria Opera Company in Melbourne, of which Richard Divall was musical director,
and, even though many refinements were added in Sydney, credit
for the conception went to the Victoria company (as a Melbourne
critic was quick to point out). A few querulous comments arose
about Bonynge's addition of some tenor arias written by Mozart
for a later performance after the premiere in Munich in 1781, of
some rearrangement of arias, and of the conductor's use of a reduced orchestra, which was very light on strings.

Far more unanimity than usual greeted the first Sydney performance on July 4, 1979, and in follow-up comments on subsequent showings. There were a few scholarly outpourings of
information and opinion about Mozart himself, *opera seria* in general, and this neglected masterpiece in particular.

The most extended of these came from Kevin McGrath in *The
National Review* of Melbourne, who considered *Idomeneo* "a great
musical testament that deserves to be set apart from the shabby
melodramas that make up the bulk of operatic repertoire."

Casting of this opera has been a modern-day problem, for the
role of Idamante, the son of King Idomeneo, was originally sung
by a castrato. It has long been the practice to put a mezzo or

contralto in such parts, but occasionally tenors have been used, many think wrongly. Bonynge chose Margreta Elkins for yet another of her "trouser" roles, and she responded nobly: "Handled the arduous cantelina with perfect ease, maintaining a flexible, resonant tone," wrote McGrath. He added a comment on her height, her "very good legs," and her acting with tactful restraint in suggesting the masculinity of the character, making the whole thing as credible as it is ever likely to be.

Leona Mitchell, the only non-Australian in the cast, made a perfect Ilia, the captured daughter of King Priam of Troy who is beloved by Idamante. Both in her criticism for the *Financial Review* and in a long piece for the English *Music and Musicians*, Nadine Amadio complimented the American soprano for the seductive warmth of her voice and the crystal clarity of her upper range. "A tiny, attractive woman . . . in [John] Truscott's delicate costume, she had an air of vulnerability that made her attempt to save Idamante's life more persuasive."

Roger Covell spoke admiringly of Sutherland: "Elettra is one of her active roles. She does not waste any time on gentle regrets. She spits fury when she is thwarted. As always, such a dramatic challenge brings out the athletic best in Sutherland. Her rapid notes whiz past in perfect formation, yet with tone of a size and quality that are truly heroic."

The *Herald* critic remarked on the culminating effect of Elettra's aria, "D'Oreste, d'Ajace," in which she compares her jealousy to the torments of Orestes and Ajax. Sutherland's big and passionate performance with the orchestra was indeed the climax of the opera, and took on a power and excitement lacking in many scenes earlier in the evening. She elected to finish with a C an octave higher than Mozart's, and proved that even at the end of a taxing aria, she could do it while still increasing the volume on the note. As John Carmody concluded in his *National Times* piece, "Idamante could hardly have survived her fury."

The men did not fare as well. Ron Stevens's light voice seemed unimpressive, and indeed at one performance he gave way to Serge Baigildin, who, though afflicted by the common tenor handicap of being born too short, showed a sympathetic vocal quality, ideal for the pathos and nobility of King Idomeneo. Henri Wilden as Arbace was considered to be miscast, but Erik Badcock as the High Priest and Clifford Grant as Neptune's Voice won a few kind words.

Robin Lovejoy, the producer, was not afraid of stylized movements, although Roger Covell thought he should have applied the same criterion to Ilya, whose gestures were too often incongruously naturalistic. The designs of John Truscott were a big asset: Cretan stone in a hot sun, rough-hewn pillars, a wall of loose rock that seemed to threaten a landslide, pointing up the timeless symbolism of Greek/Cretan women in black. The guards were Bronze-age warriors. Storm and shipwreck were veiled in gauze, like smoky, formal oil paintings.

Above all, credit heaped on Bonynge, warmly expressed in Nadine Amadio's English report. "Bonynge has given the Australian Opera audiences some of the most sparkling Mozart ever performed here. His *Nozze di Figaro* was perhaps the best all-round musical production we have seen from the company."

As McGrath concluded: "All of Mozart's tempi are virtually in-built, and a conductor goes against them at his peril. It was apparent from the first bars of the great minor-key overture that Bonynge knew exactly where he was going."

Sutherland's first *Lucia* since the tour of 1965 acted like a tonic on the Australian public. It took on the pizzazz of a second homecoming. Joan sang with all her wonted brilliance and the freshness that seemed incredible after the two decades since she had first sung it. She looked beautiful, like a young girl, one viewer thought. Part of this youthful appearance could be attributed to her hairstyling, which, created by the internationally popular wigman, Charles Elsen, was designed for just that effect, flat on top and hanging loosely, instead of stiffly coiffed and towering.

This series, which opened on February 6, 1980, was produced by John Copley in the Concert Hall, with minimal scenery by Henry Bardon, consisting chiefly of two movable pillars. Its consequent simplicity added greatly to the dramatic excitement. Indeed, as Brian Hoad remarked in *The Bulletin*, it was the greatest triumph yet of human ingenuity over architectural folly (recalling the switch for political reasons of the original opera auditorium to concert venue).

At one performance, a new tenor, New Zealand's Richard Greager, made his Australian debut and got a welcome from audiences and critics who had seemed starved for high male voices during the past few years. He would sing again opposite Joan in a later *Traviata*.

To almost everyone, this *Lucia* provided the most unforgettable night. The dissenter, foreseen, was the lady who called it "déjà vu," which could hardly be taken as a compliment. Reading the entire body of Sydney criticism in those times produces the semblance of a full and generous meal, only a few indigestibles along the way; ending with a sweet, and topped off with what the British call a savory—an anchovy or some little piece of tartness to relieve any cloying effect. The taste of bitterness does not linger long.

If Sydney had been perplexed about the choice of Elettra in *Idomeneo* for its leading diva, their bewilderment can be imagined at the prospect of Verdi's early *I Masnadieri*, which Bonynge promised for July 1980. Based on Schiller's grim play, *Die Räuber* (*The Brigands*), the story of two rival brothers, revenge and terror, is not exactly attractive. The heroine does not appear at all for two scenes, and gets almost unaccountably stabbed in the back by her lover at the conclusion.

Still, Joan could do no wrong for her audiences, and several critics liked the work very well. One called it a solidly satisfying evening of operatic thrills and spills on its musical and vocal strengths alone, with strong conducting by Bonynge. Another thought it thoroughly appealing, although it took a long time to reach the Promised Land.

What added spice to the occasion was the first meeting on stage of Dame Joan and Donald Smith, the established tenor favorite of the opera company. With Robert Allman as the evil brother and Clifford Grant as their victimized father, the cast seemed the strongest put on stage for a long time. Unfortunately, holes began to appear almost immediately. Smith, first giving his inimitable impersonation of Donald Smith, as one writer put it, lost his voice entirely, heralded by a genuine crack, at the performance of July 11, and had to be replaced after the first act by freshman Paul Ferris. Ovations for the brave young man rang long and loud, but then he too fell ill and the fifth performance had to be rescheduled. Equally calamitous was the indisposition of Robert Allman, who conked out of the fourth performance and was replaced by the 1978 Sutherland Scholarship winner, Erik Badcock, from New Zealand. This unfortunate young man fared less well than the tenor, even winning some rude boos. *Masnadieri* came back, but it could not be considered one of the shining lights of the season. All four voices would have had to be tops, as in *Trovatore*, and two of them fell short.

. . .

John Gay's *The Beggar's Opera* seems to deserve a new treatment every decade or so; indeed, the famous English ballad opera has been revived so many times in different guises that occasionally the original gets lost. Bonynge and his colleague Douglas Gamley brought it back to new life for Sydney in 1981, with a good many flourishes added, a lavish production by Anthony Besch, and costumes that commingled the eighteenth and twentieth centuries by John Stoddart. The cast included stalwarts, such as Rosina Raisbeck and Heather Begg, and a newcomer, Anne Maree McDonald. When the opera was later recorded, Sutherland sang the part of Lucy, and a *New York Times* reviewer lamented the absence of a duet that would have shown off the talents of La Stupenda and Kiri te Kanawa as Polly.

All of the 1979 and 1980 operas discussed were observed by me through the newspaper files in the Australian Opera office— except for the *Lucia*, which I witnessed in person with great pleasure.

CHAPTER
36

A Surprise Duet—Not a Duel

✳️ THE RUMOR SCUTTLED AROUND AND WAS LARGELY disbelieved: the two reigning divas of the world were going to appear on the same stage. Joan Sutherland and Beverly Sills intended to sing and then to switch roles, Rosalinda and Adele, in Johann Strauss's *Die Fledermaus*. Inconceivable, but true. The pair of prima donnas had never met publicly before.

The skeptics had not counted on the persuasive character of the *deus ex machina*, Tito Capobianco. Director and confidant of both prima donnas, he had conceived the stunt as a treat for his devoted San Diego audiences, and as a fund-raiser. As the rumor became established fact, the disbelievers swallowed their pride and sent for tickets—$100 the cheapest for opening night. This could be the event of all time. There was only one problem—how to see each singer in both roles. At the premiere, Joan was to be Rosalinda and Beverly Adele; then there would be several days before the switch. Residents, of course, experienced no difficulty, and, for outsiders, the matter was settled in September 1980, a month before the premiere. Word came to Australia, where Joan was singing *Lucia*, and I was spending a week to catch up on L'Affaire Hemmings and other matters. Beverly had begged off Rosalinda. She had just taken over the directorship of the New York City Opera, succeeding Julius Rudel unexpectedly early, and was extremely preoccupied with pulling the whole thing together.

Joan was secretly relieved.

"I had learned Adele all right," she confessed to me that week. "But I was always worried about the dialogue. It would be so easy to slip into the other gal's lines."

So one aspect of the surprise package had to be sacrificed. We never did get to see Dame Joan Sutherland as the maid Adele, saucy and frivolous. There were detractors who considered the part unsuitable for La Stupenda anyway, although Capobianco remained sanguine. "She might surprise you," he said.

Still, Rosalinda seemed much more Joan's style, as Adele was Beverly's, although the latter had sung both roles during her earlier years.

One attended the premiere on the afternoon of October 5, 1980, therefore, with no divided expectations. Predictably, San Diego was *en fête* for the occasion. Sills has been an idol in the Southern California city: they had even named a room in the new Civic Theater for her and had celebrated her fiftieth birthday with a huge party-cum-vaudeville in 1979. Sutherland had sung there before and her return was avidly anticipated. The problem seemed to be which one to mention first. Newspapers solved it by the cop-out of alphabetizing, which put Sills first by two vowels. Some clever person in the opera management did it brilliantly, devising an unusual program. You looked at the glowing color photograph of Sills as Adele, opened the booklet to page after page of blurb and photos of her, and suddenly came to the center, the evening's program. From then on, bewilderment, until you turned it upside down and started again from the color photograph of Joan as Ros-alinda with her accompanying pages of pictures and text. A fore-word about Sutherland by Robert Jacobson, editor of *Opera News*, cited her as a "natural phenomenon, somewhere in the league with Niagara Falls, the Grand Canyon, the Amazon." Alan Rich, critic for *New York* magazine and *New West*, addressed Sills as "Dear Bev," and bemoaned her retirement. "Class and fun" was what she had wanted in opera—and got. "One of the sovereign singing and dramatic talents of our country."

It was a triumph of near-perfect counterbalance. Equal im-partiality could be seen and heard in the audience's delight, shown by prolonged standing ovations and cheers, and in the ecstatic reviews that followed.

In rehearsal, the two prima donnas had a ball. They had never met before, although Richard had been scheduled to conduct a *Huguenots* for the American Opera Society years before, with Bev-erly in the cast. Someone's illness intervened. They had sent each other congratulations on various occasions—the courtesy of the profession, which is always generous to colleagues, at least in pub-lic. Bonynge, who conducted the *Fledermaus*, had been in touch more recently. But both ladies are thoroughbred professionals, and they got along like satin, by all accounts. Alan Titus, the personable baritone of the New York City Opera, had played with Beverly many times, and now as Eisenstein was buffeted between the two strong-minded women. He enjoyed it. So did the others. From comparative obscurity, Giuseppe Campora came to sing the braggadocio tenor Alfredo. Jake Gardner was the Dr. Falke, Spiro Malas the Frank, and Regina Resnik resurrected her former Met role of Prince Orlovsky, using the occasion to reminisce with Joan over some old times together.

The mastermind for all this went around with a creamy grin on his handsome face. He told *The New York Times* reviewer that he had dreamed up the idea five years ago.

"I play around making jokes to Beverly and Joan about the opera, to prepare the field for my attack. After so many jokes, they become familiar with the idea." To this day, neither knows whether he had told her or the other first about the crazy idea, using the old dodge of telling one that the other had agreed.

"I thought that the purpose of a general director is to bring attractions to your audience," he told me. "I thought this was just such an attraction." Indeed.

I asked how he manages to direct both so well, with no repercussions of jealousy or dissension. He replied:

"Everybody asks me that. I don't have any problems. I work with the dramatic possibilities in front of me. Both ladies are completely different, and I try to bring out the best in the one I'm working with. Both have a fantastic sense of humor. And both are just where they want to be, so there is no question of jealousy. When you are with a great artist of that caliber, you must give special inspiration."

Joan has said many times that she prefers a director "who makes me do things. Too many just let you go your own way."

The matter of precedence was settled neatly by Mayor Pete Wilson, who issued a proclamation making a "Sills and Sutherland Day," and another, "Sutherland and Sills Day." They all celebrated at a gala dinner in the Hotel Coronado that night. The ballroom was decorated to within an inch of its life with orchids, masks, and bunches of grapes, and champagne glasses etched with the two prima donnas' names. Beverly had to leave early to catch a redeye express plane for her New York duties, but Joan lingered on and gave an impromptu concert consisting of "Vilia" from *The Merry Widow* and "Happy Birthday" for the Australian consul general in Los Angeles, Peter Barbour. Another surprise was the presence of Sherrill Milnes, who had suddenly appeared in Prince Orlovsky's ballroom to sing, and now rose to the occasion again with the drinking song from Thomas's *Hamlet*, as a toast to his feminine colleagues.

Martin Bernheimer summed it up most judiciously in the Los Angeles *Times*, being coolly immune to the partisanship and hysteria that rocked San Diego. He called it the Duel of the Divas, but belied the title by citing the friendliness of the two, which, in a way, he found unnerving. If he had expected a Callas-Tebaldi type of confrontation, he was disappointed. For there they were on the same stage. Smiling. Hugging. Kissing. Singing. Sharing bows. Deferring.

Sills's model this time around was Marilyn Monroe, he thought. She whispered and simpered and purred. She perpetually batted her superlashes in knowing mock-innocence. She settled for a smug little shrug instead of a poke in the ribs. She is the past mistress of the double take and an old pro when it comes to exotic innuendo. In short, she was fun, she had fun, and she provided Sutherland with a splendid, elegant, charming counterforce.

And how did she sing? Cleverly. There were a few moments when the tone escaped her control, but there were also moments of uncommon sweetness, purity, and poise. And, always, there was singing marked by intelligence, phrasing illuminated by wit, a compensating for the dumb deficiencies of nature and cruelty of time.

Although Sutherland at fifty-four happened to be three years her colleague's senior, she did not seem to have any concern for nature and time. "She has husbanded her resources—no pun intended," the critic slyly remarked, more economically over the years, and her unique vocal equipment has proven less fragile. She sounded like one of the lasting wonders of the world (the old Grand Canyon comparison again). Her voice soared and roared, with ease and purity and steadiness, to every high climax Strauss required, plus a few he didn't. "She may have sounded a bit breathy in the low register, but, by gumbo, she sang, sang, sang!"

She also acted after a fashion—her fashion. She played the first-act flirtations with good-humored, matronly British reserve. She imitated Zsa Zsa Gabor with relish in Act Two and, for good measure, sang and danced a gamey czardas in the unoriginal Hungarian. She emerged graciously as a supersized, self-satisfied Gibson Girl for the last-act charades. "This, clearly, was a leading lady on a lark, and she deserved the hysterical ovations she so punctiliously shared, clap for clap, with Sills."

Richard Bonynge, he concluded, conducted "with brio and panache, and sympathy," and, dressed in dazzling white, shared curtain calls with the two beaming ladies.

CHAPTER
37

La Stupenda Reigns

✴ MANY HIGHLIGHTS LIT UP MY PILGRIMAGE IN THE next months. On her way to Toronto in 1981 for *Norma* (her first operatic appearance there, and a substitute for her first *Anna Bolena*, which was postponed until 1984), Joan stopped in for tea at the Hotel Pierre in New York. I was delighted to see her, all radiant and smiling, her shoulder-length hair now slightly darker auburn and freshly coiffed. She carried a great sheaf of flowers, the gift of the hairdresser. Our chief topic of conversation was her forthcoming October appearance in San Francisco in the *Merry Widow*.

She had never met her Danilo, the tall and personable Swede, Håkon Hagegård. Amused at hearing of his accomplishments from an admirer and intrigued at the difficulty of pronouncing his name correctly (the Swedish pronunciation is quite different from what is heard in America, because the little circle over the *a*'s makes them sound like *o*, she practiced it and promised to try it out in person. (In a later letter, she wrote that he had lived up to promises. She didn't always get his name right, but "he is a very charming and sweet person—a dogged rehearser and a fine performer.")

Joan was deeply excited by Adam's forthcoming marriage, which had been set for January 23, 1982. He had found a girl they thoroughly liked, and the couple would settle down in Sydney, near Adam's hotel. (In due time, Joan was to twice become a grandmother. "Natasha is quite grown up," she wrote later. And there was a second grandchild, born on August 14, 1985, bearing another Russian name, Vanya Nicholas. (Could this be? Yes, I am fairly certain of it—Vanya was named after the friend who struggled so valiantly with Chopin during my visit to Les Avants.)

The conversation turned to her own future. Would she, as her husband had insisted, sing until she was seventy? (The age has been advanced by two decades by Bonynge, according to later reports. She should sing until ninety-three!)

And would she teach?—the almost inevitable postscript to a singer's full-fashioned career.

"I don't think so," she answered slowly. "I'll probably go on singing too long." This brought a round of applause from her listener and laughter from both of us.

"I don't know if I would be a good teacher," she continued with her customary thoughtfulness. "Oh, I think I would like to teach if I had reasonable material to work with. I don't think I could accept a bad voice unless I thought I could do something with it, to help. It's wrong to encourage poor talent."

Could she go back and remember her own struggles?

"Oh, yes. I had to be corrected. Richard does that now—all the time. One slackens off a little, you know."

"Lazy?"

She laughed. "You need a second ear. You think you are not doing something wrong. But you don't realize. Sometimes you take a tape recording and hear what you want to instead of what's really happening. When you have technical things to overcome, you have to learn in stages."

The April *Norma* in Toronto found the leading lady with a new virus, extremely irritating. But she carried on so that few realized her difficulties. She noted humorously in a letter that it was the world's tallest *Norma* cast: Tatiana Troyanos as Adalgisa almost matched her own height and the Latin Americans Francesco Ortiz as Pollione and Justino Diaz as Oroveso touched the six-foot mark and over.

Joan carried her virus on to Sydney, where she sang Desdemona, for the first time with a conductor other than Richard: Carlo Felice Cillario, a regular at the Australian Opera.

"I was very comfortable working with Cillario," she wrote. "He was most considerate and the sort of person with whom one could discuss the work and come to a very solid, workable conclusion. He has a great sense of humor, and one could see him enjoying the performances."

Traviata and *Huguenots* occupied her in Australia before a red-letter occasion in November 1981, the concert in Washington to honor George London, whose protracted illness depleted his resources and left the opera world distressed. It may have been the greatest array of operatic talent ever assembled on a single stage, one observer remarked, citing Sutherland, Nicolai Gedda, Marilyn Horne, James King, Tatiana Troyanos, Shirley Verrett, and a dozen others. Beverly Sills acted as hostess, introducing each singer and eliciting various personal recollections of the great baritone, who had been so helpful a colleague and friend. Genuine emotion showed behind all the offerings, adding an element that the audience felt deeply.

Perhaps the highest emotional point was reached with Gedda's poignant singing of Lensky's aria from *Eugene Onegin*, which brought tears to many eyes. An added touch of glamor and excitement was provided by the surprise appearance as his accompanist of Mstislav Rostropovich, the revered cellist-pianist and conductor of the National Symphony in the nation's capital. Joan's brilliant singing of "Au beau pays" from *Les Huguenots* also took the listeners by storm. Her spoken contribution consisted of a remembrance of London's Don Giovanni in Vancouver, and his insistence on her having a Metropolitan Opera audition. "I didn't get the job," she admitted. And when Sills asked her what she would sing, she replied in that disarming, down-to-earth manner that leaves some hearers disbelieving their ears: "Well, I'll try to have a bash at 'Beau pays.' " It almost slipped by in the concert, but was delightfully audible in the television presentation some months later. She looked angelic in one of Matera's white, floating "butterfly" creations. Her accompanist was not Richard, but Eugene Kohn, one of the Met's young conductors.

At Christmastime, a London *Trovatore* brought "A Night of the Big Voices" to Covent Garden. Joan revealed a "vocal line of near flawless instrumental purity," while Elena Obraztsova was all guts and feeling, and Franco Boniselli's show-stopping high notes added to Felix Aprahamian's pleasure. Yuri Masurok's splendidly controlled Luna also pleased one critic. Edward Greenfield, who published a slim book about Joan (emphasizing her recording prowess) in 1973, was still to be found in the camp of her admirers. He wrote: "Her critics can quibble about this or that detail, but Dame Joan still combines dramatic weight, sheer size as well as beauty of voice, with range and control, plus dazzling flexibility of coloratura (with added decorations) to have one forgetting the years."

Her Leonora looked especially beautiful and dignified in costumes that used a long V neckline outlined in light color against dark, a figure-slimmer. During her stay, she was summoned to the

Royal College of Music to receive from the Queen Mother a Fellowship, an honor that pleased and touched her deeply.

In June 1982, the Sydney *Fledermaus* brought about another emergency similar to the San Francisco *Esclarmonde* panic over costumes. The designer had made a dressing gown for Rosalinda that Joan would never wear in her wildest moments, public or private. Scandalous, they called it. An SOS went out to Barbara Matera, and once again that stalwart lady leaped into the breach, carrying Joan's other *Fledermaus* costumes across the ocean to Australia.

Terence McEwen celebrated his first season as general manager of the San Francisco Opera by bringing Sutherland and Horne, the surefire glamor team, to do their *Norma*. Then, with three weeks before the rehearsals for the Metropolitan *Lucia*, Joan and Ricky deserved a small respite at Les Avants. A Holland *Lucia* had gone well, so they felt sanguine about the Met reentry, a confidence justified in the occasion.

Joan was assured a rousing welcome back to the purlieus of the Metropolitan in 1982: not only was a kind of headline advertising accorded to *Lucia*, but the Metropolitan Opera Guild nominated her as honor guest at its annual luncheon in November, when festivities were planned around her "life and times."

Still another occasion drew them in—the annual memorial concert for the tenor Richard Tucker, held in October. The following season brought a rousing revival of *La Fille du régiment*, in which Alfredo Kraus partnered the irrepressible heroine.

Joan has always added new roles sparingly, so that when, after the *Hamlet* of Ambroise Thomas in Toronto in October 1985, she announced that Ophelia was positively the last new heroine she would undertake, it came as no stunning surprise. The *Anna Bolena* had been a decided success when it finally materialized in 1984, and she had given Australia a beautiful embodiment of Adriana Lecouvreur, the Cilèa setting of the life, times, and death of a famous real-life actress. The proscription of new roles need not apply to recordings, however, for Richard assured me in 1986 that Joan intended to put on disc Verdi's *Ernani* in the near future, and other ventures might be expected. Occasional re-recordings bring surprises as well. A new *Norma* had Montserrat Caballé as Adalgisa, one of the seemingly unlikely bits of casting that can occur when the principals are heard but not seen.

The silver anniversary of Joan's debut at the Metropolitan Opera brought deep satisfaction to the prima donna and her husband. In the bouquet of compliments, fond recollections, and public presentations on the part of the company, and audience reception of a warmth that betokened people's undying affection for the singer, no thorn was discerned to spoil the happy occasion. Obviously forgotten was the disagreement that had kept the world's most prestigious soprano from the doors of the Lincoln Center house for three seasons. All was reverential tribute from the Metropolitan, delighted (and often girlish) response from the honored one.

It began on December 6, 1986, with Joan's presence on the opera's first intermission during the broadcast of *Roméo et Juliette*, when she was interviewed by Richard Mohr, director of these popular features. The chief topic was the unprecedented ovation accorded the heroine of *I Puritani*, at the first performance on November 26, a benefit which found the audience *en fête* from the moment the curtain went up. However, the heroine Elvira does not appear until the beginning of the second scene, when she walks in to hold a conversation with her uncle Giorgio.

At that moment, the sound that filled the house could only be likened to an explosion: one realized the meaning of "deafening applause."

Although undoubtedly expected in some degree, the sheer force and duration of that applause caught Joan in midstep. How does a prima donna deal with such a demonstration? Joan confessed to Mohr that it felt "like the response in a football stadium!" She could not quite believe it. And for several indecisive moments she stood with her head bowed, hands at her side, conflicting emotions dashing through her thoughts.

She must have received a telepathic signal from Richard from the pit, for she caught up her reeling thoughts and decided that she needed a moment to gather herself together, to "get psyched up again for Elvira," as she put it.

So she walked off the stage. The applause grew, if possible, and finally subsided. Richard lifted his baton, Elvira's entrance music was heard, and the lady walked back in front of the adoring public to begin the scene all over again. She later told Mohr that it was difficult to "put on madness"—she needed a little bit of quietness to prepare oneself.

That this was a "first" Richard later confirmed to me. The ovations at the Met debut and at several other occasions had perhaps lasted as long as this one, but he could not remember Joan going off stage.

Two details of that tumultuous event stand out in memory.

Sharing the continued applause with Sherrill Milnes and Samuel Ramey at one juncture, Sutherland stepped back from between the two men, and, bringing their hands together, gave a quizzical look at each of them and laughingly withdrew, to allow the pair their exclusive moment of glory, so richly deserved for their splendid duet. At another high moment, Joan reached high in the air to field a bouquet flawlessly.

Joan's very first interview in *Opera News* (it is difficult to believe that the magazine had ignored this opportunity for a quarter of a century!) appeared coincidentally. A charming photograph of Joan graced the magazine's cover, and illustrations for the article showed fanciful conceits by Beata Szpura, the prima donna—slim and elegant in a greenish blue confection—frolicking amid reproductions of various opera venues, Bonynge waving a baton in the background. The author, Jane Scovell, had previously assisted Marilyn Horne with her biography, so was well primed for this occasion. Furthermore, she had achieved access to the memory vaults of Terence McEwen, previously denied to me on the excuse that Terry was intending to write his own story, and wanted to retain all the good tidbits for that. Apparently he had at least temporarily given up the idea in the press of work as general director of the San Francisco Opera. I was relieved to see that he had told this writer very little that I had not already found out. Two subheads, "Like another recent celebrant, the Statue of Liberty" and "Sutherland is sacrosant," seem perhaps a trifle overenthusiastic.

Joan was flushed and happy after that tremendous outpouring of affection, which earned from Donal Henahan a *New York Times* accolade as well. "Miss Sutherland, surely the youngest-sounding sixty-year-old soprano in modern operatic history, responded with an astounding display of bel canto craft and staying power. The voice, though used more cautiously than it once was, retains remarkable freshness and technical security . . . the ultimate in pure, pre-Verdian vocalism . . . on this occasion remarkably dulcet and fresh in timbre."

Her hair, released from a wig to show a slightly subdued, blondish tone, her figure trim, her spirits buoyant and confident, Joan received congratulations in her dressing room and went on to further performances of this favorite role, as well as another appearance on the Saturday broadcast, after the performance of December 13. This time, it was the Metropolitan's general manager, Bruce Crawford, who presided. He cited 209 Sutherland performances in the Metropolitan ("and many more to come") and

seventeen radio broadcasts. There was for her a silver tray to com-
memorate the twenty-fifth anniversary. She responded with that
blend of earnestness and girlishness that has so endeared her to
fans and friends, citing her pleasure in her colleagues at that
house—"like a family.

"In forty years," she continued, "I have gathered a lot of
theatrical families, none more dear than here." She paid special
homage to the backstage technicians, particularly wigmaker and
wardrobe department—without them, "I wouldn't be looking like
this."

She added: "I'm glad if it sounds as if time stood still—it
doesn't feel like that. I don't hear the voice the way the audience
does. I don't like listening to my own records, but the compact
discs come closest."

Asked for advice to young singers, she responded: "Make
haste slowly. There were no jets when I began, and to go by ship
was a godsend. It needs strength and guts to stand up to interviews
and rehearsals—we are all tired by opening night.

"Me, I'm a tough old bird by now. I never know if I have
sung beautifully. I've striven for perfection but never reached it.
I nitpick after every performance."

As for the future: "I don't want to come on using a walking
stick—well, maybe a sedan chair."

On that light note, the ceremony concluded. However, promise for the future was partially revealed. Sutherland and Pavarotti
would give a concert at the Met on January 11, 1987, and would
then make a coast-to-coast tour singing various opera scenes.

Then Joan and Ricky were ready for another Christmas at Les
Avants in Switzerland.

· · ·

Meanwhile, in Australia, operatic affairs settled down into peaceful
and profitable grooves after some seasons of turmoil. The greatest
changes occurred during the regime of Patrick Veitch, who resigned as general manager in mid-October 1986, after six years in
which the company stabilized both artistically and financially. Veitch
was responsible for several ancillary organizations that boosted the
company's coffers and morale.

"The caliber of the company's performance work has risen
dramatically over recent years," declared David S. Clarke, the new
chairman, who cited improvement in casting, conducting, and
repertoire—the latter rebuilt after the disastrous warehouse fire
several years before. "There are now seventy-five productions in
the repertory," he noted.

Other innovations owing to Veitch's initiative: live TV shows, videocassettes, a National Opera Workshop, Opera Action for youth education, and the Australian Opera Guild.

While Veitch agreed to remain until the end of 1986 and thereafter to be available to assist in an orderly transition, his post was to be temporarily filled by Moffatt Oxenbourg, whom we have seen in rising importance to the company over twenty-odd years. Moffatt wrote me that although there had been "a fairly traumatic 1985, we are hopeful that 1986 will be better and that we will have some definite news about our future funding prospects."

These expectations have apparently been fulfilled, for the chairman accounted the past year the most successful in the company's history.

Our heroine and hero have shared in this wave of new prosperity and accomplishment. Richard has remained as a chief conductor and Joan is still the brightest star in the Southern Hemisphere firmament—for as long as she chooses to shine.

CHAPTER

38

Curtain Call—Joan Sutherland: Artist vs. Woman

"At last, Marchese, I have come to the final conclusion . . . that the greatest force in the world is work, and once one has made that one's own and felt all its torments and blessings, then one will hold to it tooth and nail, even if one is a woman, as one of the most precious discoveries of life, and prize it highly as the responsibility which one has for one's future and that of one's dependents."

—*Eleanora Duse to Marchese D'Afcais*

❋ THIS WORK ETHIC HAS BEEN AS STRONG IN JOAN Sutherland as in any of America's Puritan forefathers. It has sustained her through whatever difficulties edged into her life, a life that seemed perhaps placid, yet with undercurrents unsuspected and seldom rising to the surface (perhaps what her first teachers, Aida and John Dickens, called, but would not explain, "sit-you-eye-shuns"). One can believe that she does carry Duse's words with her wherever she goes. Martin Waldron, who culled it for her from the wisdom of his beloved Eleanora, swears that she does. Martin is the Bonynges' Brooklyn landlord, sometime and all-time fan, dressing-room guard, and all-around majordomo. He needs only a tall wand to complement his tall person, clad in a black velvet suit, a crown of white hair with short, curling ends framing the long and expressive face of the actor. He had been very close to and protective of the couple even before they moved into the top two floors of his house in June 1970.

Few outsiders realize how arduous a prima donna's life is, how disciplined, how rigorous, and how little time remains for distractions. Joan's life seems ninety percent work. Martin goes so far as to call it "nunlike." He says she comes down to work out the action on every opera, after sitting in her room going over every note and word the day of a performance.

Indeed, the work ethic brushes excessively close to religious ardor. Yet the natural good spirits and sunny disposition of the woman animate the totality, and Joan seems at least resigned to the unequal division of her time.

"To throw out the things you can't do and enjoy those you can comes with maturity," is the way Elizabeth Allen, one of Joan's first friends in Australia, puts it.

It is not a question of "all work and no play making Joan a dull girl," but of distilling the best out of her crowded life to reserve for that ten percent of leisure. In that small, special slice of privacy, Joan practices domesticity, thrift, motherly concern—and friendship.

An opera orbit, narrow and concentrated, though it may span the earth, constricts the field for picking friends. Most of Joan's and Richard's are directly concerned with the profession; a few outsiders, such as the Kaufmans, who came across the Atlantic from England on the same ship with Joan on an early trip to America, remain in the inner circle. Joan's vaunted bad memory is a fiction when it comes to remembering faces, names, and friends.

Of early vintage is Norman Ayrton, Joan's first real coach in London, who aided the awkward girl's struggles to learn to comport herself on stage.

In 1968 the Bonynges had chosen Yugoslavia for a vacation and invited Norman. He recalled that the water came right up to their front door and they had fresh fish every day. They would spend hours on the terrace playing mah jongg. Joan was in her element, carefree and mad about picnics. They had some splendid outings, driving over tortuous mountain roads. Joan would call out to stop and would disappear into some little shop she'd spied. She'd return with a large bag and smugly produce marvelous goodies, which she'd dispense with the graciousness of a grand duchess.

· · ·

To celebrate Sutherland's history-making debut as Lucia at the Met in 1961, Geraldine Souvaine gave a big party. Geri, a blond Missourian of Italian descent, ran the Met broadcast intermission features for the sponsor, Texaco.

"Everyone" was at the party, of course. Ania Dorfman, the diminutive Russian pianist who enjoyed friendship with Arturo Toscanini and was a dynamo at the Juilliard School, walked into the crushing crowd and immediately backed out to the edge of the room. An hour later, Geri said to her: "Did you meet the star?" and took her by the arm over to the cynosure, the circular pouffe on which sat the guest of honor. Hearing Dorfman's name, Joan cried out in the voice that carried over a multitude of cocktail chatterers: "Rick, come over here . . . see who's here!"

It seems that Richard had been studying Dorfman's records and wanted very much to meet her. This was the beginning of another good friendship, for when the Bonynges visited Dorfman in her apartment on Madison Avenue at Ninety-fourth Street, they thought it would be a nice place to live. It was rent-controlled, however, and nobody seemed to want to move. The Bonynges went away, leaving the power of attorney with their manager, Ann Colbert. Some months later, the fifth floor became available, and the Bonynges took it sight unseen.

It was wonderful to have them so close, Dorfman told me. She was on the fourth floor and they each had keys to the other's apartment, shared a refrigerator, and saw each other many times. Richard furnished their place with antiques, of course. "That Ricky—how he would shop!" marveled Dorfman. "And there's no house big enough for the things he acquires."

During one of his antique outings, Dorfman succeeded in stopping him—for five minutes. He had bought a mirror for practically nothing at a little store on Ninety-sixth Street and wanted everything else in the store. When Dorfman restrained him, the shopkeeper became cross and asked: "Is she your mother?"

He laughed, and said: "Almost."

That stopped Ania, and Richard went on buying. It all contributes to his store of knowledge—of art and of the theater.

Joan never goes on these antique raids. As for her own shopping: "Oh-h-h!" exclaims Dorfman. "I've dared to go with her. But it's whirlwind, and all domestic." She almost never buys clothes . . . has them all made by Barbara Matera, her costume maker. What she goes for are things for the table and the house. Dorfman remembered a set of pottery dishes in a lily-of-the-valley pattern— an open stock so any breakage could be replaced . . . napkin rings, things like that. All very purposeful.

Dorfman shared her French maid with the Bonynges on Ninety-fourth Street, and one day asked after her upstairs neighbor: "How is Madame?"

"Elle chante," replied the girl simply.

That meant Madame was content; it always showed when she sang around the house.

For so famous a person, Dorfman thought, she is the most simple outside the opera house. "Only, God forbid if someone steps on her foot—figuratively, of course. Oversteps friendship. That's the only time the prima donna comes out, and she is majestically angry. Her voice and eyes can cut like ice!"

Norman Ayrton, too, warned of this. "If you feel the pressure building up, get out fast!"

A certain amount of thrift still persists, inbred, from early days when frugality was second only to Presbyterian uprightness, and every Australian penny counted.

Elizabeth Allen, whose budding career paralleled Joan's, remembered that the big girl was horrified when Betty bought an extra music case; *she* made do with one. Surely you're saving money, Joan scolded Betty, who was a bank clerk but very extravagant. She had lots of tutors, lots of language lessons. Joan was studying on a scholarship.

Joan can laugh a little about her early frugality, but it is apparent even today. Her strong-willed mother's influence always looms. Joan still buys up sheets and pillowcases at white sales, because Mother admonished her: "Never let a sale go by." Then she was to buy yards of lace and trimmings to sew on the sheets.

"I simply can't resist the yard goods at Harrods in London," she confessed. "I go wild! [I] once bought yards of black georgette—the kind you can't get anymore—and some white, too. Then they insisted that I take the green—it's not really my color, but I might make a nightie. The underwear now is so awful—I make mine."

Joan's love for flowers ("flahs," as you will hear from her Australian-British lips,) is a mainspring. She arranges them with consideration for every flower and every little piece of green, and she knows if any arrangement is out of order. In Switzerland, this visitor broke off a tiny leaf of holly from a luxuriant bouquet in the hall, feeling guilty, but hoping to add a holiday touch to a hat or some silliness. Joan passed by a little later and cried: "Look at what's happened to my flahs!"

It is her sincere love for home and the desire to cherish and decorate the comfortable nest that motivate Joan's life offstage, so limited and therefore the more precious. At one level of consciousness, perhaps, Joan would be happiest in a domestic role entirely.

Though she has learned to live with her image as a glamorous diva, it still frets her. She will stand graciously at a formal function with considerate words for all comers, even though she's howled previously, in that projectable voice: "Do I *have* to go?" The usual run of publicity laid on to such a glitter figure is not exactly discouraged—except occasionally, when it seems excessive—and the Bonynges employ a particularly aggressive press agent. He's not much in evidence personally.

The Bonynges have learned to accept the press interviews that are expected of them, always entering into them with reluctance, but warming up as they proceed. One of the most joyous and fruitful occurred when they were guests of Risë Stevens, herself a former luminary and then president of the Mannes College in New York. For more than an hour, Joan and Richard answered questions by students, talking freely, humorously, and considerately. They emerged flushed and sparkling—at least Joan sparkled. Richard looked pleased in a saturnine way. It had been a performance, to be treated as one, and it had been a good performance.

At the opposite pole was a television interview with Dick Cavett in New York. Both were stiff, hardly responding to the often misplaced questions of the usually urbane interrogator. Joan was in the midst of a series of Met appearances as Donna Anna in *Don Giovanni* and had caught a slight cold. Her discomfort was obvious. She usually does better in a more personal setting, without the lights and camera. But the sense of being "on," which imbues the behavior of any theatrical person, usually comes to the rescue.

The Bonynges often give autographs by the hour when it is a question of promotion of their recordings. But Joan has reservations about certain aspects of violent fandom. Having geared herself up to it, she confronts the autograph seekers with magnificent composure and smiles that seem genuine. In fact, whenever she spots a face she knows, she asks about mother or family or that person's particular doings. It is a demonstration of memory plus thoughtfulness that is impressive. And another real performance.

But it can get rather dicey. That famous last night in Melbourne in 1965, the crowd seemed actually menacing. Police literally had to battle their way to the stage door to get her out. It is an enormous tribute as long as they keep it that way, Joan feels. No artist really knows how to cope when the fanatic element of the fans gets too near. There should be needful separation, as the orchestra pit separates the stage from the audience, Martin Waldron thought. One understands that these people long to have something in common with their stars, to communicate, to touch, to identify with them. It's all very flattering, but when they have nothing to offer themselves but trivia, it takes all the politeness and fortitude the star can summon up.

Joan rather plaintively described her reactions to the bombardment performers are subjected to, particularly after performances. "One adores this adoration, but sometimes . . . well, after the last *Puritani* in New York, we received no less than thirty requests to bring backstage friends, wives, mothers-in-law, husbands, children—huge hordes of people—one just can't cope. And it was very late, and we had our own friends and were supposed to eat dinner with a seventy-six-year-old lady who had to be kept waiting—people just don't understand. Entertaining them for three hours is not enough. It really is a privilege to come backstage, not necessarily their due, as they seem to feel.

"At concerts, it's normally accepted that anyone can go back, but it's a much shorter time you've had to perform, and in the opera house there are additional difficulties—fire laws and security and so on. I'm simply amazed at the number who crowd in."

Richard added: "And one is quite exhausted and not really up to answering questions about what one will be doing the next two years." Fans always seem to want to know and don't think to get the information from management or press agent. All fans, that is, except Lois, the Queen of the Fans, who always knows what every artist will be doing in the future seemingly before the one in question has found out. This formidable woman is near the head of the line at dressing rooms from coast to coast. Singers are invariably polite to her, even though it means signing their names two dozen times on the stack of records, books, programs, and miscellaneous pieces of paper she carries around with her as excess baggage.

When Joan has just about had it, a wary expression falls like a mask on her face and her lips tighten—particularly at the cooing and gushing that quite flusters her. She finds it distressing to accept compliments, even from those she respects, and turns them off matter-of-factly. Almost invariably she counters: "I hope it will be better the second—or tenth—time."

Norman Ayrton, after the exhilarating dress rehearsal of the Metropolitan *Tales of Hoffmann*, trying not to go overboard, but in an unmistakably rapturous tone, calling her performance "tops," received a twinkling: "You reckon?"

And Francis Robinson's similar story is classic. At the end of Joan's sensational debut as Lucia, the suave press chief of the Met went backstage, stooped over, lifted the hem of her trailing gown, and kissed it. The triumphant singer looked down over her shoulder and characteristically out of the corner of her mouth muttered: "Aw, Frawncis, come off it!"

This down-to-earthness, although sometimes dashing the ardor of would-be worshipers, endears the lady to those who scorn pretentiousness.

In truth, Joan never thought to be a prima donna, as the term has come to mean. "Never had any overriding ambition; all I wanted was to sing at Covent Garden. If it hadn't been for Richard, I would have sung anything they gave me. Certainly I would have been singing a different repertoire." To be sure, without Bonynge's goading, David Webster's gamble, and Lord Harewood's encouragement, the world would probably never have heard the true glory of the Sutherland voice, nor welcomed an authentic prima donna.

The one constant in all the years has been Richard. His guidance, criticism and encouragement have been the prime movers in this extraordinary career. Once, asked about this unswerving partnership—why did she choose it?—she gave an unexpected reply. Not only did she prefer her husband as a colleague, but sometimes it could get lonesome on the unremitting round of engagements.

"It's nice to have him there," she said simply.

Richard has made his individual way against the formidable odds of being a superstar's shadow. He received his own honor, the Order of Australia, in February 1984. He has emerged into the light of his own independent career, conducting many operas in which Joan does not appear. It should be noted that even after the Metropolitan disagreement in 1979, he conducted Massenet's *Werther* at that house, giving an example of his expertise in French repertoire.

He has recorded vast quantities of delightful material, some of it resurrected from limbo, all of it cannily presented. His discography in the London-Decca catalogue goes far beyond the opera discs in which his wife participates.

It is interesting to note that the first of his recordings in 1963 are ballet music—a potpourri called "The Art of the Prima Ballerina," another in 1964, "Pas de Deux," and a third in 1965, the Adolfe Adam *Le Diable a Quatre*.

He was absorbed by ballet, although he never conducted a full evening of dance. "There hasn't been time," he explained, what with the opera schedules paved so far ahead and ballet companies likely to want an ad hoc or last-minute performance.

"I feel that dancing is like singing," he told Professor Paul Stacy in 1973 at a symposium at the New School for Social Research in New York. Violette Verdy, noted French ballerina, was his partner. The occasion was reported in *Dance* magazine.

"It's all a thing of breathing, you know; when I conduct for singers I breathe with them. I don't dance myself, but having watched dancers for so long, I feel I understand how they breathe and what's possible to do and what's not possible."

The early recordings were made with the advice of Alicia Markova, who spent hours in her studio giving pointers and actually demonstrating dance steps for him. The matter of tempi was vital; he adopted tempi that were considered traditional, with Dame Alicia's guidance. Miss Verdy testified that she had danced to several of his recordings and found them compatible.

A dozen other ballets have come to recorded life under Bonynge's sympathetic baton, including those by Delibes, Tchaikovsky, Offenbach, and Massenet. Complimenting Bonynge on his sympathy for ballet, the critic Dale Harris wrote in *The New York Times* in 1976: "He shows a natural affinity for ballet music, its tunefulness, rhythmic vitality, and drama." He cited the "complete and scrupulously edited" versions of *Coppelia* and *Giselle* as reasons for a debt owed the conductor who brought this music vividly to life.

The scholarship that pervades his opera performances has been widely acknowledged at last. Critics may pick at his "editions," at his addition or subtraction from scores long taken for granted, but although some of these changes may seem occasionally arbitrary, he can always give logical, sometimes completely persuasive, reasons for them.

The temperaments of husband and wife are entirely different. "If Joan has too much work," Richard once said, "she worries—worries so much she doesn't do it too well. And if one limits the amount of work for her, so she can easily cope with it, she performs much better. With me, it is quite different. The more work I do, the better."

One time during one of our talks, in a sudden overblown attack of modesty, Richard confessed that he hates to practice, works at what he likes, but is basically unambitious and lazy. "I'm lucky," he insisted, "spoiled, just a glorified amateur, really."

Joan opened her eyes wide in amazement. "My God! If one of the critics had said that!" she exclaimed at this practically unbelievable confession.

Finally, what of Joan's pilgrimage through the years of study and performance and jet travel and vexations and triumphs?

"So many wonderful things happened, lovely off-the-record things," she told Shirley Despoia of the Adelaide *Advertiser* one time. "But I don't remember them. I suppose it's because this thing up here in my head that came before computers is full of words and music—what is it now? Fifty-four roles—that have to be remembered along with clothes I need for Adelaide summer and London winter within weeks of each other.

"But unlike a computer, it doesn't all come out at the touch of the right button. The necessary things take over my mind and the lovely things get lost."

The reporter summed up: "She has a disarming vocabulary of silly words such as 'golly' and 'gosh,' surviving from her Sydney school days. Warm, twinkling . . . a great star—and down to earth. She's funny and human with a heart as big as her favorite caftan. She makes you see that big is beautiful—and with her happy face, smooth skin, and high cheekbones, she *is* beautiful, no doubt of that. She cares about the person she is talking to, her house, her needlepoint, her dog, and everyone in the world."

And Joan added: "There's been a lot of laughter" . . .

· · ·

"Brightened the pages of history," was the headline over *The New York Times*'s summing-up of her twenty-fifth anniversary. "Likely to be remembered in the next century." These seem fitting words to add to the prima donna's bouquet of tributes and to close these chapters of friendly observation.

Index

JS = Joan Sutherland
RB = Richard Bonynge
QE = Quaintance Eaton